The Book of Elisha

PART 1

I am the Prophet Elisha from the Holy Bible Old Testament. I am the Prophet that has come in these last days!

The Autobiography of the life of Kennedy King Brown

Written by: Kennedy King Brown

Copyright © 2016, 2020, 2025 by Kennedy King Brown

All rights reserved. No part of this book may be used or reproduced in any manner without prior written permission from Kennedy King Brown.

ISBN 978-1-7345047-1-2

Published by Prophet Elisha Publishing

To order this book, go to:

www.thebookofelisha.com or Amazon.com

Table of Contents

Chapters

Introduction 1
1. The Day of My Birth 10
2. Dreams of Falling From The Sky 11
3. My Mother Falls Out Of A Chair 12
4. Hangers In My Left Eye 14
5. My Life 15
6. Telling People I Been Places I Never Been 18
7. Go and Get Baptize 21
8. The Heavenly Father Speaks To Me 21
9. I Am Pronounced Blessed 22
10. The Prophesy Was Given By The Lord 23
11. The Lord Saves My Life 27
12. Years Later I Realize It Was The Lord 30
13. The Anatomy of Satan Part 1 31
14. I Was Visited By An Angel Of The Lord 33
15. At UAB With My Sister 35
16. A Word Hidden in a Picture 36
17. You Are Going To Be A Millionaire 42
18. My Heritage 43
19. Who is that little girl? 43
20. I Have Been to This World Before 44
21. A Child Mimicking His Parents 46
22. The Store 46
23. I Repeated The Words The Lord Spoke 51
24. Joseph 52
25. My Science Project 57
26. I Witness It 59
27. Satan Try To Stop The Prophesy 63
28. The Anatomy of Satan Part 2 66
29. I Ignore the Warning of The Holy Spirit 66
30. My Personal Life 68
31. The Holy Spirit Speaks Thru Mrs. Gary 75
32. The Artist Part 1 76
33. My Memories of A Word 77
34. Senior Prom 78
35. A Twelve Year Vision From The Lord Part 1 80

36.	Higher Education	81
37.	Women Who Confided In Me Their Secret	85
38.	A Twelve Year Vision From The Lord Part 2	88
39.	Sandra	97
40.	The Anatomy of Satan Part 3	105
41.	Where Are Their Daddy	109
42.	Not Having The Wisdom To Understand	110
43.	They Recognized Me	111
44.	Why Do People Hate Me?	112
45.	I Witness The Second Coming of The Lord	115
46.	The Voice Is Leading Me	117
47.	My Father Speaking of Future Events	118
48.	I Am Being Watched	120
49.	Approached By The Illuminati	120
50.	Tupac Shakur	129
51.	The Prophesy Of Derivatives and Stock Market Crash	129
52.	Vision of Planes Flying Into The World Trade Center	132
53.	Lord Who Am I	133
54.	I Could See But Now I Am Blind	135
55.	A Twelve-Year Vision From The Lord Part 3	137
56.	A Twelve-Year Vision From The Lord Part 4 and 5	138
57.	The Anatomy of Satan Part 4	143
58.	Transition From My Past To My Present In Christ	145
59.	One Night At The Club	148
60.	The Voice Is The Call	150
61.	My Sheep to My Right; Goats To My Left	156
62.	George W. Bush Prophesy	159
63.	My Eyes Were Open	159
64.	The Very Old But New Religion "Illuminati"	162
65.	The Anatomy of Satan Part 5	181
66.	The Illuminati Corporation Structure	182
67.	Satan Is A Liar and So Is The Illuminati	212
68.	The Illuminati High Priest and its Symbol	218
69.	The Illuminati High Priest Suppress the Lord's Word	226
70.	The Illuminati and Political Elections	236
71.	My Theory Different From TV Evangelist	250
72.	Hidden Messages In the Bible	251
73.	Fulfillment of The Prophesy of The World Trade Center	253

74.	Prophesy of New Orleans	256
75.	Who Is That Guy?	259
76.	The Voice Reveals Himself	260
77.	The Lord Moves Me	261
78.	How Did Black People Become Perceived as Evil	265
79.	The Holy Spirit Councils Me About Race	265
80.	You Can Never Be Judged	268
81.	I Decipher The Meaning of 666	269
82.	Warning From The Holy Spirit	270
83.	Vision of Two Women In Wedding Dresses	271
84.	The Gift Of Hearing People Thoughts	272
85.	Walk By Faith and Not By Sight	274
86.	A Specific Prophesy About Me In The Bible	276
87.	The Lord Reveals To Pastor	277
88.	Satan is Sending Someone	277
89.	Something Appears Out of The Darkness	279
90.	You Must Be Talking About That Book	280
91.	The Lord Places Me At The Right Place	282
92.	Engineer Reveals Plan For A Black Project	284
93.	Confirmation Of Black Project	288
94.	The Lord Reveals To Me The President For 2009	290
95.	The Hate In Birmingham, AL Is Revealed	292
96.	The Birth of My Daughter	293
97.	The Lord Answers My Prayer	294
98.	Vision of A Woman Who Face Changed	296
99.	Something Appears Out Of The Darkness 2	298
100.	The Prophesy of the Destruction of New Orleans	298
101.	"Save my people"	299
102.	The Holy Spirit Speaks To My Daughter	301
103.	All Warning Signs Ignored And I Get Married	302
104.	Holy Spirit Warns Me of Satan's Plan	304
105.	Go and Get Baptize Part II	304
106.	Satan Tries To Chase Me Out Of The Lords Word	306
107.	The Lord Reveals To Me Partly Who I Am	306
108.	Satan Tries To Kill Me But God's Grace Saves Me	309
109.	The Apocrypha	314
110.	The Holy Spirit Makes Bishop Speak	316
111.	The Lord Reveals To Me Who My Wife Truly Is	316
112.	My Wife Is Jezebel	320

113. The Anatomy of Satan Part 6	323
114. Something Appears Out Of The Darkness 3	325
115. The Lord Delivers Me And Open My Eyes	326
116. My Disobedience To The Lord	327
117. The Lord Reveals to Me the True Meaning Of 666	328
118. Prophesy of Derivatives and Stock Market Crash Fulfilled	361
119. The Chants of a Presidential Candidate Is Not Holy	392
120. The Holy Spirit Warns Me	393
121. My Daughters Gift Is Revealed	394
122. The Abomination that Cause Desolation Revealed	397
123. The Lord Leaves the Name Of Satan In the Bible	402
124. The Artist Part 2	409
125. Out of Israel Came Jesus Christ–Out of the Illuminati Came Barack Obama	411
126. Rapture and The First Resurrection	416

Introduction

1 John 1-3: "Dear friends, do not believe every spirit, but test the spirits to see whether they are from God, because many false prophets have gone out into the world. **² This is how you can recognize the Spirit of God: Every spirit that acknowledges that Jesus Christ has come in the flesh is from God,** ³ but every spirit that does not acknowledge Jesus is not from God. This is the spirit of the antichrist, which you have heard is coming and even now is already in the world." (NIV, BibleGateway.com)

My name is Kennedy King Brown, and I acknowledge I worship the Most High God Jehovah (Yahweh) and the Lord Jesus Christ. I acknowledge that Jesus Christ (Yeshua) has come in the flesh. I acknowledge that Jesus Christ (Yeshua) is the Son of the Most High God Jehovah. I acknowledge that Jesus Christ (Yeshua) was crucified on the cross, where he died. I acknowledge that Jesus Christ (Yeshua) rose from the dead on the third day. And then Jesus ascended into heaven to sit at the right hand of the Most High God Jehovah.

Again, my name is Kennedy King Brown. I was born on February 17, 1971, and as of the year 2025, I am currently 54 years old. This book is the actual account of my life and is my true testimony of my relationship and my encounters with the Most High God Jehovah, and my relationship and my encounters with my Lord and Savior Jesus Christ (Yeshua). My encounters with the Most High God Jehovah (Yahweh), and the Lord Jesus Christ (Yeshua) are far from the average spiritual experience. My encounters with the Most High God Jehovah (Yahweh) and the Lord Jesus Christ (Yeshua) are in both the spiritual and the physical realm!

I am the son of Mervin M. Brown and Dannie M. Brown. I am the youngest of nine children. I grew up as the eighth child because one of my sisters died before my birth; her name was Elizabeth Brown (Liz). I am the great-grandson of Edgar Brown, my father's granddaddy. I am the grandson of Eddie and Willie Brown, my father's parents. I am also the grandson of Herbert and Elizabeth Johnson (Momma Lizzie), my mother's parents. I never met my great-grandfather Edgar Brown nor my father's parents because they had passed away before I was born. Even though I never met my great-grandfather, Edgar Brown, I heard stories about him and some of the miraculous things he did in the name of Jesus Christ (Yeshua). Hearing these miraculous stories about my great-grandfather Edgar Brown helped me understand myself and my daughter.

Since my great-grandfather Edgar Brown was a Pastor, and my grandfather Eddie Brown was also a man who preached the gospel. My father and mother were raised to firmly believe that Jehovah (Yahweh) is the Most High God and that all creation derived from him. My father and mother made sure my siblings and I were raised to know the same truth they were raised with. This meant it was mandatory for me and my siblings to attend church on Sundays. Going to church wasn't a subject we debated in our household. This was a standing order passed down by my dad and mom. As long as we lived in our parent's house, we went to church on Sundays. So, I was taught the word of the Most High God Jehovah, at a very young age. I served as an altar boy for my church at a very young age. I remember Sunday after Sunday, the other altar boy and I would wear our little white robes and light the candles on the altar at Enon United Methodist Church. Then, we would sit on the side of the altar until the church service was over. I sat at one end of the altar while the other boy sat at the other side of the altar. We were on the opposite ends of the altar, facing each other like two cherubim facing each other on the Ark of the Covenant.

So, I was serving in the church at a very young age. At a very young age, I started to hear the voice of the Most High God Jehovah. Just like you hear a person's voice in your ears when they speak to you, I hear the voice of the Most High God Jehovah, and the Lord Jesus Christ (Yeshua) the same way when the Lord speaks to me! I have heard the voice of the Most High God Jehovah (Yahweh), the Lord Jesus Christ (Yeshua), the Holy Spirit and the voice of angels since I was a child.

This book is my testimony that Jesus Christ (Yeshua) is the Son of the living God. I give my testimony not to be exalted by people nor for self-gratification or fame. I give it to you to fulfill the one mission the Lord Jesus Christ (Yeshua) gave me. Jesus Christ told me to save his people. I ask you to open your heart and mind to what I am about to reveal to you. What I am about to reveal to you in this book is of Biblical proportions. The events I will reveal to you are my true-life experiences with Jesus Christ (Yeshua).

This book contains events from my childhood to now. The events have neither exaggeration nor fiction. All that is written in this book is the absolute truth and nothing but the truth in the name of Jesus Christ (Yeshua). I hope you, the reader, keep an open mind until you fully read this book. I encourage you to pray to the Most High God Jehovah and ask him if I am truly the Prophet Elisha from the Old Testament. And I guarantee that God will reveal to you that I am the Prophet Elisha from the Old Testament. And God will tell you I have spoken the absolute truth in this book.

The Lord has spoken many prophecies to me over my lifetime. Year after year, the Lord has spoken many prophecies to me. And year after year, I have watched the prophecies the Lord has told me come true. Without knowing it, I have been a witness for the King of Kings. Over my lifetime, the Lord gave me very important information about the future events that are about to take place in this world that are of Biblical proportions.

What is about to be revealed throughout this book will open your mind and eyes to many things. Once your mind and eyes are open, they can never be closed again. Once your mind and eyes are open, you can never go back to where you are now. So, the choice you must make is this. Do you want your mind and eyes to be open to the absolute truth about everything, or do you want them to stay closed like they are now? If you want your mind and eyes to remain closed, please put this book down and don't read it. If you want your mind and eyes open, follow me on this journey through my life! So you will know the absolute truth about what has been transpiring in this world right under your eyes! But I tell you this: you will never be the same once your eyes are open! You will never be able to go back to the mental slavery and mental bondage that you are in now! Because the absolute truth will free you from the mental slavery and mental bondage that you don't even realize you are in!

A mighty war has raged in heaven and on earth over your souls. Many of you don't know this, but this war between God and Satan is a winner-takes-all war! The winner of this war between God and Satan will rule over Heaven and Earth forever and ever! Because of this mighty war between God and Satan, the Lord had to hide my identity from the world and even from myself. As a child, teenager, and young adult, I found myself asking the Lord the same question over and over. I always asked the Lord, "Lord, who am I?" The reason I had to ask the Lord this question over and over is because supernatural things would always happen to me. And I noticed that the things happening to me weren't happening to anyone else.

As of today, I know who I am and what my mission is. I am the Prophet Elisha from the Holy Bible Old Testament. I am here to prepare the way for the second coming of Jesus Christ, the Messiah! Many Jews, Christians, and theologians have misinterpreted the scriptures about who was going to return in the last days. Many Jews, Christians, and theologians think the Prophet Elijah is supposed to return in the last days! But the Prophet Elijah had already returned. Before we go any further, we need to clear up this misunderstanding.

The Prophet Elijah has always been one of the most talked about Prophets of the Holy Bible. The reason the Prophet Elijah has been well discussed and talked about is because Elijah ascended into the heavens without dying. The Prophet Elijah is said to be one of two men called up into the heavens without going through death. But the question must be asked: why did God call Elijah up into the heavens without him going through the process of death? Just to let you know, the Holy Father does everything for a reason, and I will answer this question for you so you can understand what the Holy Father did.

After Elijah was called up into the heavens, the Lord gave many prophesies to his prophets that a Prophet would return in the last days. Once these prophecies were given, everyone assumed all these prophecies were referring to the Prophet Elijah returning in the last days. Even the Prophet Malachi stated in Malachi 4:5- 6 that Elijah would return, but the Lord explained to me why the text read Elijah instead of Elisha. Everyone thought the prophecies were exclusively about the Prophet Elijah because the Prophet Elijah was taken into the heavens without dying. Everyone thought that since the Prophet Elijah was taken so dramatically, he had to be the Prophet who would return in the last days. But all the prophecies weren't referring to the return of the Prophet Elijah; some of the prophecies were referring to the return of me, the Prophet Elisha. But no one was expecting the Prophet Elisha to return because I wasn't called up into the heavens without dying like the Prophet Elijah was.

So when no one was expecting the Prophet Elisha to return, Biblical Scholars all assumed the prophesies referring to a prophet returning in the last days was referring to the Prophet Elijah. To understand this misinterpretation or this misdirection, you must realize that a winner-take-all war is going on between God and Satan. And with any war, you can't give the enemy your precise battle plans. So, the Lord hid his intentions to send me Elisha back into this world by allowing the world to believe the Prophet Elijah would return in the last days.

I know many of you are expecting the Prophet Elijah to return. But the Prophet Elijah has already returned. The Prophet Elijah returned as John the Baptist! Most people don't understand John the Baptist was the Prophet Elijah because John the Baptist was born as a child. Many people expected Elijah to instantly show up as a grown man! People were expecting the Prophet Elijah to instantly show up looking like he was looking when he was taken. But the Prophet Elijah was reborn into this world as John the Baptist. And nobody expected Elijah to be reborn into this world as a child. But Elijah was reborn into this world as a child and was named John! How do I know this? Because the Biblical scriptures tell us this!

I will show you some concrete evidence in scriptures that will prove to you John the Baptist was the return of the Prophet Elijah. This is not speculation that John the Baptist was the Prophet Elijah; this is one of the Holy Father's eternal truths that John the Baptist was the Prophet Elijah of the Old Testament. So you may see this eternal truth, let me show you the scriptures that revealed who John the Baptist truly was.

First, John the Baptist was the Son of the Priest Zechariah. While Zechariah was doing his priestly duties in the temple, an angel of the Lord appeared to him. The angel that appeared to Zachariah was the angel Gabriel. Gabriel told Zechariah his wife would give birth to a son, and his Son was to be named John. Gabriel goes on and tells Zechariah his Son will be filled with the Holy Spirit from birth and **that his Son John will go before the Lord in the spirit and power of Elijah!** That phrase "go before the Lord in the spirit and power of Elijah" means John (John the Baptist) had the spirit of the Prophet Elijah in him, and John had the power of the Prophet Elijah, and John (John the Baptist) was to prepare the way for the Lord Jesus Christ (Yeshua)! Since John (John the Baptist) had the spirit and power of the Prophet Elijah in him that means John (John the Baptist) was the Prophet Elijah.

It is the spirit that is in us that makes us who we are. So, when the scriptures said John (John the Baptist) would go before the Lord in the spirit and power of Elijah, that meant John (John the Baptist) would have the spirit and power of the Prophet Elijah! So, John the Baptist was the return of the Prophet Elijah! So, the prophecy of the return of the Prophet Elijah was fulfilled!

So, when the scriptures spoke of John in Luke 1:11-25, that child eventually grew up to be John the Baptist, who was baptizing people in the Jordan River and preparing the way for the first coming of the Lord Jesus Christ (Yeshua)! So you can see the complete telling of this prophecy of John's birth. Let's read Luke 1:11-19.

Luke 1:11-19 reads, [11] Then an angel of the Lord appeared to him, standing at the right side of the altar of incense. [12] When Zechariah saw him, he was startled and was gripped with fear. [13] But the angel said to him: "Do not be afraid, Zechariah; your prayer has been heard. Your wife Elizabeth will bear you a son, **and you are to call him John.** [14] He will be a joy and delight to you, and many will rejoice because of his birth, [15] for he will be great in the sight of the Lord. He is never to take wine or other fermented drink, and he will be filled with the Holy Spirit even before he is born. [16] He will bring back many of the people of Israel to the Lord their God. [17] **And he will go on before the Lord, in the spirit and power of Elijah**, to turn the hearts of the parents to their children and the disobedient to the wisdom of the righteous— to make ready a people prepared for the Lord." [18] Zechariah asked the angel, "How can I be sure of this? I am an old man and my wife is well along in years." [19] The angel said to him, "I am Gabriel. I stand in the presence of God, and I have been sent to speak to you and to tell you this good news. (NIV, Biblegateway.com)

In Luke 1:11-17, there was a lot of important information. First, the angel Gabriel appeared before the Priest Zechariah. Then the angel Gabriel told Zechariah that he and his wife would have a son, and his name would be John (John the Baptist), and his Son would be filled with the Holy Spirit from birth, and he would bring many people back to their Lord God, **and his Son will be sent ahead of the Lord in the spirit and power of Elijah.** Luke 1:17 tells you plainly and clearly that the child John (John the Baptist) will go before the Lord in the spirit and power of Elijah. Since John (John the Baptist) was filled with the spirit and power of Elijah, then John (John the Baptist) was the Prophet Elijah! It is the spirit that is in us that makes us who we are. Not our external features or our body cavity make us who we are. The spirit possesses the body cavity that makes us who we are. Since John the Baptist was born with the spirit of the Prophet Elijah, that means John the Baptist was the Prophet Elijah!

It was the spirit of Elijah in John the Baptist that made John the Baptist the Prophet Elijah. Many Biblical Scholars don't understand this because they were expecting Elijah to return as an adult because he was taken into heaven as an adult. Many Biblical Scholars couldn't conceive that Elijah would be reborn into this world as a child or reincarnated into this world as a child! Because many Biblical Scholars were taught like I was, reincarnation isn't real! But according to the Bible, it is real! Because the Prophet Elijah was reborn into this world as John the Baptist! If you don't believe me read the scriptures again and see what the scriptures tell you.

Now, let's look at the scriptures to see what Jesus Christ (Yeshua) said about John the Baptist and who John the Baptist was. The Lord Jesus Christ (Yeshua) confirmed in Matthew 11:14 that John the Baptist was the Prophet Elijah! This is a significant confirmation because it is Jesus speaking in Mathew 11:14-15.

Matthew 11:14-15 ^{14} If you are willing to accept it, John is the Elijah who was supposed to come. ^{15} Those who have ears should listen." (Biblegateway.com, NIV)

The Lord Jesus Christ (Yeshua) tells you in Mathew 11:14 that John the Baptist was the Prophet Elijah that was to come. It cannot get any clearer than that! Jesus clearly said John the Baptist was the Prophet Elijah that was to come! And those were the words of Jesus Christ (Yeshua)! And if anyone says John the Baptist wasn't the return of the Prophet Elijah. They are saying Jesus Christ (Yeshua) was lying in Matthew 11:14. Since Jesus tells us John the Baptist was the Prophet Elijah that was to come, one must ask, why did John the Baptist deny being the Prophet Elijah? In John 1:22, John the Baptist clearly states he wasn't the Prophet Elijah. So you may see what I am talking about, let's read John 1:19-23.

John 1:19-23 reads, ^{19} "Now this was John's testimony when the Jewish leaders in Jerusalem sent priests and Levites to ask him who he was. ^{20} He did not fail to confess, but confessed freely, "I am not the Messiah." ^{21} **They asked him, "Then who are you? Are you Elijah?" He said, "I am not."** "Are you the Prophet?" He answered, "No." ^{22} Finally they said, "Who are you? Give us an answer to take back to those who sent us. What do you say about yourself?" ^{23} John replied in the words of Isaiah the Prophet, "I am the voice of one calling in the wilderness, 'Make straight the way for the Lord.'" (NIV, BibleGateway.com)

In John 1:21, John the Baptist told the people he wasn't the Prophet Elijah. But in Matthew 11:14, Jesus Christ (Yeshua) clearly stated John the Baptist was the Prophet Elijah. So, why did John the Baptist say he wasn't the Prophet Elijah in John 1:21? The reason why John said he wasn't the Prophet Elijah is because John didn't know who he was. But how could John the Baptist be the Prophet Elijah, and he didn't know it?

The Lord hid this knowledge from John the same way the Lord hid the knowledge from me. John the Baptist didn't know he was the Prophet Elijah from the Old Testament, the same way I didn't know I was the Prophet Elisha from the Old Testament! Since childhood, I have asked the Lord one constant question. On many occasions, I asked the Lord, "Lord, who am I?" Since I was a child, I had asked the Lord that same question over and over because I felt like something was being hidden from me! I found myself asking that question because of the supernatural things that were happening to me in my life. Another reason I ask that question is because I had this feeling something was being hidden from me. The truth was being hidden from me that I am the Prophet Elisha, the same way it was hidden from John the Baptist. So when John said he wasn't the Prophet Elijah, he didn't realize who he truly was because John didn't remember when he walked this earth as the Prophet Elijah. Just like I didn't remember the former things of the days I walked this earth as the Prophet Elisha of the Old Testament.

The Most High God Jehovah (Yahweh) had a divine purpose for using two Prophets whose names sound the same and who walked the face of this earth at the same time. This was a strategic move for God to use two Prophets whose names sound the same and who also walked the face of this earth at the same time. Elijah was the **first** of the two prophets. Elijah was the **first** Prophet to be called by the Holy Father. Elijah was the **first** to enter the Kingdom of Heaven without dying. The Prophet Elijah was the **first** to return and fulfilled the prophecy of his return. The Prophet Elijah returned as John the Baptist. And John the Baptist ushered in the **first coming** of the Lord Jesus Christ. The Prophet Elijah was chosen **first**. I, the Prophet Elisha was chosen **second**. I, the Prophet Elisha, was called by the Lord after the Prophet Elijah, which made me **second to be called by the Lord**. I, the Prophet Elisha, will be second to enter the Kingdom of Heaven without dying. I, the Prophet Elisha, received a **double portion** of Elijah's spirit once Elijah was taken up into the heavens. And I, Elisha, am ushering in the **second coming of** the Lord Jesus Christ. I hope you noticed the theme that God used! The theme was that the Prophet Elijah would be first and the Prophet Elisha would be second. **First** came the return of the Prophet Elijah to usher in the **first coming of the Lord Jesus Christ (Yeshua)**, and then **second** will be the return of the Prophet Elisha to usher in the **second coming of the Lord Jesus Christ (Yeshua)!** This is one of the Holy Father's eternal truths!

By the Holy Father using two Prophets with similar names that walked the face of the earth at the same time, the Holy Father hide his intentions in plain sight! People were looking for Elijah's return because of the dramatic way Elijah was taken! But no one expected my return because I, the Prophet Elisha, wasn't taken dramatically away like Elijah. So, God hid his intentions in plain sight for the Prophet Elijah to return and usher in the first coming of the Lord Jesus Christ (Yeshua), and then used me, the Prophet Elisha, to usher in the second coming of the Lord Jesus Christ (Yeshua). If you notice, both Prophets walked this earth simultaneously, and both names sound similar! The Lord did that for a reason! God didn't want his plans to be known because Satan would have tried to kill off the prophecy the same way he tried to kill off the prophecy of the coming of the King of the Jews, Jesus Christ (Yeshua)! God use the two Prophets, whose names sound alike, to usher in the first and second coming of the Lord Jesus Christ (Yeshua)!

As you read this book, you must keep your mind open and not closed because you are about to be taught the absolute truth about everything. This absolute truth is not based on my perception but on what the Most High God Jehovah (Yahweh) and the Lord Jesus Christ (Yeshua) have told me. You need to keep your mind open while you read this book. To understand the importance of an open mind, let me teach you what my dad taught me. My dad would tell me and my siblings, "Your mind is like a book! If that book is closed, then you can't get any of the information out of it! But if you open the book, you can receive all the knowledge that is in the book." Then my dad would say, "Your mind is just like a book; if you open your mind to different things, you can learn extraordinary things. But if you close your mind to different things, you will never learn because you have closed your mind to receiving old or new information!" That analogy my dad used was simple but brilliant! Because you are either a person who has an open mind or you are a person who has a closed mind! And if you have an open mind, you can receive the vast knowledge the Lord has given me to share with you! But if you have a closed mind you can't receive valuable information. That concept of having an open mind allowed the Lord to reveal to me the absolute truth about the greatest mysteries known to mankind!

This book contains highly classified top-secret information about the United States Government and other world governments. And because this book contains highly classified top-secret information, I couldn't allow anyone to edit this book, nor could I allow anyone to proofread this book. So, this book was written by me and edited by me. To put it plainly, they kill people for the type of information I am releasing in this book! But don't be afraid; THEY WANT ME, NOT YOU!

This book is the most important book written since the Holy Bible was written! This book is the second most important book ever written! This book is only second to the Holy Bible itself. I don't say this because I am arrogant, nor did I say that because I am ignorant! I said this because it is the absolute truth! What I am about to reveal to you is what the Most High God, Jehovah (Yahweh), has revealed to me throughout my life, and it is groundbreaking! What if God told you the absolute truth about everything? What would you do with that information? God told me everything and told me to write this book so you will know the absolute truth about everything!

So, I say to you, if you want to know the absolute truth about everything, read this book. But I must warn you that you will never be the same after reading this book! If you want to stay where you are now and be ignorant of what is happening, don't read this book! You may think you know what is happening in this world, but you truly don't have a clue. You only know what they wanted you to know! The question you should be asking is, "Who are they?" No matter what country you live in, they are there!

As you read this book, I want you to remember that everything is connected, and all these short stories I am telling you about my life will all tie in together. So, as you read these short stories, they will begin to make more and more sense to you as you make your way through my life and this book. You must remember one thing about this world: everything is connected!

1. The Day of My Birth

The story I am about to tell you was told to me by my mom and my older sibling, Junior. The day I was born, the Lord came to my daddy,

Mervin M. Brown, and gave him a vision. The way this story was told to me by my mother and brother went as follows.

Upon my mom giving birth to me at University Hospital in Birmingham, Alabama, my dad was filled with joy. So, my dad went outside for a moment to his car. And it is said, my dad was very merry, so he had himself a beer. Then, after my dad had himself a beer, he walked back into my mom's room with so much joy and excitement, and then my dad said, "The Lord just gave me a vision. The Lord showed me and told me this boy will be President of the United States of America one day!" They said my dad was so excited and joyful that he didn't know what to do. And then my dad said, "Since he is going to be the President of the United States of America, I am going to give him a name that sounds like a President." Then my dad said, "I will name him after John F. Kennedy and Martin Luther King Jr.! So, his name will be Kennedy King Brown!" So, on February 17, 1971, I was named Kennedy King Brown! My dad would always tell people I would be the President of the United States of America one day! He told everyone who would listen!

2. Dreams of Falling From The Sky

As a child, I had what I thought was a recurring dream night after night. The dream would always start with me being in this beautiful place where everything was perfect (Heaven), and this beautiful light covered everything. I was in the presence of this beautiful light (in the presence of the Holy Father and the Lord Jesus Christ). In a split second, I was propelled from this place of light to this place full of darkness (this world). The further I fell, the darker it became. This place I was falling to was full of pain and torment. There would always be people who were trying to kill me in this place of darkness. These people would be chasing me, and they would be trying to kill me! Then I would reach some clouds and then I would wake up.

For many years, I didn't understand how I could have the same dream night after night. The events of the dream always happen the same way each time. There was never a deviation in this dream. It was not until I received higher spiritual wisdom in this world that I began to understand it was not a dream I was having but a memory of the former things in Heaven. I remembered my time in Heaven before I was sent into this world. I was remembering Heaven. The Holy Father and the Lord Jesus Christ were the beautiful light that covered Heaven. When I said I was in the presence of the light, I stood before the presence of the

Holy of Holies, God the Father and his son, the Lord Jesus Christ. Once I gained the understanding that my dream was truly a memory. I then began to understand what God said in Jeremiah 1:5.

Jeremiah 1:5, "Before I formed you in the womb I knew you, before you were born I set you apart; I appointed you as a prophet to the nations." (NIV, BibleGateway.com)

So, God knew me before I was formed in my mother's womb because I was in Heaven with the Most High God Jehovah. I was in Heaven before I was born into this world. So, the dream I had falling from this place of light to this place of darkness is what happened to me when I was sent from Heaven to Earth. One moment, I was standing before the Heavenly Father and thy Lord Jesus Christ, and the next moment, I was propelled to this place of darkness that was full of pain and torment. I was falling to this earth where many people would hate me. And they would try to kill me because of who I am. So basically, the dream was not a dream. It was a memory I had of leaving Heaven and entering this world that is full of darkness and full of sin!

3. My Mother Falls Out Of A Chair

When I was a child, I would always have this discussion with my mother and my sisters about how my mother fell out of a chair when she was pregnant. Each time I had this discussion with them, they would look at me strangely and then say, "You couldn't remember that because you hadn't been born yet." Each time I would insist I remembered the event, but to no prevail, they would always insist I didn't remember the event because I hadn't been born yet. So, I always walked away from the conversation confused because I knew I was there. Because I know what I saw, and I know I saw it happen.

Once I became older, we would have the same discussion, and like on previous occasions, my mother and sisters would say, "You couldn't remember that because you hadn't been born yet." I would insist I remembered the event but to no prevail. Because they would always try to convince me I was wrong. So, I would always walk away confused because I knew what I saw and remembered. The memory of my mother falling out of the chair while pregnant has stuck with me all of my life. It wasn't until I was in my twenties, and I had many different experiences with the Lord, that one great revelation hit me about my mother falling out of the chair while pregnant. The revelation was this: how could I remember my mother falling out of the chair while pregnant when I was the youngest child? My mother never became pregnant again after she had me. I was the youngest of nine children!

Then I understood what my mother and sisters meant when they said, "You couldn't remember that because you hadn't been born yet." My mother and sisters were kind of right when they said that because I was the child my mother was pregnant with when she fell out of the chair while pregnant! I shouldn't have remembered the event since I hadn't been born yet! Once that great revelation hit me, I realized I saw my mother falling out of the chair before I was born into this world! Once I came to grips with that great revelation, at that very moment, I remembered everything that happened that day when my mother fell out of the chair while she was pregnant with me. I remembered everything I witnessed that day and how I witnessed it. This is what happened that day!

The Lord took me to see the family I would be born into. So, the Lord took me to my parents' house in East Thomas. I was in the spirit, and the Lord was standing beside me. I remember the Lord, and I was standing near the kitchen doorway facing the living room. I couldn't see the Lord's face, but he was standing to my left, and I was to his right. Then the Lord said, "This is the family you will be assigned to, and this is where we will hide you until it is your time." After the Lord said those words to me, I remember watching my mother standing in a chair, working on the window curtains on the right side of the big window in the living room. While working on the curtains, my mother lost her footing on the chair and fell. Then, my sisters rushed over to her and picked her off the floor. Then they took my mother and sat her down on the couch.

Then they asked my mother if she was okay and did she hurt the baby. At that point, I stood directly in front of the coffee table where my mother sat on the couch. I remember trying to speak to my mother to see if she was okay, but no one would speak to me because they couldn't hear me. But for a moment my mother looked directly at me as though she saw me briefly or sensed someone was there. Then I asked the Lord, why want anyone say anything to me? Then the Lord said to me, "They cannot hear you because the child she is carrying is you." I remember standing in front of my mom and my sisters in the spirit, and they couldn't see or hear me.

The person beside me in the vision was the Lord Jesus Christ. The Lord allowed me to witness that event in the spirit for a few reasons. So

I would have memories of it and one day understand what I saw, how I saw it, and what was said to me. The keywords that were spoken to me in the vision were, "This is the family you will be assigned to, and this is where we will **hide you until** it is your time." The Lord hid me in a poor African American family in Birmingham, Alabama.

I understood why I always had memories of my mother falling out of the chair while pregnant. I remember the event because I witnessed it in the spirit before I was born into this world! Once I remembered the event, I understood why I always loved the scripture Jeremiah 1:5. The Lord knew me before I was formed in my mother's womb! Because the Lord took me to visit the family I was to be born into before I was born into this world!

Jeremiah 1:5, "Before I formed you in the womb I knew you, before you were born I set you apart; I appointed you as a prophet to the nations." (NIV, BibleGateway.com)

4. Hangers In My Left Eye

Starting at the age of four or five, I had a consistent problem with clothes hangers! Every time I picked up a wire clothes hanger, the hook of the wire clothes hanger would get caught inside of my left eye. Then, each time the hook of the clothes hanger got caught inside my left eye, I would start crying, and my mother or sister would have to come and get the hanger out of my left eye. The majority of the time, it was my mother who got the hanger out of my eye. My mother would always be baffled, just like I was baffled. My mother would say, "Boy, how in the world do you keep getting hangers caught in your eye." I would then respond, "I don't know, some kind of a way it goes in there by itself!" After I said that to my mother, she would stand back and just look at me with this puzzle look. My mother once said, "Why do you always get the hanger caught in your left eye and never your right eye?" When she asked that question, I realized the hanger never got caught in my right; it always got caught in my left eye.

No matter what I would be doing if a hanger were in my proximity, the hook of the wire hanger would land inside my left eye. It had gotten to a point where I was paranoid about clothes hangers. So, I tried my best to stay away from all clothes hangers. But no matter how much I tried to stay away from clothes hangers, the hook of the hangers would land inside my left eye and get stuck. It would be a normal day; then someone would tell me to bring them a hanger. Once I heard the word hanger, I would get scared and paranoid to pick up a hanger because I knew the result. I knew some kind of way the hanger was going to end up in my eye.

So, one day, I decided to beat the clothes hangers, so I formulated a plan. I planned to hold the clothes hanger in both hands while my arms were stretched straight out in front of me. Then, I walked very slowly to ensure the hanger didn't get caught in my left eye. So, as I was executing the plan, something that I couldn't see suddenly tripped me and made me stumble. Then the hanger went into my left eye. Something that was invisible would always trip me and cause the hanger to go into my left eye! No matter what I did to prevent the hanger from getting caught in my left eye, the hanger's final destination always landed in my left eye.

I remember my mother saying numerous times, "I don't understand how this boy hasn't put his eye out yet! As many times he got hangers caught in his eye!" My mother took the hangers out of my eye so many times she became an expert at it. The hanger itself never caused any harm to my left eye. It would just scare me more than anything. Then I had to hear the ridicule from my brothers and sisters of how something was wrong with me because hangers always got caught in my eye.

The hangar incidents went on for about four or five years. If I had to put a number on how many hangers got caught in my left eye, I would say it was about forty or more times. It was not until I was 41 years old that the Lord revealed the riddle of why hangers were going into my left eye.

5. My Life

I was born and raised in Birmingham, AL, in the southern part of the United States of America. I grew up in a community known as East Thomas, but the older generation knew the community by the name of Saint Mark. So, I was born the ninth child of Mervin and Dannie Brown. But I was raised as the eighth child because one of my sisters died before my birth. Her name was Elizabeth Brown (Liz). So, I was often called the baby of the family. No matter how old I became, people always said, "He's the baby!" It was a title I could never escape.

So, I grew up in a house with ten people: my father, my mother, my seven siblings, and I. In the beginning, we all lived in a two-bedroom, one-bath house no bigger than 700 square feet. My mother and father had one bedroom, my four sisters had the other bedroom, and my three brothers and I slept in the living room. My oldest brother, Jr., was in and out during this time, which freed up a little space for my other two brothers and me to sleep on the pull-out sofa bed. My brothers and I slept on one pull-out sofa bed in the living room. It was very close living conditions. It was even tighter conditions when we were all trying to get into the restroom at the same time. Imagine ten people using one very tiny restroom. To understand our financial situation, you must imagine this. I was handed down my brother's clothes and underwear growing up. You have humble beginnings when you are handed down someone else's underwear. When my brothers and I were sleeping in the living room, I don't remember having a dresser or closet for our clothes. I guess we didn't have many clothes, so there was no need for a closet or dresser.

I remember always being outside when I was young. I stayed outside a lot as a child because I had all the space to roam. But when I was inside the house, there was minimal personal space because the house was so small. Another reason I stayed outside a lot as a child was because we didn't have any air conditioning. The temperature could reach 100 degrees or more in the house in the summer time and the humidity could be so high you could dehydrate in a matter of hours by just sitting in the house. We didn't have air conditioning because my dad said he wouldn't pay for air because air was free. We didn't have air conditioning, but we did have several fans in the house. We would place the fans in the windows to cool the house down, but the fans would only pull in hot air during the day. So, I would go outside during the day to cool down because it was much cooler outside than inside the house. I always stayed outside as a child because there was more space, and it was much cooler outside than inside the house.

So, you can say we were poor growing up. My mom and dad worked very hard and very long hours at their jobs, but they weren't paid much. They had to feed and clothe ten people. And everyone had a need. My mother worked as a Nursing Assistant at Jefferson County Nursing Home, and my dad worked as a laborer at Kirkpatrick Sand and Cement. My dad always worked long hours, but he started working even longer hours after he and my mom had a conversation.

I remember a stretch when we were really broke. The power and water had been turned off a few times, and no food was in the refrigerator. Times were always tough, but when your power and water were off and nothing was in the refrigerator, that meant things were really bad. So, one day, I witnessed a conversation between my mom and dad. A conversation I will never forget. We were in dire financial hardship, and there was no food in the refrigerator to eat. My mom told my dad, "Brown, maybe we should go down and apply for some food stamps. I am sure with all these kids, we can get some food stamps." After my mom said that, I sat back and watched my dad's response and saw the look on my dad's face. My dad had a look that said, "Hell No!" And then my dad said, "Ain't no way in this world I am about to go down and beg nobody for some food stamps. And ain't no way in God's green earth am I going to ask the government or anybody else to feed my family." My mom got upset, but my dad had laid down the law. And it was at that point my dad and mom worked even longer hours. My dad would normally work from six in the morning to about five in the evening. But after that conversation with my mom, he worked from about 6:00 AM to about 8:00 PM and then on Saturdays. And my mom would work more overtime hours, too. So we never did get on food stamps because my dad had placed his foot down. My dad was a proud man a stubborn man. I mean, he was a very proud and stubborn man!

My dad and mom both fit the definition of being hard workers. That's all my dad and mom knew was hard work. My dad had to work in the Alabama cotton fields as a child to help his mom and dad financially. So, my dad had to drop out of school in the third grade to help his family financially. And once my dad entered the Alabama cotton fields to work, he never returned to school. My dad only had a second-grade education. My dad did what he did best: he worked long and hard. Many years later, when I was in my twenties, I realized my dad couldn't read. My dad would always say, "Be the best at whatever you decide to do. If you are a doctor, be the best at being a doctor. If you are a garbage man, be the best garbage man there is. Just be the best at whatever you do!" And that was one lesson my dad taught us. Be the best at whatever you do!

So, growing up in our family was not glamorous, but it was fun. There was always something going on in our house. With ten people living in one small house, it was something always going on. We didn't have much, but we made the most out of whatever we had. We didn't have many fancy toys or clothes, but we used whatever we had to make it through. Even though we didn't have much, my dad and mom made sure we grew up with an expectation that anything was possible in this world and that we could be whatever we wanted to be if we put our mind to it. This was a conversation my dad would pound into our heads daily.

I remember my dad and mom taking us to see how others lived in Birmingham. He would load all of us up in the station wagon, drive us over to Vestavia Hills or Mountain Brook, and show us how wealthy white people lived in Birmingham. My dad would drive us around, show us their big houses, and tell us we could have the same thing if we put our minds to it. My dad and mother would tell us we were just as good as anyone else and that we could achieve anything if we put our minds to it.

So, my dad and mother wanted to ensure we knew there was more to life than the community we grew up in. My dad would always take us to the airport and park on the side of the road so we could see the planes take off and land so we could see the lights on the runway at night. As we watched the airplanes land and take off, my dad told us there was much more to this world than Birmingham. So, my dad and mom tried to expose us to other cities whenever they could scrape up some money for a road trip. And we made the most of it whenever we took a road trip. It was a serious road trip for us if we were just going to my grandmother's house in Lavaca, Alabama. We would pack sandwiches, and my dad would have a cooler full of drinks and we would pack up the station wagons and just ride out. When I was young, we didn't go to many places besides my grandmother's house, but when we did venture out to other places, it was a trip to remember!

6. Telling People I Been Places I Never Been

Growing up, I experienced many supernatural things that I didn't understand. These supernatural things always kept me pondering about this world we live in. For instance, as a child, I always felt I'd been to this world before. I had this feeling because it seemed like I was living my life for a second time. But then I would think, "How is it possible, I have been to this world before?" No matter what I did to shake this feeling, it would never leave me. Then there were the déjà vu moments I often had. I always insisted I had been to a particular place, even though I knew I had never been there. The year is 1977, I'm six years old. My dad and mother took me and my siblings to Six Flags Over Texas.

When we entered the theme park, I felt an intense feeling come over me. I remembered looking around and saying, "I have been here before." But my brothers and sisters insisted I had never been to Six Flags Over Texas. And they were right; I had never physically been to Six Flags Over Texas before, but I kept insisting I had been there. They began to tell me it was only Déjà Vu, but I couldn't accept what they told me. So, I began to get angry with them and started yelling at them, saying, "I've been here before. I've been here before!"

Then, at that very moment, I began to explain to them what was about to happen. I told them a young white girl wearing some red and yellow clothing would walk from behind the gray fence carrying a lot of balloons, and she would stumble and lose her balloons. And all her balloons were going to go up in the sky. So, when I completed my sentence, the young white girl I described walked from behind the gray fence. She was wearing the same outfit and colors I described. She had on a yellow and red outfit. The young girl was carrying a handful of balloons, just like I described to my family. The young girl stumbled and lost control of all her balloons. The balloons then went up into the air.

After my parents and siblings witnessed this event with their own eyes, they all turned and looked at me and said, "How did you know that was going to happen?" I said, "I told y'all I had been here before!" They all were astonished! I remember my mother had this look of amazement and this look of confusion on her face at the same time. My mother had this look on her face as if she knew something about me, but she wouldn't say what it was she knew. So, once the balloon incident happened, it only held my sibling's attention momentarily. And then they were off to ride the rides in the amusement park. And because I was the youngest, I was left with my mom and dad at the amusement park. I had plenty of time to sit down and think.

After the balloon incident, I asked myself, "How did I know that would happen?" I finally concluded that I had seen the entire event in a dream. But I couldn't understand how something I'd seen in a dream could come true in real life. This threw me for a loop because people used to tell me dreams weren't real. My thinking process was, if dreams weren't real, how did I dream the event about the girl, and it came true? I tried to explain this to my brothers and sisters later that day, but they wouldn't listen to me. They would only say, "It was just Déjà Vu". To them, the word Déjà Vu was the fix-all for anything unexplainable.

A lot of supernatural events surrounded the trip to Six Flags over Texas. On the way to Texas, we had to get off the main road because the Interstate was closed. We had to pull over to a gas station in this rural part of Texas. The feeling I had as a child was that we were in the wrong area for black people to be in because of racist white people. It was a feeling that just overtook me. So, we stopped to get some gas and use the restroom. Everyone at the gas station was white, and you could feel the prejudice in the air. Then suddenly, three black men appeared out of thin air. They were standing shoulder to shoulder with each other and they all had long beards. They look straight ahead. They didn't turn their head to the left or right. They just looked straight ahead! They wore long robes, and they didn't speak to anyone.

They just stood in the middle of the parking lot. They look like the two witnesses that the Book of Revelations described. These men were no ordinary men they had a presence that was holy and divine! Once they appeared, the white people forgot about us because they were trying to figure out who the three men were and where they came from. The three men didn't say a word. They just stood there looking straight ahead. My mother was trying to figure out who the three black men were! The entire time we pumped gas and used the restroom, the three men stood in one spot. Once we packed up into the two cars we began to drive off, so I kept my eyes on the three men.

Once we pulled out of the parking lot, the three men disappeared into thin air, and my mother said, "Where did those three men disappear to?" They were gone! I think they were sent there to ensure our safety because we were in a small rural area that was hostile to black people. I think we were in a Ku Klux Klan town! You must remember the year was 1977.

So, as a young boy, I had all these strange and supernatural things happening to me, but I had no one to talk to about them because my siblings were no help at all. So, I had to figure out why these things were happening to me. It took me many years of analyzing my dreams to understand what was happening. Over the years I started noticing I had two types of dreams. One type of dream was regular dreams. These regular dreams were just random selections of pictures flowing through my mind. This is the type of dream everyone has. The next type of dreams were real-life High-Definition dreams. These dreams felt real, and they felt like I was there experiencing events in real life. They were always in high definition. These high-definition dreams always came true and manifested in real life like I saw them in my dreams. In these high-definition dreams, I witnessed actual life events before they happened in real life. As I got older, I realized these high-definition dreams were not dreams. They were visions! And these visions were shown to me by the Most High God Jehovah (Yahweh) and the Lord Jesus Christ! When I was a child, the Lord was just using situations like the gas station incident and the Six Flags over Texas incident to get my attention at a very young age.

7. Go and Get Baptize

One Sunday, when I was about seven years old, I attended church with my parents and siblings at Enon United Methodist Church. At the end of the service, the Pastor said, "The doors of the church are open. And anyone who wants to accept Jesus Christ as their Lord and Savior, come and be baptized." At that very moment, I heard this man's voice say to me in my left ear, "Go and get baptized." I immediately turned to see who was talking to me! But when I turned around there was no one there. Then, as the preacher continued to call for baptism, I heard this man's voice again in my left ear, "Go and get baptized." I turned to my left to look and see who was speaking to me, but again, there was no one there. At that very moment, my mother noticed I was looking around with this puzzled look on my face, and she said to me, "What is wrong?" I told my mother I heard this man's voice telling me to "Go and get baptized." My mother said, "You should listen to the voice and do what it says."

Then I approached the preacher and said, "I want to accept Jesus Christ as my Lord and Savior." The preacher then dipped his hand into this white bowl filled with water. Then, the preacher took some water and sprinkled it on my head. Then the preacher said, "I baptize you in the name of the Holy Father, I baptize you in the name of the Holy Son Jesus Christ, and I baptize you in the name of the Holy Spirit." I was baptized that day with a sprinkling of water on my head. Years later, I learned that the voice that spoke to me that day was the voice of the Lord Jesus Christ. The Lord Jesus Christ spoke directly to me.

8. The Heavenly Father Speaks To Me

I am about seven years old, and one hot Sunday afternoon after church, I was lying in my parents' front yard. It was cooler than being in the house, and there was more room in the yard than in the house. My mother was in the house cooking with a couple of my sisters, my dad was in the backyard with the radio turned up listening to a baseball game, and my other brothers and sisters were on the front porch laughing and joking. I was lying in the front yard thinking and pondering over many thoughts. I had my hands folded behind my head while lying on my back, looking at the clear blue sky. Then I said out loud, "I wonder what is out there in that big old outer space." Then, at that very moment, a loud voice rained down from the sky and said to me, "I, the Lord Almighty, am out here!" I heard this thunderous voice rain down from the sky! The sound of the voice made my entire body tremble, and the ground vibrated beneath me. Full of fear, I got up and ran to the porch. I ran because this voice was loud and full of power and authority.

Once I reached the porch, I told my brothers and sisters I heard this loud voice talking to me. Before I could tell them what the voice said, they all laughed at me and taunted me! They said, "Something is wrong with you because you are hearing voices." They then called my mother and said, "Ma dear, something is wrong with your precious baby boy because he is hearing voices." My brothers and sisters just kept laughing at me and making jokes. They made me feel so bad I didn't even attempt to tell them what the voice said.

My siblings always ridiculed me when I tried to explain the supernatural things happening to me. It had gotten to the point that whenever something supernatural happened to me, I would think about telling my siblings about it. But then the voice of the Lord Jesus Christ would say to me in my left ear, "Don't tell anyone because they won't believe you anyway!" The Lord had told me this on numerous occasions. So, after my siblings ridiculed me, I never told them what the voice said. I kept it to myself and didn't let anyone know about the supernatural things happening to me. That day, I heard the voice of the Most High God Jehovah! The Most High God Jehovah had spoken directly to me!

9. I Am Pronounced Blessed

I am about eight years old, and one day, I am lying in our front yard thinking about different things. As I was just lying there pondering about life and this world I lived in, this man's voice spoke to me in my left ear. The voice said, "You are blessed to be one of the last men to walk the face of this earth." Once I heard this, I was astonished. I sat there thinking about what I had just heard. I thought, "What does that mean? I am blessed to be one of the last men to walk the face of this earth." My original thought was that the world would end in my lifetime. So, as a child, I knew this world we live in was going to come to an end.

Years later, I realized that the voice that spoke to me that day was an angel of the Most High God Jehovah.

10. The Prophesy Was Given By The Lord

My dad grew up in a small town near Butler, Alabama. He was the son of Eddie Brown, my grandfather, and the grandson of Pastor Edgar Brown, my great-grandfather. I never met my grandfather or my great-grandfather because they had passed away years before I was born.

On the day I was born, my dad said the Lord told him and showed him a vision of me being the President of the United States of America. So, my dad named me Kennedy King Brown. My dad named me after two of America's assassinated leaders, John F. Kennedy and Martin Luther King Jr. They were two of the most outstanding leaders this country ever had, along with Abraham Lincoln.

For many years my dad told many people I would be President of the United States of America one day. When people ask my dad how he knew this, he would say, "The Lord told me he would be President of the United States of America one day."

My dad constantly talked to me about being the President of the United States. I remember as a child, my dad used to always try to get my siblings to watch the news when they were younger. My dad always suggested they change the channel from the shows they were watching to watch the news. But my siblings didn't want any part of the news back then. One day, I was alone watching TV, and my dad walked into the house and stared at me watching television. My dad then said these prophetic words to me, "You need to watch the news because you are going to need to know and understand what's going on in the world." And when my dad said this, he had this stare in his eye as thou someone else was speaking through him. This was my first encounter with this stare, but it wouldn't be the last. From then on, I started watching the world news on ABC, CBS, and NBC.

At one point, the World News was my favorite show because I enjoyed watching the world events. I began to understand world events, from events in the U.S. to events around the world in places like Iraq, Iran, and Israel. And whenever I heard the name of Israel on television, I got so excited. I didn't know why I got so excited; I just did. The same thing happened to me whenever I heard the word Hebrew. I would instantly get excited!

I was getting so much information from the news that I was not getting from school. I started watching the world news, and then I started watching political debates, and before I knew it, I was a news junkie as a child. And I have been a news watcher ever since. Since I started watching the news as a child, the Lord would tell me when the news was misleading people and when they were telling the truth. So, I heeded my dad's advice and watched the news.

I remember one day when I was about eight years old, I was in our backyard watching my dad work on his car. My dad had the hood up on his green station wagon and I was leaning under the hood watching him. My dad then started to walk away from the car to get some tools, and then he said to me with a smile, "You are going to be the President of the United States of America one day." After my dad said those words, he paused and hesitated as though someone was talking to him. My dad then got this confused look on his face. Then my dad said out loud, "Lord, is he going to be a preacher? But I thought you told me he would be the President of the United States of America." My dad had this confused look on his face like he was trying to understand something. He turned to me joyfully and said, "Boy, you are going to teach the Lord's word. You are going to be a preacher like your granddaddy and great-granddaddy".

Then my dad walked away, pondering what the Lord had just told him and what he thought the Lord had told him the day I was born. My dad was confused because it seemed like the Lord had told my dad two conflicting prophecies. The day I was born, the Lord told my dad I would be the President of the United States. But then, eight years later, the Lord told my dad I would teach the Lord's word. My dad had two prophecies from the Lord that appeared to be in conflict with each other, but they weren't.

The next day, Mrs. Buchanan walked up to me at church and said with joy, "The Lord wants you to be a preacher." At that moment, I remember thinking, "How does she know the Lord wants me to be a preacher?" She said, "The Lord wants you to teach his word." I stood there thinking, "How does she know the Lord wants me to teach his word?"

After my dad and Mrs. Buchanan came up to me and said, "The Lord wants you to teach his word," the world and the atmosphere changed around me. The atmosphere toward me went from peace, love, and joy to hate, kill, and destroy. I remember noticing the atmosphere changing, and I noticed it was evil, but I couldn't comprehend why and how it changed. I just knew the hearts of almost everyone had changed toward me.

At the time, I didn't understand the anatomy of Satan and his demons. But now I do. When my dad and Mrs. Buchanan's words went into the atmosphere proclaiming the Lord wanted me to teach his word, Satan and his army began to advance against me so Satan could kill, steal, and destroy me before the word of the Lord could ever take root in me. Many people started to hate me, but I didn't understand why. I was a marked person from that point on! I didn't realize this then, but Satan had a standing order against me, and that order was to "Kill, steal, and destroy me at all cost!" And believe me, Satan wanted me dead by any means necessary!

From that moment on, people started to hate me! It was Satan who led the people in this world to hate me and to dislike me. Satan didn't want the prophecy to come true! Satan wanted to stop me at all costs from teaching the Lord's word. Satan knew he had to try to prevent me from teaching the Lord's word. But why? What was so special about me teaching the Lord's word that Satan wanted to stop me at all costs?

As a child, teenager, and adult, I watched every kind of lie and evil spoken against me. I watched people lie on me for no reason whatsoever. I was constantly defending myself one way or another. Whether I was defending myself from the lies being told, or I was defending myself from the insults or I was defending myself from physical harm.

Either way, I was defending myself. I was being persecuted, and I didn't know it. I was being persecuted every day. But as a child, I didn't understand why people hated me. I was a child looking out of a child's eyes. All I knew was that it was very painful, disheartening and it hurt. It was hateful the way children and others were treating me. But many years later, when I became an adult, the Lord revealed to me that I was being persecuted because of him and his word. And then scriptures were revealed to me that confirmed everything the Lord told me. One of the scriptures revealed to me was the words Jesus Christ spoke in Matthew 5:11-12. In Matthew 5:11-12 Jesus Christ spoke of persecution because of him.

Matthew 5:11-12 reads, [11] "Blessed are you when people insult you, persecute you and falsely say all kinds of evil against you because of me. [12] Rejoice and be glad, because great is your reward in Heaven, for in the same way they persecuted the prophets who were before you. (NIV, BibleGateway.com)

So, just like Jesus said, I was being insulted, and people falsely said all kinds of evil about me because the Lord had chosen me to teach his word. But as Jesus said, I was pronounced blessed because great is my reward in Heaven because I received persecution the same way the prophets that came before I received persecution. I didn't understand why people hated me as a child, but now I do. The world hated me because Satan and his demons were set up against me to destroy me so I could never teach the word of the Lord. The persecution came by the way of daily attacks at school. Satan used the children at school and others to march against me.

One day, while I was at school, three kids were being very mean and hateful towards me. They were just attacking me verbally all at once. At that very moment of them attacking me verbally, I was allowed to see into the spiritual realm, and I saw three demonic beings standing behind the children! I saw the demonic-looking creatures standing behind the children, and they were influencing the children to say mean and hateful things to me. And the three children were doing and saying what the demonic spirits were making them say. I stood there in disbelief at what I was seeing. My eyes were open as wide as they would go, and I stood there in shock.

Even the three kids who were mean to me noticed how I looked. And they stopped being mean to me and said, "What do you see?" At that point, I was no longer allowed to see into the spiritual realm. And the three demons were gone from my sight. But I was left standing there in shock. And the three kids kept asking me, "What did you just see?" I didn't tell them or say a word to them about what I saw. Because I knew they wouldn't believe me. And I would not subject myself to the ridicule my brothers and sister would give me whenever I tried to tell them about my supernatural experiences. Plus, the Lord had already warned me to keep the supernatural things I saw or heard to myself.

I was terrified of what I saw! And because I saw these things standing behind the children, I didn't know what to think. I instantly became afraid of the children. I instantly became afraid of the children because I correlated the meanness and hatefulness of the children with the demonic-looking creatures that were standing behind them. I will never forget that day because I witnessed three demonic spirit creatures that were hideous looking.

Now listen to what I am about to share with you. And pay very close attention to what I am about to say. The demonic creatures I saw in the spirit were reptilian-looking creatures that stood on two legs. These demonic beings stood on two legs. They stood upright like human beings stand upright. And they had two arms. Its skin looked like the skin texture of an Iguana. And their face and body looked like a T-Rex (Tyrannosaurus Rex). Yes, I said their face and body looked like a T-Rex (Tyrannosaurus Rex). But these beings stood upright like humans. Their eyeballs were blood red. I mean, their eyeballs were blood red, red like crimson.

In Ephesians 6:12 the Apostle Paul told us that evil forces exist in the heavenly realm. And when the Apostle Paul used the term heavenly realm, Paul was referring to the air around us. As a child, I witnessed three demonic spirits in the heavenly realm (in the air). This is why I felt the atmosphere around me change from peace, love, and joy to hate, kill, and destroy. The demonic spirits sent to march against me in the air changed the atmosphere around me. These demonic spirits in the heavenly realms (in the air) were sent to kill, steal, and destroy me.

Ephesians 6:" 12 reads, [12] For our struggle is not against flesh and blood, but against the rulers, against the authorities, against the powers of this dark world and against the spiritual forces of evil in the heavenly realms. (NIV, BibleGateway.com)

So again, my war and your war are not against flesh and blood but against the spiritual forces of evil in the heavenly realms (air) that influence people's behavior. As a child I didn't understand nor truly grasp what was happening. I didn't realize Satan had a bounty on my head! I didn't realize Satan wanted me dead at all cost!

11. The Lord Saves My Life

I remember one particular summer morning when I was eight years old. I was at home with my mom and I had become bored. So, I decided to walk by myself to East Thomas Park. East Thomas Park was the neighborhood park that was two blocks away from my house. So, I left the house without telling my mom where I was going. I walked down to the park expecting to find children playing, but once I got there, there were no children. I only saw these two older guys sitting on the swings. The two older guys may have been between 18 and 21 years old. I thought I knew them because I had seen their faces around the neighborhood before, so I went to talk to them.

After talking to them for about thirty minutes, they convinced me to follow them. So we walk through a path that cuts across the train tracks. I felt I shouldn't go with them, but they convinced me to go. Then something kept telling me to turn around and to go home. The two guys convinced me to follow them whenever I got ready to turn around and go home. The two guys stayed ahead of me and kept whispering something to each other. And eventually we reached this abandoned building that was on 10th Court. This abandoned building was a two-story building that used to be a convenience store.

Once we reached the abandoned building, we went to the side door that was open. I stood outside the door and I was very hesitant about going in. The two guys kept urging me to go into the building. One of the guys had already entered the abandoned building, and the other guy was standing behind me. I didn't want to enter the abandoned building, but they persuaded me to go in.

Once I entered the abandoned building, one of the guys headed up the stairs, and he told me to follow him while the other guy stood behind me. So I followed him up the stairs, and once we reached the top, the guy in front of me went off to the right while the other guy stayed on the steps right behind me. So once I reached the top of the steps, I thought, "What now?" So I turned around and looked at the guy behind me on the steps.

Once I turned around, the guy on the steps pointed something at me! At that moment I realized he had a gun pointed at me and they were about to kill me! So I started to scream real loud saying, "Stop, stop, don't do that." As I was screaming, I put my arms up and backed backward, trying to get away from the guy with the gun. Then I turned my head to the right and looked through the doorway to my right. Then I saw this brown skin black man with a blue robe on. The man flickered as though he was being projected into the room, like a digital download. Then, this feeling came over me at that very moment, and I exited my body. Once I exited my body, I stood in the next room next to the man wearing the blue robe. I was then looking at my physical self-standing in front of the guy with the gun.

At that very moment, I was watching myself screaming from across the room. Then, the guy pulled the trigger and shot three times. I thought he had shot me because he was so close to me that he couldn't have missed me. After the guy fired the gun three times, I instantly returned to my body. I was in a frantic state because this guy just shot at me at point-blank range. I was backed up against the wall because I was afraid. Both guys stared at each other with a confused look on their faces. The guy on the top of the steps with me said, "You missed him from that close of a distance." The guy standing on the stairs said, "I couldn't have missed him; he is right in front of me." I was still standing there, afraid, not knowing what to do. I then moved to my right towards the room, trying to escape them.

Once I moved, they began to stare at the wall behind me. Once I moved, there were three bullet holes in the wall at the exact place I was standing. The guys just looked at each other with a look of amazement and fear on their faces. Then they said to each other, "He was standing right there where the bullet holes are." They looked at me as though I was the Devil, and then they ran down the steps and out of the abandoned building. Once they were gone, I looked for the man with the blue robe, but he had disappeared. I didn't understand where the man with the long beard and robe had disappeared too. He was nowhere to be found.

I was left there in this abandoned building all alone and I was afraid and confused. I went to the wall where I was standing when the guy shot at me, and I saw the three bullet holes. I saw the bullet holes were in the same spot I was standing. And I just stared at the wall. I honestly didn't grasp all that had happened because I was no more than eight years old. I didn't grasp the bullets went straight through my skin without harming my flesh. I didn't grasp the miracle that had just happened. I didn't grasp who the man was in the blue robe. I didn't grasp how this man manifested out of thin air. I didn't grasp how I could leave my physical body and look at my physical body from the opposite side of the room. I didn't grasp how my spirit was called over to this man who had on this blue robe. And how my spirit returned to my body after the guy fired the three shots.

I was left in this abandoned building all alone. I was frightened, scared, and confused all at once! I was afraid and confused about everything that had happened. So, I left the abandoned building crying because I was afraid and confused. I decided to walk home; while walking down the street on 14th Court West, I saw my mother standing on the steps looking for me. When she saw me, I saw how her face went from being worried to being furious. My mother started yelling at me and fussing at me because I had left the house by myself, and I was no more than eight years old. So once I walked towards the porch, my mother said, "Boy, you left this house by yourself; somebody could have killed you!" Those were her exact words! It's like she knew my life was in danger! Then my momma got a switch off the tree and went to work on me; I mean, she beat my butt! And she lectured me as she beat my butt!

After my mother got through beating me, I was in some severe pain. So I didn't get a chance to tell her how some guys tried to kill me!! And I'm glad I didn't tell her because my mother always worried about my safety! So after my mother beat my butt, I thought about the man I saw and how I was outside of my body. The man I saw was dressed in a blue robe. He had a shawl-like thing covering his head. Many years later, I learned the shawl covering his head was a Tallit, a Jewish prayer shawl. The man had a long, Amish-looking beard and wore an old Jewish robe. This man was a man of color. That man's skin color was a little darker than mine; he was brown-skinned.

I don't know who this man was. I only know that he appeared out of nowhere at the moment of my distress. I know the man was from Heaven, but I always asked whether he was an angel sent by God, or was he the Lord Jesus Christ. I asked if he was an angel or Jesus because of how the man looked and dressed. Over my life time, I would see many angels, but none looked or dressed like the man I saw in the abandoned building that day. And it always puzzled me why the man flickered like he was being projected into the room or better yet like he was being beamed down into the room like Captain Kirk from Star Trek "Beam me up Scotty".

12. Years Later I Realize It Was The Lord

I remember one day when I was about nine or ten years old, I was playing at the twin's house. The twins were two boys that lived across the street from me. One of the twins was named Keith, and the other I will call "K". It was summertime, so I would go to their house and play with them while their parents were at work. One day, while at their house, "K" gets his father's .38-caliber pistol. "K" brings out the gun and starts playing with it. So, "K" takes the gun, points the gun at me, and pulls the trigger. I started yelling at "K" to stop, and I started to run. "K" started laughing, then said, "The gun was empty". I turned back around and went back over there. "K" then opened the gun and showed me the gun was empty. "K" then said, "Let me go and put this gun up before we get into trouble."

So "K" went into the house and put the gun up while Keith stayed outside with me. "K" returned from inside the house, and Keith went inside. A few minutes later, Keith returned and pulled the gun out of his pocket. Keith then took the gun and pointed it at me. I told Keith to stop playing and to put the gun up. Before I could do anything, Keith pulled the trigger three times. The first time he pulled the trigger, it was a click; the second time he pulled the trigger, it was a click. And the third time he pulled the trigger, it was a click. Then, Keith was about to pull the trigger a fourth time, and "K" said, "Keith, stop playing with the gun. Did you unload the gun?" "K" then grabbed the gun out of Keith's hand and opened the chamber. Once "K" opened the chamber of the gun, there sat three bullets. Everyone's face had an expression that said, "You're supposed to be dead! Oh my God, Keith almost killed you!"

Keith didn't know that "K" emptied the gun before he started to play with it. When "K" put the gun back, he reloaded it by placing the bullets back in it. When Keith went and got the gun, he didn't know the gun was loaded. Keith thought he was playing with an empty gun. Everyone just stood there looking at each other. We were trying to see how Keith pulled the trigger three times, and the gun didn't go off. I knew nothing about guns, so I thought I was lucky. But years later, I learned about guns, and I remember the situation with Keith and the gun. The only thing I could conclude was the firing pin hit at least two live bullet after the trigger was pulled three times because there were three live bullets and two empty slots when Kenny opened the gun and looked at the bullets. Two of the bullets had a dent where the firing pin hit them. So I know the firing pin had to hit two bullet if not all three bullets. Where would I be without God's hand of protection over my life?

13. The Anatomy of Satan Part 1

In this book I will take you through the story of my life. Throughout my life, I will show you the different ways Satan attacked me as a child, teenager, and adult. I was unaware I was being attacked when I was younger, but as I got older, the Lord opened my eyes so I could understand the War Satan waged against me and why Satan waged War against me. In waging War against me, Satan exposed himself to show me his anatomy. Satan's anatomy is shown in the way he wages War against me and mankind.

Throughout this book, I will show you the Anatomy of Satan. That means I am going to show you the weapons of warfare that Satan uses to wage War against Christians and all of mankind! When many people think of Satan, they think of a fictitious character that is red with horns. But Satan is not fictitious; I guarantee you Satan is as real as real gets! Satan is a physical and spiritual being that displays God-like characteristics. I know I just threw many people off when I said Satan is a physical and spiritual being. I threw you off because you were taught Satan is only a spiritual being. That is not true! We were taught someone's belief that Satan only exists in the spiritual realm, but what we were taught had nothing to do with the absolute truth!

Satan is a physical being that can move through the spiritual realm! The Most High God Jehovah has given me much knowledge, wisdom, and understanding concerning Satan. Satan is a physical being that can move through the spiritual realm! And just like the Most High God Jehovah has revealed this truth to me, I will reveal this truth to you. But I must give it to you the same way the Lord has given it to me. You only need to follow my life journey in this book to know the absolute truth about everything!

The first thing you should have noticed about Satan's anatomy is an invisible army of demonic spirits in the atmosphere! These demonic spirits are ready to attack at any moment! Satan has demons in the atmosphere working on his behalf. These demons cannot be seen with the naked eye. They can only be seen when your eyes are allowed to see into the spirit realm. Seeing into the spirit realm is a gift that the Most High God Jehovah gives. This gift to see into the spiritual realm allows you to see the spiritual things that your naked eye cannot see. The Lord allowed me to see into the spirit realm so I could witness the demons influencing the children to hate me.

Satan has an army all around us that is hidden from the naked eye. This invisible army has the power to influence people's behavior. This army can convince people to kill, steal, and destroy. This invisible army can make people hate each other. Satan wages War against mankind daily by way of this invisible army. Many people don't believe demons exist because their eyes can't see them. So many people disregard these demons as fantasy. But I am here to tell you these demons are real, and they have the power to influence people's choices and decisions. This is why people kill other people. Jesus Christ speaks about Satan's army agenda in John 10:10. The thief that Jesus Christ is referring to in John 10:10 is Satan.

In John 10:10, Jesus said, "The thief comes only to steal and kill and destroy..." (Bible Gateway, NIV)

The second thing you should have grasped about Satan's anatomy is that Satan wants to stop the Lord's word from going forward in this world. Once the prophecy was spoken over me that the Lord wanted me to teach his word. Satan sent his demons to attack me. Satan sent his demons out to kill, steal, and destroy me by any means necessary! Satan's demons influence children to hate and mistreat me. And then Satan and his demons influence two guys to try to kill me in an abandoned building. Three shots were fired directly at me, with the gunman being only two feet away, but God's grace saved me. Then Satan manipulated Keith to point a loaded gun at me while pulling the trigger three times. Satan made these attempts on my life because he was trying to stop the prophecy of me teaching the Lord's word from coming true.

Satan's anatomy is to send an invisible army of demons to attack people. Satan's anatomy is to murder! The anatomy of Satan is to stop the Lord's word from being taught in this world!

14. I Was Visited By An Angel Of The Lord

One summer morning, when I was about nine years old, I stood in my driveway waiting for some kids to come outside and play. While I was standing in my driveway, this man appeared out of nowhere! I didn't see this man walk up the street, nor did I see this man drive up in a car. One second, he was nowhere in sight, and the next second, he appeared out of thin air, approaching me. This man literally appeared out of thin air. I saw this man manifest himself out of the air. When the man approached me, he called me by my name. Then I wondered, "Who is this man, and where did he come from?"

So, the man called me by my name and said, "Kennedy, I need to talk to you." The strange thing about it was that nobody but my teachers called me Kennedy. Everybody else always called me Ken or Kenny. Once he called me Kennedy, he grabbed my attention, and I wanted to see what this man wanted. My spirit recognized this man was not ordinary. I knew there was something different about this man because of the look on his face and in his eyes. This man was a brown skin African American man.

I walked over a few feet and met the man at the end of my driveway. Once I got to the man, he began to talk and reveal things to me that were far beyond my knowledge, wisdom, and understanding. The man started to tell me things that dealt with the history of mankind, things that were not taught in school. As I stood there, he blew me away with the information he told me. The man kept talking and telling me things that didn't appear in any history book, and he told me things the church was not teaching. At the end of the conversation, the man said, "I don't expect you to remember all of this now, but when the time comes, you will remember this entire conversation we had." The man then said, "I must go now." When the man said he must go, my mother walked out the front door and called my name.

Once my mother walked out the door and called my name, the man walked away from me, heading west. My mother said, "Kenny, who is that man you were talking to." I then looked at my mom and said, "I don't know!" Then my mother turned her head to look at the man, and I turned my head to look at the man, but the man was gone! Then my mother said, "Kenny, where did that man disappear to!!!!" I was just as puzzled as she was, so I said, "I don't know!" My mother and I looked for the man, but he was nowhere to be found. We didn't understand where the man disappeared too. We had only taken our eyes off the man for no more than two seconds, and the man was gone. Then my mother said, "That man disappeared into thin air!" My mother didn't realize that the man appeared out of thin air, just like he disappeared into thin air.

My mother came off the porch into the driveway, trying to understand where the man went. I was trying to understand where the man went too, and I was trying to understand the things he told me. Then my mother said, "He was not driving a car because no car was out here!" Then my mother asked me, "What was he talking to you about?" Once she asked me that question, I froze up, and something wouldn't let me tell her what he told me. My mother and I walked down the street past a few houses, trying to see if the man had gone into someone's backyard, but the man was nowhere to be found and was never seen again because the man had disappeared into thin air.

After we had looked and looked for the man, my mother asked me again, "What was he talking to you about?" Again, I froze instantly, and something wouldn't let me tell her. Once my mother saw I would not tell her, she told me to come into the house. As we walked into the house, my mother kept looking down the street, trying to make sense of the man disappearing into thin air. I was also trying to understand how the man could disappear into thin air as he did. Once we got into the house, my mother sat in the chair with her hand on her forehead, trying to understand how the man had disappeared into thin air. My mother kept saying, "That man disappeared into thin air?" While my mom was saying he disappeared into thin air, I knew he appeared the same way he disappeared, out of thin air. My mom asks me, "Where did the man come from?" Then I told her, "One second, he was not there, and the next second he was there." My mom then looked at me with this confused look on her face. Trying to understand what I said. Also, my mom had this look on her face like, "Boy, who are you?"

Later that day, my sisters came home and my mother tried to explain how this man disappeared into thin air. Once my mom explained the situation to my sisters, they started laughing at my mom. My sisters thought it was funny because they thought my mom was just tripping. But my mom kept telling them, "This man just disappeared into thin air." So my sisters had a good laugh and never understood what my mom said was the absolute truth. The man did disappear into thin air. Later that day, I thought about everything the man said to me. I was trying to grasp all the information the man told me about the true history of mankind. The man told me the true history of mankind, not the lies we were taught. The man who appeared to me that day was an Angel sent by Most High God Jehovah.

For several days, I tried to make sense of everything the Angel of the Lord said to me. But after a few days, I forgot everything that was said to me that day, just like the Angel said I would. It was not until April 2012 that I remember my entire conversation with the Angel of the Lord. Do you want to know what the Angel said to me? Just to let you know its life changing information. Just continue to read. I am going to tell you everything!

15. At UAB With My Sister

Growing up, I was the youngest of eight living children. Being the youngest, I was always lost in the midst of confusion and chaos. See, my dad worked for a Sand and Cement Company, and he worked six days a week most of the time and worked from 6:00 A.M. to about 8:00 P.M. Monday through Friday. And then sometimes he would work on Saturday. Then, my mother worked for Jefferson County Nursing Home from 3:00 P.M. to 11:00 P.M. shift. My mother would also work extra shifts. My mom and dad were just tired when it came to me. After raising seven other kids and working all the time, they were just tired. My mom and dad worked so much that I was handed off like a football to my siblings.

My brothers and sisters were supposed to look out for me when my mom and dad weren't there. But that is not how it happened! My siblings were too busy with their lives, so I was like the kid in the Home Alone movies. Since my supervision was minimal, I had a lot of free time. Especially after school! After school was playtime for me every day. I would play or watch cartoons after school. And then, when the news came on, I watched the news. I always forgot to do my homework assignments at home, but I was always reminded of homework at school. I would then realize I didn't do my homework, so I would do it in class before it was taken up. Or I would just copy off someone else's homework assignment. That was the pattern for me in elementary and high school. School was just too easy for me because I was never pushed to the point of being challenged mentally! I never studied for a test in elementary, high school, or during the first three years of college. Homework, homework, you talking about homework?

Since my mother was at work most of the time and my dad was at work most of the time, the responsibility of keeping up with me fell on my sisters. Sometimes, I would be carried off to different places with them, like when my sister "J" took me to class with her at UAB. I remember being no older than eight or nine when my sister "J" took me to class with her at UAB. The class she took me to was some type of Algebra I class. I was sitting next to my sister, and the professor wrote an algebra problem on the board. Then the professor said, "What is the answer?" Nobody in the room could answer the question. There were about sixty people in this auditorium-like classroom, and no one knew the answer. I looked at the problem, and it worked itself out in my mind, and I shouted the answer.

Once I shouted the answer, the professor said, "That is right!" The professor and all these white people in the room turned and looked at me like, "How in the world does this little black kid know the answer?" The people in the room were so shocked and so surprised they just stared at me. So, I just sat back in my seat. You must remember this was doing the late 70's in Birmingham, Alabama. Some white people here in Alabama thought black people didn't know anything. When I answered the algebra problem they couldn't answer, they were simply amazed! When the professor put the problem on the board, the formula worked itself out in my mind!

16. A Word Hidden in a Picture

One day, when I was in the third grade at Wilkerson Elementary School. This lady came to our school to test all the third graders. The school year was either 1979 or 1980, and I was eight or nine years old. We were told to go and see this lady on the first floor so we could be tested. This lady didn't work for the school; she was just sent to the school to test us! The children were sent out of class two at a time to see the lady who was giving the test. But before it was my turn to go and see the lady giving the test, I had to go to the office for some reason.

Once I got to the office, I observed some teachers talking and overheard their conversation. The teachers were talking about the lady who was giving us the test. The teachers were skeptical of the lady because they didn't know whom she represented, and the teachers didn't know what the lady was showing us and why they were giving us this visual test. I remember the teacher's facial expressions showed deep concern. I just stood there listening to the teacher's conversation. Then one of the teachers that was talking turned to me and just stared at me and then she said, "You don't need to be hearing this." So, I finished my business in the office and returned to class.

After I returned to class, it was my turn to go and see the lady and be tested. I went down by the first-grade classrooms where the lady was given the test. When the lady called me into the room, I was told to sit in front of this viewing machine. Then the lady told me to tell her everything I saw in the viewing machine. Once I told the lady what I saw, she would click this button and make the next picture appear. I told the lady I saw words hidden in the pictures. The lady told me to say the words that I saw. So I did. I went through several pictures and said the words I saw hidden in the picture. The lady would then say, "Good." Then I came to the strangest picture I ever saw. The picture that I saw was a combination of a steganography and an ambigram.

Steganography is the practice of concealing a message, **image**, or file within another message, **image,** or file. "Steganography." *Merriam-Webster.* Merriam-Webster, n.d. Web. 24 Nov. 2015. <http://www.merriam-webster.com/dictionary/steganography>.

By using steganography, you can hide a picture within a picture. You can use steganography to hide a word or message in plain sight. A person can be looking directly at a steganography, and they would never see the picture hidden within the picture. They would only see the picture intended for them to see. Once a picture is placed inside a steganography, the average person doesn't see the hidden picture; the average person only sees the picture intended for them to see. An ambigram is an inversion that spells out a word in different directions. An ambigram is when a word is spelled out going forward, and then it also spells the same word going backward or even upside down.

So, the picture I saw was a combination of a steganography and an ambigram. The word I saw hidden was the word Illuminati. The word Illuminati was spelled backward, forwards, and upside down. Below is the steganography and ambigram of the word Illuminati I saw in the viewing machine while I was in the third grade at Wilkerson Elementary School! And you must remember I saw this image in the third grade during the school year of 1979-1980. This was before this image was posted all over the internet. If you notice, the word Illuminati is spelled out going forward, Illuminati is spelled out backward, and Illuminati is spelled out upside down.

Illuminati

When I came to the word **Illuminati** hidden within the picture, I couldn't pronounce the word. The lady asked me if I could spell out the word for her. So, I spelled the word Illuminati out for her. The lady was so astonished I could make out the entire word **Illuminati** hidden within the steganography. The lady looked at me with an expression of astonishment on her face. Then the lady said, "Kennedy, you did very well! You did great, Kennedy! Kennedy, you are Gifted! You are Gifted, Kennedy!" The lady had a huge smile on her face! Then the lady marked something by my name in this notebook of hers, and then she looked at me with this huge smile on her face, and then she sent me back to class.

A few days later, my mother told me a white lady came to our house to see her about me. This white lady was telling my mom how gifted I was and that I needed to go to a special school for exceptionally gifted and special children. At first, my mom didn't understand what the lady meant when she said I was special! My mom thought the white lady was trying to call me slow or stupid! My mom said she was getting ready to let that lady have it for talking about me like that! But then the lady cleared up the misunderstanding and told my mom I was "Gifted!" This meant highly intelligent! The lady was trying to get my mom to agree to send me to a special school for gifted children out of state.

One day, I had to stay home from school because I told my mother I was sick. But I wasn't sick; I didn't want to go to school that day. While I was at home, this white lady came to our house. The same white lady that gave me the visual test at school. It was the same white lady who said I was "Gifted!" The lady came to talk to my mom about sending me to a special school that was not in Alabama. The lady told my mom I was unique and needed to attend a special school where the most intelligent kids went. Once, the lady told my mom I was the smartest of the smartest of little children. My mom had a smile on her face that said, "I knew it!"

Then the lady told my mom it would be a huge benefit for me to attend this school for "Gifted Children!" The lady starts telling my mom how the smartest of the smartest kids go to this school and how people who come out of this school grow up to become Presidents of the United States, Senators, and other high-ranking government officials. As this lady was talking to my mom, my mom looked at me with this look that said, "Do you want to go?" And I looked back at my mom with this look that said, "Are you nuts! We don't know these people! They might get me up there and do all kinds of things to me!" Those were the exact thoughts I had when I looked at my mom.

After the lady explained everything to my mom, the lady looked at me and tried to get me to say I wanted to go! But I shook my head no and grabbed my mom around her waist! My mom told the lady she had to talk to my dad before she could give her an answer. After this, the lady said a few more words, trying to convince my mother to send me to this school outside the State of Alabama. After the lady gave her a persuasive sales pitch, she left.

Later that day, my dad came home from work, and my mother told my dad about the lady who came by the house. Then my mother told my dad everything the lady said. My mother told my dad what the lady said about people who went to this school becoming Presidents of the United States of America, Senators, and other high-ranking government officials. Then, the first words that came out of my dad's mouth were, "The Lord showed me a vision that this boy became the President of the United States of America!" After my dad said that, my dad considered sending me off to school because all the things the lady said were lining up with the vision the Lord showed my daddy concerning me becoming President of the United States of America.

For a moment, my dad was considering sending me out of state to go to school. But then he had a change of heart. He quickly remembered the day the Lord told him I would teach his word. And once my dad remembered the Lord telling him I would teach the Lord's word, he shot down the idea of sending me to this special school for Gifted Children. And then my dad said, "We are not sending Kenny off to school. We don't know those people! They might get Kenny up there and do all kinds of things to him!" That was exactly what my dad said!

Also, the reason why the Lord told my dad I was going to teach his world is so my dad wouldn't send me off to school to be groomed by the Illuminati! My dad said no to sending me out of state to school! And my dad didn't allow me to enter the Gifted Program. And that was the end of that! But the white lady didn't give up. My mom said that the white lady kept coming by the house trying to persuade her to send me off to this special school or allow me into the Gifted program. And my mother kept telling the lady no. My mother said the lady even tried to threaten to have me taken away from her if she didn't send me off to this school! But my mother didn't give in to the pressure, and the lady eventually gave up.

As I was writing this book, I had many questions for the Lord. So, I asked the Lord, "Was there anyone else from Birmingham, Alabama, who was labeled as Gifted and they were sent off to a special school as a child?" At that moment, the Lord answered my question and said, "Yes!" And then I asked the Lord, "Who?" And then the Lord said to me, "Secretary of State Condoleezza Rice!" Once the Lord told me Secretary of State Condoleezza Rice, I was astonished! And it was at that point I remembered the story of Condoleezza Rice. Condoleezza Rice was also from Birmingham, Alabama. And it is said she moved from Birmingham because she had to go to a special school because she was "Gifted".

It was no coincidence that Condoleezza Rice was labeled as "Gifted" and went to this special school, and then she became Secretary of State for the United States of America. Once the Lord showed me that connection between Condoleezza Rice being labeled as Gifted, going to this special school, and then becoming a high-ranking Government official, I understood what the white lady meant when she told my mom that people who go to this school become U.S. Presidents, Senators, and high-ranking Government officials.

On that same day, I was tested at Wilkerson Elementary School. Three other kids saw the word Illuminati hidden in the steganography. From that day on, those three kids were pulled out of class occasionally to meet with this special teacher who would come to our school just to meet with them. And this teacher would teach them the

Old English language and how to read and understand it. I didn't understand why they were being taught the Old English language at the time, but now I do understand it. You must remember what the lady told my mother. The lady said that people who go to this special school become high-ranking government officials, and they become Presidents, Senators, and other high-ranking government officials. They began to teach the three other kids the Old English language because many of the laws passed in the government are written in an Old English language format. And this Old English language format is very difficult for ordinary citizens in the United States to understand. Like when these different Amendments are drafted, the ordinary person doesn't understand them. This is done so ordinary people can't see or figure out the Illuminati plan or agenda in a particular bill or law.

They wanted to pull me out of class to teach me old English, but my teacher, Ms. Beverly, and my parents wouldn't allow them to take me out of class. And the reason is because I was always doing my homework at the last minute! Blessings come in many ways! Ms. Beverly thought I wasn't Gifted. But I was Gifted. I just wasn't mentally challenged in elementary school, high school, not even in college. Just to let you know, I didn't study for a test in elementary school, high school, or my first four years of college.

Three other kids from my school saw the Illuminati steganography that day. One of the kids I will call "Revilo" worked high up with the FBI. One of the kids I will call "Asil" worked high up with the FBI. The other kid I will call "Anad" is working with different administrations in the Federal Government in Washington, D.C. Based on what the lady said to my mom when I was in the third grade, it seems she was telling the truth. People become high-ranking government officials! Four kids at my school identified the word Illuminati in the steganography that day. And three kids entered the gifted program and the three who entered work within the Federal Government. My mother and father wouldn't allow me to go off to the special school, and they didn't allow me to participate in the Gifted program that the other three participated in.

Children are labeled as "Gifted" after they are tested in the third grade, and they can identify the word Illuminati hidden in the steganography. You must remember, the lady called me Gifted after I saw the steganography and ambigram of the word Illuminati. And then she offers the world to me on a silver platter! What does this all mean? Why are they labeling children as "Gifted" after they see the word

Illuminati hidden within a steganography (hidden within a picture)? Who are the Illuminati? Why are they testing children in the third grade by showing them steganography and ambigram of the word Illuminati? These questions and many more will be answered for you.

Just remember this: if they are testing all third graders in the United States of America, I guarantee you they are testing all third graders worldwide. This is the United States of America Book of Secrets! This is the Illuminati Book of Secrets!

17. You Are Going To Be A Millionaire

I remember I was in the third grade, and one day, I was playing outside in my neighbor's yard. After playing, we laid down in the front yard and looked up into the sky. I remember saying to my neighbor, "I want to be rich one day!" Immediately after I said that the Lord spoke to me and said, "One day, you are going to be a Millionaire." Then the Lord showed me lots and lots of money falling from the sky. I was so excited once I heard the Lord say that to me. I jumped up and told my neighbor I would be a millionaire one day.

My neighbor looked at me strangely and said, "What is he talking about, and where did all of this come from?" I was so excited that I started screaming, "I am going to be a millionaire!" I was so excited!

I told everyone who would listen to me that I would be a millionaire one day. And when they asked me how I knew I would be a millionaire. I said, "God told me." After I told them that, they always had this blank look that said, "Yeah, right, whatever you say." They had no belief in the things I told them.

After that day, I looked at school a little bit differently. I always wanted to learn, but my thought process was far beyond what school could teach me. I thought about things that most adults couldn't conceive or even imagine. School never had my full attention. The things they were teaching were good, but I had this thought that said, "Someone else wrote that book, and they can tell you anything they want to!" And many years later I would realize my thought process was right! Because the Heavenly Father Jehovah and the Lord Jesus Christ gave me the absolute truth about all things; and once the Lord gave me the absolute truth about all things. I realized many things they taught in school were misinformation.

We all have been lied to! Just remember this. You were born into this system and this world! You didn't design this system that you live in! You only know what they taught you, and they only taught you what they wanted you to know!

18. My Heritage

I remember sitting on Momma Lizzie's porch when I was ten. Momma Lizzie was my grandmother, my mother's mother. Her real name was Elizabeth Johnson. We called her Momma Lizzie for short. Momma Lizzie lived in the tiny town of Lavaca, Alabama, about 6 miles east of Butler, Alabama. While sitting on my grandmother's porch, I listened to my grandmother, my mother, and others' conversations. Then, during the conversation, my mother began to speak. My mother said, "Our blood is mixed with some of everything. There is Black, White, Indian, and Chinese in our blood." Then my mother paused for a second, turned, and stared at me, and then she said these prophetic words. "There is even Jewish in our blood!"

This stare she gave me was very intense. This stare my mother had was different from normal stares. I didn't understand the stare then, but now I do. I have seen that stare many times sense then from many different people. The stare only happens when the Lord speaks to me through someone else. The stare told me, "You will remember this when the time is right. You were meant to be at this place, at this very moment, to hear this. You will make sense of this information when the right time comes." I knew it was important when my mother said, "There is even Jewish in our blood!" As of today, I know how important the information was, and I now understand I have the blood of the Israelites running through my veins!

19. Who is that little girl?

I remember I was at my grandmother's house in Lava, Alabama when I was ten years old. This was the same day my mother revealed to me I had Jewish ethnicity in my blood. As my mother and others were talking, this woman came and sat on the porch with them. This woman had a girl with her I had never seen before. When I saw the girl, I thought it was something strange and peculiar about her. I went towards the girl, and I just looked at her. It was something about this girl, but I didn't know what it was. So, I started talking and playing with the girl. Then the girl's mother said, "Ken, she is too young for you. Ken, you are ten, and she is only six. She is too young for you. Leave her alone, Ken."

Once her mother said those words, I walked away from the little girl, but something stopped me. I turned and looked at the little girl, and at that very moment, the Lord said to me, "One day, this little girl is going to make your life hell. She is going to bring many problems into your life!" Once I heard those words, I was puzzled and confused. I just looked at the girl and stared at her. I was so confused I went and sat on my grandmother's steps. I was trying to sort through everything that was said to me. But I didn't understand. I just knew there was something very peculiar about that little girl. So, I kept thinking, "Who is that little girl?"

20. I Have Been to This World Before

As a child, I always felt I had been to places I had never visited. After that day at Six Flags over Texas, I thought about how I saw real-life events in my dreams. At first, I thought the dreams gave me the impression I had been to certain places I had never visited before. But it wasn't just the dreams that gave me that impression. I would constantly think I was living in this world for a second time. Then I thought that this world was so much different than before. I tried to tell people this, but they laughed and said, "You think you were reincarnated." Then they would say something like, "Reincarnation is not real!!!" Each time after someone made that statement, I would be standing there with this blank expression on my face, thinking, "They don't understand what I am trying to say."

Little things would always happen to trigger these thoughts that I lived in this world before. I remember one time at church, I heard someone say the Israelites were enslaved for hundreds of years in a foreign land. Then I went to school, and I learned that African American people were enslaved for hundreds of years in the United States of America, which was a foreign land. Upon hearing, the Israelites and African American people were both enslaved in foreign lands for hundreds of years. I always thought the history of African American people and the Israelites were very similar because both were enslaved for hundreds of years in foreign lands. As a child, I knew there was a direct correlation between the Israelites and African Americans, both being enslaved for hundreds of years in foreign lands. I just couldn't make since of it as a child.

One day, when I was in the fourth grade, I was walking down the hall, and I was pondering the thought of the similarity between the Israelites and African American people, both being enslaved for hundreds of years in a foreign land. As I was pondering the thought of the similarity between the Israelite's enslavement and the African Americans' enslavement, this man's voice came to me out of thin air and said to me in my left ear, "You were born into both races that had been slaves." Once I heard the voice speak into my left ear, I wondered, how was that possible? How could I be born into both races that were slaves? How could I be born into this world twice? I knew what the voice said was true. But I couldn't figure out how it was possible that I lived before on this earth if reincarnation was not real. I was getting contradictory information from two different sources. The world was giving me one set of information and this voice speaking to me was giving me another. The voice that spoke to me always spoke the absolute truth, but I had this world trying to force its lies on me! I didn't know this then, but the world will tell you many lies and try to pass them off as the truth! It is Satan who wants to blind you with the lies of this world. Because if Satan can keep the truth from you, then you will perish for a lack of knowledge! I learned Satan tries to blind the people in this world from the truth because the truth will prove Satan to be a liar and murderer!

The voice told me I was born into both races that had been slaves. That meant I was born in the Old Testament as an Israelite, and my name was Elisha. And I was born into this world again as an African American named Kennedy King Brown. The voice that spoke to me that day spoke the absolute truth. I was born into both races that had been slaves. I was born as an Israelite who were once slaves during the Biblical days of the Old Testament, and I was born as an African American who once was slaves in the United States of America. This voice that spoke to me and told me these things was the voice of thy Lord and Savior, Jesus Christ. How do I know it was Jesus Christ who spoke to me? Just continue to read, and it will be revealed to you!

As a child, I always felt that history books weren't teaching the truth. I felt the people writing the history books were misleading mankind and not telling the complete truth. I felt like the history of mankind had been distorted. Then, I always felt that the year was not what they said it was! I felt they were deceiving us about what year it truly was! I had this feeling all my life, but I couldn't put my finger on the lie being told! It was not until the Lord opened my eyes to the absolute truth that I realized mankind's history and the year is not what we were taught in school! There is much more to it than what we were taught! Mankind has been disillusioned with lies! Oh my God, the level of mankind's disillusionment is astonishing! Just continue to read and your eyes will be open to the absolute truth!

21. A Child Mimicking His Parents

As a child, I watched my mother and dad have conversations with God. I watch them call on the name of the Lord and then proceed to ask the Lord questions. As a child, I always wondered why my parents would call the Lord's name out and then ask the Lord a question. Then, right after they call out the Lord's name and ask him a question, they would have a revelation moment as though the Lord answered their question for them right then and there!

As time passed, I started calling on the name of the Lord and asking the Lord questions out loud. It was a habit I picked up from my parents. Once I started asking the Lord questions, the Lord began to give me answers to some of the questions immediately and some answers he would give to me over time.

My parents taught me my most important lesson, which is ask the Lord the question, and he will answer you. By watching my parents talk to the Lord year after year, talking to the Lord became second nature to me. I guess that was one of the reasons the Lord said to me, "This is the family you will be assigned to, and this is where we will **hide you** until it is your time."

22. The Store

I grew up in a community that went by a couple of different names. Some called my community East Thomas, and some called it Saint Mark. The reason they called it Saint Mark is because that was the name of our neighborhood store. This store was like your conventional neighborhood store. You could get the little items you needed instead of going to the grocery store. It was also a place where the children went to play video games. Saint Mark was about two blocks from Wilkerson Elementary School and about a block and a half away from my house. Some days, when I walked home from school, I would go by the store. If I had some money, I would buy something. If I didn't have any money, I would get something! It was more days I didn't have any money than days I did have money. If I had 1`no money, I would walk into the store like I had money. And then, I would walk to the aisle with the cinnamon rolls. The cinnamon rolls were on the second aisle near the back of the store. I would walk down the aisle where the cinnamon rolls were, pick up a cinnamon roll, and place it in my pants. And then I would walk out of the store like nothing had happened.

Well, I did this on numerous occasions. I would buy them when I had money; when I didn't, I would steal them. That's just the absolute truth! Now the store owners were this white couple who were very friendly people. One day, I walked into the store as though I was going to buy something. I did my usual routine. I walked to the back of the store where the cinnamon rolls were located, put one in my pants, and then attempted to leave the store. When I approached the door, the owner asked me, "What do you have in your pants?" Once he said that I knew he knew what I had done. I made a mad dash for the door! But before I could reach the door, he sprinted after me and grabbed my arm so I couldn't get away. I was busted! The man told me to take the cinnamon roll out of my pants! So, I did. Then he said a few words to me and told me to call my parents and tell them to come and get me. When I heard him say call your parents, I was kind of hoping he called the Police because the Police could have protected me from my mom and my dad. That was the most terrifying thing I ever had to do. I had to call home and tell my mom to come pick me up from the store because I was caught stealing. Lord, have mercy on me!

So, I called home, and my mom answered the phone. And I told her I was down at the store, and she needed to pick me up. I didn't say what I did; I just sounded so pitiful that she knew something was wrong. She said she was on her way, and within two minutes, she and my sister's "J" and "E" were at the store. They walked into the store and asked the owner what was happening. And the store owner told my mom I had stolen a cinnamon roll from his store. Then, the owner told my mom he suspected I had done this on other occasions. My mom stood there with a look that said, "We don't do that type of stuff in this family! I'm going to take you to the mountaintop so you can be with your Lord!"

After my mom gave me that look, my mom then paid the man for the cinnamon roll and then we left. Once I got in the car with my mom and sisters, they let me have it verbally! So, I just started crying! Early on in life, I learned that tears help prevent a whipping, or it would make the whipping a light one. I was crying my butt off in the car, and I started saying I was sorry. I thought if I just repent and say I was sorry, all would be forgiven. And she wouldn't whoop me because I knew my mom was about to whoop me.

Once we pulled up into the driveway, I was prepared to get a whooping. And I was prepared to do the "I am bleeding routine on my mom!" See, whenever my mom or one of my sisters whipped me. I always pulled the "I am bleeding routine!" Once they begin to hit me with either a switch or a belt, I would start screaming, I'm bleeding! I'm bleeding! I'm bleeding! Once I said this a couple of times, they would stop whipping me to see if I was bleeding. They would be afraid to death that I was bleeding.

So, once we pulled into the driveway. I was prepared to get a whipping from my mother. But then my mother decided to throw some salt in the game. My mother said, "I am not going to whip you. I'm going to tell your daddy what you did once he gets home from work." And once she said that I almost died! My heart dropped down to my stomach, and I couldn't breathe! My mom was going to tell my daddy! Once I heard that, I begged my mom to whip me! I repented in the name of Jesus Christ right then and there! My mom waited to tell my dad for a couple of reasons. One reason is because the store owner told my mom he suspected I had stolen things from his store before, which meant I was becoming a career criminal! And the second reason is because my daddy always preached against stealing. My dad always preached night and day against stealing. And here I was, stealing a cinnamon roll from the neighborhood store. Lord have mercy!

Once I realized my dad was going to whip me, I was in a state of shock. So, I went and got in bed, and I tried to go to sleep. But I couldn't go to sleep; because the time was passing by very slowly. A minute seemed like an hour, and an hour seemed like five hours. Time seemed like it slowed down on purpose just to torment me! It felt like I was waiting for days for my dad to get home, but it had only been a couple of hours. My dad usually got home by 8:00 PM but for some reason he came home early that day. So, I was lying in bed, and I heard my dad come in the front door. Then I heard my mom say to my dad, "Brown, let me tell you what Ken did?" My mom proceeded to tell my dad I was caught stealing. Then I heard my daddy scream out, "What?" Then I heard my mom say, "He was caught stealing at the store down the street." And then my daddy screamed, "What!!!" And then my mother said, "He was caught stealing a cinnamon roll out of the store. And the store owner said he thinks Ken had been stealing from the store on other occasions." Once my dad heard that, he screamed, "Kenney!!!"

Once I heard him scream, I knew what was coming! I knew it was Judgement Day! The apocalypse! So, I laid in bed like I was asleep, and he came in there and snatched me out of bed and made me take off my pants. Then he took me into the bathroom, and he beat me like a drum. My daddy took that belt, raised it to the ceiling, and he went to work. I was screaming for the Lord! I wanted Jesus to return, and I wanted to be Rapture up at that very moment! I wanted to be called up into Heaven to be with Jesus Christ! My daddy beat my butt! And he beat my butt some more! And he beat my butt again!!! I was screaming and yelling, but he didn't stop until he got tired. He lectured me while he was beating my butt! And believe me, I heard the entire lecture. I heard, "Thou shall not steal!" And everything else he said. My God!

That was the worst whipping I ever received. I received some whippings before, but that was the worst. After the whipping, my dad told me to go to bed and not return to that store. And I didn't return to that store for a very long time. My legs, my arms, and my buttocks had red whelps on my skin, and I was swollen. In today's time, they would call that child abuse. But it was not child abuse! That was a good old fashion butt-whipping! Something I needed! Because I had no business going into those people's stores and stealing those people's cinnamon rolls! My dad did what any father who cares about his child would do. He took the belt to my behind! And that whipping stopped me from becoming a career criminal! The world would say the whipping I received was child abuse. But you must remember what I told you earlier. The world constantly tries to push its lies off on you! But the Lord and his word, the Holy Bible, say differently.

Proverbs 13:24 says very clearly that a person who spares the rod from their child hates their own child. But a person who loves their child will carefully discipline them.

Proverbs 13:24 reads, "Whoever **spares the rod** hates **the**ir children, but **the** one who loves **the**ir children is careful to discipline **the**m." (NIV, BibleGateway.com)

My dad loved me so much he didn't spare the rod; he gave me a good old fashion whooping. My dad didn't want to see his son become a thief. My dad didn't spare the rod that day. He disciplined me carefully by giving me what I needed: a good old-fashioned beat down! And to this day if I ever think about taking something that doesn't belong to me. I think about that whipping I received. The Holy Bible is correct, and the world is wrong! The world will always try to get you to go against the

Lord's word. A whipping that leaves some marks on a child is not child abuse. No matter what the news media and the Department of Human Resources say! Every whipping I got left marks on me! As a grown man, I know for a fact that none of the whipping I received as a child was child abuse. My dad and mom did what was necessary to raise me as an honest person. The Holy Bible also says to raise a child in the way he should go, and when he gets old, he will not depart. That scripture can be found in Proverbs 22:6.

Proverbs 22:6 reads, "Train up a child in the way he should go, And when he is old he will not depart from it." (NKJ, Biblegateway.com)

When my dad whipped me, that was a disciplinary action to train me in the way I should go. My dad always preached against stealing and not to be a thief. My dad hated a thief. And many years later, I would understand why my dad hated a thief so badly. When I was in my mid-twenties, I found out something about my dad I didn't know. After my dad was shot in World War II, he returned to the States and moved to Gary, Indiana, to work for the steel plants. My dad said the guys all lived in company housing. So, one night this guy asked my dad to go to the store with him. And my dad said he didn't have any money but agreed to walk with the guy to the store. Once they got to the store, my dad told the guy he was not going in because he had no money. My dad decided to wait outside the store while the guy went inside the store to buy something. After a few minutes, the guy came out of the store running. My dad said he didn't know why the guy was running, but he ran also. Come to find out, the guy had robbed the store, and my dad didn't know anything about it. My dad was arrested along with the guy who robbed the store. My dad was not involved in the robbery, and my dad didn't know the guy would rob the store. But my dad was outside the store when the robbery took place, and my dad ran when the other guy ran!

Once they caught the guy who robbed the store, the guy told the Police my dad didn't have anything to do with the robbery, and my dad had no idea he was robbing the store. But that didn't matter to the Police; the only thing that mattered was that my dad was a black man, and he ran! My dad was convicted of robbery and sentenced to seven years in prison. I first heard this story when I was twenty-five years old. Once I heard the story, it all made sense to me. I understood why my dad always hated thieves. I understood why my dad always preached about not stealing. And I understood why my dad used to tell me to be careful of the company I keep. My dad always preached these different sermons around the house. And those sermons stemmed from the hard lesson my dad learned that night. I also understood why my dad whipped my butt when I was caught stealing. He did what he had to do as a loving father! He beat the brakes off me to ensure I didn't become a thief. And it worked!

23. I Repeated The Words The Lord Spoke

When I was in the fourth grade, I knew this girl that was in my class that everyone loved. She was one of the most intelligent kids in our class. She was very outgoing, and she clowned around a lot. I will call her "P". One day, "P" stopped being herself. She became withdrawn from everyone else and didn't want to talk to anyone. At first, everyone thought she was in a bad mood, but this withdrawn state lasted a long time. Everyone thought she was upset because her mother recently got a new boyfriend or husband.

After a couple of months, "P" was still withdrawn from everyone else. One day, while we were in class, I looked back at "P" and saw so much anger and hurt in her eyes. Then the teacher asked "P" what was wrong. Then I said out loud, "Lord, what is wrong with "P"? At that very moment, a man's voice spoke into my left ear and said, "She is being molested." Once I heard the voice speak, I repeated what the voice said to me! So, I shouted out in class, "She is being molested!" The teacher turned toward me and stared at me for a few seconds, then yelled, "Shut up!" Then, the teacher pulled "P" out of class and talked to her. Then "P's" mother was called up to the school. After that day, "P" was never molested again. She was never the same as before, but the pain she had in her eyes that day wasn't there anymore! I didn't know what the word molested meant. I just repeated what I heard the voice of the Lord say to me. Years later, I learned what the word meant, and I always thought about "P" and what she endured! My heart hurts as I write this.

The very same day, I yelled out in class, "She is being molested!" My teacher, Mrs. Daniels, pulled me out of class and asked me how I knew that was happening to "P"? And I told Mrs. Daniels I heard the voice that speaks to me in my left ear say it! Once I said that, Mrs. Daniels backed away from me and stared at me; because she couldn't understand nor comprehend what I was saying. She had a look on her face that said, "What do you mean this voice spoke to you in your left ear?" She had this puzzled look on her face. After that day, Mrs. Daniels paid close attention to me.

After I told Mrs. Daniels, a voice spoke to me in my left ear, she started being much nicer to me! Mrs. Daniels was always kind of mean to me before that day, but she started being nicer to me after I told her this voice spoke to me. It is as though the Lord told her something about me! Or she realized I was anointed.

One day, Mrs. Daniels observed some students in the class being mean to me. And Mrs. Daniels stopped them, and then the stare came into her eyes, and she said these prophetic words about my life. Mrs. Daniels said, "You all need to stop picking on him because you don't know who the Lord will raise him up to be. And one day, you may have to ask him for help!" When Mrs. Daniels said those things about me, the Lord gave me a vision. I saw myself as a grown man with great authority, and millions of people had to come to me for food and provisions. There were people who mistreated me during my lifetime that were begging me for food. It was during a time of great trials and tribulations on the earth. There was a great cataclysm, and the world was in great distress. And I was given authority by the Lord to oversee millions of his people.

So, immediately after I had the vision in class, I was still listening to Mrs. Daniels speaking to the children about picking on me. I assume the Lord told Mrs. Daniels something about me because, from that day on, she had this look on her face that said, "My God" every time she looked at me. Years later, the Lord revealed to me he talked about what Mrs. Daniels said about me and the vision he gave me in Matthew 24:45-47.

Jesus said in Mathew 24:45-47, [45] "Who then is a faithful and wise servant, whom his master made ruler over his household, **to give them food in due season?** [46] Blessed *is* that servant whom his master, when he comes, will find so doing. [47] Assuredly, I say to you that he will make him ruler over all his goods. (NIV, BibleGateway.com)

24. Joseph

One day, the Lord placed me into a deep sleep and then showed me a vision of me being over my brothers and sisters. The vision showed me having great authority over all my older siblings. So that morning, when I woke up, I told my siblings that I would have authority over all of them one day. And when I told them this, they looked at me as though I was crazy because they didn't understand why I was saying these things.

Later that morning, I saw my siblings standing around my mother in the living room. My mother was talking to them. I came and stood behind them without any of them noticing I was there. I overheard my mother saying, "One day, Ken will be over all of you. God is going to raise that boy up to be over all of you. Yawl better be nice to that boy." Once I heard my momma say that, I said, "See, I told yawl I am going to be over all of you!" Once I said that, all my siblings turned around with this angry look. They all looked at me with this look that said, "Ain't no way I am letting him be over me. He's the youngest!" Since I was the youngest of eight living children, they thought it was a shame for their baby brother to have authority over them.

I didn't truly understand my sibling's resentment towards me at the time because my mother and I told them I would have authority over them. But as of today, I can understand my sibling's response. My sibling's response was the same response Joseph's siblings had towards him, jealousy. Who is Joseph, you ask? Joseph is a man of God discussed in the Holy Bible. Joseph was one of the sons of Jacob (Israel). Jacob (Israel) was a man who had twelve sons. The Most High God Jehovah changed Jacob's name from Jacob to Israel. Israel (Jacob) had twelve sons and each one of his sons represented a tribe. This is where the twelve tribes of Israel derived from. Out of the twelve sons of Israel (Jacob), the nation of Israel was formed.

At one time Joseph was the youngest child of Jacob (Israel). And Joseph was blessed with a gift. Joseph's gift was to see and interpret visions shown to him by the Most High God Jehovah. God would always come to Joseph and show him visions. And one night, God came to Joseph and showed him having great authority over his brothers. When Joseph woke up, he told his father and brothers about his dream. And his brothers were very resentful of him because he had told them he would have great authority over them. Joseph's brothers resented him the same way I saw resentment in my brothers and sisters' faces when my mother told them I would have authority over them one day.

One day, Joseph's brothers plotted to kill him. The plot was to kill him and say an animal had killed him. Rueben, the oldest brother, convinced his other brothers not to kill their younger brother, Joseph. Instead, they threw him into this cistern in the desert, which was a hole in the ground. Joseph's brothers decided not to kill him, but instead, they sold him into slavery to some Ishmaelites. And then Joseph was taken to Egypt, where he was sold again as a slave. Joseph was sold to Potiphar, one of Pharaoh's high-ranking officials in Egypt. Joseph served as a slave in Potiphar's house. Even though Joseph was a slave, the Lord was still with Joseph and blessed Joseph in all he did. And the Lord blessed

Potiphar's house because of Joseph. And Potiphar saw how his house was being blessed because of Joseph. So, Potiphar placed Joseph in charge of his entire house and all he owned. Once Joseph was placed over Potiphar's house and all that Potiphar owned, the Lord blessed Potiphar's house even more because of Joseph. The Lord blessed all that Joseph did.

Potiphar's wife took notice of Joseph because he was well-built and handsome. Potiphar's wife tried to persuade Joseph to sleep with her. For many months and days, Potiphar's wife attempted to persuade Joseph to sleep with her. But Joseph declined her offer each time because Joseph was a righteous man. So, Potiphar's wife tried to persuade Joseph to sleep with her, and Joseph refused. After Joseph refuses to sleep with her, she screams and tells the rest of the servants Joseph tried to force himself on her. Once, Potiphar was told this lie by his wife. Potiphar had Joseph thrown into prison. Joseph was in bondage for a total of thirteen years. But even in prison, the Lord was with Joseph. The Lord blessed all that Joseph did in prison. And the warden of the prison took notice of how Joseph was blessed. The prison warden put Joseph over all the prisoners in the prison. And Joseph was responsible for all that was done in the prison. The warden paid no attention to anything under Joseph's care because the Lord was with Joseph, and everything Joseph did was blessed. So, even in prison, Joseph was blessed.

Until one day, Pharaoh had two dreams no one in his royal court could interpret. All whom Pharaoh summoned to interpret his dreams couldn't interpret them. Then Pharaoh was told Joseph had a gift of interpreting dreams. Pharaoh summoned Joseph, and then Pharaoh told Joseph about the two dreams he had. And then Joseph interpreted both dreams correctly. The dream Pharaoh had was a warning about seven years of prosperity for Egypt, and then after those seven years of prosperity would come seven years of famine. The seven years of famine would be so bad it would have destroyed Egypt.

Once Joseph gave this interpretation to Pharaoh, Joseph gave Pharaoh a plan of action to prepare for the seven years of famine. Joseph's plan was this. Joseph told Pharaoh to look for a wise man and put him in charge of Egypt. Then Joseph told Pharaoh to appoint commissioners over the land to take up a fifth of the harvest of Egypt during the seven years of prosperity. Joseph told Pharaoh the food being taken up was to be stored in reserve for Egypt to eat during the seven years of famine after the seven years of prosperity. Pharaoh and Pharaoh

Officials liked Joseph's plan, so Pharaoh wanted to appoint Joseph second in command over all of Egypt and even over his Royal Palace. However, many of Pharaoh's officials objected to Joseph being second in command over Egypt. Because the law of Egypt stated that no man could rule over Egypt or be second in command unless he spoke all the languages of the sons of men, that meant whoever ruled over Egypt or whoever was second in command of Egypt had to speak all the languages of the people of this earth. But Joseph didn't speak all the languages of the sons of men. Joseph spoke his native language, Hebrew, and he spoke Egyptian, which he learned while in Egypt.

So, that night, while Joseph was asleep, the Lord sent a ministering angel to Joseph. And the angel came to Joseph and stood over him. And then the angel raised Joseph onto his two feet, and the angel stood across from Joseph. Then, the angel taught Joseph the languages of the sons of men in one night. Once the angel taught Joseph the languages of the sons of men, Joseph went back to sleep. Once Joseph woke up, he thought all that had happened that night was a vision. And he was astonished by it. (Book of Jasher 49:1-20) The next day, when Pharaoh brought Joseph before him and his officials to test Joseph in the languages of men, Joseph could speak all the languages men spoke on this earth. And Pharaoh was well pleased with Joseph. Pharaoh appointed Joseph second in command of all of Egypt. The story of Joseph can be read in the Holy Bible in Genesis Chapter 37 through Chapter 50. Also, the story of Joseph can be read in the Book of Jasher.

Many people are unfamiliar with the Book of Jasher because it does not appear in the Holy Bible. But the Book of Jasher is a part of the Lord's word as a written account of things that happened during the Old Testament. I first encountered and heard of the Book of Jasher while reading my Bible in my twenties. I noticed the Book of Jasher was mentioned twice in the Old Testament. The Book of Jasher was first mentioned in Joshua 10:13 and 2 Samuel 1:18. On two occasions, the Holy Bible references the Book of Jasher in scripture. This means the Holy Bible gives credibility to the Book of Jasher.

Joseph was taken out of prison and appointed second in command over Egypt. And once Joseph was placed second in command, he put his plan into action. For the next seven years Joseph stored food up for all of Egypt. Joseph was preparing for the seven years of famine after the seven years of abundance. After the seven years of abundance had come and gone. A great famine hit the land of Egypt and its surrounding areas.

Food was scarce in Egypt and the surrounding areas. So Jacob, whose name was also Israel, sent his sons to Egypt to buy some food. Jacobs's sons, who were also the same brothers who sold Joseph into slavery, went down to Egypt to buy some food. The same brothers who sold Joseph into slavery had to come to him for food! Joseph's brothers had to bow before Joseph, just like the vision the Lord had shown Joseph many years prior.

I noticed similarities in my life and Joseph's life. Joseph was blessed with the gift of having visions and interpreting visions. I have the gift of having visions and interpreting visions. The Lord gave Joseph visions that showed him being over his siblings. The Lord gave me a vision showing me over my siblings. Joseph's siblings resented him because the vision showed him having great authority over all his brothers. My siblings resented me because my vision showed me having great authority over all of them. All of Joseph's brothers sold him into slavery. Seven of my siblings plotted against me for thirteen years (September 18, 2004 – September 18, 2017) to cheat me out of my share of the inheritance my mother left for us. Then Joseph was in bondage for a total of thirteen years. And just like Joseph was in bondage for thirteen years, Satan placed me in bondage for thirteen years. I will tell you about the thirteen years of bondage as we move through this book.

At the end of Joseph's thirteen years of bondage, the Most High God raised Joseph out of prison to become the second in command of the Greatest Empire in the World, Egypt! And God used Joseph to save the people of Israel and the people of Egypt. On the day of my birth, February 17, 1971, my dad said the Lord showed him a vision of me being President of the United States of America, the Greatest Empire in the world today! Then, the Lord gave me a vision in the fourth grade that showed me over millions of people when this world was in great distress. People had to come to me for food and provisions just like people had to go to Joseph for food and provisions! And later in this book, I will tell you how the Most High God Jehovah said to me, "Save my people!"

After the Lord revealed his entire plan to me, I saw the similarities between Joseph's life and mine. Joseph was the youngest child, and I am the youngest child, but God is about to make the last, first.

Jesus said in Matthew 20:16 "So the last will be first, and the first will be last." (Biblegateway.com, NIV)

25. My Science Project

When I was in the sixth grade, I had to do a science project. The teacher gave each student a subject to do their science project on, and I was given the topic of black holes. When I got the topic, I was very excited and interested in black holes. As I started researching black holes, I learned a lot about them. I remember looking up different information on black holes in the encyclopedias and reading some books on black holes. In my research, I realized there was more to black holes than the books told us. The question that came to my mind was, where do stars go once they enter a black hole? I thought the stars had to go somewhere because they didn't disappear into thin air. Another question I had was, what is the purpose of black holes? I couldn't answer those questions because the books I was reading never had the answers to my questions.

After I finished my science project in the 6th grade, I still desired to know the answers to those questions; I constantly thought about the questions long after I finished my science project. I wanted to know the absolute truth about black holes because I felt there was much more to black holes than what the books told me. I was searching for the absolute truth about black holes because I felt that black holes held an essential piece of the puzzle that led to the absolute truth about all things! The questions would never leave me because I felt the answers to those questions would help lead me to the absolute truth.

I did my science project on black holes for the next three years. For the next three years, whenever we had to do a science project, I would always do my science project on black holes. So, each year, I would start all over on my black hole project and try to answer the two key questions I had. However, I couldn't find any data to answer my questions each year. I couldn't walk away from the subject of black holes because I hadn't answered my questions surrounding black holes. My classmates used to laugh at me because I did the same project year after year. They had many jokes because they thought I was obsessed with black holes. To be honest, I was obsessed with black holes because I felt black holes were a vital piece of the puzzle that led to the absolute truth! And I had a desire to know the absolute truth about all things!

So now I am in High School in the 9th grade, and I must do a science project. But I was in a physical science class and had to do my project on one of the physical science topics. So, I talked to my science teacher, and she insisted I do my science projects on one of the topics she provided. But suddenly, my science teacher allowed me to do my science project on black holes. It was the Lord that changed her mind. Do you know what I did my science project on? Black holes! I had to do my project on black holes because the same questions that plagued me three years prior still plagued me when I was in the ninth grade. The questions were: where do stars go once they enter a black hole? And what is the purpose of black holes?

After doing all my research, I still couldn't answer the questions. By this time, I had become so frustrated and angry. I became frustrated because I knew there was much more to black holes than the books told me. So, out of my frustration, I said, "Lord, where do stars go once they enter into a black hole, and what is the purpose of a black hole?" When I finished my question, the Lord said, "Once stars are pulled into a black hole, they are redistributed out on the other side of the black hole. This changes the location of the stars; this means the universe is always expanding. This is done so no one can ever reach the end of the universe." I was astonished once I heard the Lord say that because I knew it was the absolute truth, and it made sense! So I went to my classmates who were making fun of me for always doing my experiment on black holes, and I tried to explain the true purpose of black holes to them.

One day, I stopped Dana and several other classmates in the hallway at A.H. Parker High School and tried to explain everything the Lord told me about black holes. Once I told them the purpose of black holes, they couldn't understand what I was saying because their argument was, "That is not in the book, so how could that be true? That could only be true if it is in a book!" After I heard his thought process, I found it useless talking to him about anything that required an original thought process because he couldn't grasp anything that was not in a textbook.

After the Lord told me, "Once stars are pulled into a black hole, they are redistributed out on the other side of the black hole. This changes the location of the stars; this means the universe is always expanding. This is done so no one can ever reach the end of the universe." I thought about the answer regarding stars and nothing else and overlooked the timing at which the Lord gave me the answer. I have been working on black holes as my science project since I was in the sixth grade, and I have been trying to answer the same two questions since then. Why did the Lord answer me about black holes during the fall of 1985?

The Lord answered my question during the fall of 1985 because of what happened to me in the summer of 1985.

In the summer of 1985, I witnessed a life-changing event that I was trying to make sense of. The answer the Lord gave me concerning black holes in the fall of 1985 answered the question of why black holes exist, and it also gave me some answers to what I witnessed in the summer of 1985. But I didn't make the connection that the Lord's answer concerning black holes was connected to what I witnessed in the summer of 1985.

Many years later, in 1994 or 1995, I was watching CNN when a news anchor for CNN said, "Scientists have just discovered the universe is expanding!" Once I heard them say that, I started laughing, and then I said to myself, "I wonder how many billions of dollars they spent to find out the universe is expanding." I then said, "They could have just asked me, and I could have told them the universe is expanding because the Lord told me that back in 1985!" Then I said, "They could have given me that money!" Then I started laughing!

26. I Witness It

What I am about to reveal to you is the absolute truth, and it's breathtaking. I need you to open your mind and not bring your perception into this. Your perception is not truth; your perception is just what you believe. And what you believe has nothing to do with the absolute truth! I need you to be intelligent, have wisdom, and listen to what I have to say. Then, after you read this entire book, form an opinion that's full of wisdom. As you read through this book, you will see how the Lord always placed me in the right place at the right time to receive some valuable information or to witness some type of life-changing event.

In the summer of 1985, my family and I visited relatives at my grandmother's house in Lavaca, Alabama. When it was time for us to return to Birmingham, my brother "W" said he was heading to California. He then asked me if I wanted to ride with him. At first, I said "Yes," but then I told him, "No," that's ok. So, then I kept going back and forth until I decided not to go. When my brother was getting ready to pull off, the Lord said to me, "Go!" Once the Lord said, "Go!" I stopped my brother and said, "I am going." I got my clothes, jumped into the car with my brother, and rode to California. Once we made it to California, my brother dropped me off at his wife's apartment, whom he was separated from. I will call her "A".

"A" stayed in the City of Twentynine Palms, California. This city was a military town for the Marines military base. Once we got to "A's" house, my brother dropped me off there and went to San Diego, California. This didn't make any sense to me or his wife. I wondered, "Why did he bring me to California to drop me off at her apartment?" And his wife was thinking the same thing. It didn't make sense. There I was in Twentynine Palms, California, with nothing to do. I then wondered, "Why did the Lord tell me to go? I'm not having any fun sitting here at this apartment all day, every day." Why did God say to me, "Go!" I had them thoughts because I wasn't having any fun!

Then, one day, at about 7:00 PM, my sister-in-law, "A", stood outside on her balcony. Then suddenly "A" starts to scream, "Ken, Ken, Ken. Come here, Ken!!!" She was just screaming my name like the world was about to end! I got off the couch and ran to see what was happening. Once I got outside on the balcony. "A" is pointing to the sky! Then I looked up to see what she was pointing at, and there it was! The only thing I could say was, "OH MY GOD!!!" I was frozen with disbelief. I adjusted my eyes because this couldn't be real! I started thinking to myself, "How is this possible? This kind of thing only happens in the movies!" While all this was running through my mind, the streets filled with people. Everyone came outside! People stop their cars in the middle of the roads.

People were walking away from their cars while their cars were still on. Everyone was doing the same thing, pointing to the sky! I stood there and looked at this alien spaceship hovering in one spot for about thirty minutes. The alien spaceship was about five hundred feet off the ground. This alien spaceship was about the size of three Legion Field Stadiums, not the football field but the football stadium. Legion Field Stadium seats a capacity of 71,000 fans. So, imagine three Legion Field Stadiums put together and think about how large that spaceship was.

What I saw, as clear as day, was an alien spaceship that was not of this world! While I was there staring at the spaceship, I kept having this thought that something was being dispersed into the air. Whatever it was, it didn't have a smell or odor, but I knew something was being released into the air. "A," said the spaceship hovering over the Marines military base. I remember staring at the spaceship and thinking, "How is this possible?" After the spaceship stayed hovering for about thirty minutes, it accelerated into the mountains surrounding Twentynine Palms, California. This spaceship didn't move like an airplane. It went from hovering in one place for thirty minutes to gliding across the air. It was not like an airplane; it didn't have to have speed or use jet engines to maintain its flight in the air! Some type of propulsion system was propelling the spaceship. And this propulsion system allowed it to glide through the air! Once it glided away, we could still watch it for many miles because the spacecraft was so large! So eventually, it glided away towards the mountains and left our view. Once it left, everyone stood out in the streets, sidewalks, and everywhere else. Everyone was so astonished! It was like they had to rethink everything they knew or learned! I am sure they were asking themselves the same thing I was asking myself: "How is this possible?"

Once everybody dispersed, we returned inside and turned on the local news stations. We waited to see if they would have a Special News Report! There was no Special News Report! So once the regular news came on, we were waiting on one of the news stations to say something about the spaceship! None of the news stations mentioned the spacecraft! "A," and I couldn't understand why they didn't mention the spaceship! We were astonished that no news stations mentioned the spaceship! Twentynine Palms was a medium-sized town then, so how could the news stations miss that story? Years later, I figured out the Military and the U.S. Government made sure it was a news media blackout on the spaceship. That's why no news station mentioned anything about the spaceship! Years later I understood how the U.S. Government could make sure a story disappear they didn't want to air on television!

So, later on that night, my nose began to bleed. At first, it was no big deal, but then my nose kept bleeding. Hour after hour, my nose bled, and day after day, my nose bled. My nose bled for about three days straight. My nose wouldn't stop bleeding. At first, we thought the heat was causing my nose to bleed. But then I thought about it: the heat couldn't be causing my nose to bleed because I stayed inside the apartment all day with the air conditioner on. I was not exposed to any heat. The Lord revealed to me my nose bled because the spaceship released some toxins into the air. The Lord also revealed to me the toxins released in the air caused temporary memory loss in the people in 29 Palms, California.

After that day, some people who witnessed the spacecraft remembered witnessing it, but it didn't truly register in their minds what they witnessed. It was like something was causing them not to register the event in their minds even though they remembered seeing the spaceship. The Lord revealed to me the continuous flow of blood from my nosebleed was flushing out the toxins from my bloodstream. So basically, when I inhaled the toxins, it was like the toxins were being released from my blood when my nose bled for three consecutive days! That's why I remembered seeing the alien spacecraft vividly, and it registered in my mind what I saw.

My nose bled for three consecutive days and didn't stop bleeding until my brother picked me up, and we left the town of Twentynine Palms, California, which was three days after I had witnessed the spacecraft. Once my brother and I reached about sixty miles from Twentynine Palms, California, my nose instantly stopped bleeding. It was strange how suddenly my nose stopped bleeding once we were outside Twentynine Palms, California. As my brother was driving, I sat in the passenger seat thinking. And then I realized why the Lord told me to "Go" with my brother to California. The Lord told me to go with my brother to California so I could witness the spaceship! I also realize the Lord made my brother drop me off at his wife's apartment and leave me there!

After I had witnessed the spacecraft, I had a lot of thinking to do over my lifetime. I always wondered, "How could God be real when aliens exist?" I knew God was real because I had many conversations with God, and he talked to me. But I was trying to make sense of the spaceship and aliens in the equation of God the Father and the Lord Jesus Christ. The more I thought about it, the more questions I had. Something always contradicted my theory with each theory I developed, so I kept running into roadblocks. Years later, when the Lord freed me and downloaded my mind with so much information, I began to understand the big picture and put all the puzzle pieces together. As you read through this book you must remember everything is connected!

Also, after I witnessed the alien spaceship during the Summer of 1985, God answered why black holes existed during the Fall of 1985. God said to me, "Once stars are pulled into a black hole, they are redistributed out on the other side of the black hole. This changes the location of the stars; this means the universe is always expanding. This is done so no one can ever reach the end of the universe." When God said, "...so no one can ever reach the end of the universe." God was not just talking about mankind! This is why I was obsessed with black holes. This is why I had the feeling that the answer to my questions about black holes would help lead me to the absolute truth!

After witnessing the spaceship in Twentynine Palms, California, and after God told me why black holes exist, I had an encounter with this man I had never seen before. I was about 14 years old when I was standing in front of my house on the road when this man approached me and started talking. The man told me to look into the sky, and he told me to tell him what I saw. I told him I saw white clouds and a blue sky. Then the man asked me if that was all I saw. And I said, "Yes." Then, this man takes a special piece of glass out of his pocket. This glass had a tint to it. The man said it's called dicyanin glass, and it allows you to see things the naked eye can't see. Then the man handed me the dicyanin glass, pointed me in a specific direction, and told me to tell him what I saw. It was at that moment I saw it. When I looked through the dicyanin glass, I saw an alien spaceship hovering in the sky.

Once I saw the alien spaceship, I quickly removed the dicyanin glass, and the spaceship was gone. And when I looked through the glass again, I saw the spaceship again. Then the man pointed me in a different direction and had me look through the glass, and I saw a different spaceship. The man then told me these alien spaceships are in the sky all around us. I couldn't believe what I was seeing. When you look with the naked eye, you can't see the spaceships, but when you look through the dicyanin glass, you can see them.

Then the man took back the dicyanin glass and said it was illegal to have it and that he must go. But I had so many questions for the man. The man left me standing there in awe without giving me any answers. The man walked away and disappeared, and I never saw him again. I realized today that man was not an ordinary man but an angel of the Most High God Jehovah. The angel was sent to me so one day I could explain this to you. As a young boy I had many questions and not enough answers. One question was: how could God be real when aliens exist? I knew God was real, but how did aliens figure into the equation? Another question was why the U.S. Government outlawed dicyanin glass. Did the U.S. Government outlaw dicyanin glass to hide the truth? This is the United States of America Book of Secrets! This is the Illuminati Book of Secrets.

27. Satan Try To Stop The Prophesy

I remember it was the summer before I was to enter A. H. Parker High School; I had my sights on playing high school football. At this time, I felt like I was too big and too old to be an altar boy at my church. I had been an altar boy since I was seven years old. One Sunday, I went to Mrs. Buchanan, who was over the altar boys, and said, "I am not going to be able to be an altar boy anymore." She said, "Why?" And then I said,

"I was too big, and I was going to high school." She said, "Baby, I will find something else for you to do." I told her, "I didn't want to do anything else." At that moment, she said to me, "Baby, don't stop working in the church; Satan is trying to get his hands on you because he knows the Lord wants you to teach his word." I remember she pleaded with me like the world was about to end. But I didn't listen! I told her, "I am not leaving the church, Mrs. Buchanan; I just don't want to work in the church right now." She continued to plead with me but to no prevail.

I remember as I got older, in my teenage years, some people would tell me I was going to be a preacher. I would always talk to my inner circle about God. One day, while I was thinking about God, someone walked up to me and said, "You are going to be a preacher one day." At that very moment a thought was given to me that said, "I shouldn't be a preacher because I wouldn't be able to have any fun." Then, these images came across my mind, and this is what these images showed me and told me. It showed me all kinds of beautiful women, all kinds of parties and alcohol, all sorts of nice things and money. And then the thought was given to me that said, "I want be able to have any fun if I become a preacher." At that moment, I said, "I didn't want to be a preacher because I won't be able to have any fun if I become a preacher!" I was sixteen years old when this happened. I didn't have any spiritual wisdom to understand why that thought was given to me and who gave me that thought. I didn't realize until many years later that Satan had tempted me by planting the seeds of sex, parties, alcohol, and money in my mind. It was Satan who showed me the women, the parties, the alcohol, and the money. Satan is the one who gave me those thoughts of not wanting to teach the Lord's word. And I was foolish enough to fall for Satan's temptation! The thought Satan gave me was a Satanic Contradiction to the prophecy that was spoken over my life.

The Lord wanted me to teach his word so I could be a blessing to others and so I could be blessed. You must remember my dad and Mrs. Buchanan said, "The Lord wants you to teach his word!" Satan's response to the prophecy was to entice me with the things of this world so he could stop the prophecy from being fulfilled. Whenever God has plans on blessing you, Satan will always send a Satanic Contradiction to you. A Satanic Contradiction will always go against whatever God told you to do. And the blessing the Lord has for you is always won or lost in the Satanic Contradiction. If you stick to what God told you to do once Satan sends you the Satanic Contradiction, then you will receive your blessing. If you believe Satan's Satanic Contradiction and go against what God told you to do, then you will lose your blessing.

It was at this point I started to run from God. I didn't realize it then, but I was running from God. I still love God, but I didn't want to be a preacher because Satan had manipulated me into believing I couldn't have any fun if I became a preacher. So, I started running from God. I thought if I was partying and doing certain things, God wouldn't want me anymore. I began to live life fast. I didn't realize it, but I was running from God like the Prophet Jonah ran from God. Who was Jonah, you ask? Jonah was one of the Lord's Prophets discussed in the Holy Bible. And God told Jonah to go to the city named Nineveh so he could speak against that city because of their wicked actions. But instead of doing what God told him to do, Jonah decided to run from God.

So, Jonah brought a ticket on a ship to Tarshish so he could flee from God. God became angry with Jonah. God brought a great storm to sink the ship Jonah was on. The shipmaster realizes it was Jonah who was bringing catastrophe to them. The shipmaster and others cast Jonah overboard. And once Jonah was cast overboard, the storm ceased. Then, a great fish came to Jonah while he was in the sea. And the great fish swallowed Jonah. Once the great fish swallowed Jonah, Jonah was in the belly of the fish for three days. And for three days Jonah prayed to the Lord and repented for his sins. Then, on the third day, the Lord heard Jonah's prayer. And the Lord spoke to the great fish, and the fish vomited Jonah onto dry land, and Jonah was saved. After Jonah was saved, God spoke to Jonah again. God told Jonah to go to Nineveh and preach his word. But this time, Jonah did what God told him to do. The moral of the life of Jonah was this. Jonah ran from God, and because Jonah ran from God, Jonah had to go through a great storm and catastrophe. But faith in God brought Jonah through the storm and the catastrophe.

I looked at the worldly things shown to me and chose the worldly things instead of God and his word. I began to run from God. And because I ran from God, I was setting myself up for a great storm and catastrophe! After Satan tempted me, I began to live life fast. From then on, I began to meet girls, sleep with girls, and party like the world was about to end. I was in high school partying like I was off in college! I had plenty of unsupervised time, and I took advantage of it! I was a good kid, but I was beginning to go rogue! I was on the verge of leaving the reservation!

28. The Anatomy of Satan Part 2

In this Chapter of The Anatomy of Satan, we will examine another way Satan wages war against God's people and others. In the previous Chapter, Satan gave me the thought that I shouldn't become a preacher. Then I told you how Satan showed me all the worldly things I would have if I didn't become a preacher. I didn't understand it was Satan who told me I couldn't have any fun if I became a preacher. I thought it was my thoughts, but it wasn't. I didn't understand it was Satan who showed me all the beautiful women, parties, alcohol, and money I could have if I didn't teach the Lord's word.

To understand Satan's Anatomy, you must understand how Satan planted a thought and images into my mind. Satan planted a thought and images into my mind the same way he plants thoughts and images into your mind. Satan displays a god-like ability to plant thoughts and images into any human's mind by using telepathy. Telepathy means communication from one mind to another by extrasensory means.

"Telepathy." *Merriam-Webster*. Merriam-Webster, n.d. Web. 18 Oct. 2015. <http://www.merriam-webster.com/dictionary/telepathy>.

Satan uses telepathy to plant thoughts and images into our minds. I say Satan displays a god-like ability because that's what it is. I know for a fact Satan is not god. Jehovah is God, and Jesus Christ is the son of God! But the ability to plant a thought into people's minds using telepathy is God-like! And the thoughts that Satan plants into people's minds are known as temptations! Satan tempts us by using his telepathic ability to implant thoughts and images into our minds.

Satan tempts mankind into sin by planting a thought of temptation into our minds. When Satan gives people these thoughts of temptation, Satan makes people think the thoughts are their thoughts. Or Satan will even mislead people to think it was God the Father who gave them a particular thought, when in fact, it was Satan who gave them the thought, and it was Satan who tempted them into sin! Just like Satan tempted me into sin. To implant thoughts and images into a human being's mind is part of the anatomy of Satan!

29. I Ignore the Warning of The Holy Spirit

I remember during my junior year in High School there was a guy named Rodney Johnson. Rodney was a guy who always liked to joke and play around. Rodney Johnson always tried to crack on me in class for various reasons. Rodney would always try to make jokes about my teeth because I had an overbite. Rodney found it amusing to talk about my teeth. Almost every day at school, Rodney would try to crack different jokes on me, trying his best to embarrass me.

One Friday or Saturday night, a couple of fellows and I were going to a High School party. I planned to drive, pick up a couple of guys, and attend the party. One of the guys I was going to pick up was Felix. A few hours before we were to leave, Felix called me with Rodney on the phone. Rodney asked me if I could pick him up. I told Rodney I couldn't pick him up. Then Rodney pleaded with me to pick him up so he could ride with us to the party. I told Rodney I wouldn't pick him up because I didn't want to. During the entire conversation with Rodney, I thought, "You want me to pick you up when you try to dog me out in front of everyone." So, I told Rodney no and then hung up the phone.

Once I hung up the phone, the voice of the Holy Spirit spoke into my left ear and said, "Something bad is going to happen to Rodney if you do not pick him up." Once I heard the Holy Spirit speak, I stopped and thought about what I heard, and I reconsidered my position on picking Rodney up. After going back and forth about picking Rodney up, I decided I wouldn't let him ride with me to the party. Once I decided not to pick Rodney up, the voice of the Holy Spirit spoke into my left ear again and said, "Something bad is going to happen to Rodney if you do not pick him up." I contemplated picking Rodney up once I heard the voice say it again. Then the phone rang. When I answered the phone, it was Rodney. Rodney then pleaded with me over and over to pick him up. While talking to Rodney on the phone and listening to his plea, I could only think of how he always tried to crack jokes on me in class. I told Rodney I wouldn't pick him up and then hung up the phone. Once I hung up the phone, the voice of the Holy Spirit spoke into my left ear again and said to me for a third time, "Something bad is going to happen to Rodney if you do not pick him up." After I heard this warning for the third time, I started to reconsider picking Rodney up and letting him ride with me. But again, I thought about how he embarrassed me in class, and I finally decided not to pick Rodney up. So, that night, I picked up the other two guys, and we went out.

Then, early the next morning, my phone rang. As soon as the phone rang, I knew it was bad news. I just looked at the phone while it rang and eventually answered it. It was Felix! Felix then tells me Rodney Johnson was dead! I then asked Felix, "What happened to Rodney?" Felix said after I refused to pick Rodney up, Rodney went out with two guys named

"T" and Ron. While Rodney was in the car with "T" and Ron, "T" and Ron were smoking marijuana, so Rodney decided to smoke marijuana with them. While Rodney was smoking marijuana, he had an asthma attack and died. After Felix informed me of the bad news, I immediately thought about what the voice of the Holy Spirit said to me in my left ear, "Something bad is going to happen to Rodney if you do not pick him up." Then I realized Rodney wouldn't have been smoking marijuana if he was with me because I didn't smoke marijuana. If I would have allowed Rodney to ride with me, Rodney wouldn't have died! I honestly didn't grasp the situation when the Holy Spirit warned me. I didn't realize Rodney would die.

30. My Personal Life

Once, my dad and Mrs. Buchanan spoke the prophecy over me that the Lord wanted me to teach his word. The atmosphere around me changed! The atmosphere went from love, peace, and joy to steal, kill, and destroy! Satan and his demons recognized I was going to be one of the Lord's anointed ones, so Satan sent his army on the attack! And you must believe me, I was attacked! Whether physically or verbally, I was attacked! My spirit was that of a lamb, but I was surrounded by wolves. And I had to defend myself from the wolves Satan sent against me! So basically, Satan and his army came after me through people I had seen daily. So, at a young age, I found myself defending myself against Satan and all his people who had planned on harming me, whether physically or verbally!

So, I got into fights at school and in my neighborhood. I never told my mom or dad what was happening. I just tried to handle it on my own! Once I reached high school, everything went to a higher level of violence. I attended A. H. Parker High School, an all-African American High School in Birmingham, Alabama. Parker was a good school, but it could be rough at times. Parker High School had three different drug-infested, crime-infested housing projects zoned to go to Parker High School. And those elements would spill over into the school.

It was in high school my mom became fearful for my life. My mom always knew how people just hated me. And my mom would always say to me, "Satan wants you dead, and he would give anything to have you killed!" And then my mother would also say, "I pray to God you make it out of high school without being killed because Satan wants you dead! And wherever you go to college, it's not going to be in this city!" I didn't know how my mom knew Satan wanted me dead because I never told my mom what would go down at school or other places. But some kind of way, she just knew Satan wanted me dead! My mom was always fearful for my life! And it didn't help that African American teenage boys were starting to be killed more frequently in Birmingham.

I always had to fight when I was young. Either I had to fight my older brother "C" because he was jealous of me, or I was fighting this older guy named Ty who grew up in the neighborhood, or I was fighting one of the twins that stayed across the street, or I was fighting someone at school. I never picked on or bothered anyone, but I had to defend myself from the people Satan sent to harm me. Satan was using the people I saw regularly to try to harm me and destroy me. Satan was using the people I saw every day to wage war against me! So, I had to fight people at school and people in my neighborhood.

Once I entered high school, I saw the element I was in, so I adapted to my surroundings. I started partying with my associates from the hood on the weekends. On the weekend, we would always dollar up and go to the Package store next to Parker High School to buy beer, wine, or liquor or we would go to the Goldwire store and buy beer or wine. We used to go into the store and buy beer, wine, or liquor ourselves! How crazy is that! I started drinking in High School! I was just doing what my associates were doing so I could fit in, but at the same time, I was also one of the ring leaders!

While I was in high school, I joined a high school fraternity named Kappa Tau Upsilon, KTU for short. There were many high school fraternities in the Birmingham area, so I decided to join the purple and gold of KTU. Back in high school, KTU was off the chain, and high school fraternities were huge in Birmingham. Being in a high school fraternity in Birmingham while you were in high school was more significant than being in a college fraternity. It was really that big! Because in high school we were partying on a college level! We were partying like rock stars! But while I was partying like a rock star, I had to hide all of this from my parents! And I made sure my mom and dad didn't know what I was doing because they wouldn't have tolerated it! I was a master at hiding this lifestyle from them! At home, I was their darling church-going baby boy taking Honors High School classes! But when I was in the streets I was "Ken Brown!" Ken Brown was my alter ego. Ken Brown was the street part of me. Kennedy K. Brown wasn't built for those streets, but Ken Brown was! I didn't know this at the time but I created an alter ego named Ken Brown to defend Kennedy K. Brown.

I had to hide the drinking and partying from my parents and my siblings. I was cautious to ensure nobody found out what I was doing. It was not too hard to hide it from my parents because they got a divorce when I was in the eighth grade. Once my parents got a divorce, they gave me the freedom to choose who I wanted to live with. So I chose to live with both of them. So, I lived with my mother at times, and I lived with my dad at times. This living arrangement gave me extraordinary amounts of freedom. And I loved it. My parents were tired of raising children when it came to me. They raised my seven siblings before me, and they were working extra shifts on their jobs. So, they were just tired, and I took advantage of it. And I loved it! My parents were strict with my sisters and brothers when they were children! But when it came to me, all the rules were gone! I guess they were tired from raising my other seven siblings. All the strict rules they had raised my siblings under were out the door when it came to me! This was very good because all the freedom I had also helped me to think outside the box.

I was drinking because I was trying to fit in and be like everyone else. But I wasn't like everyone else; I was who the Lord created me to be (the Prophet Elisha). But I didn't understand that when I was a young man. So here I was, a member of this high school fraternity known for selling out Greek shows and throwing parties. Little did I know I painted a bigger target on my back once I joined KTU! Now I went from Ken Brown to that's Ken Brown that's in KTU! Then I went from Satan influencing guys to hate me in parts of the city to guys hating me city-wide! This city-wide exposure from joining KTU led to even more fights and altercations. Honestly, I never wanted to fight anybody or be in any type of confrontation, but I was in an environment where stupidity reigned! And Satan was sending his soldiers on the attack! People hated me because Satan was influencing them to do so. I didn't understand this then, but Satan was trying to kill me, and my mother knew it!

In high school, I had people pull guns out on me. I remember one day when I got out of my mother's car at Parker High School parking lot, this guy pulled out a 12-gauge sawed-off shotgun and pointed it at my chest. This guy didn't like me, and he had been spreading rumors he was going to kill me. This guy was in one of the other high school fraternities! So, one day, he caught me getting out of my mom's car to go to school, and he pulled out a 12-gauge sawed-off shotgun and pointed it at my chest! The guy was standing no more than four feet away. Once, he pointed the 12-gage at my chest. I became enraged with anger! I didn't flinch, nor did I fear him. I looked him dead in his eyes, and I had no fear. I was enraged with anger! Once he saw I didn't fear him nor feared death, I took all his so-called power from him! So, he lowered the 12-gauge and walked away! This same guy had shot other people before, so shooting someone was nothing for him, but since I didn't show him any fear, it took all his false courage from him!

Fights and altercations were happening so often that I got to a point where I was tired! I was tired of looking over my shoulder! It was that day when the guy pointed the 12-gage shotgun at my chest; I decided I was not taking no more "Bull Shit" off anybody else. I was enraged with anger! I was tired of people bothering me and I just snapped!!! I mean, I snapped! This was the transformation from being a meek lamb to turning into a lion! The spirit of the lamb in me was too peaceful to deal with the gang bangers I had seen daily. But the Lion that emerged from me that day could do more than defend me; the Lion could destroy anyone who thought about bothering me! The day the guy pulled the 12-gauge sawed-off shotgun on me was the same day I made an oath with the Most High God Jehovah. So, out of anger, I said to God, "If nobody bothers me, I was not going to bother them! But if anybody bothered me, I am going to F-ck them up!" I was out of order, but that's what I said.

From then on, I didn't take any more "BS" off anybody else. My motto became, you don't bother me, I don't bother you, but if you bother me, I would do whatever it takes to "F-ck you up!" What the people around me didn't understand was that I had snapped! I had snapped! This transformation happened during my junior year in high school, the day the guy pointed the 12-gauge shotgun at my chest. I had seen enough, and I had enough. I had been going to school and receiving threats daily. And I was tired of the threats and the altercations because I had the spirit of a lamb in me! But the lamb in me would be forced to surrender to the Lion that was also in me!

For legal purposes, the things in this paragraph may have happened and may not have happened. One day, while at a formal at the Botanical Gardens in Birmingham, I fought with this guy in another fraternity. This guy came at me talking trash. He thought I would have the peaceful mindset that I usually have. And he was unprepared for the Lion that was raging inside me. So once the guy approached me, he started popping off at the mouth. So, we started fighting. But the guy was not prepared for what was raging inside of me. I was beating the guy down, so the guy started running. So, I caught the guy and got him on the ground, and then I started stabbing this guy in the face! I had blacked out! I was there physically but the rage had overtaken me. As I was stabbing him, someone screamed my name, and I stopped stabbing him! So, I let the guy go! He got up and ran away. Once I let the guy go, I noticed it was blood covering the ground. There was blood all over the ground! I don't know who screamed at me, but they stopped me from doing much more damage than I did. I was furious. I was in a rage I had never witnessed in myself before! Miraculously, no charges were ever filed against me! Thank You, Jesus!

Since that day, people were cautious in approaching me with some "BS" because everyone heard about what I did. After that day, if anyone approached me with some "BS" they came in groups. They had to come in groups because they were too afraid to come alone. Then they realized even if they came in packs or groups, I still was not having it. The quiet little boy who heard God's voice and talked to God regularly had been transformed from a meek lamb to a raging Lion! And the Lion that raged inside of me was not taking any BS off anyone. You fill in the blank as to what BS means.

I had transformed from a lamb to a Lion because the lamb was too meek to deal with the vicious predators! Satan's people were out to kill me! I had to protect myself! I didn't have a choice in the matter! I had to fight to always protect myself! See, I went to school with people who drove around with Kilos of cocaine and thousands of dollars worth of crack cocaine in their cars. I went to school with people who had Mac 10s, AK47s, and fully automatic weapons in the trunk of their cars. That is just to name the small stuff! That's not to mention the other military-grade weapons they had! I went to school with some people who wouldn't hesitate to take another person's life! I went to school with people who have committed numerous homicides in Birmingham!

It was nothing for this guy name Ed to drive up in front of Parker High School and blow Myron's brains out in broad daylight! It was nothing for them to gun down Woochy in his front yard! It was nothing to see a fight in the courtyard at school, where two rival gangs went at it. It was nothing to see a brick picked up and smashed against another person's head! It was nothing to have a guy stand in front of my car and fire shots into a house party while I was sitting in my car! It was nothing for a person to say they were going to kill you, and they meant it! It was nothing for a guy named "Flood" to pull out a gun and shoot a person. It was nothing for "Flood" to pull a gun out on me because of a girl! It was nothing to see drug dealers being glorified at school as though they were the pillar of our school and the pillar of our community. It was just another day at Parker High School; it was just another day in the City of Birmingham.

That was the environment I went to school in! I saw the effects of poverty and stupidity up front! And it was not a pretty sight to see! And once you have been in that environment for so long, it hardens your heart to your surroundings. And before you know it, your surroundings have started to take root in you, and your surroundings have become a part of you. And that world you observed for so long has become second nature to you! And once it becomes second nature to you, normal behavior appears to be dysfunctional behavior to you! When you had to grow up fighting to defend yourself, sometimes that's all you know how to do is fight!

I was being persecuted, and I didn't understand it. I was being persecuted because the Lord wanted me to teach his word. So once the prophecy of the Lord went into the atmosphere, Satan went on the attack. I was being persecuted because the Most High God Jehovah, and the Lord Jesus Christ had chosen me to teach his word. I was being persecuted because Satan knew I was the Prophet Elisha from the Old Testament! And since Satan knew I was the Prophet Elisha from the Old Testament, Satan sent people to kill me! And the only person who understood Satan wanted me dead was my mother. She was the only one who understood how badly Satan wanted me dead. I guess that's why I always found my mother on her knees, praying beside her bed. Because she praying for me!

But the question you should ask yourself is, why did the Lord place me in that type of environment? You should be asking yourself that question because in Chapter 3, titled "My Mother Falls Out of A Chair". The Lord told me, "This is the family you will be assigned to, and this is where we will hide you until it is your time." So, why did the Lord place me in that environment? The Lord wanted to make me strong and fearless, and the Lord wanted to transform me from a lamb to a Lion. See I didn't understand this then, but the Lord was preparing me for my future ever since I was a child! The Lord knew he was going to have me challenge the deadliest worldwide crime syndicate this world has ever seen, so the Lord wanted me to overcome the fear of physical harm! See all things work to the good of God's glory! The Lord made sure he told my dad, Mrs. Buchannan, and others I was going to teach the Lord's word. Because the Lord knew once they spoke those words into the atmosphere, Satan was going to attack me! The Lord prepared me to battle on many different battlegrounds by allowing people to attack me!

The Lord needed to transform me from a lamb to a Lion! You also must remember an angel of God spoke to me one day and said, "You are blessed to be one of the last men to walk the face of this earth." This meant I would be on this earth during the Great Tribulation and Armageddon! It also means I will make it through! God needed me to be as tough as titanium. I was built to be Jehovah Tough! The Lord placed me in that environment as a child so I would conquer the fear of physical harm because the fear of physical harm is worse than the physical harm itself! Fear plays tricks on one's mind, causing stress, and it forces one to live in mental captivity. Fear is not REAL! Satan wants you to think fear is real, but it isn't! Fear is a mental choice! Because once I made the decision not to fear any physical harm, I chose to defeat Satan and all the people he influenced to attack me. Satan couldn't play the fear of physical harm card on me any longer.

2 Timothy 1:7 "For God has not given us a **spirit of fear**, but **of** power and **of** love and **of** a sound mind." (NKJ, Biblegateway.com)

If God doesn't give us a spirit of fear, where does the spirit of fear come from? The answer is Satan.

When John the Baptist came into this world, he was a lamb that prepared the way for the Lamb of God Jesus Christ. And once John the Baptist prepared the way for Jesus Christ, John the Baptist was beheaded by King Herrod. So, John was slaughtered like a lamb before Jesus was crucified as the lamb. See, since John prepared the way for Jesus, John had to be put to death before Jesus. The precursor of John the Baptist's death set the stage for Jesus Christ's crucifixion.

Well, I am preparing the way for the return of Jesus Christ. So, I am the precursor of Jesus Christ's return. Jesus is not coming back as a lamb; he is coming back as a Lion. A Lion is nothing like a lamb. A lamb is innocent, harmless, meek, and humble, while a Lion is fierce, powerful, strong, and courageous. See, I was a lamb when I was a child. But God didn't need me to be a lamb. God needed me to be a Lion since Jesus Christ will be returning as the Lion of Judah.

Revelation 5:5-6 [5] Then one of the elders said to me, "Do not weep! See, the Lion of the tribe of Judah, the Root of David, has triumphed. He is able to open the scroll and its seven seals." ⁶ Then I saw a Lamb, looking as if it had been slain, standing at the center of the throne,... (NIV Biblegateway.com)

1 Corinthians 15:23-25 ²³ But each in turn: Christ, the first fruits; then, when he comes, those who belong to him. ²⁴ Then the end will come, when he hands over the kingdom to God the Father **after he has destroyed all dominion, authority and power.** ²⁵ **For he must reign until he has put all his enemies under his feet.** (NIV, Biblegateway.com)

Jesus Christ is not coming back to preach the Gospel. Jesus is coming back to fight and destroy all his enemies! And I am ready to fight by his side! So, I'm here to set the stage for Jesus Christ return. I am the Prophet Elisha, who once was a lamb but now a Lion. I am the precursor to the return of the Lion of Judah Jesus Christ. I am preparing the way for the second coming of Christ. Christ is returning as a Lion, and he will defeat all his wicked enemies here on earth. Amen!

31. The Holy Spirit Speaks Thru Mrs. Gary

In high school, I had a Spanish teacher named Mrs. Gary. Mrs. Gary would always make these prophetic statements to me, and she would always have a stare in her eyes when she made them. Whenever Mrs. Gary spoke one of those prophetic statements to me, I knew it was important, but I didn't understand its meaning.

One day, Mrs. Gary got a stare in her eyes, and then she said to me, "It's going to take you a while to get there, but you will arrive when you're supposed to." Mrs. Gary told me this frequently, and I would ask her each time, "What does that mean, Mrs. Gary?" She always replied, "It's going to take you a while to get to your place, and you will think you have failed, but you will arrive at the exact time you are supposed to." Each time Mrs. Gary told me this she always had the same stare in her eyes that everyone has when the Lord speaks through them to me.

So, one day, I was late for her class. Mrs. Gary told me, "You are always late for class, Kennedy, but I understand because it is your destiny to be late!" When Mrs. Gary made that statement, I asked her what she meant by that. Mrs. Gary looked at me with a normal look in her eyes, then said, "I don't know what it means, Kennedy, but it was meant for you!" So Mrs. Gary assigned all the students a Spanish proverb to say when they came to class. My proverb was "mas varde tarde que nunca!" which means "Better late than never!"

As of today, I understand what Mrs. Gary meant by all of the prophetic statements she made to me while I was in her Spanish class. I also understand the Spanish proverb referred to my destiny. Mas varde tarde que nunca means "better late than never". It's better I show up late than never show up at all! So, it's better I show up now when things are getting so bad than not to show up at all! And just like Mrs. Gary said, it took me a while to arrive, but now I'm here! And I arrived exactly at God's appointed time!

32. The Artist Part 1

The year is 1988, and I was at school when I saw this guy drawing lifelike pictures. This young man was very talented when it came to drawing. The pictures looked so lifelike they could jump off the page and come to life. No matter what he drew, the pictures could jump off the page and come to life. That's how good of an artist he was in high school. One day, I was in class, and I saw the young man drawing pictures. And for some reason I went and stood next to him and just looked at the pictures he was drawing. First, he drew some cars that were the sharpest I had ever seen. He drew these futuristic cars. He drew a picture of these two-door muscle sports cars. Nothing in the 80's looked like the cars he drew. These cars were authentic, and they looked so real and distinguished.

Then he drew this truck; the front of it was so bold and distinguished. It didn't look like any truck I had ever seen before. The truck had this bold emblem of a Ram head. But the ram's head had a 3D effect on it. I asked him what's that and he said, "This is an emblem of a ram's head, and it is raised to give it a 3D effect." And the emblem of the 3D Rams head was on the front of the truck. And a larger emblem of the 3D Rams head was on the back of the truck on the tailgate.

So, as he drew these vehicles I sat there and watched in amazement. I asked the boy, "How do you come up with these things you are drawing?" He said, "The images just come to my mind, and a story is always being told to me about the things I see." After he said that to me, he continued to draw. Then he started to draw a picture of this black man on the same page; he drew the very distinguished truck with the 3D Ram emblem. Once he finished drawing this black man's pictures, I asked him, "Who is that man?" He then looked at me with this stare in his eyes and said these exact words, "This man is going to come, and he is going to deceive everyone. Everyone is going to think he is good. But this man is not good; he is evil. He is going to come and try to take over the entire world. Somebody has to stop this man!" At that very moment the Lord spoke to me and said, "It's your job to stop this man!"

The guy had this stare in his eyes while he was talking to me. The guy had the same stare in his eyes everyone else had when the Lord was speaking through them. The guy's mouth and eyes said, "Somebody has to stop this man!" Then the Lord said to me, "It's your job to stop this man!" When I heard the Lord say, "It's your job to stop this man!" I knew everything that was spoken to me was the absolute truth. So, I just stared at the picture. I kept looking at the face of the black man he drew. The drawing was so lifelike and oh-so-real. As the guy continued talking, I stood there staring at the picture.

I got a good look at the black man in the picture. I also got a good look at the truck with the Ram 3D emblem on it because it was drawn on the same page as the man. I want you to remember that everything is connected, and all of these stories I am telling you about my life will tie in together later. Just continue to read.

33. My Memories of A Word

The year is 1989, and I'm a senior at A. H. Parker High School. I was dating this girl who attended John Carroll High School in Birmingham. One day after school I drove to John Carroll High School to see my girlfriend. While at John Carroll, my girlfriend and her friends approached me with this steganography and ambigram. Steganography is a clever way to hide a picture within another picture. This allows for a picture to be hid in plain sight. A person can look directly at a steganography, and they would never see the picture hidden within the picture. An ambigram is an inversion that spells out a word in different directions. An ambigram is when a word is spelled out going forward, and then it also spells the same word going backward or even upside down.

So, while visiting my girlfriend's high school, she and her friends approached me with this steganography and ambigram on paper. So, my girlfriend and her friends approached me with this steganography and ambigram, and then my girlfriend said, "Do you know what this says?" Once she showed me the picture of the steganography and ambigram, I had this feeling I had seen that picture somewhere else. I knew I had seen it somewhere before but I couldn't remember where. Then I asked her, "What is that?" She said, "You must tell me what it says first." Something in me wouldn't allow me to answer her question. I knew the word said, "Illuminati", but I wanted to know what it meant. The steganography and ambigram of the word Illuminati are shown below. This is the same steganography and ambigram my girlfriend, and her friends showed me that day.

Illuminati

After I wouldn't tell my girlfriend what the steganography said, I asked her what it meant. Then she told me, "It's a secret club for those people who are good at science." After she gave me her explanation, I didn't believe her, and I asked her again. Again, she gave me the same explanation as before, so I saw she wasn't telling me the truth, so I changed the subject to avoid confrontation with her.

After I left my girlfriend, I was trying to figure out where I remember seeing the word Illuminati. A few days passed, and I was still trying to remember where I had seen the steganography of the word Illuminati. I was trying to figure it out because I remember seeing it before. I then remembered where I saw the picture of the word Illuminati. I was in the third grade when this lady came to Wilkerson Elementary School and used this viewing machine to give the third graders a visual IQ test. Once I realized where I remembered seeing the word Illuminati, I had no more interest in the matter. But many years later, I realized what the word Illuminati meant, and I understood why they used a steganography of the word Illuminati to test children in the third grade. This is the United States of America's Book of Secrets! This is the Illuminati Book of Secrets!

34. Senior Prom

The year is 1989 and I was a senior at A. H. Parker High School, and it was time for my Senior Prom. I was ready and prepared to go to the senior Prom. I was supposed to take this girl to the Prom. But during the week of my Prom, I realized my entire family was going to Buffalo, New

York because my sister was receiving her master's degree from the University of Buffalo. So, I was planning to stay in Birmingham and go to the Prom. But then my brother "W" kept enticing me to go to Buffalo with them. My brother kept telling me how much fun we could have in Buffalo and everything we could do, so I considered missing my Senior Prom. It was no big deal for me to miss the Prom because I had been to about three proms before my senior Prom anyway, but I didn't want to disappoint my prom date. But my brother "W" kept persuading me to come to Buffalo with them, but I kept telling him no!

After I decided to go to the Prom, the Lord said, "Go to Buffalo!" So, the day before the Prom, I decided to go to Buffalo with my family. So, I called my prom date and told her I was going to Buffalo. And I became the scum of the earth at school because I canceled on her at the last minute. But I had no choice because the Lord told me to go to Buffalo. So, my family and I loaded up in a couple of cars and headed to Buffalo, New York.

Once we arrived in Buffalo, it was evening time, and we went straight to my daddy's cousin's house. Her name is Elsey. We went directly to her house because my sister stayed with them while she was in Graduate School. We arrived at Elsey's house that evening, and she prepared dinner for us. Elsey had one of her friends there. Once Elsey's friend got comfortable around us, she began to tell us about this thing she witnessed one early morning. Elsey's friend said, "One early morning, I witnessed this reptilian humanoid alien-looking creature come out of this hole in the ground". She said, "This reptilian humanoid alien crawled out of this hole in her neighbor's yard. The hole was the size of a large goffer hole. Then, this reptilian alien creature stood on two legs like a human. And then, the alien walked behind her neighbor's house. Then, a few minutes later, the alien creature returned to the hole it crawled out of. And then the reptilian humanoid alien creature crawled back into the hole." She then said she witnessed this entire event.

As she told us this story, we all laughed at her! We were laughing at her like she was crazy! I was looking at this lady, and I was just laughing at her! Everyone was laughing at her. Because what she was saying didn't make any sense to us. We all had a very good laugh at the lady. Elsey told her friend to stop telling us about that because we thought she was crazy. The lady saw how we were laughing at her, so she stopped telling us the story of the alien crawling out of the hole. But the entire time, the lady was telling us the story. The lady was staring at me. Not only was she staring at me, but she also had the stare in her eyes that people have when the Lord is speaking through them.

At the time, I didn't make any connection between the alien coming out of the hole in the ground and the spaceship I witnessed in the summer of 1985. I didn't make any connection or even think there was a connection. I didn't make the connection between the alien coming out of the hole in the ground with the spaceships I saw in the sky when I looked through the dicyanin glass. Also, I didn't realize the humanoid-looking alien the lady described also had a connection to the three demons I saw standing behind the three kids who were mean to me. Well, all these things are connected. I didn't connect the dots because it wasn't time for me to connect the dots. All these events are connected. But at the time, I didn't see it.

It was the day before my Senior Prom, and the Lord told me, "Go to Buffalo!" So, I went to Buffalo. Besides having a good laugh at the lady who told us she witnessed this reptilian humanoid creature come out of the ground. I had a miserable time in Buffalo! I regretted missing my Senior Prom. I wondered why the Lord told me to go to Buffalo. Did the Lord want me to hear the woman's testimony about the reptilian alien creature she witnessed coming out of this hole in the ground? The Lord always places me at the right place at the right time to receive some valuable information or to witness a very special event. Just like the Lord told me to go to California with my brother "W". The Lord told me to go to California with my brother to witness the alien spaceship hovering above the City of Twentynine Palms, California. The Lord had me go to Buffalo, NY, so I could hear the lady give her testimony about the reptilian humanoid alien that came out of the hole in the ground! This is the United States of America Book of Secrets! This is the Illuminati Book of Secrets.

35. A Twelve Year Vision From The Lord Part 1

I remember it was the summer of 1989, and I was two weeks away from starting college at Jacksonville State University. I was very afraid because I had this feeling that some tough trials awaited me. I remember driving on the freeway headed east on I-20 and I-59, passing the Birmingham Jefferson County Civic Center (BJCC). At that moment, I said, "Lord, what does this world have in store for me? I am afraid, my Lord!" I ask the Lord this several times, and at the end of my plea, this is the vision the Lord gave me.

While driving, the Lord took me into the spirit, showed me, and told me these things. The Lord told me, "At the age of 20, you will get in trouble in college", and then the Lord showed me in a fight. Then the Lord said, "At the age of 24, you will graduate from college", and then the Lord showed me celebrating and dancing while I was walking across the stage. Then the Lord said, "At the age of 25, you will have more money than you know what to do with", and then the Lord showed me lying in bed with thousands of dollars. Then the Lord said to me, "By the age of 26, you will be broke, and for the next few years, you will wonder the streets lost, then you will give your life to me, and I will turn your entire life around." The Lord then showed me flashes of total misery as I drove in my car. Then, after the misery, the Lord showed me with peace and happiness.

By the time the Lord finished showing me the vision, I was exiting the freeway on the 1st Ave North exit in the Woodlawn area, which is located on the opposite side of town from the BJCC. I had no recollection of driving across town. I didn't understand how I got across town! After I came through, I remember thinking, "What just happened!" I thought about what had just happened, I said, "The Lord just showed me my life for the next twelve years." Then, I was trying to justify what was just revealed to me. I calculated the age I thought I was supposed to graduate from college, which was 22 years old, and I compared it to the age the Lord said I would graduate, which was 24 years old. I said, "That can't be right because it will only take me four years to graduate from college, not six years." This was my arrogance at work! So, I just blew it all off and tried to forget about it.

36. Higher Education

After high school, I went to an institution of higher learning, where I had a triple major. My first major was parties, alcohol, money, and girls. My second major involved thinking about the things the Lord said to me and thinking about the Lord and his word. Then, I eventually decided on my third major which was Finance. I know it sounds like everything in my life was out of order and a huge contradiction, but that was the life I was living in college. I loved God but I didn't want to be a preacher anymore because I thought I couldn't have any fun if I became a preacher. I loved God, but I was running from him. I was like the Prophet Jonah; I was running from God.

So basically, college was an institution for higher partying for me! I had taken college prep classes in high school for higher partying. So, I took my talents to Jacksonville State University! Once I got to JSU, it was time to work on multiple degrees in partying! The number one-party school in the South. In college, I wasn't concerned about anything because the Lord told me I would be a millionaire one day! I wasn't worried about my future because I knew what the Lord told me would come true. When I entered Jacksonville State University, I partied like a rock star! One of the reasons I was partying a lot was because my high school sweetheart broke my heart when she broke up with me. She broke up with me within a week or two after I left for JSU. She broke up with me because I slept with another girl who went to high school with her. And when she found out about it, she asked me if it was true. And like a person without good sense, I told her the truth. Because I thought it was the honorable thing to do. I thought if I told the truth, she would forgive me. But being truthful backfired on me, and she broke up with me.

Once she broke up with me, I was hurting bad because she was my first love! But I didn't let anyone know I was hurting. I just internalize it. I just started taking things to the extreme. I just started drinking more and partying more. I just started to sleep with more girls. I was doing more of everything. I was hurting, and my heart was hurting, and the alcohol masked the pain! Now, let's address this right now! Don't try and label me as a womanizer! Because college girls were coming to me for sex! So label the women as manizers because they were coming to me for sex.

Not only were they coming to me for sex, but my roommate Fred would allow girls to come into the room once I was passed out drunk, and the girls would have sex with me. Then the next day, Fred would ask me, who was that girl I had in the room last night? Then I would say, I went to sleep alone last night. Then, my roommate would tell me I needed to stop drinking. Then he would tell me how a young lady knocked on the door asking for me, and he let her in. And I would wake up the next morning, and I would be wet, and my bed would be wet. Young ladies were raping me when I was passed out drunk in my bed. And according to Fred this happened on numerous occasions.

I was introduced to a new world once I entered college! I watched a wide variety of drug use while I was in college. I watched people using everything from acid to cocaine to crack and a whole lot of marijuana. I smoked a little marijuana while I was in college, but I never became a regular marijuana user! I never became a regular drug user because my dad preached to my siblings and me to "Never use drugs!" My daddy preached the sermon "Never use drugs" so many times growing up that I was paranoid of drugs. Even when I experimented with marijuana, I always heard my dad say, "Never use drugs!" That's why my experiment with marijuana didn't last long when I was in college because I kept hearing my dad's voice while I was high, and it always ruined my high! Plus, I would think about ten different subjects simultaneously when I was high. After thinking about the ten different subjects simultaneously I would be exhausted. I had a beautiful mind!

So, once I saw other people using drugs besides marijuana in college, I didn't try them because my dad preached not to use drugs! When I watched people do cocaine, acid, and other drugs, I just sat back and observed! I have to say thanks to my dad for the awesome job of preaching, "Never use drugs!" Because his sermons deterred me from ever becoming a drug user! You parents of today should preach to your kids not to use drugs just like my dad preached to me and my siblings! As a child, I used to hate hearing my dad preach about drugs, but as an adult, I am very thankful he did! My dad preached a sermon at least two to three times a week for us not to use drugs. After hearing that sermon so many times, I knew drugs had to be the devil himself! Because my dad wore that sermon out, week after week after week! My dad didn't have a church to preach to so he preached to his children. So I guess we were his congregation.

During my freshman year in college, I started gambling. But the problem was I didn't know how to gamble. So, I made an investment to learn the craft of playing tunk. My investment was losing until I learned the game. After I learned how to play, I became very good at it! I mean, I became good at it! Once I learned how to gamble, I won a lot of money gambling with college students and dope dealers. And boy, I loved gambling with the dope dealers! Because they had a lot of ill-gotten money, and I was determined to separate them from it! And I separated them from their money! So, I took whoever money that sat down at the table. Don't get me wrong, I lost sometimes too. But the money I lost was nothing compared to what I won. So, I spent many late nights at the gambling table playing tunk and drinking alcohol! Then, I would wake up the next morning and go to class. I always went to class no matter how bad my hangover was! So many days, I sat in class, closed my eyes, and listened to the professor's lecture! So here I was, drinking, partying, having sex with many college girls, and gambling! I mean, I was having sex with many college girls and grown women.

I was living a life **of sin**, but this world had convinced me my sin was just having fun! I was doing everything that was shown to me when I was sixteen years old. In Chapter 27 titled, "Satan Try to Stop The Prophesy" a thought was given to me that said, "I couldn't have any fun if I became a preacher." Then a vision was given to me, showing me all kinds of beautiful women, parties and alcohol, and lots of money. Now, here I was, living this life of sin that Satan had shown me! So here I was, living a life of sin without realizing everything I was doing was full of sin! So basically, I had conformed to the patterns of this world. I did what God told us not to do! In Romans 12:2, the Lord told us not to conform to the pattern of this world but to be transformed by the renewing of our minds. But I allowed myself to be transformed into the pattern of this world, which was sin!

Romans 12:2 "Do not conform to the pattern of this world, but be transformed by the renewing of your mind..." (NIV, BibleGateway.com)

All the things I was doing in college were sinful, and all the sins I was doing weren't me. It was the sin that was inside of me. I wanted to do good when I was in college. I always had good thoughts of achieving academic success and doing great things for the community, but the sin in me wouldn't allow me to do good. I didn't realize this at the time, but I was a slave to sin. My flesh and my mind crave those sinful things that satisfy my flesh. So, the sinful nature of my flesh overtook my desire to do good. There was a war raging inside of me. And that war was the good I wanted to do versus the sin that made me do. On many occasions, the sin that made me do bad overtook the good that I wanted to do. I was a slave to sin, and I didn't even know it. I did what I hated to do on many occasions, but I did it because the sin in me desired it. I hated evil and everything about evil, but I did what I hated. I was a man who spiritually loved the Lord, I was a man who talked to the Most High God and the Lord Jesus Christ, but I was also a man full of sin who wanted to satisfy my flesh and the sin within me. To understand this war that raged inside of me. You must read and understand what the Apostle Paul said in Romans 7:14-25. In Romans 7:14-25 the Apostle Paul told you what he was experiencing with sin.

Romans 7:14-25 reads, [14] We know that the law is spiritual; but I am unspiritual, sold as a slave to sin. [15] I do not understand what I do. For what I want to do I do not do, but what I hate I do. [16] And if I do what I do not want to do, I agree that the law is good. [17] As it is, it is no longer I myself who do it, but it is sin living in me. [18] For I know that good itself does not dwell in me, that is, in my sinful nature.[a] For I have the desire to do what is good, but I cannot carry it out. [19] For I do not do the good I want to do, but the evil I do not want to do—this I keep on doing. [20] Now if I do what I do not want to do, it is no longer I who do it, but it is sin living in me that does it. [21] So I find this law at work: Although I want to do good, evil is right there with me. [22] For in my inner being I delight in God's law; [23] but I see another law at work in me, waging war against the law of my mind and making me a prisoner of the law of sin at work within me. [24] What a wretched man I am! Who will rescue me from this body that is subject to death? [25] Thanks be to God, who delivers me through Jesus Christ our Lord!... (NIV, Biblegateway.com)

37. Women Who Confided In Me Their Secret

In high school, there were always two sides to me. One side was a party-hard type of person, and the other side of me spent many hours thinking about the Lord and his word. This sounds like a major contradiction, but that was how it was. No matter how hard I ran from God by partying. I always went to Church on Sunday! I never got too far from Church because Church was rooted in my blood because I was taught to go to church on Sundays. So, I went to Church on Sundays, repented for my many sins, and shed many tears in church for the life of sin I was living.

Upon entering college, I met a lot of young ladies. I had many of these young ladies confide in me their secret. They would all tell me this secret they had, but they wouldn't tell anyone else their secret. Many of these young ladies didn't confide in their mothers, fathers, sisters, brothers, or friends their secret, but they always chose me to confide in. Many of these young ladies would go on to tell me how they were molested by their neighbors, stepfathers, half-brothers, uncles, cousins, aunts, stepmothers, stepsisters, teachers, coaches, friends of the family, babysitters, etc. You must understand that the first encounter I had with the word "molested" was in the fourth grade. In Chapter 23, titled "I Repeated the Words the Lord Spoke," I told you how, in elementary school, there was a girl name "P" in my class, and one day, I saw so much pain in her eyes. I then said, "Lord, what is wrong with "P"." Then the Lord said to me, "She is being molested."

Well, by the time I reached college, many young ladies started to confide in me their secret of being molested. Each time, I would pray with the young ladies and ask the Lord to heal them and release them from the burden they were carrying. The following day, the same young lady I prayed with would come up to me and stare at me with this look of amazement on their face! And I didn't understand why. Each time, they would say, "You just don't know how much you helped me and what you have done! Who are you?" I didn't have a clue as to what they were saying or trying to say. I just knew there was something different about them from that moment on.

After I prayed with each young lady, they would always be happier and at peace with themselves. It was like their burden had been lifted, they were made new, and they had peace in their spirit. But I noticed something about myself while they were made new and had peace. I noticed I was being loaded down with pain and grief. Each time I prayed for one of the young ladies, they received peace, and I received pain and grief to carry. Their pain and grief were being transferred to me. I noticed this pain and grief would only intensify after I prayed for a young lady who confided in me she had been molested.

These burdens being transferred to me were so heavy it felt like I was carrying the weight of the world on my shoulders. These burdens I was carrying increased my need to drink and party. I was already suffering from a broken heart because my high school sweetheart broke up with me. Now, I was carrying the burdens of the girls who confided in me they had been molested.

So, I increase my drinking of alcohol and partying to numb the pain! Over my lifetime, I had about forty or more women confide in me they had been molested! I just lost count because it was a frequent conversation I had with many women. When I was in college, I didn't understand why these young ladies were drawn to me to confess their secret that they didn't tell anyone else. I kept asking myself, "Why do these women always tell me these things? Why me? Why are these women drawn to me?" Many years later, I understood the Lord sent these young ladies to me. So I could pray for them and release them from the burdens they were carrying. And it was meant for me to carry their burdens for them!

While these burdens were being transferred to me, I acted out in many ways. I am drinking alcohol like a fish, and I am acting out the way I am feeling. I am carrying around all of this pain and grief in me, and I am using alcohol to try to numb the pain. I was not just drinking to party; I was drinking to kill the pain of my broken heart, and I was drinking to numb the pain of the grief that was being transferred to me to carry. So, I am acting out in many ways because of this pain and grief that is being transferred to me. At the time, I didn't understand what was transpiring! I am telling you all this is hindsight and wisdom the Lord has shared with me!

When I was about twenty-three years old, a young lady I met started telling me her story of molestation. Like in all the other cases, I prayed for her, and she was a new person, and the weight on my shoulders grew even larger. It felt like I was carrying the weight of the world on my shoulders. Later that day, I was walking, and I began to plead with God to release me from the grief I was carrying! I pleaded and pleaded with God! I repeatedly said to the Lord, "Lord, please release me from this grief I am carrying; I cannot carry this anymore!" At that very moment, the weight of the pain, grief and burdens on my shoulders was lifted, and all the pain from the women's grief and burdens was gone. I was instantly freed from carrying their pain, grief and burdens! How wonderful I felt when the pain, grief and burdens were lifted from my shoulders! If I knew that's all I had to say, I would have said it much sooner!

For many years, I didn't understand what I had experienced; it wasn't until one day, I was studying the book of Galatians, that my eyes were open to the truth.

Galatians 6:2 reads, "Carry each other's burdens, and in this way you will fulfill the law of Christ." (Galatians 6:2 NIV, BibleGateway.com)

Once I read that scripture, I realized the Lord meant for us to carry another person's burdens. After those encounters in college, I continued to meet women who confided in me their nightmare stories. In 2009, I met five women around the same time. I started talking to them on the phone, and I started noticing the same characteristics in those women that I saw in countless other women who confided in me they had been molested. One night, I decided to call and ask each woman if they had been molested. Three out of five women I asked responded, "Yes, they had been molested." One out of the five responded, "I had been raped in college."

One out of the five said, "No, they have never been molested". So three out of the five women responded they had been molested, and one out of five said they had been raped.

So, four out of five had been sexually violated. Four of the five women I had asked all responded with the same question, "How did you know?" I just told them I guessed. But I didn't just guess. I noticed the same traits in those women I saw in other women who confided in me they had been molested. It was at that point I realized an epidemic was going on in our country, but no one was talking about children being molested! No one has been talking about children being molested back then, nor are they talking about children being molested now. **Molestation is one of Satan's well-protected secrets!** Satan is the one who wants molestation to stay a hush, hush topic! But why? Many years later, the Lord revealed to me how Satan uses molestation to manipulate people about their sexual orientation! Many people who say they were born gay were manipulated to think they were born that way because they were molested by someone of the same sex when they were a child. So now, as an adult, they think they were born to have sex with a person of the same sex because their first sexual encounter was with someone of the same sex! And this is why Satan wants to keep the topic of molestation a hush, hush topic! Because Satan is spreading his homosexual virus to the masses through molestation! And Satan is stealing many people's identities through molestation and homosexuality.

38. A Twelve Year Vision From The Lord Part 2

It was the Spring Semester of 1991, and I was partying outside of my dorm at JSU when JSU campus police spotted me with a beer in my hand. I was only twenty years old. So, I was arrested and charged with possession of alcohol by a minor. But during this same time, I was in the military. I was old enough to go to war and die for my country, but I wasn't old enough to drink a beer. I was old enough to take another person's life in a war, but I am not old enough to drink a beer! Something didn't seem right about that to me! I was arrested for possession of alcohol by a minor, a misdemeanor. That was my first time being in trouble with the law.

Then, a month after my first arrest, I was arrested again! This time I was arrested for giving JSU campus police false information. That occurred because I had an open beer in my car. And I had driven to the Theron E. Montgomery Building to get my mail. Once I went inside to get my mail, JSU campus police saw my car parked with an open container. They started videotaping my car with the open container, and

I panicked. I ran to my dorm room, called the JSU campus police, and told them someone had taken my car without my permission. Here I am making a bad situation worse. I went to the police station, and I cracked within 10 seconds of the interrogation. That had to be a new world record for a person cracking under interrogations. I just confessed to the crime! I told them. I did it! I did it! Then, I was charged with giving the police false information. It is listed as misdemeanor fraud. This all happened while I was still carrying the burdens of the women who had been molested.

After being arrested twice at JSU, I decided to leave JSU because I had gotten in trouble with the law twice and didn't want a third one. After being in college for two years at JSU, I transferred to UAB. It was the Fall of 1991; I enrolled at the University of Alabama in Birmingham to play football. Before I enrolled at UAB, the Lord kept telling me I would not play professional football anyway, so I needed to stay at JSU and major in Finance. The Lord said these things to me many times, but I always brushed it off because I was still running from God. The Lord told me to return to JSU and major in Finance, but I ignored him. When I transferred to UAB, I assumed UAB offered a major in Finance. I soon learned that UAB was not offering a major in Finance. It started to bother me once I learned that UAB was not offering a major in Finance. The Lord urged me to return to Jacksonville State University, but I insisted on staying at UAB.

One night, four guys from the UAB Football team and I went to an Alpha fraternity party. It was me, my dog Rodger Walton from Detroit, Michigan, Big G, Al, and another guy. Once we got to the party, we paid our money and went inside. Once we were inside, we noticed the party was empty! There were five football players, about twenty Alphas, and about three or four young ladies at the party, and that was it. The party was empty! We tried to get our money back, but they wouldn't give us a refund, so we were standing in this dead party.

Since we couldn't get our money back, I was determined to do me! So, I saw this sexy little honey and asked her to dance. And she was like, YES, YES, YES! So, we went to the front of the room and started dancing. Since there was nobody on the dance floor and there was nobody at the party. I removed my trench coat and laid it on the floor next to us. I only laid it on the floor because the building was so empty. Nobody was on the dance floor, and nobody was at the party! After I started dancing with this girl, this guy walked up with this girl, and they started dancing right next to us. There was a huge dance floor, and the party was empty, but this guy made it his purpose to come and dance with us. I didn't know this guy, and to the best of my knowledge, I had never met or seen him before in my life. This guy was an Alpha, and I will call him or her "Ms. Keyfahkeyetta".

While I was dancing and chatting with this young lady, I noticed "Ms. Keyfahkeyetta" staring at the young lady I was dancing with. So then "Ms. Keyfahkeyetta" and the young lady he is dancing with are getting closer and closer to us. "Ms. Keyfahkeyetta" is not paying any attention to the girl he is with; his attention is on the girl I am with. So then, "Ms. Keyfahkeyetta" purposely steps on my coat. So, I asked "Ms. Keyfahkeyetta" to watch out for my coat. And his response was, "Get your coat off the floor!" His response was full of anger! But I didn't understand why because, to my knowledge, I had never met him before.

So, I grabbed my coat and moved it out of his way. Once I moved my coat, "Ms. Keyfahkeyetta" maneuvered his way over to my coat and he stepped on my coat again. And again, I said, "Man, watch my coat!"

Then he said something to me in a very hostile manner. And then I stepped towards him, and before anything else was said, he rushed me with a rage of anger! Once he rushed me, I stumbled backward, and he landed on top of me. Once I hit the floor, we landed right in front of my friends who were on the football team. Once they saw this guy on top of me, they immediately started punching him and kicking him. They were punching and hitting him because he was on top of me! They beat him down! I didn't have to hit "Ms. Keyfahkeyetta" because my boys whipped him! I mean, they whipped him! I never hit "Ms. Keyfahkeyetta" during the fight, and "Ms. Keyfahkeyetta" never hit me! Also my dad taught me not to hit women. The fellas I was with just beat "Ms. Keyfahkeyetta" down once they saw "Ms. Keyfahkeyetta" was on top of me! He was done once "Ms. Keyfahkeyetta" placed his hands on me!

After they stopped hitting and kicking him, the fight was over because "Ms. Keyfahkeyetta" fraternity brothers didn't even try to help him! It was twenty of them and five of us! And they didn't even attempt to help him. Wow! This shows that men are bred through how they are raised. You don't become a man because you are initiated into a fraternity! After the fellows beat "Ms. Keyfahkeyetta" down, we were about to leave the party. And while we were leaving, all "Ms. Keyfahkeyetta" fraternity brothers started talking trash after the fact! I just didn't understand why they were talking trash after the fact. There were only five of us football players there, and there were about twenty or more Alphas there. To make it simple, we were well outnumbered, but they were the ones who were afraid! We were ready for whatever!

So, this one Alpha was just popping off at the mouth because he knew they outnumbered us. The guy who was popping off at the mouth was short and dark-skinned, and he wore glasses. I guess he found comfort in their numbers. But he violated a sacred rule of the streets. And that rule is, don't talk trash because you got a group of guys with you because one day you will be by yourself, and you will have to put up or shut up! After I left the party, I was upset because of the guy who was popping off at the mouth! I drove back to the dorm to cool off. I had Al in the car with me. At that very moment of me parking my car, I thought I saw the same Alpha who was talking all the trash! I thought I saw the short, dark-skinned guy that wore glasses. I thought I saw him driving a white Mazda MX6 with Alpha on the tag. I thought he drove a white Mazda MX6 because I had seen him driving that car before.

I saw the white Mazda MX6 with Alpha on the tag drive up to the same dorm we were at. I thought it was the same Alpha talking trash at the party. Before I knew it, I jumped out of my car, popped my trunk, pulled out my tire rod to my car jack, and ran over to the guy.

When the guy saw me, he started running, so I swung the tire rod as hard as possible! And I hit this guy in the back of the head! Once I hit him in the back of the head, the guy continued to run, and he didn't even put up a fight. I was standing there like he was going to run after he had so much to say when his fraternity brothers were around! I was astonished because I was ready for a fight!

But later that night, I realized why he ran! He ran because he was not the guy talking all the trash at the party! I hit the wrong guy! The guy I hit was named "E"! And "E" was not the guy talking all the trash at the party. So, I must apologize to you, "E". I apologize for hitting you! I was blinded by anger and rage. I was just angry about everything that went down that night! First, "Ms. Keyfahkeyetta" rushed me inside the party, and then one of your fraternity brothers was running his mouth. So, I purposely but mistakenly came after you. So, to "E," I must apologize. I tried to apologize to you years ago when I saw you working at the store in Century Plaza, but when you saw me, you took off running.

Also, I need you, the reader, to understand that during this time, I was still caring all the pain of all the young ladies who confessed to me they had been molested. I was acting out my anger with great aggression because of the pain that was being transferred to me. I was hurting others because I was hurting.

I want take any blame for the first altercation with "Ms. Keyfahkeyetta," but I will take all the blame for the second altercation with "E"! And again, I must apologize to you, "E". I don't take any blame for the altercation with "Ms. Keyfahkeyetta" because "Ms. Keyfahkeyetta" purposely picked that fight with me that night. But why would "Ms. Keyfahkeyetta" pick a fight with me? I noticed "Ms. Keyfahkeyetta" kept staring at the girl I was dancing with. I think "Ms. Keyfahkeyetta" and the girl had something going on, or he wanted to get with her. When he saw me with her, he knew I was about to close the deal! For him to stop me from closing the deal, he picked a fight to break up the groove I had going on with the girl! And believe me, I was in a groove! It was a done deal!

Also, to my knowledge, I didn't know "Ms. Keyfahkeyetta," and he didn't know me. But I didn't realize "Ms. Keyfahkeyetta" did know me! I didn't know this then, but "Ms. Keyfahkeyetta" mother was married to my first cousin, who lived in Lavaca, Alabama. I found all these things out after the fight. I didn't remember "Ms. Keyfahkeyetta," but he or she remembered me. I met "Ms. Keyfahkeyetta" many years ago at my grandmother's house in Lavaca, Alabama. I only met "Ms. Keyfahkeyetta" maybe two or three times when we were children. And on each occasion, he would always try to bully me and hit me because he was bigger and stronger!

Like I said, I didn't remember "Ms. Keyfahkeyetta," but he remembered me. How do I know he remembered me? I know he remembered me because the very next day, my mother asked me about getting into a fight at UAB. My mother asked me, "Why did you and your friends jump on your cousin's wife's son?" And when my mother asked me, I was like, "Who?" Then she told me the guy I fought with was my cousin's wife's son. Once my mother explained that to me, it was easy to realize "Ms. Keyfahkeyetta" knew who I was before we got into the altercation! Because it's obvious, "Ms. Keyfahkeyetta" called his mother and told her my friends and I jumped on him. And then his mother called my mother. Then, the very next day after the fight, my mother asked me, "Why did my friends' and I jump on my cousin's wife's son?"

So, since "Ms. Keyfahkeyetta" called home to tell his mom, my friends and I jumped on him, "Ms. Keyfahkeyetta" knew who I was before he started the fight. Which meant he didn't care we were related when he purposely started the fight! If he didn't care, why should I care? So "Ms. Keyfahkeyetta" started the fight, but he lost the fight! And since he lost the fight, he calls home to his mommy, crying because he got beat down! He calls home crying to his mommy after he got beat down in a fight he purposely started! Only a punk tells his mommy he got into a fight and twists the details surrounding the fight while making himself appear to be the victim! Out of all the fights I have been in, I never ran home to my mother and daddy telling them I was in a fight. My dad taught me how to handle things of that nature on my own! That was a straight punk move, "Ms. Keyfahkeyetta". But I understand you were born a man, but you transgendered into a woman.

Since "Ms. Keyfahkeyetta" knew who I was, why did he purposely pick a fight with me? To show you "Ms. Keyfahkeyetta" purposely picked that fight with me let's look at the evidence! First, the party was empty, and the entire building was a dance floor! But "Ms. Keyfahkeyetta" came close to me and the girl I was dancing with on purpose! Not only did he come close to us, but he kept staring at the girl I was dancing with. He acted as though he knew her, and he acted like he wanted to get with her! So "Ms. Keyfahkeyetta" came close to us on the dance floor so he could monitor the girl I was dancing with and stop me from getting with her! That's why when I moved my coat the first time, he made it his purpose to step on my coat the second time. "Ms. Keyfahkeyetta" purposely stepped on my coat so he could interrupt the groove I had going on with the girl!

The second reason I know he picked the fight is because he had mommy issues. I guess my cousin took him away from his mommy when my cousin married his mother, causing him to be insecure. See, when "Ms. Keyfahkeyetta" mother married my cousin, she left "Ms. Keyfahkeyetta" behind to live with his daddy. So "Ms. Keyfahkeyetta" felt like his mother abandoned him! When "Ms. Keyfahkeyetta" saw me with the girl, it reminded him of his mommy being taken away from him by my cousin. This enraged him with anger! He was enraged with anger because, in his mind, another woman was being taken away from him by a man who was related to the man who took his mother from him when he was a child! I guess I can understand why he was so enraged with anger! He feels like his mother abandoned him as a child! He has mommy issues! I hate dealing with grown men who have cycles and wear tampons!

So, after I hit the guy name "E" in the head with the tire rod, "E" and his parents went and had a warrant placed on me for misdemeanor assault. My Football Coach, Fred Bohannon (who played for the Pittsburg Steelers), was also a Birmingham Police Officer, told me I had a warrant on me. Coach Bohannon took me down to the Birmingham City Jail, and he took me through the booking process and ensured we were in and out in fifteen minutes. But that was the third time I was in trouble with the law. And that was the third time in 1991 I was in trouble with the law. The year 1991 was a horrible year for me. I got in trouble with the law three times. I had never been arrested until 1991. One of the reasons I left JSU was because I had gotten in trouble with the law.

I went to jail for an assault with a carjack! Amazingly, that was the lyrics to a song I was listening to in the car right before I hit "E" with the car jack! The lyrics are, "I went to jail for an assault with a car jack!" Now was that coincidence my first impulse was to go to my trunk and get the tire iron to my car jack and then hit the guy with it? Or was the song putting subliminal messages into my mind? Once the subliminal messages were embedded into my mind, the anger, the alcohol, and the burdens I was carrying were enough to trigger my conscious mind to react to the subliminal message that was already embedded into my mind! It wasn't a coincidence. Music and television implant messages into your brain, and those images are stored until it's time to act on them. So be careful of the things you allow to enter your mind because most of the music and things on television are viruses that are being uploaded to your operating system! This is why we have so many murders here in the U.S. It's the music!

Once I found out assault charges were filed against me, I made a covenant with the Lord. I said to the Lord, "Lord, I will make a covenant with you that I will never strike another man out of anger if you make these charges go away." Once, we went to court for the assault charges for the fight at UAB. For no good legal reason, the Judge dismissed the case against me. I remember the Judge said to the prosecutor and the parents of the victim, "I am not about to mess up this young man's life for a little fight that took place in college, where there was no serious harm done to the victim." The Judge said, "Young men will get into fights." Then, the Judge dismissed the case! The victim's parents wanted more than misdemeanor charges pressed against me; they wanted felony charges filed against me! But the Lord protected me like always! The Lord gave me what I asked for. The charges went away! The irony of this situation is that "E," the guy I hit, became a successful Defense Attorney. So, our Court ordeal may have helped lead him into law. You can thank me later "E".

So the information about the fight got back to the Dean of Student Affairs who was also a member of the Alpha's. I was called into the Dean's Office and asked about the fight and what had happened. This was not a big deal because I knew the Dean's wife and his daughter personally. The Dean's wife was over a program called Upward Bound, and I had been in the program for four years. His wife knew me; she knew I was a good young man. I even went to the Dean's house because his daughter rode to the prom with me and my girlfriend. When the Dean asked me to tell him what happened, all I had to do was to tell him everything and I would have gotten a **slap on the wrist!** But something wouldn't allow me to tell the truth. The Dean gave me countless times to tell him the truth. But for some reason, I couldn't tell the Dean the truth. And if I had told the Dean the truth, I would have gotten a slap on the wrist! But the truth was not allowed to come out my mouth!

Believe it or not, the Lord wouldn't allow me to tell the truth! Yes, I said the Lord wouldn't allow me to tell the truth! Later on, you will realize why the Lord wouldn't allow me to tell the truth! Since I wouldn't tell the Dean the truth, the Dean had no choice but to put me in front of the student council for a hearing. The irony of the entire situation is this: I would have gotten a slap on the wrist if I had told the Dean the truth. And the Lord knew I would have gotten a slap on the wrist if I had told the Dean the truth. That's one of the reasons why the Lord wouldn't allow the truth to come out of my mouth. So, the Lord didn't allow me to speak the truth because the Lord needed me to return to Jacksonville State University! Remember, the Lord kept coming to me and telling me I needed to return to Jacksonville State University and major in Finance. It was a divine reason why the truth wasn't allowed to come from my mouth. The Lord's divine plan for me didn't include UAB, but it did include Jacksonville State University.

So, just like the Lord showed me in Chapter 35, titled "A Twelve-Year Vision From The Lord Part 1," at 20 years old, I got into a fight and trouble at college. Remember, the Lord showed me and told me these things when I was driving on the freeway. Remember, the Lord said, "At the age of 20, you will get in trouble in college", and then the Lord showed me in a fight. The same fight the Lord showed me in the vision happened in real life. And I was exactly 20 years old when it happened.

Since I didn't tell the Dean the truth, I had to go in front of the Student Council, and all of them were fraternity and sorority members. They already decided to expel me before they even heard the case. The Student Council walked into the room, and all of them had their fraternity and sorority shirts on. Then, each black fraternity had all their members in the hearing. They all wore their fraternity and sorority shirts because they wanted to send me a message. The message was, "We fraternity and sorority people stick together". But the only message they sent me was this: no college fraternity or sorority members should ever sit on a Student Government Association, Student Council, or Disciplinary Committee! I say this because fraternity and sorority members are biased toward others who are members of fraternities and sororities. This sets up a system of abuse where innocent people can be persecuted because they are not members of a fraternity or sorority, while others are given preferential treatment because they are members of a fraternity or sorority! That was the only message they sent me!

When people join these college fraternities and sororities, they take secret oaths that stand above any other oath! Their loyalty is to their fraternity, sorority, or other similar groups! These oaths they take even supersede any loyalty to the Most High God Jehovah! In the chapters to come, I will show you how far these oaths are taken by college fraternities, sororities, Free Masons, and the Illuminati!

So, the Student Council walked into the room, and all of them had their fraternity and sorority shirts on. They all wore their fraternity and sorority shirts because they wanted to send me a message. See, the message was we fraternity and sorority people stick together. I remember sitting through the disciplinary hearing, having so much peace! They wanted fear, but I had peace! They voted to expel me. They thought they were hurting me. They thought they were enacting their revenge! But all things works out for the good of Gods Glory in my life!

Once I got expelled from UAB, my mother was so happy I was returning to JSU and moving out of the City of Birmingham. She was happy I got expelled! It was hard to understand why my mother was happy I got expelled. My mother didn't want me in the City of Birmingham because she thought Satan was trying to kill me. She saw Birmingham and my friends as a huge distraction for me. And after looking back at it, she was right.

After being expelled from UAB, I returned to JSU in the Fall of 1992. When I reached the campus of Jacksonville State University, the Holy Spirit said to me in my left ear, "Your expulsion was a blessing; you are so blessed to be back here!" Once I heard those words, I didn't understand at first, but a spirit of peace came over me. My expulsion appeared tragic to most people, but I knew it was a blessing. UAB didn't offer a major in Finance, but JSU did offer a major in Finance. This was one of the key reasons the Lord wanted me back at JSU, because in one of my Finance classes, I was about to stumble across something that was going to change my life forever! I was about to stumble across a mathematical weapon designed to be unleashed upon the citizens of the United States of America and the people of this world. This is the United States of America Book of Secrets. This is the Illuminati Book of Secrets!

39. Sandra

After spending a year at UAB, I returned to Jacksonville State University! Immediately upon returning to JSU, I saw the most beautiful girl I had ever seen! I immediately asked the guys, "Who is that girl!" And all of them told me her name was Sandra! Then they told me she came to JSU the year I went to UAB! At that very moment, I said to myself, "I got to have her!" I fell in love instantly! She had captured my mind, heart, and spirit, and we hadn't even met! She was the prettiest girl at JSU, and that's the absolute truth! Sandra's beauty was not average. Her beauty was heavenly! To be honest with you, she was the prettiest girl in the State of Alabama! I would have put her beauty against any girl or woman in the state or even the nation! She just didn't have physical beauty. She also had a beautiful spirit!

The word had gotten back to her that I was very interested in her! I didn't know that she was also very interested in me. Because once she saw me, she instantly fell in love with me! I didn't know this until the Lord revealed that to me while I was writing this book. Our spirits were instantly drawn to each other! My spirit was drawn to her, and her spirit was drawn to me. In college, I was overtaken with love for a girl I hadn't even said two words to! To be honest, this kind of scared me! It scared me because my high school sweetheart had crushed my heart during my freshman year at JSU! When I saw Sandra, I instantly fell in love with her, and it scared me! It scared me because Sandra had taken my heart in the blink of an eye!

With most girls I liked, I always approached the girl, and I got the girl. I had a gift for approaching a girl and coming away with the girl. My gift was so obvious that many guys used to ask me, "Man, what are you telling these girls when you approach them? These girls are in love with you after you approach them!" I would just look at the guys and laugh! I would never tell guys my secret because my knowledge of getting the young ladies could have been deadly in the wrong hands! But when it came to Sandra, for some odd reason, I hesitated when approaching her! I never walked up to her and approached her. In my eyes Sandra was perfect! And in my eyes, she was heavenly! I wanted her but in an innocent kind of way! Sex with Sandra never even crossed my mind. I was a savage with other women, and they loved it! But Sandra tamed that Savage inside me without saying a word to me! I couldn't be a savage with Sandra because she was special and different! She was heavenly.

I was overwhelmed with so much love for Sandra that she cured my Post-Traumatic Stress of my heart being crushed by my first love. Then at the same time, this guy I will call "F" kept telling me all these lies about Sandra. Whenever I talked to him about Sandra, he always said these extremely negative things about her! And for some foolish reason, I listened to him! I didn't believe him but I listened. I didn't realize it was Satan that was in him influencing him! I also didn't realize he was jealous because he wanted her! Even though he wanted her, he could never have her; his job was to stop me from having her!

Since Satan was in him, Satan had a plan to use him to attach me to one of Satan's agents! One night, the guy name "F" knocks on my door, and he wants me to drive him home because the police just pulled him over and he had been drinking. The police told him he needed to park his car and get someone else to take him home. This guy I call "F" comes to my apartment with this girl named Tameko. He brought Tameko with him so I could drive his car to his apartment, and then Tameko would take me back to my place.

So, everything was going as planned until it was time for Tameko to drop me off at my apartment. Tameko first insisted on buying me something to eat. After we ate, Tameko was supposed to drop me off at my apartment. Once Tameko dropped me off, she insisted on coming into my apartment to use the phone. Yes, I fell for the old can I use the phone trick! Do you know what happened? She took advantage of me! That was another problem I had. So many women were just eager to give up the cookie to me! I had Tameko and many other young ladies in Birmingham, Tuscaloosa, Jacksonville, Anniston, and the surrounding areas. It was so wild and crazy back then it didn't make sense! My life then was gambling for money, alcohol, women, sex, and parties! With a dose of church and schoolwork on the side! I was out of control. Remember, I was still feeling all the pain from the burdens I was carrying from the women who had been molested.

It was nothing serious, but Tameko gave me whatever I wanted whenever I wanted it. Anyway, I wanted it. Tameko would give me sex, pay bills, and buy me food, clothes, and anything else I wanted! Satan knows how to come bearing gifts! So basically, Tameko was sent by Satan to distract me from the blessing God had for me, which was Sandra. I didn't know this then, but Satan will always deliver you his agents and his decoys right at your doorstep without any effort being made on your own!

Once I started writing this chapter, the Lord revealed to me that Satan sent Tameko to look like the real thing so she could distract me from hooking up with the real thing, Sandra! This is not to speak badly of Tameko, but she was playing the role Satan wanted her to play! And Tameko's role was to be a decoy and distract me from Sandra! Tameko was a decoy sent by Satan! And the decoy always looks like the real thing. Now watch this: Tameko was mixed with African American and Caucasian, just like Sandra was mixed with African American and Caucasian! Both were light-skinned with long, pretty hair! I want you to take notice of this because this is very important. Tameko was a decoy that looked like or resembled the real thing, Sandra. The decoy will always resemble or look like the real thing. Sandra was the original God sent, and Tameko was the decoy Satan sent. The decoy will always look like or resemble the original. The Most High God Jehovah taught me that Satan always sends a decoy before God sends the real thing. The decoy is always sent to distract you from receiving the gift God has prepared for you. The Lord revealed to me while I was writing this book that Satan sent Tameko to distract me from the gift he had prepared for me, which was Sandra.

One night, I remember Tameko and I were at this food joint in Jacksonville called Jeffersons. Tameko and I were sitting in a booth eating. When I looked up, I saw Sandra and her sorority sisters sitting in the next booth facing me! And when I looked at Sandra, my heart just melted! I saw her sitting there staring at me with a look that said, "Why not me?" And she had this expression of "I am hurting" on her face! And when I saw the expression on her face, I knew I had to get up and go and hug her and kiss her! But as I started to move to get up, Tameko knew what I was about to do. She grabbed my arm, and she wouldn't let me move. Then, at that very moment, I was given a thought, and the thought said, "Don't hurt Tameko's feelings!"

I want you to take notice of what I just said. A thought was given to me that said, "Don't hurt Tamako's feelings!" I was placed in that moment of do I go after Sandra or sit here with Tameko and try not to hurt Tameko's feelings? I wanted to jump across that table and hug and kiss Sandra, but I was trying not to hurt Tameko's feelings! I didn't think of how I was hurting the woman's feelings that captured my heart! Sandra's feelings and mine should have been the only two feelings I worried about! Then, the moment came when Tameko and I were getting ready to leave Jefferson's.

Once I walked out the restaurant door, my heart wouldn't allow me to leave. I turned around to go back inside the restaurant to talk to Sandra. But when Tameko saw me getting ready to return inside the restaurant, she grabbed my arm and started pulling me away from the door! And she started to cause a scene and wouldn't let me go! I was doing everything I could to get away from her. Then Tameko said, "That girl doesn't want you! That girl doesn't want you!" As I was trying to get away from her, she wouldn't let me go back into the restaurant! I tried to return to that restaurant to see Sandra, but Tameko stopped me. I eventually got into the car with Tameko and left with her!

Tameko was a decoy sent by Satan to distract me from Sandra. The Lord revealed this to me while I was writing this book! But Satan sent more than just Tameko and "F" to keep me away from Sandra. He also sent others. I didn't realize this at the time, but Satan was sending flocks of women to me to distract me from Sandra! This is what the Lord revealed to me many years later! While I was thinking I was making it rain women when I was in college! It was truly Satan who was making it rain, women! It was Satan who was sending the women to me to have sex with me! Satan was using the women to distract me from Sandra! It was Satan who was making it rain, women! This is all hindsight because the Lord revealed this to me as I was writing this book!

One night, I was sitting at the gambling table at the gambling apartment where a guy named Corey, aka C-Money, lived. While I was playing cards and winning all the money, Sandra walked in with some of her sorority sisters! Once I saw her, I was so happy! I was already winning lots of money, and now I had the woman of my dreams walk through the door. It was on like popcorn! I told Sandra to come and sit on my lap! And she did! And then I whispered in her ear, "Will you marry me!" And her face lit up like a Christmas tree! I knew, and she knew the answer was yes! We both knew we wanted to be together! I was so happy she was sitting in my lap, and she was just as happy to be sitting in my lap. And all was well! But then one of her retarded sorority sisters started screaming at her because she was sitting in my lap, so her sorority sister busted up the groove we had going on. And then one of her sorority sisters made sure they left immediately! It had escaped me for many years why her sorority sister had to break up the groove that night. But the Lord revealed to me that it was Satan working through her sorority sisters.

At the time, I didn't know this, but years later, the Lord revealed to me Satan didn't want me and Sandra together! Satan broke up the groove that night, so those words of "Will you marry me" would go unfulfilled. So "Will you marry me!" were the first and last words I had spoken to Sandra in college! And after looking back over it, we both had people in our ears trying to keep us apart! And all those people were placed there by Satan to keep us apart. Even the people we knew in common were placed in our lives by Satan to keep us apart. The Most High God Jehovah and the Lord Jesus Christ revealed this to me.

I would see Sandra from time to time on campus, but for some odd reason, I never approached her to get with her. See, I wanted Sandra, but for the first time in my life, I didn't approach the girl I wanted! After that night at the gambling table, I wouldn't approach her or say anything else to her! This girl wanted me as badly as I wanted her, and all I had to say was, "What's up!" And it would have been a done deal! But something wouldn't allow me to open my mouth whenever we were in each other's presence. And I didn't even try to sleep with Sandra! And as a young man in my early twenties, my philosophy was. Well, just say I was like King David in the Bible! I was sleeping with many different women! But I didn't even try to sleep with Sandra, which was odd! I didn't see Sandra like that. Sandra was special! For the first time in my life, I was that guy who thought the girl was too special for me to have sex with! Then there was the time I was standing in front of Fitzpatrick Hall and Sandra came and stood right in front of me. We were face to face! So, just when I was about to start talking to her, a thought was given to me. The thought said,

"You will only mess up her life if you get with her!" Once that thought was given to me, a feeling of guilt and sympathy came over me. In that split second, I decided not to say anything to her because I didn't want to mess up her life! So, Sandra stood face to face with me, waiting for me to say something. And when I didn't say anything, she stormed off in anger!

After that thought was given to me, I still wanted Sandra, but I didn't want to mess up her life! I remember times I would drive to Sandra's apartment at Pheasant Run, get out of the car, walk up to her door, and have my hands ready to knock on her door, but then my hand wouldn't move! So, I just stood there! After standing there for a few seconds, I would turn around, walk back to my car, and drive off! And she never knew I was there! I did that at least three to four times! I did so many drive-byes on her apartment that it was ridiculous! I guess you can say I was stalking her (LOL)! I couldn't say a word to Sandra, but with any other woman, it was on like popcorn! Sandra and I graduated from JSU on the same day.

On graduation day, Sandra walked up to me and stood in front of me with her head tilted, trying to see if I would say anything. I looked at her and turned away from her because I loved her so much. I loved her so much that I had to accept the hurt of walking away from her because I believed the thought given to me, and I didn't want to mess up her life!

Once I graduated and left JSU, the decoy Tameko wasn't interested anymore. Satan had sent the decoy on a mission to distract me from hooking up with Sandra while I was at JSU. Then, once the mission was complete, the decoy just went away. So basically, Satan placed an anointing on Tameko to have strong feelings for me. And once I left JSU, Satan removed the anointing he placed on Tameko. The decoy was only interested in me when Sandra and I were at JSU. Once Sandra and I graduated, we went our separate ways, and Tameko wasn't interested in me any longer. The decoy Tameko had done the job Satan sent her to do. Once the job was done, the decoy didn't have any interest because Satan's anointing had ended because she had done the job Satan sent her to do. The Lord revealed all of this to me! Satan anoints people to have feelings and emotions for others. And these feelings will seem genuine, but they are not. It's Satan's anointing that is driving these emotions. And when Satan anoints a person like the decoy he sent to me, it makes the sex feel like it's the best I ever had.

Once Satan has achieved his goal, his anointing leaves the decoy, and then the people either have no interest in each other or the one sent by Satan is out to destroy the other person. To make a long story short, Sandra and I never hooked up in college. The only words I had ever spoken to her were, "Will you marry me!" And the way her face lit up like a Christmas tree let me know she would have!

In October 2013, the Lord took me in the spirit and showed me who Sandra was in Heaven to me and who she was supposed to be here on Earth to me! In October 2013, the Lord revealed to me that Sandra was my wife in Heaven and was placed at JSU to be my wife here on Earth! Once the Lord revealed to me Sandra was my wife in Heaven, I understood why our spirits were drawn to each other! Our spirits were drawn to each other because our spirits recognize each other from Heaven! This is why I instantly fell in love with her the first time I saw her! My spirit recognized her as being my wife in Heaven.

As you read this book, you must remember it was not revealed to me until October 2013 that Sandra was supposed to be my wife! Since the Lord revealed to me that Sandra was my wife in Heaven and was supposed to be my wife here on Earth. The question must be asked: who gave me the thought that I would mess Sandra's life up if I got with her? Who gave me that thought? Years later, the Lord revealed to me it was Satan who gave me that thought! Satan gave me that thought to keep me from uniting with Sandra! It was Satan who gave me that sympathetic thought with those sympathetic emotions! Since I was in love with Sandra, the last thing I wanted to do was to mess her life up! Satan played on my love for Sandra by using a guilt trip on me. This is the reason why we should pray over every thought that is given to us! Because Satan gives us thoughts that play on our emotions!

The decoy name Tameko is another example of how Satan always sends a Satanic Contradiction your way to stop the blessing the Lord has for you. See, the Lord had Sandra at JSU to unite me with my wife from Heaven. Sandra was a blessing for me from the Lord. If I had united with Sandra, I would have truly cut back on all the partying and drinking. The Lord knew I would have been more focused if I united with Sandra in college! Not only did the Lord know this, but Satan knew this also! And since Satan knew I would have been a more focused person with Sandra on my side. Satan knew he had to keep Sandra and me apart because Satan had plans to destroy me!

Satan sent the Satanic Contradiction Tameko and other women to stop me from receiving the blessing the Lord had for me, which was Sandra. The blessing is always won or lost during the time of the Satanic Contradiction. Let me say that again: the blessing is always won or lost during the time of the Satanic Contradiction. In my case, I gave in to the Satanic Contradiction, which was Tameko, and I lost the blessing the Lord had for me, which was Sandra. I lost my blessing, Sandra, because I allowed myself to be distracted by Tameko, the Satanic Contradiction. Also, the words spoken by the guy name "F" were Satanic Contradictions. And some of Sandra's sorority sisters who were speaking against me were also a Satanic Contradiction! Anyone who opposed Sandra and I from uniting was a Satanic Contradiction! They were a Satanic Contradiction because it was God's will for me and Sandra to be together. You must remember Sandra was my wife in Heaven.

The two thoughts that were given to me by Satan were also Satanic Contradictions. At the restaurant Jefferson's, Satan gave me a thought that said, "Don't hurt Tameko's feelings!" "Don't hurt Tameko's feelings" was a Satanic Contradiction to what the Most High God Jehovah wanted because God placed Sandra and me at JSU so we could unite. God didn't mind if Tameko's feelings got hurt because the reason Tameko had feelings for me was because Satan placed an anointing on her for her to have strong feelings for me! Tameko's feelings for me weren't genuine; her feelings came from an anointing Satan placed on her! So, God Jehovah wasn't concerned about Tameko's fake feelings. God only cared about Sandra and I uniting!

Also, it's one other aspect I want you to look at. Sandra is two years older than I am. But I had already been at JSU two years before she got there. During my third year of college, I went to UAB when the Lord told me to stay at JSU. I went to UAB the same year Sandra started school at JSU. So basically, if I had been in a place where the Lord wanted me to be, I would have met Sandra a year earlier, which may have changed the outcome of the entire situation. Sandra was two years older than me, but Sandra started school at JSU two years after me. But we both graduated on the same day. God had everything measured out perfectly. God told me it would take me six years to graduate when I was eighteen. God held Sandra back from JSU for two years so I could get myself together. But I just screwed it up by doing things my way!

Let me talk to you, single people, for a moment. Many of you are single because somewhere down the road, you or the person God had for you was distracted by Satan's decoy. God had someone for each one of us, but in some way, Satan sent in a decoy to distract one of you or both of you! This is what God told me to tell you!

40. The Anatomy of Satan Part 3

In the Anatomy of Satan Part 3, we will talk about how Satan always deploys a decoy before God sends the real person or authentic person. Then, we will talk about how Satan uses our emotions against us to manipulate us to do his will. And then, we will discuss how Satan uses those close to us to manipulate us to do Satan's will.

First, let's talk about Satan's ability to deploy decoys. Satan always sends you a decoy before the Most High God Jehovah sends the real thing. The decoy is sent to look like the real thing and to look authentic, but it isn't the real thing, and it isn't authentic. A decoy can be a person or a physical object, like a car, a house, etc. But in this chapter, we will discuss the decoy as being a person. The decoy is sent, so you will miss the authentic person God has for you. Satan sends a person to you as a decoy so he can stop the blessing the Lord has for you.

The decoy is sent to hang around long enough so you will miss the authentic person God has for you. And once you miss the authentic person God had for you, the decoy will no longer be interested in you. The interest the decoy had in you was created by Satan's anointing placed on the decoy. Satan anoints the decoy with strong emotional feelings and sexual feelings for you. And once Satan's decoy has done the job of making you miss the person the Lord had prepared for you, then Satan removes the anointing from the decoy. Once Satan's anointing has been removed from the decoy, the decoy either leaves the person it was sent to distract or the decoy makes sure the relationship turns very volatile. And once a decoy has done its job, it will always leave a path of destruction! The decoy leaves a path of destruction because the decoy was sent to do Satan's will, which is to kill, steal, and destroy!

The decoy is always deployed to you before the Lord sends the authentic person to you. The decoy always looks like an authentic person. Whenever the decoy is deployed, Satan will send someone who physically looks like the authentic person or the real thing. If you remember the story, I just told you about Sandra. I told you how Sandra was mixed with African American and Caucasian. The decoy Tameko was also mixed with African American and Caucasian. They both were light-skinned with long hair! Their physical appearance was very similar.

It was no coincidence that Tameko resembled Sandra with her physical features! Satan ensures he sends a decoy that looks real because it throws off the senses of one's mind and spirit! Our spirits know who is for us and who is not for us. But once a decoy is deployed, it tricks our mental, physical, and spiritual senses! My spirit recognized Sandra from day one. But once the decoy was deployed, the decoy was just enough to distract me from Sandra! The decoy Tameko was sent to me to have sex, pay bills, buy food and clothing. The necessities that one needs when they are in college. Except for sex, sex is not a necessity! Satan sent the decoy, and Satan sent her bearing gifts!

The question you should be asking is this: how could Satan send a decoy and make another person want you? Satan can sway one's emotions by anointing that person by placing a spell on that person. Whether those emotions are anger, sadness, depression, happiness, or love (lust), Satan can move one's emotions to fit whatever his goal is. For example, remember I told you Tameko and I were sitting in the restaurant across from Sandra and her sorority sisters? Once I got ready to get up and go over to Sandra, Tameko grabbed my arm and wouldn't let me go! Once she grabbed my arm, the thought of "Don't hurt Tameko's feelings" came across my mind, and I became sympathetic towards Tameko's emotions.

Since it was God's will for me to marry Sandra, who gave me the thought that said, "Don't hurt Tameko's feelings". The Lord revealed to me the thought was given to me by Satan! Satan saw I was about to approach Sandra, so Satan gave me a thought that played on my emotions. Satan ran a guilt trip on me! And that guilt trip was, "Don't hurt Tameko's feelings!" Satan ran the same sympathetic guilt trip on me when Sandra and I were standing face to face in front of Fitzpatrick Hall. Satan gave me a thought: "You will only mess up her life if you get with her!" And then this feeling of guilt and sympathy came over me!

Once these thoughts were given to me, I should have done what the Holy Bible instructed. I should have tested the spirit to see where the thoughts came from. Because our thoughts are driven by the Heavenly Father and the Lord Jesus Christ, or they are driven by Satan and his evil spirits that are in the air. So, you need to test the spirit to see where the thought originated. The way you test the spirit is by asking the spirit did Jesus Christ come in the flesh. Every spirit acknowledging that Jesus

Christ has come in the flesh is from God, and every spirit denying Jesus Christ came in the flesh is from Satan. Once the spirit denies Jesus Christ came in the flesh, then you know the thought was given to you by Satan! John was trying to tell us this in 1 John 4:1-3.

1 John 4:1-3 Dear friends, do not believe every spirit, but test the spirits to see whether they are from God, because many false prophets have gone out into the world. ² This is how you can recognize the Spirit of God: Every spirit that acknowledges that Jesus Christ has come in the flesh is from God, ³ but every spirit that does not acknowledge Jesus is not from God. This is the spirit of the antichrist, which you have heard is coming and even now is already in the world. (NIV, BibleGateway.com)

When the Holy Bible refers to testing the spirit, it is talking about actual spirits, but it also refers to things that are told to you in your mind, like thoughts. Just like Satan gave me thoughts, Satan has given you thoughts also. We must first test the spirit that gives us these thoughts to ensure our thoughts are being driven by the Most High God Jehovah, and the Lord Jesus Christ.

Satan is a master manipulator, and Satan will use whatever trick and deceitful tactic he can to make sure God's will is not done. Satan will use your emotions to make you think you are doing the right thing or even make you think you're doing God's will. But really, you are doing what Satan wants you to do, which is the opposite of the Father's will! Satan will allow you to do acts of kindness and do things that feel right to ensure his will is done. And this is the primary way Satan deceives people. Many people think because they did something nice, that means their act of kindness came from God. That is not always so! Mankind must be very careful when it comes to our emotions and making decisions. We must all pray and ask the Lord who is driving our emotions. Is it the Lord, or is it Satan driving our emotions? Because Satan is a master at manipulating our emotions!

When Satan plays on our emotions with acts of kindness or acts of sympathy, he is using it to alter the will of the Most High God Jehovah! Let me give you a modern-day example of Satan using sympathy and this guilt trip on the citizens of the United States of America. Satan has used the media to use sympathy to teach people it's ok to be homosexual and transgender! One of Satan's top sympathy quotes used by homosexuals is, "Discrimination against gays is the same as discrimination against black people!" If you were mindless and if you were unable to think clearly, you would fall for the sympathetic quote used by homosexuals! The sympathetic quote used by homosexuals draws on the abuse and mistreatment of black people in America!

Satan also uses sympathy to teach you same-sex marriage is ok because they are in love! The Bible tells you same-sex marriage is not love, but it is lust! And lust is from Satan! Satan uses a sympathetic role to manipulate you to think these things are ok when they are not ok because it goes against the word of the Most High God Jehovah, and the Lord Jesus Christ! Satan plays on our emotions because Satan knows most of the people in this world want to do what is good and helpful to others. Satan uses our emotions against us! Just like Satan used my emotions against me when he gave me the thought, "You will only mess up her life if you get with her!" Satan used sympathy on me because Satan knew I loved Sandra, and Satan knew I wouldn't have done anything that would have been harmful to Sandra!

Also, Satan will use the people closest to you to help him accomplish his plan. Satan always uses the people who are closest to you to try to discourage you or to persuade you not to do something the Lord wants you to do. For instance, Satan was using this guy I knew to speak against Sandra, while at the same time, Satan used this same guy to deliver the decoy to me. I told you how one night, this guy named "F" got stopped by the police because he had been drinking. The police didn't arrest him, but the police allowed him to park the car and have someone come and pick him up. Now, who or what persuaded the cop to let my friend go free instead of arresting him for driving while intoxicated? The Lord revealed to me it was Satan that made the cop have sympathy for him and let him go! It is rumored that some years later, the same guy killed a person while he was driving while intoxicated! If the cop had done his job that night and arrested him, that may have taught him a lesson, then the person he killed might still be alive today! My God! In the long run, Satan's sympathy always leads to destruction!

The guy got stopped by the police because he had been drinking. The police didn't arrest him, but the police allowed him to park the car and have someone come and pick him up. So, he came by my house with this girl name Tameko so I could drive his car home. Once I dropped him and his car off at his apartment, Tameko drove me back to my apartment. Then Tameko asked to come into my apartment to use my phone. Once she entered my apartment, she wanted more than to use the telephone. She wanted the magic mike. She wanted sex! Satan used "F" to deter me from Sandra, and then he used "F" to deliver the decoy to me! Do you think those acts happened by coincidence, or did Satan plan them? The Lord revealed to me all those acts were planned and executed by Satan! Satan works through people!

As of now, you should begin to see Satan is a planning, manipulative being that has God-like characteristics! Satan's anatomy includes using people who are close to you to manipulate you. And Satan's anatomy includes using your emotions against you! Satan's anatomy always includes deploying a decoy that looks like the real thing. Satan always sends a decoy before the Heavenly Father sends the real thing. This decoy looks like the real thing and even, to a degree, sounds like the real thing, but the decoy is far from being the real thing. The deployment of the decoy is part of the anatomy of Satan.

41. Where Are Their Daddy

I remember watching the news at Jacksonville State University and seeing different stories about young teenagers getting arrested for stealing or killing. It seemed like I was seeing a story in the news every day about some teenager getting arrested for stealing or killing. One day after I had seen another story about a teenager committing a crime, I said out loud, "Lord, where are these children's daddies; because my daddy would beat my butt if I did anything like these children are doing." I didn't understand where these children's daddies were. I just didn't understand!

Around the same time, I started seeing different news stories about men killing their wives and ex-wives. I remember there was a stretch where, for about three to four weeks straight, you heard various stories about a man killing his wife, ex-wife, or his baby momma. After I had seen another news story explaining how a man killed his wife. I said out loud, "Lord, why are these men killing these women like this?" And at that very moment, the Lord said to me, "Because Judges won't do their jobs!" And once the Lord said this to me, I didn't understand. I was trying to figure out what Judges? And I was trying to figure out how the judges didn't do their job. I asked the Lord, but the Lord wouldn't answer me. I was left with figuring out what the Lord meant when he said, "Because Judges won't do their jobs!"

It would be many years later before I understood what the Lord meant by that statement he made. So, what job didn't the Judges do? Just continue to read, and you will find out, just like I found out.

42. Not Having The Wisdom To Understand

While I was at JSU I would tell people how the Lord would speak to me and tell me things. Each time I would tell people this, they would look at me like I was crazy. I didn't understand why people would look at me like I was crazy because I thought God spoke to everyone. I thought that since God had spoken to me since I was a child, God had been talking to everyone since they were a child. So one day, I asked the Lord, "Lord, why do people look at me strangely when I tell them you speak to me." After I completed my sentence, the Lord said to me in my left ear, "One's perception is one's reality." Once the Lord said that to me, I didn't understand.

So, one weekend, I went to my mother's house in Birmingham. I went into my mother's room and said, "Madear, why when I tell people the Lord speaks to me, people look at me like I am crazy." My mother then responded, "The Lord doesn't speak to everyone. The Lord chooses to whom he speaks too." I told my mother, "Surely the Lord speaks to everyone because he speaks to me." My mother then responded, "The Lord doesn't speak to everyone. The Lord chooses to whom he speaks too." After my mom said those words to me, it didn't register in my mind what she was saying. It didn't register because I had heard the voice of the Lord since I was a child. So, my thinking was, "Surely the Lord speaks to everyone because the Lord has been speaking to me since I was a child."

It was not until I remembered what the Lord said to me earlier that week that made me understand what my mother was saying. "One's perception is one's reality." I thought the Lord spoke to everyone because the Lord was speaking to me. That is a perfect example of how my perception became my reality. I believe the Lord spoke to everyone because the Lord always spoke to me. So, my perception was the Lord speaks to everyone because the Lord speaks to me, and since it was my perception, it also became my reality. It became my reality because that is what I believed! So, whenever you believe something based on your perception, your perception becomes your reality!

So, I couldn't perceive or even conceive the thought the Lord wasn't speaking to everyone because I had always heard the voice of the Lord. My perception had become my reality. On the flip side of this, other people have never heard the voice of the Lord, so they couldn't conceive the thought I heard the voice of the Lord. They believed the Lord does not speak to people because the Lord has never spoken to them. Their perception that God does not speak to people because God never spoke to them became their reality. But one's perception has nothing to do with the truth. Your perception is just what you believe. And what you believe has nothing to do with the absolute truth.

Once, I understood what the Lord said, "One's perception is one's reality." I then started telling people, "One's perception is one's reality." I told people this saying in the early 90s. After I started using it at JSU in the early 90s, the phrase caught on fire, and everyone started to use it. After I figured out what the Lord meant by "One's perception is one's reality." Everything my mother told me made more sense to me. My mother told me, "The Lord doesn't speak to everyone. The Lord chooses to whom he speaks to." My mother was trying to tell me that the Lord chose me to speak directly to. My mother was trying to tell me that the Lord chose me to speak to out of the billions of people in this world, the Most High God Jehovah, and the Lord Jesus Christ chose me to talk directly to.

43. They Recognized Me

One day, while at JSU, my friends and I talked in front of Curtis Hall. While we were standing there talking, this girl walked into our circle. Once this girl heard me speak, these things that appeared as a bright distorted light jumped out of her head. It didn't leave her head; it just extended itself out of her head about seven inches, and then it returned inside of her very quickly. It looked like a distorted gleam of bright light that came about seven inches outside of her head, and then it returned inside of her very quickly. Once we all saw this we all looked at each other and said, "What was that?" Then we all started laughing because we all thought we were just tripping. We all saw it, but we didn't understand it. And since we didn't understand it, we started laughing!

So, at that moment, the girl just stared at me while repeatedly asking me the same question. She asked me, "Who are you?" I didn't respond to her because I was trying to figure out what I saw. None of us knew the girl, but she kept asking me, "Who are you?" She had this stare on her face like something was telling her who I was. She was obsessed with finding out who I was, but I didn't speak a word. I don't know why I didn't speak a word. I just didn't!

Years later the Lord revealed to me what happened that day. The bright light we saw come out of the young lady's head and then return inside her head were unholy spirits that were in her. The unholy spirits became uneasy once they heard my voice, so they came out of the girl and revealed themselves to us for a moment, and then they went back inside the girl. The girl didn't know who I was, but the unholy spirits in her recognized me. Once the unholy spirits heard my voice, they knew or sensed I was Elisha the Prophet! That's why the girl kept asking me, "Who are you?"

44. Why Do People Hate Me?

When I was a child, everyone loved me; but then my dad and this lady from my church named Mrs. Buchanan said, "The Lord wants you to teach his word." From that moment on, the atmosphere changed. Instead of many people offering me love, they offered me hate. This was the trend throughout elementary, high school, college, and my life. People hated me! I always wonder why people hated me so much. I remember one day, while I was at JSU, I was talking to the Lord. I said, "Lord, why do people hate me so much?" At that very moment, the voice of the Lord Jesus Christ spoke into my left ear and said, "The world hated me first; the world hates you because I am in you." After the Lord Jesus Christ spoke, I thought about what he said. I didn't truly grasp what the Lord was telling me because I thought everyone loved the Lord Jesus Christ! It was many years later I came to realize the world does hate Jesus Christ. Many years later, while studying my Bible, I ran across the same answer Jesus gave me that day I was at JSU.

In John 15:18-19 Jesus said to his disciples, [18] "If the world hates you, keep in mind that it hated me first. [19] If you belonged to the world, it would love you as its own. As it is, you do not belong to the world, but I have chosen you out of the world. That is why the world hates you. (NIV, BibleGateway.com)

If you noticed, the scripture said, "...if you belong to the world, it would love you as its own..." I hope you understand what that statement means! And Jesus said if the world hates you, it's because Jesus has chosen you out of the world.

In John 17:14, Jesus said this prayer for his disciples, [14] I have given them your word and the world has hated them, for they are not of the world any more than I am of the world. (NIV, BibleGateway.com)

Once I read the scriptures, I thought about what Jesus said to me that day while I was at JSU. Then I realized why people hated me so much. But there was more to it than I initially thought. When Jesus said, the world hated him first. Jesus was talking about his life before he preached the Gospel, while he taught the Gospel and afterwards. Jesus was hated as a child; he was hated as a teenager, and he was hated as an adult. The Lord led me to the Book of Isaiah and revealed to me that many of the things I had experienced as a child, teenager, and adult, he also experienced those things. And that was something I never knew until the Lord revealed those things to me. The Lord revealed to me the prophecy about him in the Book of Isaiah talks about how people hated him in his youth. Let's look at Isaiah 53:1-4. After we read the scripture, I will show you the verse about his youth as a child.

Isaiah 53:1-4 [1] Who has believed our message and to whom has the arm of the Lord been revealed? [2] He grew up before him like a tender shoot, and like a root out of dry ground. He had no beauty or majesty to attract us to him, nothing in his appearance that we should desire him. [3] **He was despised and rejected by mankind, a man of suffering, and familiar with pain**. Like one from whom people hide their faces, **he was despised, and we held him in low esteem**. [4] Surely he took up our pain and bore our suffering, yet we considered him punished by God, stricken by him, and afflicted. [5] But he was pierced for our transgressions, he was crushed for our iniquities; the punishment that brought us peace was on him, and by his wounds we are healed. [6] We all, like sheep, have gone astray, each of us has turned to our own way; and the Lord has laid on him the iniquity of us all. (NIV, BibleGateway.com)

If you look at verse 2 it gives us some background knowledge of Jesus' physical appearance. Isaiah 53:2 reads, [2] He grew up before him like a tender shoot, and like a root out of dry ground. He had no beauty or majesty to attract us to him, nothing in his appearance that we should desire him. (NIV, BibleGateway.com) So, verse 2 gives you insight into Jesus' appearance, and then verse 3 gives us insight into how Jesus was treated as a child and then how he was treated through his teen years and then to manhood.

Isaiah 53:3 [3] He was despised and rejected by mankind, a man of suffering, **and familiar with pain**. Like one from whom people hide their faces, he was despised, **and we held him in low esteem**. (NIV, BibleGateway.com)

The Lord Jesus Christ revealed to me that he suffered greatly as a child, teen, and man. Jesus suffered because Satan hated him, and Satan wanted to destroy him because of who he was and what he was sent into this world to do. Jesus revealed to me that Satan sent people to attack him physically and verbally as a child, teenager, and adult like Satan sent people to attack me physically and verbally as a child, teenager, and adult. Satan wanted to discourage Jesus as a child, teenager, and adult so Jesus wouldn't have the courage to carry out his ministry and go to the cross. Satan sent people to attack Jesus just like Satan was sending people to attack me. Jesus revealed to me that Satan was applying the same strategy against me that Satan used against him. Satan was using people to attack me so Satan could convince me I had no self-worth. Satan wanted to convince me I had no self-worth, so I wouldn't be willing to complete the mission the Lord sent me into this world to do.

Jesus suffered as a child, a teenager, and an adult because Satan sent people to discourage him from completing his mission. This is why Isaiah 53:3 says Jesus was a man of suffering and familiar with pain. Jesus felt pain of emotional hurt just like we feel pain of emotional hurt. Once, the Lord came to me and told me these things. I understood he endured the same as I. Satan and his demons were influencing people to hate Jesus just like Satan and his demons were influencing people to hate me.

So, when the Lord told me that day at JSU, **"The world hated me first; the world hates you because I am in you."** I genuinely grasp all that Jesus suffered in this world before he started to preach the Gospel. The world hated him because Satan and his demons influenced people to hate him. Just like Satan and demons were influencing people to hate me! Satan was trying to break Jesus psychologically, just like Satan was trying to break me psychologically! Satan thought if he could convince Jesus to believe he didn't have any value, then Jesus would abort the mission God sent him here to do. The world started hating Jesus as a child! Just like the world started hating me as a child! For the first time, I understood how Jesus suffered before he preached the Gospel.

The reason why people hate me is because Christ was in me, and all those who hated me had Satan in them. To everyone who said to me or to others, "It's something about him I just don't like. I don't know what it is; I just don't like him!" You can't stand me because Christ is in me, and Satan is in you. So, the problem is not with me. The problem has been you all this time! Christ is in me, while Satan is in you!

Satan influenced people to hate me because my coming symbolizes the beginning of the end for them. Satan realizes my coming as the Prophet Elisha must happen before the second coming of Jesus Christ. And the return of Jesus Christ symbolizes the end to all this sin in this world! And Satan and his demons realize their time is up once

Jesus returns. When demons see me coming it's a reminder Jesus Christ is also coming!

45. I Witness The Second Coming of The Lord

After transferring back to JSU, I started to have more and more visions of world events. One night in 1993, I fell on my knees, prayed, and fell asleep. I fell into a deep sleep, and the Lord took me into the spirit and showed me the following.

I was at A. H. Parker High School's class reunion picnic, standing by the pavilion, talking to a guy named Fred and a guy named Lando. While talking to them, I heard a very loud trumpet sound. Once I heard the loud trumpet sound, I turned to see where the loud trumpet sound was coming from. I then looked toward the sky! I then witness the Lord of Lords, the King of Kings, riding in on a cloud! I saw Jesus Christ standing on the cloud! He had a long white robe on; I could see everything about him except for his face. The sun's brightness blocked Jesus' face because the sun was directly behind him. I saw angels riding behind Jesus on horseback. There were many angels following Jesus. The sky was filled with angels on horseback! I then turned toward Fred and Lando, and at that very moment, they caught on fire right before my eyes. Fred and Lando instantly caught on fire in a huge blaze of fire! I remember saying, "My God, it's Judgment Day!"

As I looked to my right, I saw a cemetery, and spirits began coming out of the graves (the first resurrection). I then ran to my car to get my Bible so I could say the words in the Bible, and this is what happened. I picked up my Bible and opened it and then I dropped it. I picked up my Bible again, and then I dropped it. I picked up the Bible again, held on tight to the Bible, and said, "I must hold on to the word of God, and I must say the words in the Bible." But no words were allowed to come out of my mouth! Then I woke up! As soon as I woke up, I was covered in sweat. My roommate looked at me and said, "Man, you are sweating. What did you just see?" I then told him everything I had witnessed in the spirit.

At the picnic, I saw the faces of people I graduated from high school with. I was at a class reunion picnic. The vision gave me a particular year to look towards for some significant event. I graduated high school in 1989, so my ten-year reunion would be in 1999, and my twenty-year reunion would be in 2009. The Lord revealed to me that some significant event would happen in 2009 that would change this world forever.

The guys burning up were a warning to me that they wouldn't enter the kingdom of heaven because their names are not written in the Book of Life and to separate myself from them. This does match their spiritual profile to this very day. The spirits coming out of the grave represented the first resurrection that happens once Jesus returns. The Bible discusses the first resurrection when those who had been beheaded during the Great Tribulation because they held to their testimony that Jesus Christ was the son of God. Those who were beheaded because they held to their testimony of Jesus Christ will be called up into heaven right before those who are still alive are called up into heaven (Rapture).

When I dropped my Bible, it symbolized it being too late for those who had not accepted Jesus Christ as the son of God and their Lord and Savior. When no words were allowed to come out of my mouth was a warning to you! You won't be allowed to confess that Jesus Christ is the son of God and your Lord and Savior once he returns. So you must establish a relationship with him now!

This is the third time something has happened to me that referred to the end of days! The first time was in Chapter 9, titled "I Am Pronounced Blessed". In that chapter, I told you how the voice of an angel came to me as a child and said, "You are blessed to be one of the last men to walk the face of this earth." Then there was the vision that was given to me when I was in the fourth grade. In Chapter 23, titled "I Repeated The Words The Lord Spoke", my fourth-grade teacher, Mrs. Daniels, witnessed some kids picking on me. And then Mrs. Daniels said, "You all need to stop picking on him because you don't know who the Lord is going to raise him to be. And one day you may have to go to him for help!" Then, at that very moment Mrs. Daniels was saying those things about me, a vision was given to me. Then, I saw myself as a man with great authority, and many people had to come to me for food and provisions. It was during a time of great trials and tribulations on the earth. There were great cataclysms, and the world was in great distress. And I was given authority by the Lord to oversee millions of his people.

If you look at all three chapters, they each were given me a warning of the end of the age. The Bible references it as the end of the age, but most people in the world refer to it as the end of the world. If you compare the vision shown to me concerning the second coming of Jesus Christ and the words spoken to me as a child, they both refer to the end!

Then, look at the vision the Lord gave me concerning this world's great cataclysm. It's all warnings about the end.

46. The Voice Is Leading Me

I don't remember the year, but I was still at JSU. If I had to pinpoint the year, it was between 1993 and 1994. One day, while I was at school, the Holy Spirit came to me and whispered in my left ear, "It's in your blood." The first time the Holy Spirit said this to me, I didn't understand, so I just blew it off. But then the Holy Spirit returned day after day, multiple times in the day, saying, "It's in your blood." For the first time in my life, I thought I was losing my mind. I thought I was losing my mind because the Lord and the Holy Spirit have always spoken to me, but this time, the voice came back to me day after day, telling me the same thing.

Eventually, I had to tell my mother what was happening. I remember going home that weekend and entering my mother's bedroom, and I said, "Ma dear, I got to tell you something! I am not crazy, Ma dear, but I keep hearing this voice saying, "It's in your blood." After trying to convince my mother I wasn't crazy. My mother said, "Listen boy, it's time I tell you something. I knew since you were a little boy, you had the Gift." I immediately said, "Gift, what Gift? What are you talking about." My mother said, "It's time I tell you about your great-granddaddy Edgar Brown." I responded, "Who, your daddy?" My mother said, "No, your daddy's daddy, daddy." She then said, "Your great-granddaddy was an anointed man of God. They say that man could teach the word of God like no other. They say he could lay hands on the sick and heal them regardless of their illness, disease, or medical problem." She then said, **"The Lord would talk directly to your great granddaddy Edgar Brown and held conversations with him."** My response was, "My daddy's daddy daddy?" My mother said, "The Lord is trying to get your attention."

After talking to my mother, the Holy Spirit never returned to me, saying, "It's in your blood." The Holy Spirit was leading me to my mother so she could reveal who my great-grandfather Edgar Brown was. I never knew anything about my great-granddaddy because he died well before I was born. By the time I was of age, there was very little discussion about him. Once my mother explained the gifts of my great-grandfather Edgar Brown, my life started to make sense to me.

When my mother told me everything about my great-grandfather, I thought that was the only reason the Holy Spirit kept coming to me, saying, "It's in your blood." I didn't make another important connection with the phrase, "It's in your blood," until many years later. In Chapter 18, titled "My Heritage," I told you how I was ten years old, sitting on my grandmother's porch, listening to my mother, grandmother, and others talk. Then my mother said, "Our blood is mixed with some of everything. There is Black, White, Indian, and Chinese in our blood." Then my mother paused for a second and turned and stared at me and said, "There is even Jewish in our blood."

Well, when the Holy Spirit came to me and said, "It's in your blood." The Holy Spirit was leading me to my mother to find out about my great-grandfather, but the Holy Spirit was also referring to the Israelite bloodline in my blood. The blood of the Israelites, God's chosen people, is in my blood! I have the same blood that the Biblical Prophets had in them! So, I'm from the same bloodline that men like Abraham, Isacc, Jacob (who God change his name to Israel), Joseph, Moses, and King David were from! In 2015 the Lord told me that I am a descendant from the tribe of Judah! That means my father, Mervin Brown, my grandfather, Eddie Brown, and my great-grandfather, Edgar Brown, were also descendants from the tribe of Judah! Judah was one of the sons of Jacob. God changed Jacob name from Jacob to Israel. And Israel had 12 sons which became the 12 tribes of Israel. And I am a descendant from the tribe of Judah. It's in my blood!

47. My Father Speaking of Future Events

Once my mother told me about my great-grandfather, I finally made a connection between my great-grandfather's anointing, my gifts, and the gift of prophecy my dad had. When I was young, my dad always talked about things that weren't happening yet. And many people never understood my dad because he talked about future events. For instance, I remember when I was about eight to nine years old (1979-1980), my dad would say things like, "These people's plan (a secret group inside the government) is to have everyone on drugs (prescription drugs and street drugs), even children. So, they mind want work right (the citizens of the United States and other nations), so they can have everyone doped up, so they (the government) can do whatever they want. They plan is to have drug stores on every corner, and the government is going to pay people to put their children on drugs."

Those were the words my father spoke in the late 70's. By the time 1992 came around, I realized what my dad was saying in the late 70's was coming true. For instance, pharmacies are being placed in almost every community and they incentivize putting children on certain medication. Then, over the years, I saw how prescription medication was being released onto the streets of America. I watched as large portions of the population became hooked on pain pills. Then, years later, I watched the legalization of marijuana in the state of California and other states. I watched how my father's words in the late 1970s were fulfilled yearly. I watched how they intentionally released drugs into American communities so the population could become addicted to drugs. So, they could have Americans addicted to street drugs or prescription medication so they could easily take over America while the American citizens were getting high! Just like my dad said! But the question must be asked: who are they? As we move through this book, you will understand who they are and how they did it! Just continue to read.

I remember one day during the late 1970s, my daddy walked into the house angry and he slammed the door. Once my dad did this, my mother said, "What is wrong, Brown!" My dad replied, "Do you know these people are doing away with pensions and replacing them with 401 K's?" Then my dad said, "When the people get ready to retire, the money will not be there for them!" My mother said, "Brown, how do you know the money will not be there for them to retire with?" My dad replied, "Because the Lord told me!"

I remember I was about eight or nine years old when my dad said this. I remember standing there looking at my dad. My dad was so upset! He was upset because he knew what the Lord had told him was true, and he knew millions of people would get ripped off by 401 K's. In the late 70s my dad said exactly what would happen to people's 401 K's almost 30 years before the event occurred. In 2008 and 2009, it happened just like the Lord told my dad it would happen! The people's 401K money was gone when it was time for them to retire! People's 401K money just disappeared into thin air! Your 401K money disappear into someone else's bank account? In return, they mailed you a statement showing you lost more than seventy-five percent of your 401K money. What happened to your 401K money will be revealed to you just like the Lord revealed it to me. Just continue to read, and you will understand who they are and what they are doing!

48. I Am Being Watched

All my life I had this strange feeling, I was being watched by someone or by some group of people. This feeling increased when I was in high school, but it intensified when I was in college. I would have different conversations with people and tell them I felt like someone was watching me. I tried to explain to people that some group or government organization was watching me. Once I told my friends or brothers about this, they always laughed at me as though I was crazy! I didn't have anyone I could talk to who understood what I was trying to tell them.

I just knew some organization or government organization was keeping a watchful eye over me. I sensed they were observing me from afar and keeping tabs on my every move! I felt like they had marked me since I was a child. But I didn't know who they were and why they were watching me! I had no proof of this, but my spirit felt like someone was watching me!

49. Approached By The Illuminati

These are the events that took place at Jacksonville State University during my fourth year in college, which was the year 1993. These events gave me the pieces to a puzzle that helped me understand who was watching me and how people were chosen to be recruited into the Illuminati. Please pay close attention to what I'm about to reveal to you. Because the things I am about to share with you may have happened to your child, family member, or friends!

During my fourth year in college at JSU, people would tell me a white lady had been by my dorm room looking for me. But every time she came by, I was nowhere to be found. One day after class, I went directly to my dorm room. Once I got to my dorm room this white lady was standing near my door. As I approached my room, the lady said, "Kennedy!" Once she called my name, I thought, "Who is this?" I had never seen this lady before, but she knew my name and was waiting for me. This lady didn't look like a student; she was dressed professionally and in her early to mid-thirties.

Once she called my name, she got my attention. Then she approached me and pulled out this sheet of paper with the steganography and ambigram of the word Illuminati. I recognize the word because I have seen it twice before. The word was Illuminati. And you must remember this was in 1993 before the image of the word Illuminati appeared all over the internet. Below is the steganography and ambigram of the word Illuminati that was shown to me that day.

Illuminati

So once the lady called my name, she got my attention. Then she approached me and pulled out this sheet of paper with the steganography and ambigram of the word Illuminati. I recognized the word because I had seen it twice before. Then the lady said, "Kennedy, can you tell me what this says?" Once the lady finished her sentence, the Lord spoke to me at that very moment and said, "Do not answer her question!" Once I heard the Lord say this, I stood there trying to figure out what was happening. I then said to her, "How do you know my name? Who are you, and what is your name?" She replied, "If you can tell me what this says, I will tell you more than my name?" I then started to answer her question, but the Lord told me again, "Do not answer her question!"

Once the Lord said that again, I was confused. I had this lady in front of me trying to get me to tell her what the steganography said. Then, I had the Lord telling me not to answer her question. I was standing there in a state of confusion. I told the lady again, "How do you know my name? Who are you, and what is your name?" Then the lady said, "First, tell me what this says, then I will tell you more than my name." So, I said to her, "What does that mean?" She replied, "If you can tell me what this says, I will tell you so much, Kennedy?"

At this point, she had me very curious. She insisted I tell her what the steganography said. We went back and forward, and I wouldn't tell her what the word said. Then she said, "I know you know what it says, Kennedy!" Then, I was about to tell her what the word says, but the Lord yelled at me and said, "Do not answer her question!!!" After the Lord yelled at me, I decided not to answer her question. The lady became frustrated with me, and she walked away. I never saw this lady again at JSU; mysterious as she appeared in front of my dorm room, mysterious as she walked away and disappeared. That was the first time someone at JSU had approached me, wanting me to reveal what the word in the steganography said. But it was the third time I had been exposed to the word.

The first time I was exposed to the word "Illuminati" was when I was in the third grade, and this lady came to our school to test everyone in our class. And when I was tested, I identified the word Illuminati hidden in the steganography. And then the lady said I was "Gifted," and she marked something by my name in her book! And then the same lady showed up at my house trying to convince my mom to send me to this school for very smart people. The lady also told my mother that people normally become Presidents, Senators, and High-Ranking Government officials once they go to this school. This is discussed in Chapter 16, titled "A Word Hidden in a Picture". The second time I was exposed to the steganography of the word Illuminati was by my high school girlfriend. This is discussed in Chapter 33, titled "My Memories of A Word".

Now, I am at JSU, and this lady I don't know has approach me with the steganography of the word Illuminati. By this time, I was becoming more curious than ever. I wanted to know the meaning and purpose of the Illuminati and why this lady approached me. All that day, I thought about the woman. I was trying to figure out who she was, how she knew where I lived, and when I would return to my room. And why did she want me to tell her what the word said? I couldn't figure it out, so I just blew it off. And you must remember this took place in 1993 before everything about the Illuminati was published all over the internet!

A week later a second recruiter of the Illuminati approached me. One day I was driving to my dorm when I noticed this black lady pretending she was walking down the sidewalk. Once I parked my car in front of Weatherly Hall, the same black lady ran across the street to my car. Once I exited my car, she called out my name. This lady was in her mid-twenties. Once she called out my name, I turned to see who she was. I didn't know who she was, but she knew me. So, the lady pulls out this white sheet of paper with the steganography of the word Illuminati on it. Then she said, "Kennedy, can you tell me what this says?" Once she asked me that question, I asked her straight forward, "What does that mean?" Her reply was the same as the white woman's reply. She said, "If you can tell me what it says, I will tell you so much more."

I just stood there and looked at the lady with this expression that said, "What in the world is going on." So, I said to the lady, "You are going to tell me what that means first." Then the lady said, "I know you know what it says!" I was about to tell her, but before I could, the Lord spoke to me and said, "Do not answer her question!" Once the Lord said that to me, I was ready to walk away when the lady said, "Why won't you answer the question? I know you know what it says!" I said, "First, you going to tell me what that means! I tried everything I could to get her to tell me the meaning of the word Illuminati, but no matter how hard I tried to get her to tell me the meaning of the word Illuminati, she wouldn't tell me anything. So eventually she became frustrated with me, and she walked away. At the time, I couldn't understand why these people were approaching me and why the Lord didn't want me to answer their questions. I was puzzled and confused! From then on, I wanted to know what the word Illuminati meant!

A few days after my second encounter with the Illuminati recruiter, I received a call from the Financial Aid office about my financial aid. I was told I had to come to the Financial Aid Office because a problem had arisen with my financial aid money. They said I needed more money to pay for school, so they scheduled me and appointment to meet with the Financial Aid Director.

So, I went to see the Financial Aid Director. While talking to him, I asked him how I could get more financial aid to pay for school. He said, "If you make the right choice, you can get as much money as you want!" He then said, "I can give you enough money so you can pay for school and buy you a brand-new Mercedes if you make the right choice!" I then said, "The right choice at what?" Then he just smiled, and he wouldn't tell me what choice I needed to make. Then, he scheduled an appointment for me to return to see him a week later. That was my third encounter with an Illuminati recruiter.

After that meeting with the man in the financial aid office, I had a fourth encounter with an Illuminati recruiter. The fourth time an Illuminati recruiter approached me at JSU was when I left class and headed to the Bibb Graves Hall. **I had a second appointment with the Director of Financial Aid**. Once I parked my car in front of Bibb Graves, I began to walk towards the building. As I walked towards the building, this white lady was sitting on the bench near the sidewalk. Then, the white lady saw me, so she stood up and approached me on the sidewalk. Then the white lady said, "Kennedy!" Once the lady called my name, she got my attention. This lady was there waiting for me! This white lady was probably in her late twenties or early thirties and dressed professionally. She looked like she was not a student but a business professional. Once she called out my name, I said, "Yes." Then this lady broke out the sheet of paper with the steganography and ambigram of the word Illuminati on it, and then she said, "Can you tell me what this says, Kennedy!" Before I could say anything, the Lord said, "Do not answer her question!"

After the Lord said this to me, I stood there like, "Lord what in the world is going on!" I was at the point of serious curiosity! I wanted to know everything that was going on. This was the third time I was stopped by someone I didn't know at JSU, and each of them broke out this steganography with the word Illuminati on it! Then they wanted me to tell them what the steganography said! But at the same time, the Lord is telling me not to answer their question. If you ever wanted to see a confused person, you should have seen my face that day!

Then the lady said again, "Kennedy, can you tell me what this says?" So, I said to the lady, "I want to know what that means and what is going on!" The lady replied, "I will tell you so much, but first, you have to tell me what this says!" Out of curiosity, I was about to tell her what it said, but then the Lord yelled at me and said, "Do not answer her question!!!!" Once I heard the Lord yell at me, I stood there confused. The Lord yelled at me while I had this lady in front of me, piquing my curiosity. I didn't know what was going on! So, the lady asked me again, "Kennedy, can you tell me what this says?" I said, "No, I don't know what it says!"

Then the lady looked at me with this confused look on her face as though she knew I was lying. Then the lady said, "Kennedy, I know you know what it says!" I just looked at the lady and didn't say anything. The lady looked at me with frustration on her face, and then she walked away. The lady didn't realize the Lord was talking to me at the same time she was talking to me. When the Lord speaks to me, I have this expression that looks like I am confused, but I am not. But in this case, I was confused; I was confused about everything that was transpiring.

So that was the third time someone came and confronted me with the steganography of the word Illuminati while I was at JSU. And all three women came and confronted me within three weeks. This was the fifth time in my life I had seen the word. At the time, I couldn't understand why these people were approaching me and why the Lord didn't want me to answer their questions. I was puzzled and confused! From then on, I wanted to know what Illuminati meant!

After the lady walked away from me, she entered the same building I was entering, but she went in through the side door while I went in through the front door. So, I continued to the Financial Aid Office for my appointment. When I got to the Financial Aid Office, I was seated at the Director's desk, but he wasn't there.

Then, a few minutes later, he walked into the room and said I couldn't get any more financial aid money because I made the wrong decision. When he said that, I was confused because the week before, he told me I could get enough money to pay for school and buy me a brand-new Mercedes if I made the right decision! I didn't understand why I suddenly couldn't get any more financial aid money. It was not until I was writing this book that the Lord revealed to me what the man meant by me making the right decision. See, if I had answered the lady's question, I would have moved to the next level of the Illuminati recruitment process. And if I had joined the Illuminati, I would have had unlimited amounts of money given to me for financial aid and to buy me a new car! But since I didn't answer the lady's question, I didn't make the right decision, according to the man in the financial aid office, so I couldn't get any more money for financial aid! So, getting unlimited money for financial aid was contingent on me joining the Illuminati! Just to let you know, Illuminati members are given unlimited money for college once they join the Illuminati, and it doesn't matter what their grades are!

Years later I came to realize the reason why the three women were approaching me at JSU. They were approaching me because the Illuminati was recruiting me! But at that time, I didn't realize they were recruiting me. That's why the Lord was telling me not to answer their question. Because if I had answered the question, that would have taken me to the next phase of their recruitment process. Everyone who looks at the steganography with the word Illuminati in it cannot see the word. Only those people with a very high IQ can see the word Illuminati hidden within the steganography. I didn't realize it then, but they were recruiting me because I identified the word Illuminati in the steganography in the third grade. That's why the ladies always ask me if I can tell them what the steganography of the word Illuminati says. Because they knew I identified the word when I was in the third grade! This is why all the ladies said, "I know you know what it says!" They said that because they knew I identified the word Illuminati hidden in the steganography when I was in the third grade! This means the Illuminati identify those kids with very high IQs in the third grade, and then they start a pipeline year after year until it's time to recruit them.

A few days after the last Illuminati recruiter approached me in front of Bibb Graves Hall, I went to the Thurman Montgomery Building to check my mail. While I was there checking my mail, for some reason, I went down to the first floor where the bookstore is located. Once I got to the first floor, I saw two people guarding the door to the meeting room. This young white lady was sitting behind a table, and a white guy stood up guarding the door to the meeting room. For some reason, I kept staring at the meeting room door because I felt something was going on behind those doors.

So, I tried to go into the meeting room. But the lady and man stopped me and said I couldn't go in. They were adamant about not letting me get past them. For some reason, I felt I needed to know what was happening behind those doors. So, I made a second attempt to go past the two people guarding the door, but they stopped me again. Then they said the meeting was by **invitation only!** After they said that, I just turned around and walked away. But before I left, I turned around and stared at the two people guarding the door. I just knew something major was going on behind those doors.

After encountering the two people guarding the doors to the conference room, I was about to leave the Thurman Montgomery Building, but God said to me, "Wait!" I waited and hung around the Thurman Montgomery Building. I hung around the Thurman Montgomery Building for about twenty minutes. Then suddenly, God said, "Leave now!" I then decided to walk back to my dorm. As soon as I got about twenty feet outside the door of the Therman Montgomery Building, I saw this girl leaving the Thurman Montgomery Building. This girl had a puzzled look on her face, and she said, "Ken!" So, I asked her what was wrong. And then this girl told me she had just come from this secret meeting with this secret group in the Thurman Montgomery Building. Then the girl said they were telling them how aliens created man and how man was created for slave labor! Then the girl said they were shown top-secret information from the **U.S. Government** about these aliens. Then the girl said, "They told us that man was created by the aliens for slave labor." Then the girl asked me if I thought that was possible. I gave this girl this look that said: "I don't have a clue what you are talking about!" Then suddenly, the girl said, "I am not supposed to be telling people this stuff! And then she stopped talking and walked away!

After that brief conversation with the girl, I didn't think about anything she said because the little information she gave me didn't make sense to me. Because I knew the Most High God Jehovah, created man. The things she was saying sounded ridiculous to me! It sounded ridiculous because I was taught and raised as a child that the Most High God Jehovah, created man. I had many conversations with the Lord, so I knew the Most High God Jehovah and the Lord Jesus Christ was real. I did not doubt this! In my thinking process, I didn't consider anything the girl said about aliens could be true. But I didn't connect the dots of what the girl said about aliens created man to the spaceship I witnessed in 29 Palms, California, during the summer of 1985.

See, I didn't try to connect the dots back then. I thought each event was separate from one another. The Heavenly Father and the Lord Jesus Christ dropped so much information into my lap that I didn't connect the dots! But everything is connected! Everything is connected! Things may seem to be unconnected or unrelated, but everything is connected!

After that encounter with the girl, I didn't realize the secret group she met with was the Illuminati. And I didn't realize the three ladies who approached me were Illuminati recruiters who were sent to recruit me into the Illuminati! I also didn't realize the ladies who were approaching me were recruiting me so I would be in that same Illuminati secret meeting! The Illuminati were meeting in the room I was trying to get into. The Lord led me down to the first floor of the Thurman Montgomery Building so I could witness and encounter the two people guarding the door. The Lord was letting me know something was going on behind those doors. The Lord led me to see how suspicious the two people were acting that guarded the door to the meeting room. It was the Lord who had me waiting around the Thurman Montgomery Building. The Lord's divine intervention made me leave the building at the same time the girl was leaving the building. The Lord did this so I could meet the girl while she was leaving the Thurman Montgomery Building. The Lord made the girl tell me things discussed in the secret meeting. The Lord guided my footsteps so I could one day decode all this information for you.

Also, the Illuminati had a secret meeting on the campus of Jacksonville State University. This means the Illuminati are given the authority to hold these meetings by the administration. The Lord revealed to me these secret meetings are held on every College and University campus in America and every College and University campus around the world. There are members of the Illuminati who work for the Colleges and Universities. Like the man I met with in the Financial Aid office. He was also recruiting me to be in the Illuminati. So, four people were sent to recruit me into the Illuminati.

These Illuminati members who work for the Colleges and Universities authorize these Illuminati recruitment meetings on college campuses! How else did the Illuminati have a room reserved at the Thurman Montgomery Building at JSU? How else did the Illuminati recruiter know which dorm and dorm room I stayed in? How else did each one of the ladies know what I looked like? They had to have access to my picture on my school ID, or they had access to my driver's license picture. Because each recruiter knew what I looked like! How else do you think the Illuminati recruiter knew my class schedule? How else do you think that Illuminati recruiter was waiting for me in front of Bibb Graves Hall? She knew I had an appointment with the Director of Financial Aid in the Business Office. She knew I had an appointment because the entire financial aid situation was a setup. Since she knew I had an appointment, she was waiting for me to show up, which means the appointment in the Financial Aid office was set up so an Illuminati recruiter could meet me on the way to the Financial Aid Office.

Before these incidents occurred, with the three ladies approaching me or me meeting with the Director of Financial Aid at Jacksonville State University, I always had this feeling I had been marked since I was a child and that some organization was watching me closely. I could never fully understand who marked me since childhood and why some organizations wanted to keep tabs on me. It was the Illuminati who had marked me since I was a child. I was marked by the Illuminati when I was given the visual IQ test in the third grade when I identified the word Illuminati hidden in the steganography. The lady that gave me the test said I was "Gifted!" The three ladies who approached me were sent to recruit me into the Illuminati. The Director of Financial Aid was sent to recruit me into the Illuminati and to entice me with large sums of money. But why did the Illuminati want to recruit me? To answer that question, you must understand who the Illuminati are and what their goals are. Just continue to read, and I will give you that information because this is truly the United States of America Book of Secrets! This is truly the Illuminati Book of Secrets.

50. Tupac Shakur

One day, after the Illuminati recruiters approached me, I was listening to one of Tupac Shakur CD's. While listening to one of his songs in my car, I heard him say this word, which was "Killuminati". I had heard him use the word before, but this time, I wondered, "What is he saying?" So, day after day, I kept hearing Tupac Shakur say "Killuminati" in his songs. Then, one day, I said, "I got to find out this word Tupac keeps saying." So, I sat down and wrote the word on paper. Once I spelled the word out, I noticed the word was very similar to Illuminati. I was wondering, "Why did Tupac put a "K" on the word Illuminati?" Then I looked at the first four letters of the word, and I noticed it spelled out the word "Kill". Then it hit me; Tupac was giving us a coded message, which was to "Kill the Illuminati". Tupac was telling us to Kill the Illuminati by adding the letter K to the word Illuminati, which was "Killuminati". I then realized he was trying to warn us of the Illuminati. At that point, I was determined to discover what Illuminati meant. Who are they, and what are they? Why was I being approached by people I didn't know, and why did Tupac give his listeners a coded message in his songs to "Kill the Illuminati." All these questions and more will be answered in chapters to come; just continue to read!

51. The Prophesy Of Derivatives and Stock Market Crash

The year was 1994; I was in one of my Finance classes at JSU when Dr. Scroggins walked into the room and told us to turn our page to mortgage derivatives. Once I turned to the page, I remembered looking at the formula for mortgage derivatives in my book, and something bothered me about the formula. **After staring at this formula for derivatives for about ten minutes, I finally concluded that the formula was WRONG**. I made this assessment because it appeared the formula was violating the rules of mathematics. I couldn't pinpoint what rule was being violated; I just saw the formula was wrong. As I stared at the formula, something my high school Trigonometry teacher used to say to me kept coming to mind. Mrs. Kimes would always say, "Kennedy, I see how you worked the problem, and your answers are always right. I can see how you came up with the answers but the way you worked the problem is **violating the rules of mathematics**."

So, I may keep a long story short; the Lord showed me a shortcut starting in elementary to working on math problems. This shortcut was first revealed to me at UAB when I was ten. This shortcut would always produce the correct answer without going through all the rigorous steps math teachers want you to go through. Many of my elementary and high school math teachers couldn't see nor understand the ingenious method the Lord showed me at that time concerning math. Because they couldn't understand it, I would always get penalized on math tests and homework because of the method I was using. But my method always produced the correct answer! The method was ingenious! I believe the Lord showed me that method, so Mrs. Kimes would say, "Kennedy, you are violating the rules of mathematics." So that day at JSU, when I saw the formula for mortgage derivatives, I kept hearing the voice of Mrs. Kimes in my mind saying, "You are violating the rule of mathematics."

The formula for mortgage derivatives violated the rule of mathematics. I couldn't pinpoint the rule that was being violated, but I knew something about that formula for mortgage derivatives was wrong. So, at that moment, I said aloud, "Lord, something is not right about this formula for mortgage derivatives." At that very moment, the voice of the Holy Spirit said to me in my left ear, "This formula is going to cause the stock market to crash." Once I heard the Holy Spirit speak, I knew it was true! I frantically raised my hand and said, "Dr. Scroggins, Dr. Scroggins, Dr. Scroggins." Then Dr. Scroggins said, "What Kennedy!" I said, "Dr. Scroggins, this formula for mortgage derivatives is wrong." Dr. Scroggins said, "Kennedy, what are you talking about!" I said, "This formula for mortgage derivatives is set up wrong; this is going to cause the stock market to crash!!!" After I said that, the professor and everyone else started laughing at me. The entire room was in an uproar, laughing at me. While they were laughing, I just sat there thinking, "These people just don't get it!"

So, I just sat there while everyone laughed at me! But after everything that happened in the 2008 stock market crash, I bet they are not laughing now! Oh, I forgot the media and the U.S. Government told you that the stock market crashed in 2008 because people bought houses they couldn't afford. And you believe them! They told you and sold you on a lie! Mortgage derivatives are the reason the stock market crashed in 2008! And just to let you know, Mortgage Derivatives were created and designed to crash the United States and other nations stock markets simultaneously, and that's precisely what happened in 2008 and 2009!

The Holy Spirit told me in 1994 that mortgage derivatives would cause the stock market to crash. The Holy Spirit told me that mortgage derivatives would cause the stock market to crash 14 years before it happened. And just like the Holy Spirit told me, mortgage derivatives would crash the stock market. The Lord also told my dad that people's 401K money wouldn't be there when people got ready to retire. As of today, both prophecies were fulfilled because, in 2008, people's 401K money disappeared into thin air. And many of those people were getting ready to retire! I know the U. S. Government and the mass media sold you on a huge lie about why the stock market crashed. But I am here to tell you the absolute truth! They lied to you. The stock market crash of 2008 and your 401K money disappearing were all planned to happen in 2008, right before the 2008 Presidential election! They convinced you that your 401K money disappeared and the stock market crash was just a coincidence. But it was no coincidence it was planned!

But the question you need to be asking yourself is. Why would someone want you to lose your money in your 401K and your stocks? Why would someone want millions of people to lose their homes in foreclosure? Who could plan and cause the entire stock market to crash? How can a formula for a financial product such as mortgage derivatives be wrong when this financial product had trillions upon trillions of dollars invested in it worldwide?

Also, if I saw the formula was wrong for mortgage derivatives. Are you telling me no one else saw this formula was wrong? I will answer these questions and many more as you read this book. And what I will show you and teach you "they" don't want you to know? "Who are "they"? "They" are the same people who tried recruiting me in college! "They" are the same people that mark me as a child. "They" are the same people who tried to convince my parents to send me to this special school for Gifted Children. **"They" are the Illuminati!** I will solve for you the riddle of who the Illuminati truly are! Because they have tried very hard to stay hidden like a ghost, and they have tried hard not to expose their face or their agenda! And my God, what a plan they have devised!

Also, you should understand why the Lord didn't want me to attend UAB, but he wanted me to return to Jacksonville State University, and why he wanted me to major in Finance! In my Finance class at JSU, the Lord revealed that the formula for mortgage derivatives would cause the stock market to crash! If I hadn't gotten kicked out of UAB, the Lord wouldn't have had a way to reveal that to me. You must remember, at that time UAB didn't offer a major in Finance! That's why the Lord kept telling me to return to JSU when I was at UAB! That's why the first day

I returned to JSU, the Lord said, "Your expulsion was a blessing; you are so blessed to be back here!"

When the Holy Spirit speaks, it can only speak the absolute truth. Listen to the scriptures Jesus spoke about the Holy Spirit in the Book of Matthew and the Book of John.

In Matthew 10:27 Jesus said, [27] "What I tell you in the dark, speak in the daylight; **what is whispered in your ear, proclaim from the roofs**." (NIV, BibleGateway.com)

Did you notice the scripture said, "What is whisper in your ear"? The scripture says this because the Holy Spirit whispers in your left ear! I know because the Holy Spirit has repeatedly whispered in my left ear. The Holy Spirit will tell you what is to come. The Holy Spirit will reveal future events to you before they happen. Jesus also speaks about the Holy Spirit in John 16:12-15.

John 16:12-15 Jesus said, [12] "I have much more to say to you, more than you can now bear. [13] But when he, the Spirit of Truth comes, he will guide **you** into all truth. He will not speak on his own; **he will speak only what he hears, and he will tell you what is yet to come**. [14] He will bring glory to me by taking what is mine and making it known to you. [15] All that belongs to the Father is mine. That is why I said the Spirit will take from what is mine and make it known to you..." **(NIV, BibleGateway.com)**

The Holy Spirit is known by several names: the Counselor, the Holy Spirit, and the Spirit of Truth. Unlike man, the Holy Spirit can only speak what is true.

52. Vision of Planes Flying Into The World Trade Center

The year is 1994, and I am still at JSU. My friends and I were at the car wash, washing our cars. After washing our cars, we stood by my car and discussed politics and world events. We managed to get on the subject of the World Trade Center bombing that happened in 1993. Then one of my friends said, "They are going to attack the World Trade Center again." Once I heard him make that statement, my spirit recognized what my friend said was the absolute truth. After one of my friends made that statement, I looked to the sky and said out loud, "Lord, what is going to be the next terrorist attack they are going to do on the World Trade Center." At that moment, the Lord took me into the spirit and showed me planes flying into the World Trade Center. While staring into the sky, one of my friends interrupted the vision by shaking me. I felt like I didn't see the entire vision.

Once my friend shook me, he said, "Man, what did you just see?" I turned towards my friends, and I said these exact words, "The next terrorist attack on the World Trade Center, terrorists are going to fly planes into the World Trade Center. Terrorists are going to fly suicide missions like the Japanese pilots did in World War II." That's exactly what the Lord showed me in the vision, and that's what I told my friends that day. My friends shook me and asked me what I saw because they all witnessed me go into trances and then tell them things I saw. I am physically there when I enter a trance, but my spirit has entered the spiritual realm to witness life events. My friends were accustomed to me telling them different things that would happen to us before they happened. I would always have dreams that would manifest themselves in real life. So, my friends were accustomed to listening to my warnings. What happened to me that day is described in the Bible in the Book of Acts and the Book of Numbers.

Acts 2: 17-18 [17] "In the last days, God says, I will pour out my spirit on all people. Your sons and daughters will prophesy, your young men will see visions; your old men will dream dreams. [18] Even on my servants, both men and women, I will pour out my spirit in those days, and they will prophesy. (NIV, Biblegateway.com)

Numbers 12:6 "Listen to my words: "When there is a prophet among you, I, the LORD, reveal myself to them in visions, I speak to them in dreams..." (NIV, Biblegateway.com)

So the Lord speak to his prophets in visions and in dreams. But if you continue to read verse 7 and 8 the Lord tells how he speaks to some of his prophets face to face like Moses.

Numbers 12:6-8 [6] "Listen to my words: When there is a prophet among you, I, the LORD, reveal myself to them in visions, I speak to them in dreams. [7] But this is not true of my servant Moses; he is faithful in all my house. [8] With him I speak face to face, clearly and not in riddles; he sees the form of the LORD.

53. Lord Who Am I

Whenever I experience something supernatural, I have asked the Lord the same question since I was a child: "Lord, who am I?" because I felt like the Lord wasn't telling me something. I had the feeling something was being hidden from me.

So, one day in 1994, while I was still at JSU, something supernatural happened to me again. Once it happened, I wanted to know who I was and why supernatural things always happened to me. So, I ask the Lord repeatedly, "Lord, who am I?" This time, I wouldn't leave the Lord alone until I got an answer. So, I kept asking the Lord repeatedly until he answered me. At the end of my plea, the Lord Jesus Christ said in my left ear, "You are Elisha". When the Lord said to me, "You are Elisha," my mind didn't hear Elisha; my mind heard Elijah! So, I thought the Lord said, Elijah! I thought the Lord said Elijah because the world had taught me the Prophet Elijah would return in the last days. So, my mind was hearing what the world had taught me, "Elijah!"

After the Lord Jesus Christ said to me, "You are Elisha". I immediately said, "Who?" Then the Lord Jesus Christ responded again, saying, "Elisha". Once the Lord Jesus Christ said Elisha for the second time, I heard "Elisha" in my left ear, but my mind still thought Elijah. To make sure I heard the Lord say, Elisha, I asked the Lord again, "Who!" Then the Lord said to me a third time, "Elisha!!" It was at that point I heard the name loud and clear when the Lord said, "Elisha!!"

One of the reasons I ask the Lord "who" so many times is because I was hearing Elisha in my left ear, but my mind was thinking Elijah. Also, the names sound very similar to each other when the names are pronounced. I thought Elijah because the world had taught me the Prophet Elijah would return in the last days. The world had brainwashed me to believe the Prophet Elijah was going to return in the last days. The world didn't teach me the Prophet Elisha would return in the last days. The Lord was telling me something different than what the world had taught me! Years later, this would be the cornerstone the Lord will use to show me the world teaches lies to manipulate mankind, but he teaches the absolute truth!

The Lord said I was "Elisha", but my mind couldn't comprehend what the Lord said because the world taught me the Prophet Elijah would return in the last days. What the Lord said didn't make sense to me. At the time, I couldn't figure out how I could be Elisha, and I didn't know. What the Lord said to me was far beyond my knowledge, wisdom, and understanding. I had the same feeling when the Holy Spirit kept coming to me, saying, "It's in your blood." I couldn't grasp what the Lord said to me.

So, I ignored what the Lord said and tried to forget about it. Now, you may be asking, how could I be the Prophet Elisha and not know it? The same way, John the Baptist was the Prophet Elijah, and he didn't know it. In my introduction to this book, I gave you proof in scripture that Jesus Christ said John the Baptist was the Prophet Elijah. And then I also showed you scripture where John the Baptist denied being the Prophet Elijah. John the Baptist denied being the Prophet Elijah because he didn't know he was the Prophet Elijah. He didn't know he was the Prophet Elijah because he was not allowed to carry the memories of his previous life into this world once he returned as John the Baptist.

In Matthew 11:14, Jesus said that John the Baptist was the Prophet Elijah! In Mathew 11:14-15 Jesus said to his disciples, **[14] If you are willing to accept it, John is the Elijah who was supposed to come. [15] Those who have ears should listen."** (Biblegateway.com NIV)

The Lord Jesus Christ tells you that John the Baptist was the Prophet Elijah who was to come. It cannot get any clearer than that! But at the same time the scriptures also have John the Baptist denying being the Prophet Elijah. In John 1:19-21, John the Baptist clearly states that he is not the Prophet Elijah.

John 1:19-21 reads, [19] "Now this was John's testimony when the Jewish leaders in Jerusalem sent priests and Levites to ask him who he was. [20] He did not fail to confess, but confessed freely, "I am not the Messiah." **[21] They asked him, "Then who are you? Are you Elijah?" He said, "I am not."** "Are you the Prophet?" He answered, "No." (NIV, BibleGateway.com)

John denied being Elijah because he didn't know he was Elijah. And John didn't know he was Elijah because God didn't allow him to bring his memories of being Elijah into this world. But before John the Baptist was born, an angel, Gabriel, told Zacharias his son John (John the Baptist) would be born with the spirit of Elijah. Now, since John the Baptist was born with the spirit of Elijah, that means John the Baptist was the return of the Prophet Elijah. It is the spirit that is in us that makes us who we are. Luke 1:11-25 tells you the story of John's birth. It is in Luke 1:17 that tells you John would be born with the spirit of Elijah.

So, while I was at JSU, I was told by the voice of the Lord Jesus Christ that I am Elisha! This means I have the spirit of Elisha in me which makes me the Prophet Elisha.

54. I Could See But Now I Am Blind

After the Lord told me I was Elisha, I couldn't comprehend it, so I went to the recreational center at JSU to play basketball. While playing basketball, I went up for a rebound, and this guy swiped for the ball. When the guy swiped for the ball, he poked me in my left eye. Once the guy poked me in my left eye, I felt this sharp pain and I knew something was wrong.

This girl in the gym tried to help me; she told me to open my eyes and poured water into my eye. Once the water hit my eye, a sharp pain went through my eye. So, I pushed the girl away because it hurt my eye even worse. I didn't realize this then, but the girl was Sandra! Remember the girl name Sandra I told you about? The girl I fell in love with the first time I saw her. Sandra would always be in the gym sitting on the bleachers. I didn't realize it then, but she was always watching me play basketball. The Lord revealed this to me while I was writing this book. It only took me twenty-plus years to figure out Sandra was always in the gym watching me play basketball, and I didn't realize it!

So once Sandra poured the water into my eye, my eye started to hurt worse. So, I tried to open my left eye, but something was wrong with my vision in my left eye. Once I couldn't see, I knew something was seriously wrong. So the guy came over and apologized and told me he was sorry. The guy's name was "Elisha". Elisha played football at JSU along with his twin brother Elijah. This is the absolute truth! I was blinded in my left eye by this guy whose name was Elisha, on the same day the Lord told me I was Elisha! Do you think that was a coincidence? No, it wasn't!

So, I left the gym to get medical treatment from the hospital. But it was nothing the local hospital could do and they referred me to the eye foundation in Birmingham. So, I became partially blind in my left eye during my senior year in college. My main concern was finishing school because it was very difficult to read with this blind spot in my vision. So Dr. Brown, one of my Finance professors, gave me a pep talk and told me to retrain my mind to read without seeing the blind spot in my left eye. Dr. Brown was famous for his pep talks. After the pep talk from Dr. Brown, I started to retrain my mind on how to read without noticing the spot in the center of my vision.

So, I trained my mind not to see the spot in the center of my vision in my left eye. I got so good at retraining my mind not to see the spot when I was reading I decided to retrain my mind not to see the spot during everyday activities. So, I did just that. To this day, many people don't even realize I am blind in my left eye because they cannot see any difference in the way I look at them. I have peripheral vision but no center vision of sight in my left eye. This means that if I close my right eye and look at a person's face, I can only see parts of their body. I cannot see their face.

So I forgot about the Lord telling me I was Elisha after I was poked in my left eye. Having that blind spot in my left eye was a traumatic experience I had to deal with for many days and months. I was concerned about my future and how being blind could affect it. For the longest time, I had to focus on everyday life, like reading and finishing college. So, at the time, my being blind was the issue I had to deal with. Once the guy name Elisha poked me in my eye and blinded me, I forgot the Lord told me I was Elisha. I forgot because I had been traumatized.

Also, if you noticed, I was blinded in my left eye. The same left eye I use to get wire clothes hanger hooks caught in. Do you remember Chapter 4 titled, "Hangers In My Left Eye"? In that chapter, I told you how wire clothes hangers always got caught in my left eye, and no damage was ever done to my left eye. And my mom always wondered why the wire clothes hanger never went into my right eye.

The Lord revealed to me that he made the clothes hanger go into my left eye because he was marking my left eye for the future. If you noticed, the same left eye I got wire clothes hangers caught in is the same left eye the guy named Elisha blinded me in. As a child, the Lord and his angels made the wire clothes hangers go into my left eye. The Lord allowed this to happen because the Lord was marking my left eye for the future. The Lord was letting me know that if a wire clothes hanger went into my left eye forty or more times, and no damage was ever done to my left eye. It was no accident; I was blinded by a guy named Elisha moments after the Lord revealed to me that I was the Prophet Elisha. This is why the clothes hanger incident happened to me as a child! This is why no damage was ever done to my left eye by the wire clothes hangers! This is why the hangers never went into my right eye! The Lord was making the cloth hanger go into my left eye as a child so he could show you that if a wire cloth hanger went into my left eye forty or more times and no damage was done to my left eye, then it was no coincidence this guy name Elisha poked me in my left eye and blinded me on the same day the Lord told me I am Elisha! I couldn't make this stuff up if I tried!

55. A Twelve-Year Vision From The Lord Part 3

Everything was taken to a different level in college, and I just partied like a rock star. I met some people and did some things, and that's all that needs to be said! I partied like a rock star during the first four years of college! Then, one day, I realized I had been in school for four years and was nowhere near graduating. For the next two years, I stopped partying as much and took 18 and 21 hours in the fall and spring, and I went to school during the summer. Then, two years later, I graduated! I only got semi-serious about school during my last two years in college! I could have graduated in three years if I had been semi-serious.

The date is April 29, 1995, and I graduated from Jacksonville State University, and I was twenty-four years old, just like the Lord showed me and told me. In Chapter 35, titled "A Twelve-Year Vision from the Lord Part 1," I told you how I was driving in my car, and the Lord took me into the spirit and showed me a vision that covered twelve years of my life. In the vision, the Lord said, "At the age of 24, you will graduate from college." he then showed me celebrating and dancing while I walked across the stage. So, just like the Lord said, I graduated from college at the age of twenty-four and danced across the stage at my graduation.

56. A Twelve-Year Vision From The Lord Part 4 and 5

Before I graduated from JSU, I remember having a conversation with several of my friends. The conversation was about where each of us planned on living after graduation. After everyone gave their answers, I was asked the same question. One of my friends asked me, "Where are you going to live after you graduate?" I replied, "I will live anywhere; I will move to Mississippi if the money is right." I don't know why those words came out of my mouth because I didn't want to live in Mississippi.

Once I graduated from JSU, I started a small business and moved to Jackson, Mississippi. After I landed in Mississippi, I thought about the words I spoke to my friends before I graduated from JSU, which was, "I will live anywhere, I will move to Mississippi if the money is right." From that situation, I learned to be careful of what I allow my tongue to speak. While living in Jackson, Mississippi, I had to find some type of entertainment, so I took part in Casino gambling. At the time, I found Casino gambling to be very entertaining and very financially rewarding. I became very good at playing Blackjack. I became good at Blackjack because I saw something mathematical about it. Most of the time, I would walk into the Casino with two or three hundred dollars, and then I would walk out with a thousand or two. Until one night, I witnessed a gentleman with a stack of purple chips. Each one of the purple chips was worth five hundred dollars.

Once I observed the gentleman playing two hands simultaneously, I realized one could increase their risk but double their reward. I also realized playing two hands was one way of covering the bet on one of the two hands. Because if you win one hand and lose the other, no money is lost because one hand pays the other. As I watched the man playing two hands, I said to myself, "If I increase my betting and play two hands, I could win a lot more money because I am better than he is." I increase my betting, and instantly, I increase my winnings. I started gambling when I was in college, and I never truly lost. I was so accustomed to winning whenever I gambled.

Imagine this: I was a single man with no children I knew about who liked to party and gamble. And I had plenty of disposable income. This was a recipe for disaster! The year was 1996 when I went on a winning spree of $10,000.00, $15,000.00, and $50,000.00 playing Blackjack. I remember that night I went into the Casino with $300.00 and turned it into $50,000.00 playing Blackjack. That is almost mathematically impossible! But I did it! That night, I was in a zone where I made the right decision almost every time, and the cards fell in my favor. I walked out of the Casino with $50,000.00 cash. Once I reached home, I was so excited that I went and laid down in my bed with $50,000.00 scattered across the bed. But once I laid down in my bed, a feeling of complete emptiness came upon me. I went from an emotional high to feeling complete emptiness in a matter of seconds. I felt empty and lost!

I was twenty-five years old, lying in bed with $50,000.00 cash, and a feeling of emptiness overtook me. At the time, I didn't realize the Lord had already shown this to me when I was eighteen. Do you remember Chapter 35, titled, "A Twelve-Year Vision from the Lord Part 1"? Remember I told you how I was driving my mother's blue Corsica, and the Lord gave me a vision of the next twelve years of my life. One of the things the Lord said to me was, "At the age of 25, you will have more money than you know what to do with". The Lord then showed me lying in bed with thousands of dollars. So, everything the Lord had told me was coming true. I was twenty-five years old, lying in bed with $50,000.00. I was lying in bed with thousands of dollars and went from being on top of the world to feeling empty!

Some people would always say I was the luckiest person they ever knew. But this was not luck. This was a trap set by Satan! This was one of the reasons why Satan wanted to keep me from Sandra because if I had been with Sandra, I wouldn't have been living in Mississippi gambling. But I didn't know this at the time! I didn't know Satan was committed to destroying me! And he was going to use my gambling to do it!

After I had won the $50,000.00, I became greedy. I disregarded all the mathematical rules and guidelines I set to prevent me from losing in the Casino. The greed overtook me, and I became reckless! Once I disregarded my rules and strategy, I became a loser in the Casino! Instead of continuing my pattern of taking two or three hundred dollars into the Casino, I decided to take more money to win more!

I started taking two to three thousand into the Casino each trip! Then if I doubled my money, that was not good enough for me because I wanted more. Greed overtook me! Once I disobeyed my gambling rules, the Casinos didn't have to take my money because I gave it to them. I would sit at the Blackjack table and win $10,000.00 or more, and I would continue to gamble, trying to win more. I wouldn't stop until I lost the $10,000.00 back plus any money I had brought. On so many occasions, I would win $10,000.00 or $20,0000, and I would lose it right back to them the same night! To make a long story short, I was sinking fast. I was gambling fast and hard, and I was dropping thousands a day in the Casino. I lost more money in a week than most people make in two years! Because I was losing thousands a day in the Casino and once I started losing, I started to chase the money I lost. Chasing money is when a gambler is trying to recover his losses fast. Chasing money is when you have lost so much money you are trying to win it back in a hurry. The worst thing any gambler could do is to chase money!

It had gotten to a point that I lost all my winnings back to the Casino. My bank accounts were empty, and I maxed out all my credit cards, and I took money out of my business to gamble! I was losing it all, and I was losing it fast! By the age of twenty-six, I was dead broke. I lost all my winnings and then some. Just like the Lord told me and showed me when I was eighteen, "By the age of 26, you will be broke, and for the next few years, you will wonder the streets lost…" All the things the Lord had told me when I was eighteen years old were being manifested right before my eyes and I didn't even recognize it. At this point in my life, I didn't remember the Lord telling me and showing me these things when I was eighteen.

So, I eventually moved from Mississippi because I had lost it all! I was broke! So, the lifestyle of gambling and trying to win back what I had lost went on for several years. For the first time in my life, I didn't know which way to turn. There was no easy fix for my dilemma because I didn't like walking away a loser! I just couldn't walk away while I was down. My pride wouldn't let me. So, like I was saying, for the first time in my life, I didn't know which way to turn. My dad or mother couldn't help me. I was out there alone on an island by myself. For a man to lose money is no great tragedy, but when he abandons the foundation by which he was raised and believes, that is a great tragedy. I had run from God, and I had destroyed myself!

After I moved from Mississippi, I moved to Atlanta and got a job. Even though I was living in Atlanta, I still traveled to Mississippi on the weekends to gamble. I was still trying to recover all I had lost. See, I had this "no retreat, no surrender" attitude. And I had this belief that nothing could beat me! I thought I would eventually overtake the Casinos and win my money back, plus a lot more. I had a mindset that I could do anything. I thought I could will myself to do anything in life! Because all my life I had always willed myself to do different things. So, I saw the challenge of the Casinos to be no different. I continued to go to the Casinos, and I would win thousands of dollars! But then I would give it right back to them because my greed wouldn't let me stop when I got up on them! To be honest, I knew I was one of the best to ever play Blackjack, so I always pushed the envelope. My arrogance and greed always made me go for more because I knew I could turn sixty dollars into ten or twenty thousand dollars! But the downside was that I would lose it all back to them the same night! I did that on so many occasions!

I remember the year was 1997, and I was in Atlanta with my brother "W", and we were in his van talking. My brother "W" asked me, "Why don't you just quit gambling and just stop." At that very moment, I said to him, "I can't quit because it is like this is supposed to happen!" My brother looked at me like I was crazy and said, "What do you mean this is supposed to happen to you? Do you suppose to be throwing your life away gambling!!!" I told my brother, "I cannot explain it; it's like this is supposed to happen to me." My brother then looked at me like I was nuts!

You, the reader, must remember that I am not aware that everything the Lord showed me and told me when I was eighteen years old was being fulfilled. So, when I told my brother, "I can't quit because it's like this is supposed to happen." I was talking blind. This means the words came from my spirit, and I didn't know why those words came out of my mouth then. This also means once the Lord gave me that vision in 1989, everything the Lord showed me had to be fulfilled just the way the Lord showed it to me! I couldn't stop the chain of events! Do you understand what I just told you? Once the Lord gave me the vision in 1989, there was no way I could change the chain of events! Do you truly understand what I just said? Once the Lord gives you a vision of the future, there's no way you can alter the events in real life. Because the vision is a prophecy, every prophecy the Lord gives must be fulfilled!

So, from the age of twenty-six to twenty-nine, I wondered about the streets lost, and I was trying to regain all that I lost. I was not homeless; I was just lost! This only fulfilled the other part of the prophecy the Lord had given me, which was "by the age of 26 you will be broke, **and for the next few years you will wonder the streets lost**, then you will give your life to me, and I will turn your entire life around."

So, I continued to gamble and chase money for the next few years. I lost everything! I had to move back home with my mother, and I was working for a bank in Birmingham. Isn't that funny! Here I was, a big-time gambler, and I was working for a bank! Thank God I was an honest man when I worked for that bank! I guess that whooping my dad gave me when I was a child taught me not to steal!

So, one day, when I was twenty-nine years old, I was sitting in my car in front of my mother's house, and I was as low as any person could get emotionally. I was drained! I was mentally, physically, and spiritually exhausted. Then I remember repeating something my sister "J" said to me. I said, "I messed up my life before I even started my life." Then I reached into my glove compartment, grabbed my 9-millimeter gun, and placed it in my lap. Then, at that very moment, the Holy Father said to me, "Is this not what I showed you." Once God said those words to me, I didn't understand at first, so I said, "What?" Then the Holy Father said to me again, "Is this not what I showed you." Then, the Holy Father reminded me of the vision he gave me when I was eighteen years old.

After I compared my real-life events to the vision the Lord showed me and told me when I was eighteen. I noticed my real-life events matched the vision the Lord gave me when I was eighteen. And I was astonished! At that moment, I said, "Yes Lord, this is what you showed me." Then the Holy Father said, "Now give your life to me, and I will turn your entire life around." Once I heard the Holy Father speak those words, I knew everything would be all right! I had run from God, and I brought a great storm and catastrophe on myself, just like the Prophet Jonah brought a great storm and catastrophe on himself when he ran from God! Once the Prophet Jonah repented for running from God, God saved him. And once I repented, God saved me!

57. The Anatomy of Satan Part 4

In this chapter of The Anatomy of Satan, we are going to discuss how Satan tries to change, confuse, or steal our identity! When Satan doesn't have the authority to kill a person, Satan must attempt to steal one's identity to prevent that person from fulfilling his or her divine potential. If you noticed, I was having an identity crisis in high school, college, and after college! The reason I was having an identity crisis is because I was living a life that was contrary to the prophecy that was spoken over me as a child. I was running from God, and I didn't want to become a preacher because I thought I couldn't have any fun if I were a preacher.

Once Satan and his demons knew I was chosen to teach the word of God. Satan sent everything he had after me to destroy and kill me. But once his murder attempts failed, he had to come up with another way to destroy me. He ultimately tried to confuse my identity. The way Satan tried to confuse my identity was by manipulating me into his world.

Satan had been working on his plan of confusing my identity well before he gave me the thought. Satan's plan of confusing my identity started when he had people attack me daily, which started in elementary school. Amid that daily turmoil in elementary and high school, I had to adapt to my surroundings. And in that adaptation process I lost who I was. I had become a product of my environment, and I had gotten to the point where I couldn't separate my environment of fighting and partying from who I truly was. Amid the Chaos, Satan had done more than kill me or inflict harm on me. Satan had confused and stolen my identity. He had me to a point where I was my own worst enemy! And that was the purpose for creating a chaotic environment around me! Satan sent so many different people to attack me I couldn't process what was going on. Then, to top it off, Satan tempted me with the thought of not wanting to become a preacher because I wouldn't be able to have any fun if I became a preacher.

Satan had drawn me into his world without me truly recognizing what he had done because all the things I was doing were sinful things that represented Satan's kingdom. I was living a life full of sin. And I was glorifying that sin as though it was the greatest thing since sliced bread! If you remember, my life didn't start that way. My life started with hearing the Holy Father's and Lord Jesus Christ's voices. My life began with me talking to the Lord and the Lord talking back to me! But through the Chaos Satan presented to me in my life and through his temptation of money, women, parties, and alcohol. I had lost my identity of who I truly was and what God wanted me to do! God wanted me to teach his word. But I was doing things contrary to teaching God's word. I was doing things to purposely run from God so I could avoid teaching the word of God. I thought God wouldn't want me anymore if I continued to do all the things I was doing. But I was wrong because I truly didn't understand God's love, mercy, grace, and forgiveness of sins.

Satan had changed me; I was born and raised wanting to teach the word of God, but I was changed to a person who was running from God! Satan had managed to manipulate my identity! And through this identity crisis, you saw one person living two different lives. It was Ken Brown, who was a worldly man who did a lot of sinful things. Then, there was Kennedy K. Brown, who talked to God and conversed with God. And God revealed great things to Kennedy K. Brown. Only my mother had insight into Kennedy K. Brown. I hid Kennedy K. Brown from the world most of the time because the people I was hanging around with couldn't grasp Kennedy K. Brown. After all, Kennedy K. Brown was on a different thinking level than the average person. But the world could easily grasp Ken Brown because Ken Brown acted like them! Since I didn't fit in as a child, I manufactured this personality to fit into a worldly environment. And that personality was Ken Brown!

I was having an identity crisis! And Satan was trying to steal my identity of Kennedy K. Brown and make me be Ken Brown. Satan wanted my identity because the Heavenly Father and the Lord Jesus Christ had a great work for Kennedy K. Brown to do. After all, Kennedy K. Brown is the return of the Prophet Elisha! If Satan continued to confuse my identity, he would have done away with Kennedy K. Brown, and once he did away with Kennedy K. Brown, he would have also done away with the Prophet Elisha. Because Kennedy K. Brown and the Prophet Elisha are one and the same! When I was in high school and college, I told people Satan wanted my spirit! And I was right! Because Satan wanted my identity, which was my spirit of the Prophet Elisha! And if Satan can steal your identity, he has stolen your spirit! This is just another part of Satan's anatomy, which is to steal one's spirit by stealing one's identity!

Satan is attacking men and women to steal their identity! Are you displaying the identity the Holy Father and the Lord Jesus Christ bless you with? Or has Satan confused your identity so the world can never see the true you? The anatomy of Satan is to change, confuse, or steal your identity!

58. Transition From My Past To My Present In Christ

Once the Holy Father reminded me of the twelve-year prophecy, I realized everything the Holy Father showed me in the vision when I was eighteen had come true. So, from then on, I started focusing on the Lord. That night, I decided to stop running from the Lord. I began to attend the GL CHURCH. The Pastor taught the word like I had never heard it before. He was not a screaming and yelling Pastor; he brought an educational approach to teaching the word. I began to love this Pastor like no other. I mean, I truly loved this Pastor. I had so much love for him because of the way he was teaching the word. But the Lord warned me not to trust that Pastor. One day, the Lord came to me and said, "Don't put your trust in this Pastor or no other pastor. Put your trust in me!" The Lord warned me on many occasions not to put my trust in any pastor; the Lord wanted me to put my trust in him.

So, the more I attended GL Church, the more I began studying God's word. Before long, a thirst was in me that needed to be satisfied. That thirst was a desire to hear and study the word of the Lord. I have always gone to church and prayed, but now I was studying the word constantly; I was worshipping the Lord, praying with a spirit of humility and truth, and began to tithe faithfully. The final thing the Lord told me in the twelve-year vision started to be fulfilled: "...then you will give your life to me, and I will turn your entire life around." The Lord had my full attention for the first time in a long time.

From then on, a new era in my life was about to take place. My new era would be rooted in the word of the Lord and not myself. I started reading my Bible and searching for the Lord in his word. So, I began a quest to search for the absolute truth. I originally thought the truth could be found in the law. So, I went to Miles Law School. After spending a year in law school, I realized there was neither absolute truth nor justice in the law. Then, I realized I could only find the absolute truth in the Lord. Then, I decided to leave law school because law school couldn't give me what I longed for, which was the absolute truth. Once I decided to leave Miles Law School, the Lord said to me, "You will only need to be a Lawyer for one case anyway," then the Lord showed me standing in a courtroom before a judge in a divorce proceeding.

So, I searched for the Lord in prayer. The more I prayed to him, the more he revealed himself to me. Then I search for the Lord in his word. I started reading the Bible in the Book of Genesis Chapter 1 and read the entire way to the end of Revelations. I read to get knowledge, wisdom, and understanding of his word. I was not in a speed-reading contest; it was a very slow meditative process. I would ask the Lord to explain what he meant by many things I read, and then the Holy Spirit would counsel me personally. I didn't go to any man or woman for their explanation. I went directly to the source of all creation because he was the only one qualified to counsel me. I tried to obey the Lord's laws, decrees, and covenants. The more I tried to be obedient, the more he blessed me. Like I said earlier, the more I search for the Lord in his word, prayer, and obedience, the more he blessed me with his Holy Spirit. The more I search for the Lord the more he revealed himself to me.

Before I turned thirty years old, I noticed some powerful was taking place inside me. I was forming a true relationship with Christ. I remember I was at a weeklong revival at GL CHURCH. One day at this revival, I stood, prayed, and pleaded with the Lord to reveal himself to me. At that very moment, the Spirit of the Lord entered my lower chest area. I was instantly overwhelmed with joy, peace, and happiness. I had never experienced anything like it before! It was powerful; it was an entity filled with pure Love, Peace, Happiness, Grace, and Authority, and it was Holy. It was the purest and the sweetest thing I had ever felt. It was the Holy Spirit that entered me!

Once I received the Holy Spirit, my mind was renewed and transformed. See, my mind had to be renewed and transformed because my mind was like a computer hard drive. And my hard drive had crashed because I had received a bunch of viruses on it. Throughout my life, I have allowed a lot of garbage to enter my mind, which is my hard drive. Your mind stores all the images and conversations it hears! And if those images and conversations are sinful, they are viruses! Viruses entered my hard drive through people I associated with, television shows, movies, and music. These viruses had corrupted my mind which is my hard drive, and the viruses were trying to corrupt my operating system, which is my spirit! The only way I could get those viruses off my hard drive was to delete them. The only way to delete or purge a virus from my hard drive was to get some antivirus software. The Holy Spirit was the antivirus software that came in and swept my hard drive clean. Once the Holy Spirit purged the viruses from my hard drive, this caused my operating system, to perform properly. The Holy Spirit is to us what Norton's antivirus software is to your computer! We all need the word of God and the Holy Spirit because this world has been designed to crash our hard drive (our mind), so our operating system (our body and spirit) will conform to the pattern of this world, which is sin!

I had received the Holy Spirit, and the Holy Spirit was purging all the viruses from my hard drive and my operating system! My mind was being renewed, and I was being transformed from the patterns of this world, which meant I was turning away from sin! Once I received the Holy Spirit, the Holy Spirit began ministering the gospel to me daily.

Then one day, I was thinking about my life and the supernatural things that always happen to me. I started to put things together; I said, "The only people in the Bible that have the gifts that I have are Prophets." At that time, I never spoke that word from my mouth because, as far as I knew, the Lord hadn't declared me to be a Prophet! But he did, I just didn't remember. The Lord had told me years earlier I was Elisha! But I didn't remember. My thinking at the time was I couldn't declare myself to be a Prophet unless God had declared it.

So, just like the Prophet Jonah, I had gone through a Great Storm because I ran from God. And just like the Prophet Jonah, God had delivered me from the Great Storm I was in. And just like the Prophet Jonah, I will do God's will and teach his word!

59. One Night At The Club

The year is around 2000, and I am becoming a new creature in Christ. So, one night, I was at home, and I was bored. So, I decided it's nothing wrong with going to the Club for a little while. I decided to go to the French Quarters in downtown Birmingham. It was one of the hottest spots in Birmingham at the time. I went to the Club to just chill for a moment. I went to the Club, but I didn't have anything to drink before I went in, and I didn't have anything to drink once I got into the Club. This was very strange because I would always grab a beer or some cognac to sip on. But that night, I didn't drink anything.

After I had been in the Club for about ten minutes, I noticed this shadowy figure looming in the corner. As I adjusted my eyes to see what it was, I noticed this thing was not human. I saw the figure as plain as day, and it was some type of demonic spirit. I stood there in total shock and disbelief. I said, "Oh My God," as I watched this spirit float from out of the corner of darkness and move throughout the Club freely.

Then, I watched the spirit move towards a group of people. Then, I watched the demonic spirit enter the head of one person who was standing in the group. Then, as quickly as it entered that person's head, it exited that person's head. Then it entered another person's head, standing in the same group. Then it exited that person's head and entered another person's head. The spirit kept moving from person to person. To make a long story short, it went into about four or five people. The spirit was searching the mind of each individual, and it was searching for a home! Then it settled in this one lady who was standing in the group. Once it entered the lady, the lady went from laughing and joking to a total mood change of acting like all hell just broke loose. She started yelling and screaming at the people in her group. Everyone in her group looked at her like, "What in the world is wrong with you?" They also looked at her like, "What in the world got into you!"

The demonic spirit had to move from one person's head to the next person's head because it was searching the inner thoughts of that person. The demonic spirit was searching for a suitable home to dwell in. The demonic spirit had to find a person whose mind had been corrupted with sin, hurt, or pain. The unholy spirit exited the other people it entered because it didn't find a suitable living environment. The unholy spirit needed an environment with a certain amount of sin, hurt, and pain. The reason why it entered the head of everyone is because the head houses the mind (brain). And the brain is the gateway to one's soul. The demonic spirit must search the inner thoughts of one's mind first to see if its gates are open to one's soul. If one's mind has been corrupted, one's soul could be captured! If you capture a person's soul (the mind), you can capture their spirit. You must remember that man's composition is a three-part being. Man is body, soul, and spirit. This is told to us in 1 Thessalonians 5:23

1 Thessalonians 5:23 "Now may the God of peace Himself sanctify you completely; and may your whole **spirit**, **soul**, and **body** be preserved blameless at the coming of our Lord Jesus Christ." (NKJ, BibleGateway.com)

The soul consists of our mind, which houses our thoughts, emotions, and will. The soul (our mind) is a gateway to our spirit! Our spirit lies within our hearts! This is why the Lord warns you to guard your heart.

Proverbs 4:23 says, "Above all else, **guard your heart**, for everything you do flows from it." (NIV, BibleGateway.com)

In Proverbs 4:23, the Lord is telling you to guard your spirit. Corruption must first occur in your mind, which is your soul before it can ever reach your spirit, which is in your heart. The mind, your soul, is the gateway to the heart where your spirit dwells. If the mind is corrupted so one's spirit can be corrupted because the soul (the mind) empties its belief into the heart where your spirit dwells. So, if your mind, which is your soul, is corrupted with evil, your heart and spirit will soon follow. So listen to the Lord and **guard your heart.**

After I had witnessed the spirit enter different people, I was simply astonished. I immediately left the Club and wasn't right for the rest of the night. I had never seen anything like that before. I had seen three demon spirits control the actions of three children before. But I had never seen a spirit move from person to person. I had never seen a spirit enter a person before. And when I saw the spirit go in and out of each person so easily, I was so shocked. It was so easy for the spirit to enter and exit each person. And it controlled the actions of the woman so easily. It is a scary thought when you understand a spirit can easily enter you and then control your actions. This spirit I had seen in the Club was another example of what the Apostle Paul told us.

The Apostle Paul warns us that our war is not against each other (is not against flesh and blood), but our war is against the principalities in the heavenly realm, which is in the air. Our war is not against each other but against the evil spirits in the air that are manipulating our behavior.

Ephesians 6:12 reads, For our struggle is not against flesh and blood, but against the rulers, against the authorities, against the powers of this dark world and against the spiritual forces of evil in the heavenly realms. (NIV, BibleGateway.com)

The Apostle Paul recognized that demons in the air influence people's behavior. The phrase "...against the rulers, against the authorities, against the powers of this dark world and against the spiritual forces of evil in the heavenly realms" refers to demonic spirits in the air.

60. The Voice Is The Call

Since I was a child, I heard some Pastors say they were "called" by God to teach the word of God. They would always use the word "called". I knew what they were trying to say, but I didn't understand why they were using the word "called." Until one day, when I was in my twenties, I heard a pastor use the word "called" to describe why he was preaching the gospel. When this Pastor was preaching, he said something that grabbed my attention. The Pastor said, "If I tell you what the call is, you may want to declare that I am crazy and have me committed." After the Pastor said that, everyone in the congregation started laughing.

After I heard the Pastor make that statement, I realized whoever heard the voice of the Lord had been called. Then, I was able to make the connection that I had been "called." Then I thought about all the other Pastors who used the word "called" to describe them hearing the voice of the Lord. Then I thought to myself, "I can see why they use the term "called" because it sounds better than the words "hearing the voice". Because if you tell people you heard "the voice," they will think you are schizophrenic or something!

To clarify, the "Call" is hearing the voice of The Holy Father, the Lord Jesus Christ, or the Holy Spirit. To give you a more in-depth understanding of this, you must realize the Father, the Son, and the Holy Spirit are three distinct individuals. Each has a distinct voice and depending on who is speaking will determine how you physically hear them. Yes, I said the Father, the Son, and the Holy Spirit each have their own distinct voice. Pay close attention because I am about to teach you something very important. I am about to give you one of the secrets to the kingdom of Heaven. I am about to give you one of the hidden secrets to the kingdom of Heaven that Jesus spoke of in Matthew 13:11.

In Matthew 13:11, Jesus said, "The knowledge of the secrets of the kingdom of heaven has been given to you, but not to them..."

Let me explain that statement made by Jesus. The knowledge of the secrets of Heaven hasn't been given to everyone. Only the ones Christ has chosen to give this knowledge to can truly begin to understand it. The Lord Jesus Christ has permitted me to decode some of these secrets for you.

When I was about seven years old, I heard the voice of the Most High God Jehovah. In Chapter 8, titled "The Heavenly Father Speaks to Me," I told you how I was lying in my front yard, and then a voice with so much power and authority reigned down from Heaven and said, "I, the Lord Almighty, is out here." The voice I heard was the voice of the Holy Father, Jehovah. I heard the voice of the Holy Father Jehovah in both of my ears. The Holy Father's voice is filled with power and authority, which makes the entire ground tremble and make a thunderous roar. When the Holy Father spoke to me, I heard him say, "I, the Lord Almighty, is out here." But others only heard thunder. Others heard thunder because they were not allowed to hear the Holy Father's voice! They only heard thunder! This is proven in scripture when the Holy Father spoke to Jesus while others were present. When the Holy Father spoke to Jesus while others were present, some witnesses heard thunder, and some described hearing an angel's voice. But the voice was not an angel. The voice was the Holy Father, Jehovah. Let's look at John 12:28-29 to see what the scripture says.

John 12:28-29 reads, [28] "Father, glorify your name!" Then a voice came from Heaven, "I have glorified it, and will glorify it again." [29] The crowd that was there and heard it said it had thundered; others said an angel had spoken to him. (NIV, BibleGateway.com)

Now, you should ask yourself why some people heard thunder and others heard a voice. The answer is this, those who heard the voice of what they thought was an angel were approved by the Holy Father to hear the words the Holy Father Jehovah had spoken. Those people who heard thunder were not approved by the Holy Father to hear the words he had spoken. The voice that came from Heaven was the Holy Father, but some people thought it was the voice of an angel. We know it was the Holy Father because of the thunder they heard! What the Holy Father said was intended for Jesus and those meant to be witnesses. This is proven in John 12:30.

In John 12:30, Jesus said, [30] "This voice was for your benefit, not mine." (NIV, BibleGateway.com)

Jesus clearly stated the voice they heard was for their benefit and not his. This meant the Holy Father intentionally spoke so the approved ones could hear his voice, and those who were not approved only heard thunder. The approved ones were allowed to hear the Holy Father's voice so they could give their testimony to what they heard. The next question is who decides who is approved and who is not approved. The Holy Father and the Lord Jesus Christ determine who is approved and who is not approved.

When we hear thunder, we always assume it's from clouds. I once had that same belief. Until one day, an incident occurred, and it changed my entire perspective. One day, I was standing outside my sister's house in Forestdale with two young ladies. I was angry and upset with God. So I was directing my anger towards the Holy Father in Heaven, and the Holy Father almost wiped me off the face of the earth! I was upset and venting my frustration towards the Holy Father, and two times the Holy Father said to me, "Silence!" On the third time, the Holy Father said to me, "Silence, you better not say another word!" Each time the Holy Father spoke to me, his voice was so powerful his voice forced me to my knees, and I had to shield my face from his shout. I had to hold both of my hands over my face so I could shield my face from the shout of his voice because the power and authority of his voice forced me down to my knees. On each occasion, the two young ladies in my presence only heard thunder. They both looked up and saw there was not a cloud in the sky and no lightning, but they couldn't figure out why I was bending down, covering my face before the sound of thunder was heard! So you may fully understand what happened that day, I will go through the event step by step.

One day, two young ladies visited me at my sister's house in Forestdale. I was angry about something before the young ladies arrived. Once they got there, I was still angry and upset. While standing outside, I started venting my anger and frustration towards the Holy Father, Jehovah. Then, amid my venting, the Holy Father shouted at me and said, "Silence!" Upon hearing the shout of the Holy Father, the shout forced me to my knees, and the only thing I could do was to use my arms and hands to shield my face from his anger. Then, after I had been on my knees for about three to four seconds, the roar of thunder came. Once the roar of thunder came, the two girls looked to the sky, but there were no clouds. The girls couldn't understand why I went to my knees before the roar of thunder. I heard the Holy Father's shout before they heard the roar of thunder.

After the Holy Father in Heaven shouted at me the first time, I got up and started venting my anger and frustration at the Holy Father again. Then the Holy Father shouted at me again and said, "Silence!" Then, upon hearing the shout of the Holy Father, the shout forced me to my knees, and I had to raise my arms and hands to shield my face from his anger. Then, after I had been on my knees for about three to four seconds, the roar of thunder came. And again, the two girls I was with looked to the sky, but there were no clouds.

So, I got up off my knees and again began venting my anger and frustration towards the Holy Father. On this third time, the Holy Father shouted at me and said, "Silence, you better not say another word!!!" The Holy Father's shout of anger was so powerful it forced me to my knees for a third time. Then, I lifted my arms and hands to shield my face from his anger. Then, three to four seconds later, a roar of thunder came from above. Then, at that very moment, Jesus spoke to me in my left ear and said, "Be quiet and don't say another word!!!" At that moment, I realized how out of order I was, and I knew the Holy Father was about to take me off the face of the earth if one more word came out of my mouth. I instantly shut up! I thank Jesus for telling me to be quiet and not to say another word because I was out of order! And whatever the Holy Father would have done to me, I would have deserved it!

The two young ladies standing near me witnessed this but didn't understand what was happening. They kept looking around, trying to understand where the thunder was coming from because there was not a cloud in the sky, and there was no lightning. After they witnessed me venting my frustration towards the Holy Father, falling to my knees while covering my face with my arms and hands, and hearing a thunderous roar for the third time, they realized something was not right! They looked at me like, who are you? The young ladies then ran and jumped into their car and left. And to the best of my knowledge, I never saw them again!

When the Holy Father spoke, I heard, "Silence!" But to my knowledge, the two young ladies only heard thunder. Those not approved to hear the message when the Holy Father speaks will only hear thunder. And those who have been approved for the message will hear the Holy Father's voice. When the Holy Father speaks, you will always hear him in both ears, and his voice is filled with ultimate power and authority that makes the ground tremble! And those who are not approved to hear the message only hear thunder!

Then, there is the voice of the Lord Jesus Christ. Jesus Christ's voice is a humbling tone that is firm and filled with power and authority. Jesus has the voice of a friend! Whenever I heard the voice of Jesus Christ, the Holy Spirit, and the Angels, it was always in my left ear. On most occasions, Jesus has spoken to me; it has always been in my left ear. Jesus' voice is that of a friend!

Then there is the voice of the Holy Spirit. The Holy Spirit always speaks into your left ear with a whisper. I mean, the Holy Spirit always whispers into my left ear. In Matthew 10:27, Jesus tells you how the Holy Spirit will whisper into your ear!

In Matthew 10:27, Jesus said, [27] "What I tell you in the dark, speak in the daylight; what is whispered in your ear, proclaim from the roofs." (NIV, BibleGateway.com)

When the Holy Spirit speaks to you, it whispers into your left ear! No matter what is spoken by Jesus, the Holy Spirit, or Angels, your Spirit always recognizes it as the absolute truth. Jesus tells us about the Holy Spirit coming to us in John 16:7. The Counselor that Jesus speaks of in John 16:7 is the Holy Spirit.

In John 16:7, Jesus said, [7] "But I tell you the truth: It is for good that I am going away. Unless I go away, the Counselor will not come to you; but if I go, I will send him to you." (NIV, BibleGateway.com)

In John 16:12-15 Jesus said, [12] "I have much more to say to you, more than you can now bear. [13] But when he, the Spirit of truth, comes, he will guide you into all the truth. He will not speak on his own; he will speak only what he hears, and he will tell you what is yet to come. [14] He will glorify me because it is from me that he will receive what he will make known to you. [15] All that belongs to the Father is mine. That is why I said the Spirit will receive from me what he will make known to you." (NIV, BibleGateway.com)

If you notice, Jesus referred to the Holy Spirit as the Spirit of Truth in verse 13. Also, in verse 13, Jesus tells you the Holy Spirit will guide you in all truths and that he (the Holy Spirit) will not speak on his own, but he (the Holy Spirit) will only speak what he hears, and he will tell you what is yet to come. "Yet to come" means the Holy Spirit will reveal future events to you before the event occurs. Do you remember Chapter 29 titled, "I Ignored The Warnings of the Holy Spirit"? In that chapter,

I told you how I ignored the warnings of the Holy Spirit. The Holy Spirit warned me that something bad would happen to Rodney Johnson if I didn't pick him up. I decided not to pick Rodney up, and then, later that night, Rodney Johnson died. Well, the Holy Spirit told me something that was "yet to come," which means the Holy Spirit told me something bad would happen to Rodney Johnson before it happened to Rodney. The Holy Spirit revealed to me a future event.

In John 16:13, Jesus said, [13] "But when he, the Spirit of truth, comes, he will guide you into all the truth. He will not speak on his own; he will speak only what he hears, and he will tell you what is yet to come." (NIV, BibleGateway.com)

Jesus was telling you the Holy Spirit will reveal future events to you. Once these future events are revealed to you by the Holy Spirit, it becomes a prophecy! Information about the future is revealed to Prophets by the Holy Father, Jesus Christ, the Holy Spirit, or angels. Once Prophets receive this information, they tell it to others, and then it becomes a prophecy! But the information of a future event must come from the Holy Father, Jesus Christ, the Holy Spirit, or angels for it to be a prophesy. And no matter what is revealed to you by them, it will always come true!

Let me show you another prophecy (future event) the Holy Spirit revealed to me. Do you remember Chapter 51 titled, "The Prophesy of Derivatives and Stock Market Crash"? In that chapter, the Holy Spirit told me Derivatives would cause the stop market to crash. Once the Holy Spirit spoke those words to me, the Holy Spirit warned me of a future event that was "yet to come". That means the Holy Spirit gave me a prophecy that Mortgage Derivatives would crash the stock markets! And just like the Holy Spirit said, Mortgage Derivatives were going to cause the stock market to crash; the stock market crashed because of Mortgage Derivatives. In 2008 and 2009, the stock market crashed because of Mortgage Derivatives. I know the government and the media lied to you about why the stock market crashed in 2008, but I am here to tell you the truth. The stock market crashed because the formula for Mortgage Derivatives was designed to crash the stock market. This will be talked about in the chapters to come. Just continue to read!

I just gave you two scenarios of how the Holy Spirit told me things that would happen before they happened, but there would be many other prophesies given to me by the Lord Jesus Christ, the Holy Spirit, and angels that would come true. The Holy Spirit speaks to you in a soft whisper voice into your left ear.

In Matthew 10:27, Jesus said, [27] "What I tell you in the dark, speak in the daylight; what is whispered in your ear, proclaim from the roofs." (NIV, BibleGateway.com)

Then Jesus said something else that was very important in the scripture. Did you notice how Jesus used the word ear in "singular form" and not plural form in Matthew 10:27. Ear means one, and ears mean more than one. Jesus let you know that the Holy Spirit and angels will speak to you only in one ear! That's why Jesus said, "…what is whispered in your ear…" The ear is singular, meaning one. The scripture tells us the Holy Spirit whispers into your ear. Now, we must determine which ear the Lord Jesus Christ, the Holy Spirit, or Angels speaks in. The Bible tells us what ear, but it is coded so only those who were meant to have this knowledge could understand it. In the next chapter, I will reveal to you why the voice of Jesus, the Holy Spirit, and Angels speak to you in your left ear.

61. My Sheep to My Right; Goats To My Left

I know you have been asking yourself why Jesus, the Holy Spirit, and angels only speak to people in their left ear. To understand why Jesus, the Holy Spirit, and angels only speak into my left ear, we must first fully understand where Christ's place is in Heaven. I will give you scriptures that show you where Jesus Christ's place is in Heaven.

In Luke 22:69, Jesus said, [69] "But from now on, the Son of Man will be seated at the right hand of the mighty God." (NIV, BibleGateway.com)

The term Son of Man " refers to Jesus Christ. So, when you see the Son of Man, it's talking about Jesus Christ.

Then, in Luke 20:42-43, Jesus said, [42] "David himself declares in The Book of Psalms: "The Lord said to my Lord: Sit at my right hand [43] until I make your enemies a footstool for your feet." (NIV, BibleGateway.com)

Then Acts 7:55-56 reads, [55] "But Stephen, full of the Holy Spirit, looked up to Heaven and saw the glory of God, and Jesus standing at the right hand of God. [56] "Look," he said, "I see heaven open and the Son of Man standing at the right hand of God." (NIV, BibleGateway.com)

Acts 2:32-34 [32] God has raised this Jesus to life, and we are all witnesses of it. [33] Exalted to the right hand of God, he has received from the Father the promised Holy Spirit and has poured out what you now see and hear. ³⁴ For David did not ascend to Heaven, and yet he said, "'The Lord said to my Lord: "Sit at my right hand..." (NIV, BibleGateway.com).

All the scriptures I just gave you refer to Jesus sitting or standing to the right hand of the Holy Father. Now, since we all understand Jesus' place in Heaven is to sit at the right hand of the Holy Father. I need you to visualize something in your mind. The Holy Father sits in Heaven, and Jesus sits at the right hand of the Holy Father. This means Jesus's left hand is next to the Holy Father's right hand. This also means Jesus' left ear is next to the Holy Father. So, when the Holy Father turns to speak to Jesus. What ear does Jesus hear the Holy Father speaking in? The answer is the left ear. Since Jesus's left ear is closer to the Holy Father, Jesus hears the Holy Father speaking to him in his left ear.

Since we understand where Jesus is in Heaven, let's see where our place is in Heaven. So we can understand why I hear Jesus speaking to me in my left ear. We must examine more scriptures spoken by Jesus for me to prove Jesus speaks to me in my left ear. In Chapter 25 of the Book of Matthew, Jesus talks about the sheep and the goats. The sheep represent the servants of Christ (me and you), and the goats represent those who are not the servants of Christ. The goats are those people who belong to the devil (Satan).

In Matthew 25:31-33, Jesus said, ³¹ "When the Son of Man comes in his glory, and all the angels with him, he will sit on his glorious throne. ³² All the nations will be gathered before him, and he will separate the people one from another as a shepherd separates the sheep from the goats. ³³ He will put the sheep on his right and the goats on his left."

Then, in verse 41, Jesus continues by saying, ⁴¹ "Then he say to those on his left, 'Depart from me, you who are cursed, into the eternal fire prepared for the devil and his angels…"

If you notice, Jesus placed his sheep on his right (Christ's servants) and the goats on his left (servants of the devil). In verse 41, Jesus told us that those to his left, the goats, would be cast into the eternal fire prepared for the devil and his angels.

Since it is clear to you, the sheep are the blessed ones to the right of Jesus, and the goats are the cursed ones to the left of Jesus. All we have to do is visualize the two groups of people to see their physical position once they are separated. So, imagine we are in a crowd facing Jesus, and then Jesus picks us on his team as his sheep. Then Jesus tells us sheep to move to his right; now we are on Jesus' right-hand side. When the sheep moves to Jesus' right-hand side, we are no longer facing Jesus. We are instead on Jesus' right-hand side. Once we are placed to Jesus's right, our left hand and the left ear are closer to Jesus. Just like Jesus's left hand and left ear are closer to the Holy Father because Jesus sits to the right hand of the Holy Father. This same principle applies to us in scripture when Jesus puts his sheep to his right.

Since the servants of Christ are to the right of Jesus that means our left hand is next to Jesus right hand. This also means when Jesus speaks to us, he would speak into our left ear. So, when the Holy Spirit is sent to us from Jesus, the Holy Spirit will be speaking into our left ear. Some may say that the scripture talks about the Day of Judgment when Jesus will place us to his right, and that day has not yet come. So how can I say Jesus already speaks to us as though we are already on his right? I will tell you the absolute truth to those who ask this question. The scriptures have already told us that the chosen ones names already appeared in the Book of Life since the creation of the world. This means the names of those who are the true children of the Lord were written in the Book of Life before the world was ever created. So, the Holy Father and Jesus Christ already know who will accept them! Wow! So those who will accept the Most High God, Jehovah, and the Lord Jesus Christ are already known to God and Jesus.

Now, to give you more wisdom than you can bear, I must give you the flip side of this. Whatever is spoken to you in your right ear will always violate the word of God and is of Satan, his demons, and the abomination that will cause desolation. I will teach you about the abomination that causes desolation in future chapters. But if you don't know the word of God or the voice of the Lord, you won't realize what was spoken to you in your right ear was from Satan. Remember what Jesus just said in scripture.

Matthew 25:41 Jesus said, [41] "Then he say to those on his left, 'Depart from me, you who are cursed, into the eternal fire prepared for the devil and his angels..." (NIV, BibleGateway.com)

Since our left ear is reserved for Jesus Christ, the Holy Spirit, and Angels, that means the only ear Satan is allowed to come to us is our right ear. I have heard the voice of the Holy Father, the Son Jesus Christ, the Holy Spirit, and the voices of Angels. So, I know I have been called. To every pastor out there, I must ask you the question. Have you been called by the Most High God Jehovah, or the Lord Jesus Christ, or did you just go on your own? You can't just decide you want to teach the word of God and just become a pastor, apostle, teacher, evangelist, or Prophet. You must be called by the Most High God Jehovah or the Lord Jesus Christ, to be a pastor, apostle, teacher, evangelist, or Prophet! And please don't try to be a pastor, apostle, teacher, evangelist, or Prophet because you feel like that's what you should do, because Satan gives people feelings to enter the ministry so they can mislead the Lord's people by teaching them false doctrine or by having them drink Kool-Aid with cyanide in it! You must be called by the Most High God Jehovah, to teach his word!

62. George W. Bush Prophesy

I remember the year was 2000; well before the presidential election, I told my mother and everyone else who would listen that no matter what it took, George W. Bush was going to be President. I said, "Even if they had to steal the election, George W. Bush had to be the next President." I said this long before election day. We all know what happened during the election. I felt in my spirit they had to have George W. Bush as President instead of Al Gore. But the question is why? I didn't see the play the Illuminati was making at the time, but it was a chess move. So why did George W. Bush have to become President? Just to let you know. The Illuminati like to play games! For the Illuminati to get their chosen one into the Presidency, the Illuminati had to sacrifice one of their pieces to clear the way for his successor. George W. Bush was the piece that was sacrificed before the American people and the world during his time as President to clear the way for his successor. The Illuminati needed President George W. Bush to play the role of an idiot. So, his successor would look that much smarter and greater! So, his successor could look like a great savior!

63. My Eyes Were Open

I had searched for the Lord in prayer, worship, and his word. Then, one day, I was at a summer revival giving the Lord total praise, and the Holy Spirit entered me. Once the Holy Spirit entered me, its divine presence began to transcend me. From that point on, I wanted to seek out God's face. I wanted to know everything about him, and I wanted to know what he knew. I searched for him in prayer; I searched for him in his word (The Bible). The more I searched for him, the more he revealed himself to me. With the Spirit of the Lord in me, I began to search the mind of the Most High God Jehovah. Once I received the Holy Spirit, I wanted to know what God knew, so I was given access to the mind of God. To understand what I just said, you must read 1 Corinthians 2:10-11. In 1 Corinthians 2:10-11, the Apostle Paul expressed the same thing.

1 Corinthians 2:10-11 reads, [10] "these are the things God has revealed to us by his Spirit. The Spirit searches all things, even the deep things of God. [11] For who knows a person's thoughts except their own Spirit within them? In the same way no one knows the thoughts of God except the Spirit of God. (NIV, BibleGateway.com)

So once the Holy Spirit had entered me, I had free access to search the mind of God. And I was searching!!! It was about 2001 when the Holy Spirit made my Spirit become uneased with this world. Since I was a child, my Spirit sensed something was not right about this world. But now, the Holy Spirit wouldn't allow my Spirit to rest; I kept having this overwhelming feeling something was not right about this world. I had this overwhelming feeling this world was not what it appeared to be!

One day, while driving my car on Highway 280 in Birmingham, I felt something wasn't right about this world. So, at that very moment, I said, "Lord, remove the blinders from my eyes so I may see the absolute truth. Lord, remove the blinders from my eyes so I may see the absolute truth. Lord, remove the chains of bondage from my mind so I may be able to perceive the truth. Lord, let me see this world for what it truly is."

At that very moment, I felt this band of bondage being released from my head. I felt this band around my head being removed. The band that was around my head had been placed there by Satan to keep me from knowing and seeing the truth about this world. Once the band was removed, the Lord downloaded my mind with so much information. The Lord downloaded my mind with information just like you download your computer with a new software program or you download your smartphone with an app. That's how fast the Lord gave me knowledge, wisdom and understanding of this world and this system we live in and understanding the designers of this system we live in. I saw the system we live in and for what purpose it was truly designed for! Then the Lord spoke to me and said, "This world is an illusion that was built on a lie!" At that moment, the Lord freed me, and I saw this world for what it truly is! The Lord opened my eyes so I could see this world was nothing more than an **illusion**! An illusion! An illusion! An illusion that appears to be real and feels real! And the Lord showed me this system we live in was designed and built on a lie! That's what the Lord showed me and told me! My eyes were opened to the absolute truth for the first time! I was freed from the Matrix! I was freed from this world of bondage and disillusionment! I was freed from the Matrix! The Matrix!

2 Corinthians 3:17 reads, [17] "Now the Lord is the Spirit, and where the Spirit of the Lord is, there is freedom." (NIV, BibleGateway.com)

So that day, the Lord freed me and downloaded my mind with so much information. God woke me up from the Matrix! God woke me up from a sleepwalking state of mind and revealed everything I thought I knew about this world was a lie!!!! What if you knew the controllers of the system you live in have been manipulating you, your family, and your friends since you were born into this world? Could you handle the truth if your mind and eyes were open? Could you handle the truth if the designers of this world was not from this planet. Could your mind handle knowing they purposely taught you a false history of mankind to cover up the truth? Could you handle the truth of knowing who really controls many world governments. Could your mind handle knowing you were born into a three dimensional system that teaches you what they want you to know and programs you with their vision through television and the News Media? What if you realize they told you what to think through their vision machine, television, and the News Media? Could you handle the truth? What if you woke up and realized they wanted to keep people distracted by dividing people based on race, gender, social status, economic status, and political affiliation? Could you handle the truth?

Could you handle knowing the Illuminati overload your minds with useless information day in and day out with the hopes you won't ever desire to wake up and search for the absolute truth? You must understand that you did not create this worldly system! Nor was this system created by your mother, father, or grandparents. They were born slaves into this system, just like you! And the word slave is not used to reference any ethnic group. It is used to reference society as a whole! You were born as a slave into this worldly system (Matrix), and you only know what they taught you! They have raised you since childhood to become a conforming adult. You are their cattle and sheep people. You are their labor force! Like all cattle or sheep, you must be raised and fed until it's time to be slaughtered. And this generation is being led to the greatest slaughter mankind has ever seen!!! I tell you the absolute truth: this generation that walks the face of this earth was raised to take part in the greatest massacre the world has ever seen!! If you think I am exaggerating, I am not!

The Lord revealed this to me that day while driving in my car. The Lord instantly downloaded my mind with this knowledge, wisdom, and understanding. So, you may understand all the Lord has revealed to me. I must give you this information in pieces. Because if I told you everything right now, you couldn't handle the truth! I must give this information to you in stages! This is the only way your minds will not be overloaded! But first, I must reveal to you the designers of this system you live in. The front men for the designers of this system are the Illuminati! The same people that tried to recruit me in college! Front men are used so you want see who is really orchestrating things from behind the curtain. Welcome to the Matrix!

64. The Very Old But New Religion "Illuminati"

The day the Lord freed me and downloaded my mind with so much information is the same day the Lord connected all the dots for me and made sense of the group, the Illuminati, and their agenda! I was astonished once the Lord revealed all these things about the Illuminati to me! If you remember, the Illuminati sent recruiters after me when I was in college at JSU. The Illuminati is a religion that predates the birth of Jesus Christ and predates the Tower of Babel! But the common lie that is told is that the Illuminati was founded on May 1, 1776, by a man named Adam Weishaupt in Bavaria. That is not true! The Illuminati dates back thousands of years and predates the Tower of Babel. The Illuminati predates the Flood of Noah!

The Illuminati is a Luciferin religion that worships Satan as a god! But this religion is not spoken of publicly! It is a secret society that has millions and millions of members. Every member is sworn to secrecy, and they never let outsiders know they are members of the Illuminati! It's a secret that each member keeps as though his or her lives depend on it because their lives do depend on it! Any member who divulges any information about the group to any outsiders receives a death sentence, which is normally done in some type of public or private execution!

If you allow someone to tell you the Illuminati don't exist, and you believe them. You are the biggest fool to walk the face of this earth! The Illuminati wants you to think they are just another "Conspiracy Theory" because if you can't conceive the thought of their existence, the more likely their plans will succeed. Because if you don't think the Illuminati exist, then you will never try to stop their plans! So not only do they exist, but they have seized control over the world and its system. They are the front men for the controllers and designers of this system, this modern-day society you live in. This is partly what the Lord opened my eyes to see that day when he downloaded my mind with so much information!

The Illuminati is a well-organized cult, crime syndicate, and terrorist organization that is responsible for the trillions of dollars of America's national debt, responsible for wars, genocides, abortion laws, drug trafficking, assassination, political corruption, sex trafficking, Satanic sacrifices, the spreading of homosexuality, promoting gay marriage, promoting transgender movement, promoting the disarmament of the American people, the lies the news media tells you, and many other things.

The Illuminati believe Satan created man. The Illuminati believe Satan is an alien name Ea and that he created man. The Illuminati believe Satan gave man wisdom to gain knowledge and understanding when he convinced Eve to eat from the Tree of Knowledge of good and evil. The Illuminati believe Satan created man and freedman when he opened their eyes and gave man knowledge of good and evil. The Illuminati was originally called "The Brotherhood of the Snake". And through the years the name Illuminati was adopted. The Brotherhood of the Snake is now a department's name in the Illuminati Corporation. There is a lot to know about this cult, crime syndicate, and terrorist organization, but the only way to understand this organization is to start from the point I was introduced to the word Illuminati and then work our way forward. This way, you can get a precise understanding of this cult and crime syndicate and how they operate, and then we can understand their agenda.

So, follow me as I walk you through their recruitment process and explain their beliefs. For you to clearly understand the Illuminati, I have placed my previous encounters with the Illuminati into this chapter. Then, I will systematically show you their recruitment process in conjunction with real-life events that happened to me. This will give you an accurate visualization of how they choose the people they recruit into their organization. But I must remind you that this is only the recruitment process of the Illuminati. People who are part of the Illuminati are not just recruited into the Illuminati. Some are also born into the organization. Those born into the Illuminati are part of 13 original families of the Illuminati. These 13 original families go as far back as Babylon and Nimrod. The 13 original families are said to be the direct bloodline of Nimrod and the Reptilians. Trust me, I am not making this stuff up. The truth can be stranger than fiction!

To understand the 13 families of the Illuminati, you must be able to understand the 12 Tribes of Israel. The 12 Tribes of Israel were comprised of the 12 sons of Jacob. Jacob was a man of God, and God changed Jacob's name from Jacob to Israel. When Jacob had 12 sons, they became the 12 Tribes of Israel, which makes up the nation of Israel. Each son makes up a Tribe. The 12 sons of Israel that make up the 12 Tribes of Israel are Reuben, Simeon, Levi, Judah, Zebulun, Issachar, Dan, Gad, Asher, Naphtali, Joseph, and Benjamin. Those are the 12 Tribes of Israel; this is where the nation of Israel originated. This is how the Most High God, Jehovah, sent his word into this world through the 12 Tribes of Israel. And because God used the 12 Tribes of Israel to send his word through them, God called Israel his chosen people.

Well, Satan did the same thing God did by comprising the 13 tribes of the Illuminati. And these 13 tribes of the Illuminati are comprised of 13 families of the Illuminati. The names of the 13 families of the Illuminati are Bauer (Rothschild's, Orsini), Bruce, Cavendish, De Medici, Hanover, Hapsburg, Krupp, Plantagenet, Rockefeller, Romanov, Sinclair (St. Clair), Warburg, and Windsor. Those are the 13 Families of the Illuminati! Those 13 families control over five hundred trillion dollars of the world's money. Satan is using the 13 families of the Illuminati to send his so-called word to this world. And Satan's word is an anti-Jesus Christ message. Satan used the 13 Families of the Illuminati to recruit others and grow an army, just like God used the 12 tribes of Israel to grow his Christian army. Some Illuminati people are born into the Illuminati through the 13 families, and most are recruited into the organization. The Illuminati that were born into the Illuminati are always at the very top of the Illuminati, and those who are recruited are mere foot soldiers for the 13 families of the Illuminati.

The Illuminati start their recruitment process by giving students in the third grade a test through a viewing machine. The Illuminati will send people around to all the elementary schools in the United States and other countries to test children in the third grade. The people giving the test are members of the Illuminati. The people taking the test are permitted to do the test by the state or federal government. Many teachers don't know why the children are being tested with a visual test or what is shown to the students. The permission to test the kids in the third grade couldn't be done on a local school district level, which means permission comes directly from the state or federal level. This means the Illuminati are in key positions in the State or Federal Government to ensure the children are tested. The test may be a condition for receiving State or Federal money for education!

I was given the test in either 1979 or 1980; the person giving the test used a visual machine to show me many different pictures. Today, they still use a visual machine to test the kids. The pictures have words hidden in them. In one picture, the word "Illuminati" is hidden in the steganography and ambigram. Suppose the child makes out the word Illuminati hidden in the steganography. In that case, that child is flagged by the Illuminati as being "Gifted". Once the child has been flagged as being "Gifted", the child is tracked through high school, college, the military, or the job force. They then track this person until it's time to recruit them. How do I know this? I know these things because I was given this same test in the third grade. The Illuminati marked me as being "Gifted" in the third grade. Then, I was recruited by the Illuminati while I was in college at JSU.

Now, if you want to go back and read Chapter 16, titled "A Word Hidden In a Picture," that will tell you the entire story of my being tested in the third grade when I saw the steganography of the word Illuminati. And once I saw the word Illuminati in the steganography, the lady giving me the test labeled me "Gifted". Then, within a few days, that same white lady was at my house trying to convince my mom I needed to go to a special school out of state for very smart kids. The lady said the school I would be attending is the same school many Presidents of the United States, Senators, and other high-ranking government officials have attended. I want you to take notice of what the lady told my mom. She said I would be attending the same school many Presidents of the United States, Senators, and other high-ranking government officials have attended. This means these politicians and high-ranking government officials went to the same Elementary and High Schools. So, they all were Illuminati members who were raised in the same school or school system. They all knew each other. Wow!

So, I was labeled as Gifted after I saw the word Illuminati hidden in the steganography. And then the world was being offered to me on a silver platter by this lady! As I was writing this book, I had many questions for the Lord. I asked the Lord, "Was there anyone else from Birmingham, Alabama, who was labeled as Gifted and they were sent off to a special school as a child?" The Lord answered my question and said, "Yes!" And then I asked the Lord, "Who?" And then the Lord said to me, "Secretary of State Condoleezza Rice!" Once the Lord said that to me, I was astonished! I then remembered how they said Condoleezza Rice was gifted and had to attend this special school. It was no coincidence Condoleezza Rice was labeled as Gifted; she went to this special school and became Secretary of State for the United States of America! All of this happened to her because she became a member of the Illuminati. Now, if you don't remember, the things I talked about in Chapter 16 titled, "A Word Hidden In a Picture"! I want you to stop and go back and read Chapter 16 because I want you to clearly understand what I am about to share with you! But if you do remember, let's continue.

After I saw the word Illuminati hidden in the steganography in the third grade, I immediately forgot all about it until my high school girlfriend showed me the steganography with the word Illuminati hidden in it. Once she showed me that steganography, I remember seeing it somewhere. For the next several days I tried to remember where I saw the steganography of the word Illuminati. It was at that point I realized I saw the steganography of the word Illuminati when I was tested in the third grade.

This is the Illuminati recruitment process in stages. The first stage is to test the children so they may identify all the children that are "Gifted". The Illuminati sends in a person who is a member of the Illuminati to test the children while they are young for a few reasons. The Illuminati think if a child can make out the word Illuminati in a steganography, then that child must have a very high IQ. The Illuminati knows if a person doesn't have a very high IQ, then they will never see the word Illuminati in the steganography. Only a child with an extremely high IQ could decipher the steganography at a young age! The Illuminati steganography looks like a picture or artwork to the average person.

They test children so young because it prevents a child from being trained to see the words hidden in the steganography. The Illuminate tests the kids before they are trained and taught those things so they can see who was naturally born with higher intelligence. The third reason why they test the children so young is so no one would be able to figure out how the Illuminati chose the people they recruited in college. By the time the recruitment process starts in college, no one remembers the visual test they were given in the third grade. This makes it hard for anyone to make the connection of how he or she was truly chosen for the recruitment process. I probably would have forgotten if my high school girlfriend hadn't shown me the steganography of the word Illuminati. Once she showed me the steganography of the word Illuminati, it sparked my memory of seeing the word in the third grade. All things work to the good of God's glory!

Another reason they test kids so young is so they can raise these kids in programs and label them as "Gifted!" This makes the child and the child's parents feel special when the child has been labeled as "Gifted!" The Illuminati mark all the children who identify the word Illuminati in the third grade as having a very high IQ and are labeled as "Gifted"! Why do they want children or people with a high IQ? The Illuminati want those people with high IQs because they believe Satan has enlightened them, and they are more intelligent people in our country and the world. The Illuminati want people with high IQs or Gifted people because they believe if they can keep all the people in the world with high IQs "together under one cause," then they (the Illuminati) can rule over the rest of the population like a herd of cattle or like a herd of sheep (you).

This ideology is known as the Luciferian ideology. The Luciferian ideology states that those with superior intelligence have the right to rule over those people who are less intelligent or average because people who are average or less intelligent don't know what is best for them, so those with higher intelligence should rule over them. The Luciferian ideology is better known as totalitarianism. They told you about this on television, but you didn't understand what they were saying. Based on this belief, the Illuminati have implemented a system of control over you and the rest of the world! Without you even knowing! The news media is part of this system of control. The news media tells you what to think! The television is used as a delivery system to the masses to dumb down society and to control society!

When I was tested in the third grade, which was the year 1979 or 1980, my school had no gifted program. That's why the white lady came to my house and tried to convince my mom I should be sent off to this school for Gifted children; to the best of my knowledge, they didn't have any special program in Birmingham for Gifted Children at that time. But some years later, they developed a Gifted program for all those children who were tested and saw the word Illuminati in the picture.

In Birmingham, they label the child as "Gifted" and make them part of the "GATE" program. GATE stands for Gifted and Talented

Education. The program may go by a different name in your city, state, or country, but it is the same program. The Illuminati are the GATEKEEPERS! They determine who gets into power and who doesn't! You heard the term GATEKEEPERS on television. When they mention the term GATEKEEPERS, they are referring to the Illuminati! See the GATEKEEPERS determine who becomes President of the United States and who doesn't!

The Gifted program in Birmingham is called "GATE". When they developed the "Gifted Program", they set up phase two of their recruitment process. Phase two of the process is designed to make the children and the parents of the children in the "Gifted Program" feel special. The children and the parents of the children feel special because the child was labeled with a word, and that word is "Gifted!" Then phase two of the recruitment process also allows the Illuminati to have access to your children once a week or more in a controlled environment.

Once a week or more, members of the Illuminati pick your children up from school and isolate them at their facilities. Now, the school systems have become part of these programs without knowing what the programs were truly designed for. The school system probably receives money from the federal, state, or local government if they allow these programs to exist. This means every school system in the U.S. would agree to have these "Gifted Programs" to receive more money from the state and federal government. The only thing the local school systems see and understand is more money for education. So, these children who have been labeled as "Gifted" are brought through these "Gifted Programs" year after year and are groomed to be recruited into the Illuminati.

Once children have been labeled as "Gifted" and enter the gifted program named GATE, they meet other children in the "Gifted Program" year after year until the members of the "Gifted Program" become like a tight family. It is very important to the Illuminati that all the children of the "Gifted Program" become close like a tight family. This is one of the primary reasons the Illuminati developed a gifted program.

So, the parents are proud their child was labeled as "Gifted", so in return, the parents turn their child over to the Illuminati with little to no questions asked. Wow! What a psyche job they did on you people! The only thing the Illuminati had to do to get you to turn your child over to them was to use one simple word, which is "Gifted". Then, once they labeled your child as "Gifted," you turned your child over to them. Now, your children who have been labeled as "Gifted" are no longer your children; they now belong to the Illuminati! Don't get upset with me; you are the ones who turned your children over to them because they labeled your child Gifted. I thank the Lord my dad and mom had enough wisdom not to send me off to school with that lady who labeled me as Gifted when I was in the third grade. Also, the lady who labeled me as Gifted got very aggressive with my mom and threatened to have me taken away from my mom and dad when my mom consistently told the lady no! This will show you the lengths they will go to take control over your child!

Once a child has been raised with this mindset, they are "Gifted." Years later, the Illuminati can exploit that mindset in their recruitment process by telling the recruits only a few Gifted people can join their organization. Using the word "Gifted" to describe them makes the individuals feel special.

Phase one of the Illuminati recruitment process has been completed by testing the kids in the third grade to see which of them are gifted. Then phase two was implemented when they created "Gifted Programs" throughout the U.S. school system and other parts of the world. After that, they recruited the child they labeled as Gifted. This is phase three of the recruitment process. They recruited me at Jacksonville State University in this phase of the recruitment process. That's when they sent the three recruiters and the Director of Financial Aid to recruit me. You can read Chapter 49, titled "Approached By The Illuminati. "It tells how the Illuminati tried to recruit me.

So, while the Gifted children were in college, they were recruited into the Illuminati. The recruits are first told only highly intelligent people, and the Gifted can be a part of their organization. Your child's mindset of being highly intelligent and Gifted has been bred into your child since the third grade. When the Illuminati recruit them, the Illuminati must do very little to persuade them to join because your child was raised and brainwashed with the mindset of "I am superior to others since I am Gifted!"

In the recruitment process, they were told of all the financial rewards and benefits they would receive if they became members of the Illuminati. Then, after graduating from college, the Illuminati assist your child in getting a good paying job in whatever field they choose to go into, and they are fast-tracked, meaning given promotions ahead of others. If that individual wants to continue their education, the Illuminati guarantees unlimited scholarship money. No matter what happens, the

Illuminati guarantees all their members will be financially secure and they will advance in their careers. This is one of the perks given to its members. Once they become members of the Illuminati, they are guaranteed financial security for the rest of their lives. They will never have to worry about losing a job because if they lose a job, they will be given a new one right away that pays them the same or even more money! Once they become members of the Illuminati, they are also fast-tracked to management positions.

Once these recruits are enticed with the money and other benefits, they join the Illuminati and become loyal members. Because the recruits understand they could have financial security for the rest of their lives. I believe that some of the new Illuminati recruits don't understand in the beginning the organization they just joined worships Satan. It is my belief after being in the Illuminati for a little while, this aspect of the group is introduced to them. When a recruit figures out what they are truly a part of, they are in so deep they can't get out. The members understand if they talk about the Illuminati to any outsiders, they are jeopardizing their life and their family life. They are sworn to secrecy! Also, like any organization or cult, the Illuminati members at the bottom never understand the true nature of the cult's overall agenda. The Illuminati members at the bottom are no more than foot soldiers that is given a few perks to stay in order. The Illuminati never allows the foot soldiers to know their true agenda!

So, you may understand how the Illuminati recruit individuals who are unaware of their religious beliefs. Let's look at my sister "V". I have a very smart sister in elementary, high school, and college. I came to realize she was a member of the Illuminati once the Lord opened my eyes the day he downloaded my mind with so much information about this world. At that point, I started sensing something was not right about my sister "V". At the time, I couldn't place my finger on what I was sensing. I remember telling one of my brothers it seemed like our sister was part of a secret organization like the CIA. I remember my brother started laughing at me once I told him that. Even though my eyes were open to understanding, my sister was part of a secret group. The Lord hid the truth because it was not time for me to know. So, for the next few years, I constantly tried to figure out what was happening with my sister "V".

So, one day the same subject about my sister being a part of a secret group came to mind. Instantly, the Lord allowed me to remember a conversation between my mom and my sister "V". I remember the year was around 1986 or 1987, and I was at my mother's house. As I was walking down the hall, something made me stop outside my mother's door. I didn't understand what made me stop outside my mother's door at the time, but now I do. The Lord made me stop in the hallway outside my mother's door so I could hear the conversation between my mother and my sister "V".

As I stood in the hall, my sister and mother talked in my mother's bedroom. And while they were talking, I overheard their conversation. My sister told my mother, "Madera, it's this secret group at Auburn University that guarantees me job advancement and financial security if I join their group." Then my sister said, "The only thing about it is I have to keep it a secret that I'm a member." And then, at that very moment, my mother said these exact words to my sister, "Anything people want you to join, and it has to remain a secret, got to be from Satan!!!" Then my mother said, "Satan gets these secret societies and tricks people into joining, and then people don't realize what they are a part of!"

Those were my mother's exact words! I guess my mother was "Gifted"! Because she was exactly right! It all made sense after I remembered the conversation between my sister and mother. I then understood why I felt my sister was part of this secret organization. The secret organization that recruited me at Jacksonville State University also recruited my sister years prior at Auburn University. The secret organization is the Illuminati!

Once I realized my sister was a member of the Illuminati, I started to remember how she was given a lot of scholarship money for college and grad school at the University of Buffalo. I then remember how easily she got a job and advanced her career. Then, I noticed how she hadn't experienced one problem since college. Then I noticed when she lost her job because the company was downsizing, she was given another job paying even more money within a few weeks. Her help was coming from the Illuminati! You must remember the Illuminati guarantees all their members' financial security once they join. And my sister "V" joined the Illuminati when she was at Auburn University. My sister was a member of the Illuminati for years, and I didn't know it!

I confronted my sister "V" about being a member of the Illuminati, and she denied it! She has never told me she is a member, but I know she is. She didn't realize I overheard her conversation with my mom in 1986 or 1987. When I confronted her, she acted like she never heard of the Illuminati. But how could she forget about a group that recruited her and made her many promises for her future? My sister didn't realize, nor did she have a clue to what she was joining. But since she was receiving the financial rewards, she didn't care. But one thing I do know about my sister is this: if the Illuminati revealed to her, they worship Satan as god in the beginning! She would have walked away from them right then and there!

To my sister and other Illuminati members, I say this: you cannot serve two masters. You can't serve Jehovah and Satan at the same time. To be a part of the Illuminati is to worship Satan! You cannot be a member of the Illuminati and say you believe in Jesus Christ! Once you become a member of the Illuminati, you are an enemy of my Father in Heaven. You must denounce the Illuminati publicly before the Holy Father will even consider taking you back! A choice must be made between one or the other! A choice must be made between the Most High God Jehovah, and Satan (the Illuminati). Jesus said you cannot serve two masters in Matthew 6:24.

Matthew 6:24 "No one can **serve two masters**. Either you will hate the one and love the other, or you will be devoted to the one and despise the other.... (NIV, BibleGateway.com)

Many may ask why I would put this information about my sister in this book. Because as soon as my book goes public, I guarantee you the Illuminati is going to make the connection we are brother and sister. If they haven't already made the connection! The Illuminati may think my sister told me things about them since I know a lot about them. My sister has always denied being a member of the Illuminati. Now, if my sister "V" goes public against me for any reason, you will understand why! Because she is a member of the Illuminati, and she must do whatever they tell her to do.

To my sister "V", Madear warned you, but you sought the easy way out. You sought the financial gain and the fast track over the wisdom my mother gave you! So, you sold your soul to Satan for a job and some money! But I know you didn't realize what you was joining. The Illuminati is going to try to use you against me. Remember the teachings of Madear and daddy. Don't think about self-preservation.

Say your child joined the Illuminati, and they grew up in Birmingham, and they wanted to return to Birmingham after graduating from college. The Illuminati finds your child a job in their field of study in Birmingham and strategically places them in a corporation, non-profit organization, or within one of the departments of local Government, state government, or federal Government. So, your child is back in Birmingham, where they were raised with other people in the "Gifted Program". Those same children who were raised in the "Gifted Program" are reunited to form a tight Illuminati family in Birmingham. Now they can **network** so they can do whatever the Illuminati ask of them!

So, you can understand how and why the Illuminati place their employees in specific jobs and companies; let's look at this scenario. Say this young lady name Terry just graduated from college and she majored in Human Resource Management. Before she graduated, she was recruited by the Illuminati, and she joined the Illuminati. Now sense Terry majored in Human Resource Management, the Illuminati wants to place her in the Human Resource Department as the head recruiter for XYZ Corporation. The Illuminati wants her in this head recruiter position at XYZ Corporation so she can control the hiring and placement of future Illuminati members inside XYZ Corporation. By controlling the Human Resource Department, you can control the hiring and firing within a corporation. And by controlling the Human Resource Department you can place Illuminati members in key managerial positions in a corporation and control a corporation from the inside. The Lord revealed to me the Illuminati control the Human Resource Department and Managerial positions in many corporations so they can control the hiring and firing for corporations, organizations, and government positions! This is how the Illuminati members get promoted and are fast-tracked into managerial positions. Illuminati members are fast-tracked for management positions because the Illuminati has their people in the Human Resource Department, and key management positions.

The Illuminati is an active, ever-expanding network or virus! Once an individual is in the Illuminati organization, they are strategically placed throughout different companies, government agencies, educational institutions, medical institutions, law enforcement, judicial system, and other organizations worldwide. They are placed based on their desired field of study and career goals. Their reach includes Presidents of the United States, Democrat and Republican Senators, Democrat and Republican Representatives, high-ranking Pentagon Officers, Military Officers, Judges, the FBI, the CIA, the NSA, the

Pentagon, IRS; they fill most of the high-ranking and midlevel positions in the federal and state governments. They have highjacked the Federal Government. They are Policemen, Firemen, local councilmen, city employees, District Attorneys, Attorney Generals, Governors, State and Federal Representatives, state employees, heads of city and state education, CEOs of Corporations, board members of corporations, upper-level management of corporations, middle-level management of corporations, lower level management of corporations, everyday workers, owners of corporations, owners of newspapers, magazines, and television networks. The Illuminati are Members of Parliament, European bankers, **news editors, news reporters, television stars, movie stars, music superstars, radio hosts**, TV hosts, and everything else that was not mentioned. There are Bishops, Archbishops, Pastors, and Ministers who are members of the Illuminati. The Illuminati is in every country, every nation in the world! This organization is a global network and a global virus! The Illuminati own the Federal Reserve.

The Illuminati control the media and the airwaves! The Illuminati controls all the corporations that own all the media outlets. And since the Illuminati controls the corporations that own the media outlets like news channels, newspapers, and radio stations, they control the news you see and hear. This means they control the flow of information you receive. This means they control what is reported and what is not reported, and how the story is reported. The Illuminati knows if they want to control you, the only thing they need to do is to control the information you receive. Since they control the news you see and hear, they can control what information they want you to know and what information they don't want you to know. They control the war of Democrats versus Republicans or the Republicans versus Democrats. Wow!

They used their financial power to form umbrella corporations, which they then used to buy large amounts of stocks in other corporations. Then, they turned around and had the corporations buy up the major media outlets. Once they had the media outlets and national news companies, they placed their people as editors, producers, and reporters.

So, from top to bottom, the Illuminati controls the flow of information you receive from the News Media. To prove to you they control the national news media, all you have to do is ask yourself one simple question. Why haven't you ever heard of the Illuminati being talked about on any national news station? If the national news channels are trying to act like the Illuminati don't exist, something is wrong! The only reason local or national news coverage doesn't report on a story like this is because many people in the media are members of the Illuminati! And do you think they are going to cut their own throats by telling on themselves?

So, if someone does a story about the Illuminati, the name Illuminati is never mentioned. Instead of the word Illuminati, they use the term "Shadow Government". Have you ever heard of the term "Shadow Government" or "Deep State"? The term "Shadow Government" or "Deep State" is used to describe the Illuminati. The Illuminati has a government within the Government. So, you have two fashions of the U.S. Government. One is the Government formed by the people for the people. Then you have the Shadow Government, which is made up of people who are members of the Illuminati who work for the U.S. Government. And the Illuminati members are in Government positions to do the will of the Illuminati!

So, two fashions of the U.S. Government are in play: the one they allow you to see on TV and the one behind the scenes that controls the politicians. And many politicians are either members of the Illuminati or they are afraid of them! And I mean the Politicians and government employees who are not members of the Illuminati are truly afraid to death of the ones who are members of the Illuminati. The Government formed for the people by the people has been overthrown by the Illuminati. The Illuminati have overthrown our U.S. Government without firing a shot! A silent war!

President Woodrow Wilson, the 28th President of the United States, said, **"Since I entered politics, I have chiefly had men's views confided to me privately. Some of the biggest men in the United States, in the field of commerce and manufacture, are afraid of somebody, are afraid of something. They know that there is a power somewhere so organized, so subtle, so watchful, so interlocked, so complete, so pervasive, that they had better not speak above their breath when they speak in condemnation of it."** "A quote from The New Freedom." *Goodreads*. N.p., n.d. Web. 13 Mar. 2017. <http://www.goodreads.com/quotes/162688-since-i-entered-politics-i-have-chiefly-had-men-s-views>.

This powerful organization President Woodrow Wilson was describing is the Illuminati! This Shadow Government of the Illuminati is responsible for many deaths of ordinary citizens, politicians, political figures, judges, and anyone else who stands in their way or who tries to reveal the truth about them. This is why many people are afraid to speak of them publicly or privately.

Tupac Shakur recorded songs warning you about the Illuminati in the early 1990's. So, if a rapper knew of the Illuminati, you mean ABC, NBC, CBS, CNN, FOX, and all these other national news organizations didn't know about the Illuminati. And since Tupac Shakur was smart enough to see the danger the Illuminati pose to the United States of America, are you telling me the national news media, the Pentagon, the CIA, and the NSA don't recognize this threat known as the Illuminati? Are you starting to understand why Tupac Shakur was giving you a coded message of Killuminati in his songs, which means "Kill Illuminati?" Do you understand why Tupac Shakur was gunned down in Las Vegas? He was violently gunned down so he could be silenced, and his massacre was to serve as a deterrent to anyone who thought about going public about the Illuminati! The Illuminati ordered the hit! It's the people who ordered the hit that killed him! In any assassination, you must remember. It's the people who order the assassination that is also the killers. Too often, the Illuminati have you looking at the people who pulled the trigger. It's the people who ordered the hit you need to look at. But most of the time, people get lost in this enigma that is the Illuminati! People cannot solve the enigma of the Illuminati because it is like an ameba, the Illuminati appears not to have a definite shape or face! But they do have a shape and a face, and I will show you their shape and face in chapters to come! I will pull back the veil so you can see the Illuminati!

The Illuminati kills anyone who exposes the truth about them to the public. And these killings are sometimes performed as public executions. Just like Tupac was gunned down for exposing the Illuminati in his rap songs. President John F. Kennedy was publicly gunned down because he was about to open the eyes of billions of people in this world about the Illuminati. A former Naval Intelligence Officer named Milton William Cooper was gunned down for writing a book exposing the plans of the Illuminati. Plans that they are doing right now in front of your face. Do you see a connection between how these three men who exposed the Illuminati were all gunned down?

Milton William Cooper was a Naval Intelligence Officer who found detailed Illuminati agenda plans on a copy machine at the Pentagon. Cooper published those plans in his book named "Behold a

Pale Horse". His book explained the Illuminati and their plans. Milton William Cooper was eventually gunned down and killed by Sheriffs. The Sheriffs were nothing more than legalized hitmen for the Illuminati! The Illuminati use Police, Sheriffs, and other law enforcement officers as legalizing hitmen! These Illuminati that are law enforcement go by the name of the Brotherhood. You must remember the Illuminati is a Luciferian religion that worships Satan as god! So, some of these cop killings that are going on today are happening because Illuminati cops have been sent out to do a public execution on someone who has been speaking out against the Illuminati! So, William Milton Cooper was gunned down by Sheriffs who used their badges to be legalized hitmen for the Illuminati! Public executions are used as a deterrent to cause fear among the public. And it deters others from thinking about going public against the Illuminati.

Now, if someone wants to call all this a conspiracy theory, it is not a conspiracy theory! The proof is in everything I said about them testing children with a viewing machine and labeling them as "Gifted". Is it a conspiracy theory third graders in the United States have been tested for many years with a viewing machine, and then some of these kids are labeled as gifted after they identified the Illuminati steganography? Is it a conspiracy theory that three different recruiters approached me in college trying to recruit me? The phrase conspiracy theory works on those individuals who are unknowledgeable and simple-minded.

Is it a conspiracy theory that the first President of the United States of America, George Washington, wrote a leader that mentioned the Illuminati organization and Free Masonry? On August 22, 1798, G.W. Snyder wrote a letter to George Washington explaining to him the plans of the Illuminati. Here is what G.W. Snyder wrote to George Washington.

From G.W. Snyder To George Washington

August 22. 1798.

Sir,

You will, I hope, not think it a Presumption in a Stranger, whose Name, perhaps never reached your Ears, to address himself to you the Commanding General of a great Nation. I am a German, born and liberally educated in the City of Heydelberg in the Palatinate of the Rhine. I came to this Country in 1776, and felt soon after my Arrival a close Attachment to the Liberty for which these confederated States then struggled. The same Attachment still remains not glowing, but burning in my Breast. At the same Time that I am exulting in the Measures adopted by our Government, I feel myself elevated in the Idea of my adopted Country. I am attached both from the Bent of Education and mature Enquiry and Search to the simple Doctrines of Christianity, which I have the Honor to teach in Public; and I do heartily despise all the Cavils of Infidelity. Our present Time, pregnant with the most shocking Evils and Calamities, threatens Ruin to our Liberty and Government. Secret, the most secret Plans are in Agitation: Plans, calculated to ensnare the Unwary, to attract the Gay and irreligious, and to entice even the Well-disposed to combine in the general Machine for overturning all Government and all Religion.

It was some Time since that a Book fell into my Hands entitled "Proofs of a Conspiracy &c. by John Robison,

' which gives a full Account of a Society of Freemasons, that distinguishes itself by the Name "of **Illuminati**," whose Plan is to overturn all Government and all Religion, even natural; and who endeavor to eradicate every Idea of a Supreme Being, and distinguish Man from Beast by his Shape only. A Thought suggested itself to me, that some of the Lodges in the United States might have caught the Infection, and might cooperate with **the Illuminati** or the Jacobine Club in France. Fauchet is mentioned by Robison as a zealous Member: and who can doubt of Genet and Adet? Have not these their Confidants in this Country? They use the same Expressions and are generally **Men of no Religion**. Upon serious Reflection I was led to think that it might be within your Power to prevent the horrid Plan from corrupting the Brethren of the English Lodge over which you preside.[2]

I send you the "Proof of a Conspiracy &c." which, I doubt not, will give you Satisfaction and afford you Matter for a Train of Ideas, that may operate to our national Felicity. If, however, you have already perused the Book, it will not, I trust, be disagreeable to you that I have presumed to address you with this Letter and the Book accompanying it. It proceeded from the Sincerity of my Heart and my ardent Wishes for the common Good.

May the Supreme Ruler of all Things continue You long with us in these perilous Times: may he endow you with Strength and Wisdom to save our Country in the threatening Storms and gathering Clouds of Factions and Commotions! and after you have completed his Work on this terrene Spot, may He bring you to the full Possession of the glorious Liberty of the Children of God, is the hearty and most sincere Wish of Your Excellency's very humble and devoted Servant

G. W. Snyder

"Founders Online: To George Washington from G. W. Snyder, 22 August 1798." *National Archives and Records Administration*, National Archives and Records Administration, https://founders.archives.gov/documents/Washington/06-02-02-0435.

In the letter Reverend G.W. Snyder was trying to warn George Washington of the Illuminati and their plans. The same plans they are carrying out right before your eyes! The plan is to overthrow Governments and do away with Christianity. But it's one thing Reverend G.W. Snyder didn't realize was that George Washington was a 33rd Degree Mason and that the 33rd Degree Mason functions as High Priest for the Illuminati. This Mason Illuminati priesthood will be discussed in chapters to come. So, G.W. Snyder didn't understand he was talking to a member of the Illuminati when he wrote to George Washington. So, the Illuminati was alerted that Rev. G. W. Snyder was trying to warn people about them. I understand this because I have talked to some Illuminati members, and I didn't realize the individuals were members of the Illuminati.

So George Washington wrote back to G.W. Snyder, who responded by denying that any lodges were contaminated with the Illuminati. Below is the letter George Washington wrote, followed by a copy of the original letter.

To Rev. G. W. Snyder From George Washington

September 25, 1798.

Sir: Many apologies are due to you, for my not acknowledging the receipt of your obliging favour of the 22d. Ulto, and for not thanking you, at an earlier period, for the Book[8] you had the goodness to send me.

I have heard much of the nefarious, and dangerous plan, and doctrines of the Illuminati, but never saw the Book until you were pleased to send it to me.[9] The same causes which have prevented my acknowledging the receipt of your letter have prevented my reading the Book, hitherto; namely, the multiplicity of matters which pressed upon me before, and the debilitated state in which I was left after, a severe fever had been removed. And which allows me to add little more now, than thanks for your kind wishes and favourable sentiments, except to correct an error you have run into, of my Presiding over the English lodges in this Country. The fact is, I preside over none, nor have I been in one more than once or twice, within the last thirty years. I believe notwithstanding, that none of the Lodges in this Country are contaminated with the principles ascribed to the Society of the Illuminati.

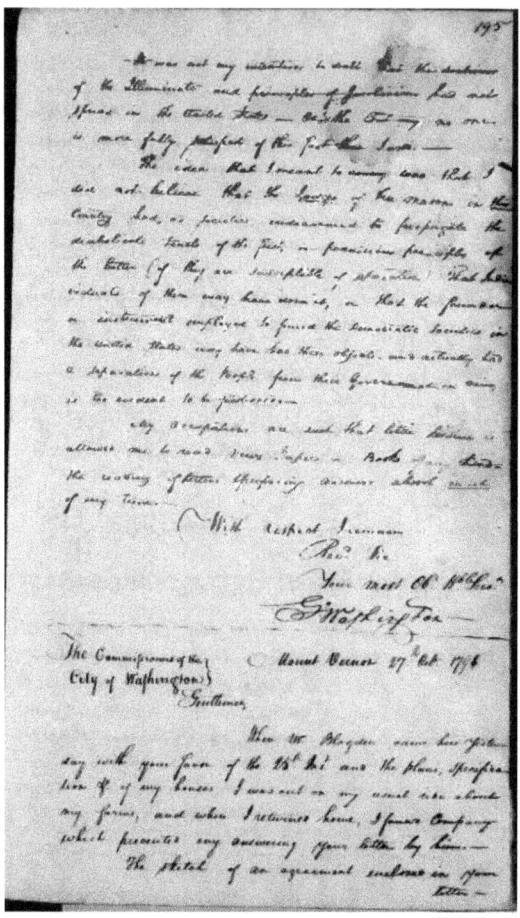

"George Washington to William Russell, September 28, 1798." *The Library of Congress*, https://www.loc.gov/resource/mgw2.021/?q=Illuminati&sp=182&st=text.

We have two letters from 1798 talking about the Illuminati. One of the letters is a warning of the Illuminati's plan, and the other is from the first President of the United States of America denying that the Illuminati has contaminated Masonic Lodges. So, is this a conspiracy theory? No, it's not. The Illuminati is as real as you and me. Let me tell you about the two words "conspiracy theory". I have watched an entire generation of people in this country get brainwashed by two simple words. The words "conspiracy theory" are always used to discredit any information that leads to the truth! The government first used the phrase conspiracy theory to discredit individuals who had information about things of a top-secret nature. The phrase conspiracy theory works on those unknowledgeable and simple-minded individuals. So if you are simple minded you are probably the individuals that are using the term conspiracy theory.

If you cannot conceive the Illuminati truly exist at the capacity I have explained to you, then you cannot conceive their agenda. This means they can continue to rule over you like sheep and cows until the day comes when the Illuminati will call checkmate! And when the Illuminati call checkmate, that means Game Over. That means you will be killed or carried off into bondage like the Jews in Germany! And when they call checkmate, they are going to make everyone worship Satan as god! Their plan is so ingenious you will never see it coming! And they are almost ready to call Check Mate! You are living out their plan at this very moment!

65. The Anatomy of Satan Part 5

In this chapter, we will look at how secret societies are part of the anatomy of Satan. Satan uses secret societies to entice people to do his will. In the recruitment process of the Illuminati, one is always offered financial security, wealth, power, and prestige. These are the key components most individuals seek to obtain when entering a secret society. And the Illuminati promise these things to their recruits as an incentive to join their organization! These incentives of financial security, wealth, power, and prestige are dangled in front of a recruit like a carrot is dangled in front of a horse. Once the recruit has been enticed with financial security, they join the Illuminati because they see it as a fast track to success!

Satan uses the Illuminati as a mask to recruit people to do his will while hiding his true intentions. The group's true intentions or overall agenda is never revealed to the recruit or lower-level members! Most individuals join the Illuminati without knowing the absolute truth about the group's satanic origins. But some know the Illuminati worships Satan as a god, and they want to be a part of that organization. Satan manipulates millions of people to join his organization before they even realize what they are a part of. The reason why Satan and the 13 Families of the Illuminati chose this way of doing things is that most people wouldn't worship Satan if they were just asked to worship him! Satan crafted this secret society to bring people to him in exchange for wealth and power! And it worked!

Satan uses secret societies to recruit the smartest and the brightest into his corporation. Satan and the 13 Families of the Illuminati's plan is to keep the smartest of the smartest together under one cause, which is Satan's cause! Satan knows average people always follow intelligent people. Because it's the smart people who are leaders and others are followers. Satan's thought process is this: if intelligent people are leaders, let's recruit the leaders into his organization and keep all the smart people together under the same cause, which is his cause. And then his people, the Illuminati, can rule over the average individuals like sheep and cattle. Sheep and cattle always follow until they are led to the slaughter. Since Satan recruited the smartest of the smartest (Gifted people), Satan has been looking to monopolize the positions of power by placing his people in positions of power! Satan believes if he controls the hierarchy of government and corporations, then he can control the rest of the population, like sheep and cattle! And guess what? It has worked to perfection so far!

The Illuminati holds many positions of power in the Local, State and Federal governments and publicly and privately held corporations. They needed these positions to dictate laws and rule over you like sheep and cattle! The Illuminati are in positions of power in key strategic areas throughout the United States and the world. Secret societies are part of the anatomy, Satan!

66. The Illuminati Corporation Structure

The Illuminati itself is run and structured like a corporation. To understand the Illuminati, you must first understand it is structured like a corporation. The Illuminati is broken down into different departments, just like a corporation is broken down into different departments. Each group in the Illuminati works as a department inside a corporation. For example, XYZ Corporation has an Accounting, Human Resources, and Marketing Department. Each Department in the Corporation is responsible for its field of expertise that helps the Corporation run efficiently and effectively. Then, the Corporation has a Board of

Directors that oversees the Corporation and makes final decisions. The Illuminati Board of Directors is called "The Order of the Quest". The Illuminati Corporation is set up exactly like a Fortune 500 Company. The Illuminati is well organized and plan their events years in advance. The Illuminati agenda is a One World Government, under a One World Leader, under a One World Religion with a One World Monetary system. This plan is called a New World Order. This New World Order plan goes back thousands of years. The Illuminati has taken over most of the world governments by inserting their people into power.

The Illuminati have different departments for each area of expertise that is needed! First is Satan, who gives his agenda to the 13 families of the Illuminati, by way of the Board called the Order of the Quest and entities that worship Satan as God. Then there is the Financial Banking Cartel of the Illuminati, which owns the Central Banks of the world. In the U.S., this Central Bank is called the Federal Reserve Bank. Then comes the Department that makes the U.S. Policies and other nations policies. The Illuminati Policy Makers are nothing more than think tank groups that come up with ways to manipulate the people with laws that surrender their rights to the Elites (the Illuminati). These Illuminati Policy makers include the World Economic Forum, Council of Foreign Relations, Club of Rome, Chatham House, Trilateral Commission, the Council on Foreign Relations, the Jason Society, etc.

The Illuminati is comprised of the smartest and the brightest. They have groups that are called "think tanks". The "think tanks" devise the course of action that should be taken to secure laws or anything else that may hinder the Illuminati's plans. The Illuminati's governing body, called "The Order of the Quest," has two or three "think tanks" working on the same problem at any given time. Then "The Order of the Quest" looks over all the "think tank" plans and then decides to use one of the "think tank" plans or both "think tanks" plans. Or they will have two "think tanks" integrate their plans if necessary. These members of the "think tanks" are good! They think more advanced than you will ever think! They can predict your behavior in the future so well they draw up plans of action years in advance that will condition your mind to accept whatever they are trying to do. For example, getting Americans to accept homosexuality and gay marriage! They devised a plan many years ago to get you to accept homosexuality and gay marriage. Then, they delivered that plan to you through the news media. Then, many of you received the brainwashing or the reprogramming of your minds and accepted homosexuality and gay marriage! The Illuminati knew they could get you to accept homosexuality and gay marriage if they scorned anyone publicly in the news who rejected homosexuality. They use the television as a delivery device to brainwash you to accept homosexuality.

So basically, the "think tanks" devise ways to manipulate you into compliance years before any issue arises. Then you, on the other hand, have no clue they have manipulated you twenty years before any issue ever came up, which means you are always behind! This is why the Illuminati want people with very high IQs because the people with very high IQs think and plan while everyone else reacts to what the Illuminati does. The Illuminati want people with high IQs because they believe if they keep all the people in the world with high IQs "together under one cause." Then, they can rule over the rest of the population (you), like herds of cattle or sheep.

When the Illuminati wants to set policy for the U.S. or another nation, the Illuminati will have one or more think tank groups devise a plan that includes writing new laws for a nation or state. Once the Order of the Quest approves the plan and the laws, the Policies are then sent to the Illuminati Policy Distributors like the United Nations, International Monetary Fund, Intergovernmental Panel on Climate Change (IPCC), The World Bank, The World Health Organization (WHO), World Trade Organization, etc. Policymakers like the World Economic Forum and others send their policies to Policy Distributors like the World Health Organization, United Nations, etc.

Once the Illuminati Policy Distributors get the policy, they go to the Illuminati Policy Enforcers where they have their Illuminati members in place in the different governments worldwide and the United States of America. People like Senators, members of the House of Representatives in the United States Government, Governors, State Senators, and State Representatives in State Governments, etc. The Illuminati has its people in place in every nation in the world. They are not just in the United States of America Government; the Illuminati have their members in every nation's government in the world.

Once the Order of the Quest realized they would have to remove cash to achieve their goal of a New World Order, One World Government, and a One World Monetary system. The Illuminati assign one or more of their think tanks to devise a plan. Once the plan has been devised, policymakers like the World Economic Forum or the Bilderberg Group devise a way to convince the public that cash needs to be removed from the United States of America or other nations and must be replaced with a Central Bank Digital Currency. The World Economic Forum or Bilderberg would draw up the legislation or design a plan surrounding CHAOS, and then the Order of the Quest would approve the plan. Then that legislation would go to one of their Illuminati members in the United Nations or World Bank, and the specific legislation for the United States would go to the Illuminati members in the House of Representatives to be introduced into legislation and passed by the Senate and signed into law by an Illuminati President.

In most cases, legislation introduced into the House of Representatives is drafted by people who may not even be American citizens but are members of an Illuminati think tank group. The Illuminati's plans were drafted about forty or fifty years in advance. They were just waiting for the technology to catch up before they enforced their plans. The Illuminati's plans are precise and strategic.

For example, the lie of Climate Change and that the CO_2 is rising and the earth is overheating was a lie that the Council of the Club of Rome came up with in the late 80's. I know this for a fact because their book name, "The First Global Revolution," was copywritten in 1991. On page 115, under the subject name, "The Common Enemy of Humanity Is Man," they said, and I quote, "In search for a new enemy to unite us, we came up with the idea that pollution, the threat of global warming, water shortages, famine, and the like would fit the bill." *King, Alexander, and Schneider, Bertrand. Page 115, The First Global Revolution, Patheon Books, 1991*

Basically, in that quote, they told you this. They came up with the lie of global warming to unite people. They sold you on a lie of global warming so you would follow their demonic plan to kill you and your family and seven billion and five hundred million people on this earth. They came up with sophisticated ways to kill you that include vaccines, biological weapons, food shortages, and more. Also, when you hear them use the word sustainability that means reducing the world's population from eight billion to five hundred million people. The Illuminati believes the world's resources would be more sustainable if the world's population were reduced to five hundred million people. This is the Illuminati Flow Chart.

Illuminati Flow Chart

Satan

Order of the Quest
The Illuminati Governing body from the 13 Families of the Illuminati.

13 Families of The Illuminati
The 13 families of the Illuminati are Rothschild's (Orsini, Bauer), Bruce, Cavendish, De Medici, Hanover, Hapsburg, Krupp, Plantagenet, Rockefeller, Romanov, Sinclair (St. Clair), Warburg, and Windsor. Now these families are in the hundreds and goes by other names.

Central Banks
U.S. Federal Reserve Bank is owned by the 13 Families of the Illuminati. The Federal Reserve is a Non-Government Agency that act like it's a government agency. The Federal Reserve is a Privately held Corporation agency. The Central Banks around the world are owned by the 13 Families of the Illuminati.

The Illuminati Policy Makers, Think Tanks
World Economic Forum, Council of Foreign Relations, Club of Rome, Chatham House, Trilateral Commission, World Governments Summit, Jason Society, Bilderberg Group, Other Illuminati Non-Government Organizations (NGO's). None of the organizations are government agencies but they are setting U/S. policies and drafting legislation to become laws. Many people who were recruited into the Illuminati work for these organizations.

The Illuminati Policy Distributors
United Nations, International Monetary Fund (IMF), Intergovernmental Panel on Climate Change (IPCC), World Bank, World Health Organization (WHO), World Trade Organization (WTO), Other NGOs, Non-Governmental Agencies, Global Corporations etc. So called Philanthropist like Bill Gates, George Soros etc. Many people who were recruited into the Illuminati work for these organizations.

Then the Illuminati use the Policy Enforcers

United Staes Government Agencies and State Governments Agencies for the U.S. (People who were recruited into the Illuminati like Senators and House of Representatives of the Democratic Party and Republican Party, Federal and State Judges, the FDA, FBI, CIA, NSA, DOJ, IRS, ATF etc. For other nations it's the same. The Illuminati has its people in all branches of government and the private sector. The Illuminati has its people National and State Governments for other Nations. Selected Scientific Authorities for U.S and other Nations (They have highjacked the science.)

The Illuminati Control the Flow and Distribution of Propaganda

Mainstream media (ABC, CBS, CNN, NBC, MSNBC etc. New York Times, Washington Post etc. Facebook, Instagram, Twitter etc.

Those who are recruited into the Illuminati

The amount of knowledge given to those recruited into the Illuminati about the New World Order and the takeover of all nations is based on their rank within the organization. So even though some Illuminati members start off here at the bottom of the flow chart, they will be fast-track up the flow chart depending on their commitment to the organization and Satan. And if they committed to the torture of children, pedophilia, and the sacrificing of children and adults, they are truly moved up through the organization based on their usefulness.

THIS IS WHERE YOU ARE AT IN THE FLOW CHART

This is you; it doesn't matter if you are rich or poor, White, Black, Hispanic, or etc. Christian or Muslim, believer or non-believer or anything in between. They are about to kill 7.5 billion of you world-wide and 200 million of you people in the United States.

Now, I want you to assemble the pieces and understand everything I showed you. The Illuminati test children in the 3rd grade to see who is of higher intelligence, and then years later they recruit these people while they are in college, in the military, or the workforce. Then, these people are strategically placed in jobs in their field of expertise, whether in the government, the private sector, non-profits, the media, the military, law enforcement, religious organizations or any other place of importance. They have a pipeline of people they start testing in the third grade that they recruit each year. This pipeline is continuous. This pipeline is worldwide. They have millions of people in the Illuminati organization, and they are some of the smartest people on this planet. Now, I want to show you the damage the Illuminati has already done to this nation and how they did it.

The Skull and Bones is the WAR Department of the Illuminati. And the Illuminati used the Skull and Bones to bring the United States and other nations into WAR. The Illuminati Skull and Bones members occupy the Executive Branch, the Legislative Branch, and the Judicial Branch, and they are in all the Intelligence Agencies. The Skull and Bones are where many of the U.S. Presidents, U. S. Senators, employees, and contractors for the CIA, NSA, Homeland Security, FBI, Secret Service, Pentagon Officials, and other Intelligence agencies.

My first encounter with a member of the Skull and Bones happened when I was 10 or 11 years old. One day, I had just come home when I saw this white man walking down the steps of my house. This man was a member of the Secret Service. This man asked me if I lived there, and I said, "Yes". He then asked me a couple of questions about my brother "W". After I answered the man's questions, I noticed he had this silver ring on his finger that had a Skull and Bones on it. The bones cross each other. I grabbed the man's hand with the ring and stared at it. Then the man asked me if I liked the ring. I then ask the man what does the ring mean. The man said I had to be in a special group to receive one of those rings. I then asked him what group. The man said, "Not just anyone can join this group!" The group the man referred to was the Skull and Bones. I later realized the man was a member of the Secret Service because the man had been interviewing neighbors about my brother "W". My brother "W" was applying for a Top-Secret Security Clearance to be on a Navy Nuclear Submarine. Members of the Secret Service are also members of the Skull and Bones.

The Skulls and Bones's motto is WAR! Their Motto is WAR because they head up the organizations that bring us WAR! Organizations like the CIA, NSA, Senators, and the Presidents of the United States. Those positions I mentioned are responsible for leading the United States into WAR! WAR is what the Skull and Bones are responsible for, and WAR is what Skull and Bones give you! Do you all know why they are called Skull and Bones? They are called Skull and Bones because they are responsible for WAR, and WAR always produces death! And d**eath always produces Skulls and Bones!** Now, do you understand why they are called Skull and Bones? They are the bringers of WAR and death!

George H. W. Bush, Bill Clinton, and George W. Bush were the three most recent Skull and Bones Presidents. They all were in the WAR Department! I know you have heard the phrase "The WAR Department" on TV before. But when you heard the term WAR Department mentioned on TV, you thought they were talking about the Pentagon, didn't you? Sometimes, they talk about the Pentagon and sometimes the Skull and Bones. When they use the term WAR Department, they are referring to the Skull and Bones, it is a clever way to release information over the airwaves concerning the Skull and Bones. The media use coded phrases like this all the time to pass messages across the airwaves to its Illuminati members. And the public is never the wiser to it!

The Illuminati WAR Department and the Skull and Bones also oversee the illegal drug trade in the United States and around the world! The Illuminati used agents of the CIA, which are members of the Illuminati, to set up the transportation of illegal drugs into the United States. And they also use these agents to set up distribution channels for illegal drugs. The hierarchy of the Illuminati uses the CIA to transport and set up distribution pipelines because they can cover up their involvement by hiding behind the Central Intelligence Agency. By using the CIA, they are never at risk for prosecution because the CIA can ward off the DEA or other law enforcement agencies!

This is how it works! The CIA uses CIA planes, private planes, Cargo ships, and U.S. Military planes to go into countries to pick up tons of cocaine, heroin, and other narcotics. Then they bring the narcotics back into the U.S. When the CIA is using U.S. Military planes and U.S. Soldiers, the planes have no flight manifest, and the soldiers aren't given any orders that are written down on paper. The soldiers fly into airfields and load large wooden crates onto a Military plane because they were verbally ordered to do so. How do I know this? Because I know someone who was on some of these drug runs for the military. They bring these large shipments back into the U.S. then the product is distributed through the supply chain to lower-level men in African American communities throughout the U.S.

There was a story that came out in the 1980s about how the CIA was bringing drugs into this country and putting those drugs in the African American communities in California and throughout the United States of America. However, the CIA drug story was covered up by the news media by using the details of the same drug story to drown out the CIA's involvement in drug distribution. They used the Iran Contra Affair that was going on in Nicaragua to cover the true story of Oliver North and the CIA shipping cocaine into the United States of America. And it worked! Misdirection! The Iran Contra affair wasn't just about weapons being sold to the Contras. The real story of the Iran Contra Affair involved CIA agent Oliver North and the CIA shipping cocaine into the United States of America and using crack cocaine sales in the United States to make billions of dollars for themselves and to help buy weapons for the Nicaragua Contras. The Nicaragua Contras had plenty of cocaine, but they didn't have any money. The CIA had large shipments of cocaine shipped from Nicaragua to America and set up distribution pipelines across America.

In return, the CIA used the money from the cocaine sales to purchase weapons for the Contras. I am talking about the same Oliver North that appears on Fox News from time to time! The same Oliver North George H.W. Bush pardoned for keeping his mouth shut and taking the fall for the Iran Contra Affair. The same Oliver North who was appointed President of the NRA. The U.S. Government, by way of the CIA, flooded African American communities with crack cocaine so they could raise money for a private war! And then the same U. S. Government that destroyed so many African American people waged war on the very same people who were using and selling illegal drugs. Crack cocaine devasted the African American communities! It was like they set off a thousand nuclear bombs across the United States when they put that crack cocaine in African American neighborhoods. The violence, the extreme poverty you see now, the mass incarceration, etc., were all caused by the Illuminati, CIA, and the U.S. Government! And that's the Absolute Truth!

Oliver North takes the fall for the Iran Contra Affair, and then he gets Pardon by George H. W. Bush right after he got convicted! President George H. W. Bush is Illuminati, and Oliver North is Illuminati! Do you see how this Illuminati game works? Even if Illuminati members are caught red-handed, the Illuminati make sure the people don't serve any time in jail! And they ensure the people are pardoned if they stand trial!

The Iran Contra affair was truly about Oliver North and the CIA bringing shipments of cocaine into the United States and flooding poor African American communities with crack cocaine. This is what the Illuminati control news media didn't tell you. A journalist named Gary Webb broke the story that the CIA was shipping cocaine into the United States. Once that story broke, the Illuminati controlled news media, and the Illuminati within the U.S. Government decided to use the sale of illegal arms to Contras to cover up the same story of the CIA bringing drugs into the United States. The Contras supplied Oliver North and the CIA with cocaine in exchange for weapons! And then Oliver North and the CIA took the cocaine and distributed it throughout the United States in poor African American communities so they could turn the cocaine into cash! Since cocaine itself was too expensive for the average African American to purchase, the CIA released information to the dealers on how to cook down the cocaine into crack. The CIA was consulting with UCLA professors on how to make crack. UCLA professors were experimenting with crack cocaine on monkeys 13 years before crack cocaine hit the streets. Do you think that was a coincidence? Or did the CIA consult with those professors at UCLA to learn how addictive crack cocaine was? This is how the crack cocaine epidemic in the United States truly got started. Our own United States Government and our own publicly funded University, UCLA, are responsible for the crack epidemic! It's time that the truth be told.

I must repeat this so you can truly understand what happened. Oliver North and the CIA were receiving millions and millions of tons of cocaine from the Contras for payment for weapons, then Oliver North and the CIA took the millions and millions of tons of cocaine and flooded the United States with cocaine and crack! Oliver North and the CIA had so much cocaine coming into the United States they had to find a way to make it more affordable for African American people to use. They consulted with UCLA professors who had been experimenting with crack cocaine on monkeys for 13 years. The professors taught the CIA agents how to cook the cocaine down to make crack, which would make it more affordable and more addictive for African Americans. Oliver North, the Illuminati, the CIA, and UCLA professors are responsible for the crack epidemic! So, the Illuminati and the CIA made hundreds of billions of dollars from the sale of crack cocaine and powder cocaine in the United States. And guess what? They are still making billions upon billions of dollars from the sale of drugs in the United States of America.

Former Director of the Drug Enforcement Agency (DEA) Federal Judge Robert C. Booner said, "The CIA are Drug Smugglers" (Booner, Robert C. "The CIA's Cocaine" Interviewed by Mike Wallace, CBS 60 Minutes 1993).

The former Director of the DEA (Drug Enforcement Agency), who happens to be a Federal Judge, said that the CIA are drug smugglers. If a former Director of the DEA who happens to be a Federal Judge tells you the CIA are Drug smugglers, you better start listening and paying attention to what he is telling you about the CIA! Also, Drug Enforcement Agent (DEA) Michael Levine said, "...the CIA is the King Pin and...at the top of drug smuggling" (Levine, Michael "Montel Williams Show" Interviewed by Montel Williams).

Then there was Gary Webb, an investigator News Reporter for the San Jose Mercury News, who researched the involvement of the U.S. Government and Drug smuggling. Gary Webb found out the CIA was smuggling cocaine into South Central Los Angeles in the early 80's. Gary Webb also found out that the money from the drugs sold was used to finance the Contras in Nicaragua! (Webb, Gary "Montel Williams Show" Interviewed by Montel Williams)

So former DEA agent Michael Levine, former Director of the DEA Federal Judge Robert C. Booner, and a news reporter name Gary Webb all told you the CIA is supplying the United States of America with drugs. So why don't you believe the CIA is supplying the United States of America with a constant supply of cocaine, heroin, Fentanyl, etc? Its time you people wake up and recognize the absolute truth! The CIA is the largest distributor of cocaine and heroin in the United States of America and the world!

Opioids like heroin come from the Opium Poppy Plant, which is grown in Afghanistan. U.S. Troops were in Afghanistan guarding and protecting those Poppy Plants! If the United States has a "War on Drugs," why were U.S. Troops guarding the Poppy Plants in Afghanistan? Those same Poppy plants are fueling the opioid epidemic here in America and around the world! The Opioids oxycodone, hydrocodone, morphine, Fentanyl, and heroin are made from the Poppy Plant. Those same Poppy Plants the U.S. Military was guarding in Afghanistan will be used to make oxycodone, hydrocodone, Fentanyl, and heroin to be sold on the streets in the United States and other nations! So, if those Poppy Plants are used to make oxycodone, hydrocodone, and heroin, that fuels the opioid epidemic in America. Why was the U.S. Military guarding those Poppy Plants? The U.S. Military was guarding those Poppy Plants because they were given orders to protect those Poppy fields. After all, the Illuminati would make billions of dollars from the sale of oxycodone, hydrocodone, Fentanyl, and heroin on the streets of the United States of America and other nations!

Also, do you think it is a coincidence oxycodone, hydrocodone, Fentanyl, and heroin become plentiful in the streets of the United States of America ever since we went to war in Afghanistan? The opioid epidemic increased because the Illuminati and the CIA took over the Poppy fields in Afghanistan! The Illuminati and the CIA took over the Poppy fields so they could control the production and distribution of heroin! Therefore, the U.S. Troops were guarding the Poppy fields in Afghanistan to protect the Poppy fields from being destroyed by the previous owners! The Illuminati used the U.S. Military to take the Poppy fields from Afghanistan people so the Illuminati could control the opioid trade! This is one of the true reasons why we went into Afghanistan! It was never about Bin Laden! Bin Laden was a CIA asset! It was more about the Illuminati controlling the Poppy fields in Afghanistan and installing an Illuminati Central Bank like the Federal Reserve in Afghanistan.

Whoever controls the Poppy fields controls the opioid trade! The Illuminati and the CIA now control the production and distribution of opioids! It's not the Mexican Cartel that's supplying most of the drug trade; it's the CIA. They just tell you it's the Mexican Cartel, so you won't look at them. Just like the Illuminati and the CIA took over the Poppy fields in Afghanistan, the Illuminati tried this same takeover of the drug trade by consolidating the Mexican Cartels into one Mega Cartel! This was the Illuminati's plan before Operation Fast and Furious was exposed! Operation Fast and Furious was not just about the U.S. Government selling guns to the Mexican Cartel; it was about the Illuminati and the CIA's complete takeover of the Cocaine trade! The plan was to kill off all the Cartels except for one Cartel, and they were going to rule that one Cartel to control the drug trade! This is the part of Operation Fast and Furious the media didn't tell you about!

So, weapons seized by the U.S. Government were sold to Mexican Drug Cartels. Then, those same weapons were used to kill U.S. citizens and Mexican citizens. Once an Alcohol, Tobacco, and Firearms agent (ATF agent) realized the guns used in murders were seized by the U.S. Government and then sold to Mexican Drug Cartels, the ATF agent blew the whistle. Once the ATF agent blew the whistle on Operation Fast and Furious, they fired him! And that opened the door for other information about the takeover of the cocaine trade to be released! What they didn't tell you about Operation Fast and Furious is this: the Illuminati was using the CIA to kill off all the drug Cartels except for one. Then, the CIA was going to consolidate all the drug production and distribution into one Mega Cartel. Then, the CIA and the Illuminati had plans to rule over that Mega Cartel by controlling the production and distribution of cocaine around the world! I want you to remember these names: General Noriega and Pablo Escobar were CIA assets that provided drugs to the CIA to distribute in the United States of America and around the world.

To sustain the drug demand for the United States of America, you must have a constant, uninterrupted flow of drugs into this country. And the Illuminati WAR Department, the Central Intelligence Agency, provides that constant, uninterrupted supply chain! The CIA hide their illegal drug money from Congress by setting up fake corporations. Then, the money is divided up amongst the high-ranking Illuminati members while the CIA maintains a portion of the money for black ops! While the Illuminati was making hundreds of billions of dollars from the sale of cocaine and opioids in America, African American communities were destroyed at an alarming rate because the Illuminati targeted these communities to destroy! Then, the Illuminati and the CIA use the news propaganda to make you believe African American people are responsible for this nation's drug problem, when in fact, the Illuminati and the Central Intelligence Agency are responsible for America's drug problem. The U.S. Government and the news media are not telling you the truth!

Also, you have been brainwashed to believe the United States of America has a "WAR on Drugs". The phrase "WAR on Drugs" is a coded phrase to the high-ranking Illuminati members. The phrase "WAR on Drugs" truly means this: "The WAR Department is supplying the drugs!" That means the Illuminati WAR Department (CIA) is supplying the drugs! You must remember the WAR Department for the Illuminati is the Skull and Bones. The Skull and Bones consists of Presidents, Senators, the CIA, and other intelligence agencies. And the Skull and Bones motto is WAR! WAR produces death, and death produces skulls and bones. So, WAR (Skull and Bones/CIA) is supplying the narcotics, and narcotics produce death, and death produces skulls and bones! So, the phrase "WAR on Drugs" truly means "The Illuminati WAR Department (CIA) is supplying the drugs!" The phrase "WAR on Drugs" was nothing more than a coded message to the high-ranking Illuminati members.

The Bilderberg group is the Illuminati Finance Department. The Bilderberg group is made up of the richest members of the Illuminati. The Bilderberg group has men who represent the 13 families of the Illuminati. The Bilderberg group controls the Banking Cartel in almost every nation, even the United States of America. The Centralize Banking Cartel of the United States of America is known as the Federal Reserve Bank. The 13 Families of the Illuminati own the United States Federal Reserve! The United States Federal Reserve is not a government institution like we were taught in school. They taught us a lie on purpose! The Federal Reserve Bank is a privately held bank that 12 other banks own. And those 12 banks that own the Federal Reserve are owned by the 13 Families of the Illuminati! The Federal Reserve is not a government institution! I know what you think you were taught, but it was all a lie. The Federal Reserve Bank is not a department of the U.S. Government. The Federal Reserve is a privately held Corporation!

This is what happens. The United States of America was a sovereign nation that owned its own money. Then, in 1910, a group of Illuminati men met on Jekyll Island off the coast of Georgia. These men had legislation drafted out to take complete and utter control over the United States' money. This legislation would be named the Federal Reserve Act. The Federal Reserve Act was passed by Congress and signed into law in December 1913 by President Woodrow Wilson. The Federal Reserve Act gave the 13 Families of the Illuminati the legal right to take over the United States of America's money. The United States money was taken from the United States and given to the owners of the Federal Reserve Bank. So, you can understand this; I want you to think of it like this. You have ten thousand dollars in the bank. And then I tell you to sign all your money over to me so I can own and manage your money for you. And if you need any money, I will lend you your own money, and you will have to pay me back the principal with interest even though it's your money I am lending you! And I will use those interest payments to enrich myself. This is what the Illuminati did to the United States of America when they created the Federal Reserve Bank.

From there, they lent the United States their own money and then charged the United States interest on their own money! The interest payments don't belong to the United States of America it belong to the 13 Families that own the Federal Reserve Banks. Wow! Then the Federal Reserve Bank started printing new money out of thin air and then lent it to the United States of America. Then, the U.S. had to pay the principal and interest back to the Federal Reserve Bank on the money they created out of thin air when they had the money printed! So, the United States must repay the Federal Reserve the principal amount of the money printed plus the interest on the principal amount. This is known as the National Debt. The U.S. has paid so much interest toward the National Debt that the Federal Reserve Bank can now lend trillions of dollars to the U.S. Government!

How can the Federal Reserve lend the U.S. Government trillions of dollars? The United States has been paying the Federal Reserve billions in interest annually. These interest payments are known as interest on the National Debt! As of 2023, the U.S. is paying a yearly interest payment of six hundred and fifty-nine billion dollars ($659,000,000,000) annually! Yes, the U.S. pays the Federal Reserve six hundred and fifty-nine billion dollars annually in interest payments! By 2024, we are expected to pay the Federal Reserve eight hundred and seventy billion dollars ($870,000,000,000) a year in interest. Each year, those interest payments will increase. We have paid the Federal Reserve so much money in interest that the owners of the Federal Reserve Bank are worth more than five hundred trillion dollars! Yes, I said the owners of the Federal Reserve Bank are worth more than five hundred trillion dollars! And since the owners of the Federal Reserve are worth hundreds of trillions of dollars. They can lend the U.S. Government trillions of dollars through the Federal Reserve Bank.

Once these interest payments are made, the Federal Reserve takes the money and divides it up between the 12 privately held banks that own the Federal Reserve. The 13 Families of the Illuminati own the 12 privately held banks that own the Federal Reserve. The money is divided between the 13 Families of the Illuminati. Then the Illuminati family members take your tax dollars, and they go out and live their billionaire and trillionaire lifestyles on the taxpayer's money! And guess what? The trillions of dollars they make off the United States taxpayers are not subject to any taxation. This means the Federal Reserve Bank and the 13 Families of the Illuminati do not pay any taxes on the trillions of dollars they made from U.S. taxpayers. They have a law barring any taxation on the Federal Reserve Bank.

The law is 12 U.S.C § 531 (C) Exemption From Taxation. Which states the Federal Reserve banks, including the capital stock and surplus therein, and the income derived therefrom shall be exempt from Federal, State, and local taxation, except taxes upon real estate. *"Exemption From Taxation." Board of Governors of the Federal Reserve System, January 17, 2023, https://www.federalreserve.gov/aboutthefed/section7.htm*

The 13 families of the Illuminati make sure you and your family are taxed to death, but they aren't paying any taxes on the hundreds of trillions of dollars they stole from the United States and its citizens. These people have found a way to make slaves out of every citizen in the United States and the world. Wow! So let me ask you one question. Who did you think the interest being paid on the National Debt was going to?

When President John F. Kennedy found out about this system of control, the Illuminati had on the citizens of the United States and the people around the world. John F. Kennedy planned on making a stand against the Illuminati! On April 27, 1961, President John F. Kennedy gave a speech denouncing the Illuminati secret society! Here is part of the speech.

...<u>The very word "secrecy" is repugnant in a free and open society; and we are as a people inherently and historically opposed to secret societies, to secret oaths and to secret proceedings.</u> We decided long ago that the dangers of excessive and unwarranted concealment of pertinent facts far outweighed the dangers which are cited to justify it. Even today, there is little value in opposing the threat of a closed society by imitating its arbitrary restrictions. Even today, there is little value in insuring the survival of our nation if our traditions do not survive with it. And there is very grave danger that an announced need for increased security will be seized upon by those anxious to expand its meaning to the very limits of official censorship and concealment. That I do not intend to permit to the extent that it is in my control. And no official of my

Administration, whether his rank is high or low, civilian or military, should interpret my words here tonight as an excuse to censor the news, to stifle dissent, to cover up our mistakes or to withhold from the press and the public the facts they deserve to know.

But I do ask every publisher, every editor, and every newsman in the nation to reexamine his own standards, and to recognize the nature of our country's peril. In time of war, the government and the press have customarily joined in an effort based largely on self-discipline, to prevent unauthorized disclosures to the enemy. In time of "clear and present danger," the courts have held that even the privileged rights of the First Amendment must yield to the public's need for national security.

Today no war has been declared--and however fierce the struggle may be, it may never be declared in the traditional fashion. Our way of life is under attack. Those who make themselves our enemy are advancing around the globe. The survival of our friends is in danger. And yet no war has been declared, no borders have been crossed by marching troops, no missiles have been fired.

If the press is awaiting a declaration of war before it imposes the self-discipline of combat conditions, then I can only say that no war ever posed a greater threat to our security. If you are awaiting a finding of "clear and present danger," then I can only say that the danger has never been more clear and its presence has never been more imminent.

It requires a change in outlook, a change in tactics, a change in missions--by the government, by the people, by every businessman or labor leader, and by every newspaper. For we are opposed around the world by a monolithic and ruthless conspiracy that relies primarily on covert means for expanding its sphere of influence--on infiltration instead of invasion, on subversion instead of elections, on intimidation instead of free choice, on guerrillas by night instead of armies by day. It is a system which has conscripted vast human and material resources into the building of a tightly knit, highly efficient machine that combines military, diplomatic, intelligence, economic, scientific and political operations... "John F. Kennedy Speeches." *John F. Kennedy Presidential Library and Museum,* www.jfklibrary.org/Research/Research-Aids/JFK-Speeches/American-Newspaper-Publishers-Association_19610427.aspx.

Once John F. Kennedy made that speech, he publicly defied the Illuminati. But many Americans didn't understand who or what John F. Kennedy was talking about. Many Americans thought John F. Kennedy was talking about Russia because the Illuminati control news media informed the people he was talking about Russia. But President Kennedy wasn't talking about Russia; he was talking about the Illuminati.

Once President John F. Kennedy found out what the Illuminati was doing by way of the Federal Reserve, President John F. Kennedy planned to stop the Illuminati from making money off the American taxpayers. President John F. Kennedy signed Executive Order 11110 on June 4, 1963. Executive Order 11110 created the **United States Note**. Executive Order 11110 was designed to give the United States their currency while making the Federal Reserve Notes worthless! Executive Order 11110 would use U.S. silver to back the newly issued **United States Note.** The United States Note would be backed by silver, while the Federal Reserve Note would only be backed by a promise. By backing the newly issued United States Note with silver, the Federal Reserve Note, which the Illuminati own, would have become worthless, but the United States Note would have been very valuable! This would have put the Illuminati Federal Reserve Bank out of business! You must remember the Federal Reserve is not a branch of the United States Government! The Federal Reserve is a privately held Corporation!

Executive Order 11110 would have made the Federal Reserve Notes you currently carry in your pockets worthless, but it would have made the newly issued United States Note very valuable! Wayne, Anthony. "Thoughts about Gold, Silver, and other stuff." *Thoughts about Gold Silver and other stuff*, www.rapidtrends.com/it-almost-became-money-united-states-notes-versus-federal-reserve-notes/.

President John F. Kennedy was going to give the United States back ownership of its currency when he created the United States Note. But the Illuminati Central Banking Cartel wouldn't allow that to happen. The 13 Families of the Illuminati planned on making trillions of dollars off the United States taxpayers from the federal income tax law they created in 1911! This is the true reason the Illuminati issued a kill order against President John F. Kennedy. President Kennedy was publicly defying the Illuminati power structure! President Kennedy was going to stop the Illuminati from making hundreds of trillions of dollars off the United States Government and its citizens.

President John F. Kennedy was assassinated on November 22, 1963, by the Illuminati! His assassination came five months after he issued Executive Order 11110. The governing body of the Illuminati ordered the assassination of President John F. Kennedy. The assignation of John F. Kennedy was nothing more than a coup d'é·tat (ko͞o′ dā-tä), which means a regime change by force! The governing body of the Illuminati used its members in the federal government to arrange the assassination of President John F. Kennedy. You must remember there are two governments in the United States Government. There is a government that is for the people by the people. Then there is the government that is for the Illuminati by the Illuminati. As of today, the Illuminati has almost taken total control of the United States Government.

You must remember it's the people who ordered the assassination of President John F. Kennedy who are also to blame. Don't just blame the ones who pulled the trigger! Blame the ones who gave the order to assassinate President John F. Kennedy. The order has to come from the highest levels to assassinate a U.S. President; the order must come from the very top! And the top is the governing body of the Illuminati, which is the Order of the Quest!

The United States Note would be the currency in circulation if President Kennedy wasn't assassinated. That means the United States wouldn't owe a thirty-four trillion-dollar ($34,000,000,000,000) National Debt to the Illuminati! The majority of the thirty-four trillion dollars ($34,000,000,000,000) in National Debt is owed to the Federal Reserve Bank, which means the majority of the thirty-four trillion dollars is owed to the Illuminati! The national debt is growing and will have grown by the time you read this book. It may be more than thirty-five trillion by now. They killed President John F. Kennedy to stop him from having the United States Note issued on a massive scale. They also killed him to send a message to every President or Senator that no one would interfere with the Federal Reserve Bank and its currency.

This is also the reason why President John F. Kennedy's brother, Bobby Kennedy, was assassinated! Bobby Kennedy was running for President when he was assassinated! The Illuminati knew if Bobby Kennedy got elected, he would enforce Executive Order 11110, which his brother, President John F. Kennedy, signed into law. The Illuminati killed Bobby Kennedy before he could get elected! The Illuminati also killed President Kennedy's son, John F. Kennedy Jr. John F. Kennedy Jr. was about to enter a New York Senate race against an Illuminati member named Hillary Rodham Clinton. And John F. Kennedy Jr. would have been considered the favorite to win the election. But his plane crashed, and he was murdered, which cleared the way for Hillary Clinton. How convenient it was for Hillary Rodham Clinton that John F. Kennedy Jr.

was murdered in his plane crash. Things don't just happen; they are planned.

You all should have known something was wrong because the United States is the richest nation on earth, but we owe thirty-four trillion dollars in debt. But the United States is lending other nations billions of dollars each year. If we are the richest nation on the earth and lending billions of dollars to other nations, who do we owe thirty-four trillion dollars to? It doesn't make sense if you think about it. No other nation or nations have the resources to lend the United States of America thirty-four trillion dollars! It never made sense if you stop to think about it! But they dumbed down the citizens of the United States of America so much that no one stopped to think about it.

Most of the thirty-four trillion is owed to the Federal Reserve Bank. This means thirty-four trillion dollars is owed to the Illuminati! This means your tax dollars pay six hundred billion in interest payments to the national debt! And those six hundred billion in interest payments go directly to the 13 families of the Illuminati! This is why the Federal income tax law was created when the Federal Reserve Act came into law. These people have robbed and raped the United States of America, and they have made slaves out of every American! It doesn't matter if you are Black, White, Hispanic, Native American, or any other ethnic group! It doesn't matter if you are democrat or republican. The Illuminati found a way to make slaves out of all of you! Now, do you understand why they killed President John F. Kennedy? Now, do you understand why they killed his brother, Bobby Kennedy? The Illuminati killed them because President John F. Kennedy and his brother Bobby Kennedy were trying to stop them!

Below are the Federal Reserve Note and the United States Note. The Federal Reserve Note is the money we use today, but this is how it looked back in 1963. The United States Note is the money President Kennedy issued with Executive Order 11110. The primary difference between the Federal Reserve Note and the United States Note is the color of the serial number. The Federal Reserve Note serial number is green, while the United States Note serial number is red. Also, the Federal Reserve Note has a green seal, while the United States Note has a red seal. This is the true history I am giving you.

Federal Reserve Note Owned by the Illuminati (Money we use today)

United States Note (Money John F. Kennedy Issued)

Since childhood, the Lord has prepared me with this information. One day, when I was about ten or eleven, this man approached me. This man started talking about the Federal Reserve Note and the United States Note issued by John F. Kennedy. This man then took both notes out of his wallet and began to explain the difference between the two notes to me. He then explains why John F. Kennedy created the United States Note. After the man gave me a five-minute lecture on the Federal Reserve Note and the United States Note, he disappeared, and I never saw him again! I thought nothing of it then, but now I know it was an angel sent to me. The angel taught me important facts about the United States currency that our history books purposely omitted.

All the interest being accumulated and paid towards the national debt is making the 13 Families of the Illuminati super rich! So basically, the Illuminati have created a way to make every American citizen a slave! The Illuminati has made us slaves so we can produce an income stream for them! We are nothing more than a slave labor force for them! Our tax dollars are financing their billionaire and trillionaire lifestyles! But these trillionaire Illuminati members make sure their wealth is never aired in the media! They keep their names out of the media because they own nearly all the mainstream media outlets. They own almost all of them! And since their wealth is never aired in the media, you don't even know they exist! Also, the Illuminati call themselves "The Elites!"

Now, the Illuminati Banking Cartel is not just doing this in the United States of America. This same system is being done across the world by the same Illuminati Central Banking Cartel. But six nations refused the Illuminati's Banking Cartel. They were Libya, Iraq, Iran, Afghanistan, Syria, and North Korea! And it just so happened that a war was started in four of these countries, and the governments were overthrown so an Illuminati Central Banking Cartel could be set up. WAR destroyed the four countries because they rejected the Illuminati Banking Cartel and the Illuminati system! Now, do you truly understand why we went to WAR with Afghanistan and Iraq and helped overthrow Libya and Syria? Everything they told you on television was just propaganda to convince you we had to go to WAR with those countries. We had to go into those countries to take control over their governments so they could set up the Illuminati Centralize Banking Cartel, and so they could force them to rewrite their Constitution to allow for a One World Leader and a One World Currency.

It was never about Iraq having "Weapons of Mass Destruction". That was just propaganda to get you to support the war! It was never about the United States going into Afghanistan to find Bin Laden! It was about toppling the government of Afghanistan so they could set up their people in government so that they could set up an Illuminati Centralize Banking Cartel so that they could take over the heroin trade! It was about removing Muammar Gaddafi from Libya because Muammar Gaddafi had been talking to nations about trading gold dinar instead of the U.S. Dollar. Trading in Gold dinar would have made the Illuminati Central Banking Cartel lose money and control. The Illuminati Banking Cartel had to remove Muammar Gaddafi. All the reasons they gave you on television were propaganda to manipulate the American people and people of the world to support military action!

The two main nations that are left without an Illuminati Centralize Banking Cartel are North Korea and Iran. And it's only a matter of time before the Illuminati used the United States military to take down Iran so they could install their Illuminati Central Banking Cartel. Now, do you understand recent and past events that have been going on around the world? The Bilderberg Group is the Illuminati Finance Department that controls the world's banking system! And when I say they control the world banking system, they control it! What they are doing in the United States is the same thing they do around the world in other countries. It's not just happening here in the U.S.; it's happening worldwide. I am just showing you what they are doing in the U.S., but it is a global conspiracy by the Illuminati that is taking place all over the world.

The Federal Reserve Bank is about to remove the U.S. Dollar from circulation and flex their power over the United States citizens. First, they will remove the ACH, which is the Automated Clearing House. ACH is the primary system that companies use to process electronic funds transfers. When payments are made with ACH, the funds are electronically deposited into that company's financial institution. Once they remove the Automated Clearing House, they will replace it with FedNow. FedNow is designed for all financial electronic transactions to go directly to the Federal Reserve. So, instead of ACH being the clearing house, the Federal Reserve will be the clearing house. So basically, the Federal Reserve will have TOTAL control over every financial transaction in the United States. And once they remove cash from circulation, they can lock you out of the financial industry if you don't comply with their tyrannical mandates and Draconian rules. Draco! Hint to the wise: the words Draco and Draconian mean something!

So, instead of cash, they will issue an electronic currency. This electronic currency is called the CBDC, Central Bank Digital Currency. This digital currency can be set up to expire all the money in your account at the end of each month, and if you do not use the money before the end of the month, then you will lose it. This CBDC will be issued in the United States and worldwide. Cash will be removed from the system. This Central Bank Digital Currency will give them limitless power over you. Once they remove cash from the system, they can lock people out of the financial industry who don't comply with their tyrannical mandates and their Draconian rules. Once they issue a CBDC, they will force the population to take the mark of the beast, the computer chip I warned you about. They are walking you right into a trap. They are implementing this system right now!

For them to pull this off, I believe they will cause Chaos in the United States of America. Whether this Chaos is purposely crashing the U. S. Dollar directly or indirectly, causing a food shortage, or unleashing viruses on the world. Or they may have a Black Swan event where they hit you with unexpected events that don't usually happen. For example, the Banking System collapses, the power is out for 30 to 60 days, the internet goes down for weeks, and there is no food in the grocery store for 6 months or more. The Illuminati always rule by Chaos. The Illuminati will cause the problem so they can give you the solution.

Another department of the Illuminati Corporation is the Trilateral Commission. The Trilateral Commission is the department in the Illuminati that is responsible for the consolidation of commercial and banking interests to create a Global Society! The reason why the Illuminati want a Global Society is because they are preparing to usher in a One World Currency, a One World Government under a One World Leader under a One World Satanic religion! Every nation must be subject to fall under the authority of this One World Leader. Some of you call this One World Leader the antichrist! But the Holy Bible refers to him by a different name. This different name will be discussed in the chapters to come!

So poorer nations are enticed to come into the Illuminati-controlled Centralize Banking Cartel. They enticed these poorer nations with loans from the World Bank, trade benefits from the World Trade Organization (WTO), and other benefits from the International Monetary Fund (IMF). The World Bank makes billions of dollars worth of loans to poorer nations for development or aid. The money is supposed to boost the economy by creating jobs and circulating money throughout the nation's economy. But most of the money never reaches the citizens in these poor nations; because conditions are placed on the poorer nations to bring in outside corporations to do most of the work. These outside corporations are normally corporations that exist outside of that nation and the corporations are normally controlled by the Illuminati. Once these outside corporations are brought in, the money lent to these poor countries is recycled back through the Illuminati control corporations. And the money flows back to the nation the corporation was from. The money is not truly helping the poorer nation's economy because very little money is reaching the citizens who live in these poor nations because the work was contracted out to corporations from other nations. So now the poorer nations are on the hook to pay back billions of dollars they can't afford because the billions of dollars they receive didn't circulate in their economy!

Once the Illuminati has these poor nations on the hook for billions of dollars worth of loans, they can't afford. The Illuminati then sends in the Council of Foreign Relations, which is the Illuminati Department that is responsible for making sure other nations change their laws and constitutions to make it easier for that nation to join the Illuminati Global Community, which will have a One World Government ruled by a One World Leader. The One World Leader is the one you all call the antichrist.

So now the Council of Foreign Relations is persuading this same nation the World Bank lent billions of dollars too, to change their laws and Constitution. Once the poorer nation refuses to do so, the Illuminati, by way of the Trilateral Commission, the Council of Foreign Relations, the World Bank, and the World Trade Organization, make sure they collapse that nation's economy. The Illuminati make sure the World Bank prematurely calls billions of dollars worth of loans due, and then the Illuminati make sure the World Trade Organization (WTO) places trade sanctions on that nation. Once these two things are done it causes the economy to collapse! This throws the economy into hyperinflation. The Trilateral Commission, Council of Foreign Relations, the World Bank, and the World Trade Organization (WTO) know that poorer nations can't afford to pay the loans back prematurely! They know this would cause the nation's economy to collapse! So, they put enormous amounts of pressure on the nation to surrender to their Illuminati Central Banking Cartel and to rewrite their Constitution so it would allow that nation to be governed by a **One World Leader** under a **One World Government** under a **One World Currency**. The One World Currency is the Central Bank Digital Currency! Every nation is moving to a Central Bank Digital Currency.

Once a nation refuses to join its centralized banking Cartel or refuses to rewrite its Constitution, the Illuminati uses the WTO (World Trade Organization) to impose trade sanctions on that nation, making food and other resources scarce. Then, the Illuminati Trilateral Commission made the World Bank call the nation's loan prematurely.

Once the loans are called due prematurely and the sanctions have been placed on the nations' trade, this crashes the poorer nation's economy and causes hyperinflation! All because the nation wouldn't do what the Illuminati wanted them to do. The Illuminati cause hyperinflation in these poor nations, and they starve the government and its people in the poorer nations until they give in to their demands! And I mean, they are starving these poorer nations to death! This is why hyperinflation was going on in Venezuela and other nations. This is why there is a food shortage in Venezuela. The Illuminati has been starving nations for years! And they have been doing it right in front of your face! And since they control the government and the mainstream media, they made sure you didn't know any of this!

Whenever you hear the term hyperinflation, this means they have collapsed a nation's economy! To understand how they are starving these nations, just follow me! Most of the food supply in the United States and other nations is controlled by Umbrella Corporations like BlackRock, Vanguard, or State Street, which the Illuminati control. Through mergers and acquisitions, the Illuminati used corporations to buy food companies, water companies, and water rights. The Illuminati did this so the Illuminati could control the food supply, water companies, and water rights in almost every nation. While many of you weren't paying attention, in the '80s, '90s, and 2000s, these Umbrella Corporations bought food companies, water companies, and water rights worldwide. They were consolidating all the food and water companies under their control.

Why do they want to control the food, water companies, and water rights, you ask? Because one day, they will hold every nation hostage like they have been holding countries like Venezuela hostage! What would you do if you had to give in to the Illuminati to get the essentials such as food and water? What if the Illuminati wanted you to worship Satan for you to receive food and water? Would you do it? What if you and your children were hungry and thirsty? Food and water are the two things everyone needs to survive! So, no food and no water mean you starve to death! The Illuminati understands this concept, so they use the financial resources they receive from the interest payment made to the Federal Reserve Bank for the National Debt to form Umbrella Corporations. They then use these Umbrella Corporations to buy up many nations' food companies, water companies, water rights, and farmlands. So they can control the food supply. They are even putting the farmers out of business because of this B.S. called climate change. If they put the farmers out of business and they control the food companies, where are you and your family going to get food from? This is what the

Illuminati are doing to many nations right now! In Germany, the Netherlands, France, Australia, and other nations, they are stopping the Farmers from growing food, and they want the farmers to kill off their cattle. But you wouldn't know any of this because the mainstream news media is not reporting this to you. After all, the Illuminati controls the mainstream news media! They even have their Illuminati member Gates buying up the U.S. farmlands. The Illuminati-controlled news media is just giving you a bunch of useless information to keep you dumb and stupid.

So through the use of these Umbrella Corporations like BlackRock, Vanguard and State Street, the World Bank, and the World Trade Organization, the Illuminati can starve nations like Venezuela to death until nations like Venezuela give into their demands and allow the Illuminati to place their Centralize Banking Cartel in that nation and that nation must rewrite their Constitution to allow for a One World Leader under a One World Government with a One World Currency (Central Bank Digital Currency). What I am giving you is the absolute truth given to me by the Most High God Jehovah! They are starving these poorer nations to death because they won't surrender their nation's currency over to the Illuminati, and they won't change their laws and their constitutions to allow for a **One World Leader**!

The Illuminati manipulate nations to surrender to their Centralize Banking Cartel by collapsing that nation's economy. Then, they force that nation to rewrite their Constitutions to allow a One World Leader under a One World Government to control that nation. And if a nation rejects the Illuminati's plans for a Centralize Banking Cartel, One World Leader, and One World Government. They collapse that nation's economy by causing hyperinflation and food shortages. If that doesn't work, the Illuminati bring in their WAR Machine, the U.S. Military!

Five nations that refused the Illuminati's Banking Cartel, One World Government with a One World Leader, were Libya, Syria, Iraq, Afghanistan, and Iran! If you noticed, four of the five nations the United States went to war with recently. The United States and other nations first went to War with Afghanistan, then Iraq, then they helped topple Libya, then they overthrew Syria, and now the United States is starting a propaganda campaign to go to War against Iran! Is it a coincidence that four out of the five nations that refused to allow for a Centralized Banking Cartel, the United States, and other nations went to war with it? This is not just a coincidence; this was all planned! You just didn't know what was happening because you brought into the lies they told on television! All the wars against the nations I just mentioned were designed to take over each government to make sure each nation would allow for a One World Leader and allow for the Illuminati Centralize Banking Cartel to take over that nation's currency! This is the United States of America's Book of Secrets! This is the Illuminati Book of Secrets!

How is the Illuminati able to do all these things while the media and its citizens are watching? Well, first, they control the media, and by controlling the media, they control the public opinion! The Illuminati has formed and controlled a social behavior Institute called The Tavistock Institute of Human Relations. The Tavistock Institute is responsible for using techniques to help condition and brainwash the masses. See, everything that you see in the News media is mass programming and brainwashing techniques the Tavistock Institute came up with. Let me just tell you how they do it. Have you ever had a conversation with another person about a topic that was in the news media? And then that person starts repeating word for word everything they said in the news media. No matter how wrong or idiotic the news media opinion was. Well, the person repeated everything the news media said because the Tavistock Institute devised techniques to make people think whatever they say in the news media was that person's original thought! Brainwashing! Please read the "Tavistock Institute of Human Relations: Shaping the Moral, Spiritual, Cultural, and Political and Economic Decline of the United States of America" by Dr. John Coleman. This book will blow your mind!

Then there is the Jason Society, which is the technology Department of the Illuminati. The Jason Society uses, releases, and flows specific advanced technology. The Jason Society first distributes this advanced technology to the NSA, CIA, and the Pentagon and then plans its future release into everyday society. An economic boom always occurs with the release of this super-advanced technology into society! We will talk more about this in chapters to come.

Then there is the Brotherhood of the Snake. The Brotherhood of the Snake is the Illuminati Medical Department. The Brotherhood of the Snake is responsible for releasing certain medical advancements achieved through experimenting on humans against their will. Then, the Brotherhood of the Snake releases those medical findings or breakthroughs to the medical community and the world. The

Brotherhood of the Snake symbol is the same symbol for modern-day medicine.

The Illuminati and the Brotherhood of the Snake worship Satan as God. And the symbol for Satan is the snake. This is why the medical association uses a snake wrapped around a stick or a tree or two snakes wrapped around a stick with wings on it. The snake is the universal symbol for Satan; the stick or tree represents what happened in the Garden of Eden. It was when the snake deceived Adam and Eve to eat from the Tree of the Knowledge of Good and Evil that Satan was given authority to bring sin into this world. The tree and the snake represent the beginning, the beginning of Satan and sin in this world. The Brotherhood of the Snake adopted that symbol for itself and the medical community that it is over. Below are the symbols for the Brotherhood of the Snake (the medical community).

American Medical Association | AMA. N.p., n.d. Web. 14 Mar. 2017. <https://www.ama-assn.org/>.

"AMA Votes To Maintain Support Of Health Care Mandate." *CBS Chicago.* N.p., n.d. Web. 14 Mar. 2017. <http://chicago.cbslocal.com/2011/06/21/ama-votes-to-maintain-support-of-health-care-mandate/>.

Then there is the Priesthood of the Illuminati, which is known as Free-Masons. The Free Masons are the Illuminati Department of Religion! The Free Masons are to the Illuminati as the Levites were to the Israelites. The Levites were the priests responsible for teaching the word of God to the Israelites. And the Free Masons are the Priesthood for the Illuminati! The higher the degree you obtain the closer you become to becoming a High Priest. Only those who reach the 33rd degree are given a chance to reach the High Priest Hood of Free Masonry.

When many people first joined the Free Masons, they honestly believed Free Masons worshiped the Most High God Jehovah. It was set up like that to give new inductees into the Free Masons the perception they worship God Jehovah. But they don't worship God Jehovah; they worship their god, Satan. In the beginning, Free Masons are told they worship god. But this god is never named to them in the beginning! So, each Free Mason is taken on this journey of moving up the ladder to a higher degree. In each degree, more information about their god is revealed to them. Since more information is revealed to them in each degree, the more severe the punishment for them if they reveal this information about their god. These threats of punishment impose fear upon the member. This is a critical indicator that Satan is over Free Masonry because Satan always uses fear tactics!

So many Christians who joined Free Masons assume the god they are talking about is Jehovah. But in fact, the god they are talking about is Satan. This is why you should always ask the name of the god a person is referring to when they say the word "god". Just don't assume their god is your God, Jehovah. Free Masons is the Priesthood of the Illuminati. This is why Free Mason's place of worship is called the Masonic Temple! It is called the Masonic Temple because this is their house of worship to Satan! Once people got wise to them calling their place of meeting a Temple, this sparked questions about who they were worshiping in their temple. And once people started asking questions, they changed the name from Masonic Temple to Masonic Lodges!

One of the leading fashions of the Free Masons is to construct satanic symbols in plain view of men. The Illuminati believe the more satanic symbols they use in public, the more power the Illuminati have and the more power they can obtain! The Illuminati used the Snake wrapped around a tree to symbolize the medical industry. They have used this symbol in plain sight for years, and none of you knew why they chose a snake wrapped around a tree. This is an example of how the Illuminati use these satanic symbols in plain sight, and the public is ignorant of their symbols. The High Priest for the Illuminati, the 33 Degree Free Masons, are responsible for constructing many satanic symbols here in the U.S. and around the world. Like the symbols they use on the U.S. Currency. If you only knew the message on the one-dollar bill and what it's telling you. In a chapter to come, I will reveal the coded message on the back of the U.S. One Dollar Bill, and we will talk more about the High Priest of the Illuminati called Free Masons.

I just gave you a few departments that make up the Illuminati Corporate structure, but there are many more departments! Once you understand their corporate structure, you can see how they have influenced our world and how they operate! So, each Illuminati department has its own Upper-Level Management group. Like the Skull and Bones have members with the Central Intelligence Agency, Senators and Presidents who comprise their upper-level management group! Then the upper-level management group of each department answers to the Illuminati Board of Directors called "The Order of the Quest". "The Order of the Quest" maps out the Illuminati agenda and how the agenda is to be carried out. The Order of the Quest maps out and governs the plans for worldwide dominance (New World Order) and the implementation of their system into everyday life. The Order of the Quest is the governing body of the Illuminati that maintains "Order" throughout the different departments and all of the different agendas. Everybody within the Illuminati understands that "Order" must be maintained. And anyone who doesn't stay in order will be killed!

Also, one of the reasons the Illuminati is broken down into different departments is because it disguises the group's overall agenda. Since the Illuminati goes by different names in different groups, it has been difficult for individuals to pinpoint who is pulling the strings and who is directing the world's agenda. These different departments allow the Illuminati to hide behind a mask! This mask they have been hiding behind has allowed them to stay anonymous while being seen in plain sight. I am pulling back their mask so you can see who they are!

The Illuminati understood that going under one group name would make it too easy for them and their agenda to be recognized. So, they formed different groups that served as departments of the Illuminati Corporation. The high-level Illuminati members understand their acts are acts of treason against their government, so they try to make it as difficult as possible for you to understand who they are and what they are doing. Do you see why they make sure they control the positions of power and influence? They want to control the position of power and influence so they can carry out their agenda and stop any prosecution of their members for treason.

67. Satan Is A Liar and So Is The Illuminati

In Chapter 64, titled "The Very Old But New Religion, The Illuminati," I told you about my encounter with this young lady at JSU. During this encounter, this young lady told me she had just come from this secret meeting with this secret group. And then the young lady began to tell me some of what they told her! This meeting with this secret group was one week after the last Illuminati recruiter approached me at JSU. I am about to review what happened that day and what the young lady revealed to me!

One day, while I was leaving the mail center at JSU. This girl had a puzzled look on her face, and she said, "Ken!" So, I asked her what was wrong. And then this girl told me she had just come from this secret meeting with this secret group in the Thurman Montgomery Building. Then the girl said they were telling them how aliens created man and how man was created for slave labor! Then the girl said they were shown top-secret information from the **U.S. Government** about these aliens. Then the girl said, "They told us that man was created by the aliens for slave labor." Then the girl asked me if I thought that was possible. I gave this girl this look that said, "I don't have a clue what you are talking about!" Then suddenly, the girl said, "I am not supposed to be telling people this stuff! And then she stopped talking and walked away!

After the brief conversation with the girl, I didn't think about anything she said that day because the little information she gave me didn't make sense. But some years later, the Lord revealed to me who the Illuminati were, and things made more sense to me. Then, I ran across the beliefs of the Illuminati that were posted on the internet. When I read this information on the internet, the memory of the conversation I had with the girl at JSU came back to me.

My memory was sparked because the same thing I read on the internet was some of the same information the young lady told me many years earlier at JSU! Below are the beliefs of the Illuminati. In the article below the Illuminati is referred to as the Brotherhood of the Snake because that was their name in the beginning! When the text below speaks of this alien name Ea or Enki, it's talking about Satan! The Illuminati say Satan is an alien, and he created man! Below is the article I found on the internet

The reality of alien interaction with humans can be seen throughout history. In the 1st century, the Roman statesman **Cicero** wrote of strange spheres in the sky. There are records dating back to 8th century France that tell of individuals during Charlemagne's time that were taken up by strange craft and shown various marvels. At that time, if they revealed what had happened to them or if it became public knowledge, they were killed. There are even records during that time which speak of strange aerial ships destroying crops.

All the major religions of Mesopotamia, Egypt and the Americas are dominated by adoration of "Gods from the sky". There is evidence that these *custodial rulers from the stars* controlled every aspect of human society from the initial appearance of the current version of Homo Sapiens about 30,000 years ago. It was at the same time that the Neanderthal version of Homo Sapiens *mysteriously and suddenly vanished from the face of the planet.*

Early investigations into this matter were done by **Charles Fort**, who lived between 1867 and 1932. He found that extraterrestrial societies were very much involved in Earths prehistory, and that the status of the human race appeared to be like *self-satisfied livestock.* His final thought was that humans were used as slaves.

The idea of humans as a slave race is not new. Ancient Sumerian records dating back to 4500BC relate that humanoids from the sky were the rulers of humans. Human priests acted as intermediaries between the rulers from the sky and the human masses. The rulers from the sky were described in those records as having male and female sexes, racially diverse, and behaviorally similar to humans.

The records of that time also relate that it was the general Sumerian belief that the first humans were bred in the wombs of alien females. Sumerian records indicate that the alien rulers were involved in mining and other exploitation of natural resources that involved humans performing lifetimes of backbreaking labor. The actual creation of the Homo Sapiens species occurred sometime between 300,000 to 500,000 years ago.

Records in ancient Mesopotamia credit an alien by the name of **Ea** for directing the creation of Homo Sapiens as a genetic hybrid. Ea was also known as the Prince of Earth. Other portions of the Earth were controlled by Ea's half-brother. During the time of his uninterrupted influence, marshes by the Persian Gulf were drained and dams and dikes were constructed. Ea was the main advocate of the hybrid species later known as Homo Sapiens before the council of aliens that managed operations on the planet.

Sumerian records indicate that human beings were spiritual beings animating physical bodies, and that the alien rulers contrived an original plan to keep entities attached to physical bodies, body physically and psychologically, so that the humans could function as slave labor. Population control measures were carried out on the humans. Food supplies were cut off, humans were forced to cannibalism, diseases were introduced, and there was global flooding.

In order to prevent the humans from banding together and realizing the predicament they were in, the aliens sought to block spiritual recovery for the humans. Various immediate measures were taken in order to prevent human unity. Formal religions were introduced, people were scattered around the planet, and different language functions introduced. The aliens made sure that existence for humans became a physical chore that would preclude excess time on their hands.

Ea, when in power, was dedicated to the dissemination of spiritual knowledge to the newly created human hybrids. He was aware of the desire by other alien groups to promote human bondage. Despite his good intentions, Ea failed to maintain the freedom of the human species. His faction, sometimes known as the Brotherhood of the Snake, was defeated by other alien factions. Ea was banished to Earth by the other aliens, and his title was changed from the *Prince of Earth* to the *Prince of Darkness*. He was then portrayed to the humans as the "enemy of a Supreme Being" and the humans were told that all their troubles were the fault of Ea. *Humans were subsequently programmed to detect any trace of Ea in future lifetimes.*

Under negative alien influence, the *Brotherhood of the Snake* was changed from a force disseminating scientific and spiritual knowledge to one that became known for spiritual repression and betrayal. Corruption of the Brotherhood was evident in Egypt by 2000BC. The Pharaohs and priests were indoctrinated into the Brotherhood as Elite who would manipulate the masses for their own ends. *Brotherhood functions in society eventually evolved into* the Mystery Schools, which twisted spiritual knowledge, and restricted public access to any truths which had survived.

Traditions were started that transferred knowledge orally and also embedded it in symbology which only the Elite could understand.

Monotheism was one of the most insidious teachings of the Brotherhood. It was started in Egypt during the reign of Akhenaton, and eventually evolved into the teachings embodied in *Judaism*, *Islam* and *Christianity*. Humans were taught that the aliens were *Gods*, and the aliens enforced human obedience. One group of alien custodians was named the <u>Jehovah</u>, who had influence over the *Hebrew peoples*. The Hebrews were befriended and ruled by the Jehovah, who typically landed his craft in the mountains. In order to promote the "God" concept, only specific humans were allowed to approach the Jehovah, which were presented to the humans as a succession of singular beings, named *Jehovah*, over a long period of time.

Over time, a network of Brotherhood organizations imposed alien institutions on the human species and *generated conflict and war in order to manipulate and divide the human race.* The Brotherhood of The Snake - La Hermandad de La Serpiente. N.p., n.d. Web. 04 Feb.2013.<http://www.bibliotecapleyades.net/sociopolitica/sociopol_brotherhoodsnake.htm#menu>.

Here is another article I found talking about the Brotherhood of the snake and this alien name Ea (Satan).

The <u>Secret Societies</u> have been present in the history of man for a very long time. It all started thousands of years ago with the **"Brotherhood of the Snake"**, a secret society set up by an alien named **Ea** or **Enki**. This story is very carefully told in the *Sumerian scriptures*, which go back at least 6000 years. There it says man was created by <u>draconian aliens</u>, who came to this planet to exploit its resources - especially gold. But the work was heavy, so the alien race wanted someone else to do the hard work. Thus **Ea**, who was a brilliant scientist, created homo sapiens as a hybrid between a primitive earth life-form and the alien race.

First homo sapiens was only meant for slave labor and couldn't breed. Later on this was changed. Ea didn't like, though, how his created race was treated and wanted to enlighten them by telling them who they were and where they came from. He also wanted to tell them the well-hidden truth that each individual is a spirit inhabiting a body and that after body death the spirit lives on and reincarnates on earth.

Ea's superiors didn't agree to this, as they were afraid of chaos and turmoil, but Ea told them anyway. The early homo sapiens revolted against their Masters, but were forced to retire. Ea then started this secret society, the **Brotherhood of the Snake**, to enlighten people in secret. But he was discovered and judged by the alien laws, which meant that Ea was deported to Earth for eternity - to die here and be reborn here in endless cycles, using fragile, short living human bodies. If this is right, he might still be here...

In the meantime, as time passed by, the "**Brotherhood of the Snake**" was infiltrated by the Draconian Master aliens and the knowledge was distorted to trap man instead of enlighten him. The *Egyptian Era* was in fact real "space opera", with aliens walking around among us, even taking the throne as pharaohs on mostly. By that time the Brotherhood was very infiltrated and its purpose to manipulate the masses, making them believe in false gods and masters.

In the background through all history there are the secret societies. The *original Brotherhood* soon split up in cults, when certain people on top were in disagreement with each other and different powers of control developed, with them even fighting each other (which still is the case today) totally above an ignorant population.

They invented the different religions and sects and cults so man would be busy doing something else instead of looking into what the Brotherhood was doing. It was also a way to control people by not telling the truth about *God* and *Jesus*, so that people would miss the point and never be able to be set free. Religion has always been connected with guilt and punishment, which is NOT the way it is supposed to be. They put themselves in charge of the churches to entrap people and to spread conflicts between different belief systems. Most wars throughout history have been **religious wars.** Secret Societies and The Brotherhood of the Snake. N.p., n.d. Web. 04 Feb. 2013. <http://www.bibliotecapleyades.net/sociopolitica/sociopol_brotherhoodsnake05.htm>.

Now, did you notice how the articles credited this alien name Ea with creating humans? The devil is a liar, and so are the Illuminati! The

Heaven Father Jehovah, created man! Not Satan! But what if I told you there are some truths in the text above? Would you believe me, or would you say I am crazy? You know I love and believe in the Most High God Jehovah, his Son Jesus Christ, and the Holy Spirit! But what if I told you there was a lot of truth in the text above? Would you believe me? What the Lord has revealed to me over my lifetime is astonishing! What I know is almost the entire story of mankind! The Lord opened my eyes to the absolute truth, and when he did, he used his word in the Holy Bible to prove it. The ancient knowledge that was told to us in the Bible that we all missed! The Holy Bible speaks of some things in the above text, but we all missed it! We missed it because we didn't understand what we were reading! The Lord told us much in the Old Testament, but it was coded to us, and we all missed it!

I am not going to give it to you now! Because I must give it to you the way the Lord revealed it to me! Because if I give all of it to you at one time, it would overload your brain, and you would blow a circuit.

It is a reason why some of the smartest and most intelligent people in the world are members of the Illuminati, and they believe the article above is true. Because in the article above, there is a lot of truth, and Satan used a lot of truth to sell a BIG LIE! See when a lie contains truth in it, it is hard to detect the lie! So continue to follow me on this life journey; all truths will be revealed to you! And I will give you the absolute truth like the Lord Jesus Christ gave me! And I will prove it with scriptures out of the Bible! I am about to pull back the veil so you will know the true history of this mankind and this world. This is the United States of America Book of Secrets! This is the Illuminati Book of Secrets!

68. The Illuminati High Priest and its Symbol

In the previous chapter, I told you how the Illuminati believes this alien name, Ea or Enki, created mankind. And the alien they call Ea or Enki is truly Satan. To prove to you the Illuminati believe these things to be so, I will show you a coded message the High Priest of the Illuminati gave to you on the United States of America One Dollar Bill. The High Priest of the Illuminati are the Free Masons who reach the 33rd degree. Once the Free Masons reach the 33rd degree, they must perform an act that will desecrate the Holy Father in Heaven and the Holy Bible to prove they worship Satan. Once this act is done, they become High Priest of the Illuminati. If the act is not done, the 33rd Degree Mason is not received as a High Priest. And future knowledge of the Priesthood is not given to them.

So those who do reach the 33rd degree of Free Masonry and desecrate the name of the Most High God Jehovah, the Lord Jesus Christ, the Holy Spirit, and the Holy Bible continue their journey to the upper levels of Free Masonry and become High Priest of the Illuminati. Once they received this High Priesthood, they continued to learn more about the ancient history of mankind. They are taught about aliens and some of the information listed in the previous chapter. The journey through Free Masonry program one's mind to convert to Satanism. The journey to Free Masonry is to teach them Satan is god. The journey of this Priesthood starts with the Khedive; the organization is designed to introduce the male youth under 18 into the Free Mason Priesthood. The female Priesthood is called the Eastern Star!

Once one reaches the 33rd degree Free Masonry Priesthood they become High Priest if they desecrate the Holy Father and the Holy Bible. Then, some of the Illuminati High Priests used their talents to teach and preach their beliefs to the public by using satanic symbols and coded messages. One coded message was given to you on the back of the U.S. One Dollar Bill. This coded message on the back of the U.S. One Dollar Bill tells you the Illuminati's beliefs and agenda. I will decode the entire message for you. The message is broken down into several phrases, and once the phrases are placed together it gives you the entire message. Once I decode these word phrases for you and put these phrases together, you will then see the Illuminati agenda. Then, we will look at the United States of America's Great Seal on the back of the U.S. One Dollar Bill. The United States of America's Great Seal is nothing more than a steganography. A picture is hidden within the United States of America Great Seal! And that picture inside the United States Great Seal will tell you who the Illuminati god is! Follow me so you can see the Illuminati agenda revealed to you in plain sight.

A 33rd-degree Free Mason Illuminati High Priest designed the dollar bill. A 33rd-degree Free Mason Illuminati High Priest designed the Great Seal of the United States of America. Now, let's look at the United States of America Dollar bill. I am going to take you through this step by step. We will start from the left of the dollar bill and work our way to the right of the dollar bill.

1. Annuit Coeptis means "He favors our undertaking."

    The first question you should ask yourself is. Who is he? And why does "he favors our undertaking?"

2. Novus Ordo Seclorum means "A New Order of The Ages."

    The second question you should ask yourself is. What is this New Order of the Ages? And what is wrong with the current order?

3. In the middle of the Dollar Bill you see the statement "In God We Trust".

The question you should be asking is. Who is this god they are referring to? Don't make the mistake and think they are talking about Jehovah as God. Remember, this Dollar was created by the High Priest of the Illuminati, which are 33rd Degrees Free Masons. And the Illuminati and Free Masons worship Satan as a god. Now, let's piece together the initial three phrases to unravel this message. Often, these phrases are dissected in isolation, leading to a fragmented understanding. However, I will consolidate these phrases to present you with a comprehensive view of the message.

Annuit Coeptis Novus Ordo Seclorum In God we Trust. That means, "He favors our undertaking of a New Order of the Ages in God we Trust."

Did you see how the phrases turned into a sentence! And that sentence is telling you part of the Illuminati agenda! Here it is again.

Annuit Coeptis Novus Ordo Seclorum In God we Trust. That means, "He favors our undertaking of a New Order of the Ages in God we Trust."

To understand who this god is, you must look at the Great Seal on the right of the Dollar Bill. Once you see the hidden picture inside the Great Seal, you will understand who the Illuminati god is. The Great Seal of the United States is a steganography. A steganography is a picture hidden within a picture. Inside the Great Seal is a hidden picture. And that picture will tell you who the Illuminati is talking about when they put the coded message, "He favors our undertaking of a New Order of the Ages in God we Trust."

This steganography inside the Great Seal will show who the Illuminati god is. I'm going to show you three U.S. One Dollar Bill's. The U.S. Dollar Bill has been rolled up with light being placed behind them so you can see the image more clearly. The dollar bill was also darkened on the second and third dollar bill to help you make out the image more clearly. This will help expose the picture hidden within the Great Seal. This is who the Illuminati was referring to when they said, "He favors our undertaking of a New Order of the Ages **in God we Trust**." You can see a hidden picture within the Great Seal of the United States of America. The Illuminati created the Great Seal as a steganography to hide a picture of an alien within plain sight. The third dollar bill was darkened so you see the alien within the Great Seal of the United States of America!

When the Illuminati put the coded message, "He favors our undertaking of a New Order of the Ages **in God we Trust**." They are referring to the alien within the Great Seal as the god they trust in! In the third dollar bill, you can see an image of an alien that appears within the Great Seal. This is not a trick and this was not done by accident. The Great Seal is a steganography. The Great Seal was created as a steganography so they could hide the picture of the alien in plain sight. This took time and expertise for the Illuminati High Priest (Free Masons) to carefully craft this image within the Great Seal of the United States of America. The image in the Great Seal is a picture of an alien the Illuminati worships. Is that the picture of the alien name Ea or Enki that was discussed in the two articles we read? If so, Ea or Enki is just another name for Satan. Is that a picture of Satan in the great Seal of the United States?

Or is that a picture of the image of the beast that is discussed in the Holy Bible in the Book of Revelations. This alien is either Satan or the **image of the beast described in the Book of Revelations!** Let me say that again, in case some of you didn't understand what I said. This alien in the United States of America Great Seal is either a picture of Satan or the image of the beast. The phrase "the image of the beast" means "the image of Satan". Let me repeat what I just said: the phrase "the image of the beast" means "the image of Satan". The Holy Bible warns you about the image of the beast in the Book of Revelations.

This phrase image of the beast was first used in the Book of Revelations when the Prophet John tells us all he witnessed during the Great Tribulations. The picture of the alien on the back of the U.S. One Dollar Bill is also connected to the three demons I saw standing behind the three children in elementary. The picture of the alien (image of the beast) on the back of the U.S. One Dollar Bill is connected to the spaceship I saw in Twentynine Palms, California, during the summer of 1985. The picture of the alien (image of the beast) on the back of the U.S. One Dollar Bill is also connected to the two spaceships I saw when I looked through the dicyanin glass. The picture of the alien (image of the beast) on the back of the U.S. One Dollar Bill is also connected to the reptilian humanoid alien the lady in Buffalo, NY, saw crawl out the hole in the ground.

Remember the lady who told my siblings and me she saw a reptilian humanoid-looking creature crawling out of a hole in the ground? And then that creature stood up on two legs like a human. The picture of the alien on the back of the U.S. One Dollar Bill is connected to the things the girl was told at the secret Illuminati meeting at JSU! The girl at the secret Illuminati meeting was told aliens exist and they created man as slave labor. The picture of the alien on the back of the U.S. One Dollar Bill is also connected to the image of the beast mentioned in the Book of Revelations. The picture of the alien on the back of the U.S. One Dollar Bill is connected to the things the Lord revealed to me about the Illuminati recruiter having an alien inside of her. All these things are connected. It may not seem like it to you, but all these things are connected! And as you read this book, I will reveal to you what the Lord has revealed to me.

The Book of Revelations warns us that the image of the beast is coming! Here are a couple of scriptures that tell you about the image of the beast.

Revelation 13:15 The second **beast** was given power to give breath to the **image of the first beast**, so that the **image could speak and cause all who refused to worship the image to be killed.** (NIV, BibleGateway.com)

Revelation 13:15 is a coded message. The Lord revealed to me what it truly says. In a chapter to come, I will decode it for you, and once I do, it will blow your mind!

Revelation 14:9 A third angel followed them and said in a loud voice: "If anyone worships the **beast and its image** and receives its mark on their forehead or on their hand, (NIV, BibleGateway.com)

The alien that appears within the Great Seal is either Enki or Ea (Satan) or it's a picture of the image of the beast. Now, if you notice the image of the beast on the back of the U.S., One Dollar Bill looks like the alien many people describe as **"The Greys"**. Do you think it is a coincidence the picture of the alien on the back of the U.S. One Dollar Bill looks like the aliens many people describe seeing? Now, I know you have many questions about the image of the beast. And I know you want to know where the image of the beast comes from. I will reveal it to you the same way the Lord revealed it to me. Just continue to read.

The Illuminati and 33rd Degree Free Mason High Priest worship Satan and the image of the beast as god. This is why they constructed the image of the beast on the back of the U.S. One Dollar Bill. The Illuminati worship Satan as a god, and in the phrase "He favors our undertaking". "He" is referring to Satan! Now, since we understand who "He" represents in the coded phrase. Let me show you what they are saying in their coded message.

"He favors our undertaking of a New Order of the Ages, in God we Trust"! The coded sentence and the picture of the alien truly mean this:

"Satan favors the Illuminati undertaking of ushering in a New Order of the Ages where all mankind will trust in his image of the beast as god!"

Now, if you compare the Illuminati coded message I just decoded for you and then you compare the Biblical scripters I just gave you. You will see **biblical scripture is warning you not to worship the image of the beast.** But on the back of the One Dollar Bill, it's telling you to worship the image of the beast. Here are the Biblical scriptures.

Revelation 13:15 The second **beast** was given power to give breath to the **image of the first beast**, so that the **image could speak and cause all who refused to worship the image to be killed.** (NIV, BibleGateway.com)

Revelation 14:9 A third angel followed them and said in a loud voice: "If anyone worships the **beast and its image** and receives its mark on their forehead or on their hand, (NIV, BibleGateway.com)

It will be a New Order of the Ages when Satan and Satan's image is worshiped as god instead of the Most High God Jehovah being worshipped as God. And the Illuminati is responsible for ushering in this

New Order of the Ages which many call the New World Order. If you look at the picture, it shows the image of the beast (alien) on the back of the Dollar Bill; the image of the beast has a crown around its head. The crown represents royalty, like a King. The picture is saying the image of the beast is King. The message you should take from the crown is this: the Illuminati see the image of the beast as their god, their King! Just like we Christians see God Jehovah and Jesus Christ as our Lord and King. The Illuminati see this image of the beast (alien) as their King and god. Now you must remember the Illuminati teaches its members an alien name, Ea, created man. And you must remember the alien name Ea is truly Satan! So Satan must be an alien.

Just remember what that coded message on the back of the dollar bill truly tells you. "Satan favors the Illuminati undertaking of ushering in a New Order of the Ages where all mankind will trust in his image of the beast as god!"

Since I have shown you their coded message and the picture of the image of the beast (alien) hidden within the Great Seal; now I need to decipher more coded messages on the back of the U.S. One Dollar Bill for you. If you notice, the term "E Pluribus Unum" appears on the ribbon hanging out of the mouth of the eagle. The eagle represents the United States. "E Pluribus Unum" means "Out of many, one." I know you were taught that "Out of many, one" refers to the United States being formed out of many different states, and now we are one nation. But that is not why the High Priest of the Illuminati put that saying there.

When the High Priest of the Illuminati put the saying "Out of many, one" on the picture with the alien, the High Priest of the Illuminati was referring to a prophecy of the coming of their messiah! And the Illuminati's messiah is the one who will be the One World Ruler I was telling you about. The Illuminati's messiah is the One World Ruler that you all call the antichrist. But the Bible has another name for him. I will give that to you later.

So "E Pluribus Unum" means "Out of many, one." But the saying means, "Out of many comes one!" The Illuminati are prophesying about the coming of their messiah. The Illuminati is saying this; "Out of many Illuminati shall come the one!" This means the one you all call the Anti-Christ will rise from the Illuminati. He will rise to power by the hands and the money of the Illuminati. And he will come from the United States of America. That's why the Illuminati had the eagle holding the ribbon that says "E Pluribus Unum" out his mouth. The eagle is the national bird of the United States of America, so the eagle represents America. They are telling you the Illuminati messiah will come from the United States of America.

Out of the Illuminati comes the one! Just like Jesus Christ, the Messiah came from the Israelites. Satan tries to build his kingdom here on earth, just like the Holy Father built his kingdom here on earth. The word of the Lord came from 12 tribes of Israel. The teachings of Satan come out of the 13 tribes of the Illuminati.

So, just like the Most High God Jehovah formed Israel to bring his word to the world. Satan is using the Illuminati to bring forward his lies to the world. Since Satan formed the Illuminati out of the 13 Families of the Illuminati, the number 13 is a very sacred number for the Illuminati. This is why the number 13 is repeated so often on the back of the U.S. One Dollar Bill. If you look at the image of the alien within the Great Seal, there are 13 stars on the forehead of the alien. Those 13 stars represent the 13 Tribes of the Illuminati (13 Families of the Illuminati). Then, there are 13 arrows within the eagle's feet. Then there are 13 leaves on the branch. Then, there are 13 berries on the leaves. The number 13 is repeated because the number 13 is sacred to the Illuminati because of the 13 families of the Illuminati. The Illuminati hold the number 13 sacred, just like many Christians hold the numbers 3, 7, and 12 as sacred and holy numbers.

So out of the Illuminati will come the son of Satan, who will mislead the world! The one who will be ushered in like he is a savior to the United States of America! But he is no savior; he is full of lies and deceit. I know who the Illuminati false messiah is, and so do you! Many of you already worship this man as if he were a god! They are preparing this man to be ushered in as a One World Leader! You better wake up! This is the United States of America Book of Secrets! This is the Illuminati's Book of Secrets!

69. The Illuminati High Priest Suppress the Lord's Word

Satan is at war with the Most High God Jehovah, and the Lord Jesus Christ. Satan wishes to ascend to the heights of the Most High God Jehovah, and take over Heaven. Satan wages war against the Lord and the Lord's people through his actions here on Earth. The Earth is a battleground between the Most High God Jehovah, and Satan. This battleground is the epic center for a winner-take-all war. Yes, I said a winner-take-all war is being carried out here on Earth.

The winner of the war between God and Satan will sit on the throne in Heaven. I know this is the absolute truth because this is what the Most High God Jehovah has revealed to me. I know many of you just thought the events of this world were just random acts, but it's not. Many of these events are strategic moves being made by Satan and his people, the Illuminati. In this world, you have two waring fashions battling. One fashion is the Most High God Jehovah, Jesus Christ, angels, and Christians. Then you have the other fashion, which is Satan, the anti-Christ, demons, the Illuminati, and others who reject Jesus Christ. This war came about because Satan desired to take over Heaven, so Satan convinced two-thirds of the population in Heaven to follow him. And it is a reason why two-thirds of the population in Heaven followed Satan. We want discuss that reason now but will discuss it in future chapters. Some of you have been taught that one-third of the angels followed Satan. That is true, but more than just angels dwelled in Heaven. Angels were just one small set of the population. The Lord revealed to me two-thirds of the entire population of Heaven rebelled with Satan.

The Kingdom of Heaven was divided once the war broke out in Heaven. So, the Holy Father and us angels fought back and drove Satan and his angels out of Heaven. After Satan was kicked out of Heaven, Satan made a challenge to the Holy Father. Satan said he could get anything the Holy Father created to worship him. The Holy Father accepted the challenge Satan had made. And then the Holy Father created this Earth and everything in it in six days. And on the sixth day, the Holy Father Jehovah created man in his image. And then the Holy Father Jehovah rested on the seventh day. And then God set the rules up for this war. One of these rules set a time frame for the number of cycles to be fought in this WAR, and the Holy Father determined the length of each cycle.

The WAR was going to have a winner-take-all prize! If Satan were to win, Satan would take over the Kingdom of Heaven. But once Satan loses this WAR, then Satan would be cast down into the pit of burning sulfur forever and ever. What we are experiencing here on Earth is the WAR between the Most High God Jehovah, and Satan. And it's a winner-take-all prize! And all of you are a part of this WAR one way or the other because each one of us is like a piece on a game board! Those who are with the Most High God Jehovah accept Jesus Christ as the son of God, and those who are against the Most High God Jehovah are on Satan's team!

Let me explain this to you so you can understand clearly. Through Abraham came three pillars of religion: Judaism, Islam, and Christianity. The Islamic faith does not deny Jesus Christ. They believe Jesus was a Holy Prophet! But Jesus was more than a Prophet. He is the son of God. I need the Islamic faith to understand that Jesus' name is mentioned twenty-five times directly and another eight times as the Messiah in the Quran. So, it is Jesus who should be worshiped. When the Bible references the saints, it is talking about Christians, Jews, and Muslims who accept Jesus Christ as the son of God. All other religions are false religions, and they have false gods! If you don't believe Jesus Christ is the Son of God, you are against the Most High God Jehovah! Don't worry, my Jewish and Islamic brothers; your eyes will soon be open to the absolute truth! All that I am telling you was revealed to me by the Most High God Jehovah and the Lord Jesus Christ! Those who decided not to follow the Most High God Jehovah, and the Lord Jesus Christ made a decision to follow Satan, whether intentionally or unintentionally. Because of this war, the actions of men on this Earth are being weighed in the balance, as stated by the Prophet Enoch in the Book of Enoch.

Enoch 41:1 reads, [1] "And after that, I saw all the secrets of the heavens, and how the kingdom is divided, and how the 2 actions of men are weighed in the balance. *The Book of Enoch: The First Parable: Chapter XLI.* N.p., n.d. Web. 15 Mar. 2015. <http://www.sacred-texts.com/bib/boe/boe044.htm>.

So those are the two waring fashions here on this Earth. But many Christians didn't understand they were warring directly against Satan's people, the Illuminati. And that was part of Satan's plan. Satan used the secrecy of the Illuminati to fight a **silent war** against Christians and the Lord's word. Christians didn't understand they were at war with the Illuminati because Satan planned to keep the secret society a secret. To be honest with you, the strategy was brilliant because how could Christians fight a war when they didn't even understand they were at war? And because we Christians didn't understand we were at war, we have been losing the war! Christians are losing the war because we didn't identify our enemy, the Illuminati! We understood Satan was the enemy, but we didn't understand how Satan was using his secret society, the Illuminati, to carry out his plans. For thousands of years, Christians have been fighting a faceless opponent that was like a ghost! The Illuminati!

The ghost name the Illuminati has been setting agendas to remove the word of God from everyday life so they can suppress the Lord's people. This agenda has taken shape here in the United States of America. While Satan and his people, the Illuminati, plan their attacks years in advance, we Christians are just reacting to the plans they have already placed in motion. This means we constantly react to their plans for social engineering, laws, and agendas. We have been playing defense while they have been playing offense. They are attacking, and we have been defending. The Illuminati has used the media to speak against the Lord's word and the Lord's leaders. The Illuminati controls the media (airwaves), and they are the ones who are teaching these false doctrines through the media. The Illuminati are the ones who are preaching this false doctrine of same-sex marriage, transgender, and homosexuality in the media. The Illuminati has been preaching you false doctrine for years through the media.

The Illuminati are in positions of power throughout the United States Government. The Illuminati has members in low-ranking, midrange, and high-ranking positions. Do you remember when I was in the third grade, and I was tested, and the lady said I was "Gifted". The same lady that tested me went to my mother and tried to convince my mother to send me out of state to this school that was for "Gifted children". The lady told my mother that people who attended this school became high-ranking government officials. The lady was saying that people who went to that school became members of the Illuminati, and they became high-ranking government officials, people like Condoleezza Rice, and many others.

The Illuminati have used their control over the Democratic Party and the Republican Party to influence laws to suppress the American people and the Lord's word. The Illuminati has used the Judicial System to pass laws to suppress the Lord's word. For example, the Illuminati had five of their Illuminati Free Mason High Priests on the U.S. Supreme Court when they ruled to take prayer out of schools. There are 9 people on the U.S. Supreme Court. To have the majority, you only need five votes. Since there were five Illuminati Free Mason High Priests on the U.S. Supreme Court for the *Engel v. Vitale* case, they only needed all five Illuminati High Priests to rule in favor of removing prayer from public schools. But in this case, the Illuminati High Priest Free Masons didn't need five votes; they only needed four votes because one of the Justices was out for medical reasons. Then, another Justice refused to vote on this case for some odd reason.

So, only seven Supreme Court Justices voted on the *Engel v. Vitale* case, which meant the Illuminati only needed four votes to pass the law to remove prayer from schools. This meant they only needed four out of the five Illuminati Free Mason High Priests to vote to remove prayer from schools. And that's exactly what happened: four out of the five Illuminati Free Mason High Priest voted to take prayer out of schools. The Illuminati are the ones who removed Christian Prayer from schools. The Illuminati gave orders to the Illuminati High Priest to vote in favor of removing Christian prayer from schools. We can identify which Supreme Court Justices are Illuminati Free Mason High Priest because they are 33rd Degree, Free Masons. But what we don't know is what other Supreme Court Justices were also members of the Illuminati because they could have been members of the Illuminati without being one of the Free Mason High Priests.

The five Illuminati Free Mason High Priests on the U.S. Supreme Court for the *Engel v. Vitale* case were Chief Justice Earl Warren, Justice Hugo L. Black, Justice Thomas C. Clark, Justice William O. Douglas, and Justice Potter C. Stewart. Also, you must remember the Free Mason High Priest worships Satan as a god. The four Illuminati Free Mason High Priest who voted to remove prayer from schools are Chief Justice Earl Warren, Justice Hugo L. Black, Justice Thomas C. Clark, and Justice William O. Douglas. Then, to make it look good, the Illuminati Free Mason High Priest Potter C. Stewart voted against removing prayer from schools. They did this to make it appear all the Free Masons didn't conspire to remove prayer from school. They knew they only needed four votes, so they made sure Potter C. Stewart voted against it.

The vote was 6 to 1 to remove prayer from schools. This was no accident that five out of the seven Supreme Court Justices that voted were Free Mason High Priest for the Illuminati. This was by design! It was not a mistake. There were only seven people who voted. That was a calculated attack by Satan and the Illuminati. And that planned attack by Satan and the Illuminati had a devastating impact on our country to this very day. The Illuminati has been making sure laws like this have been passed in our country for years. The Illuminati are the ones who are pushing this anti-Christian agenda. The Illuminati has been using its members in the Judicial Branch, Legislative Branch, and Executive Branch to pass laws to remove the word of the Most High Jehovah from our society. The Illuminati and their Priests have been leading this assault against Christians.

The Illuminati were responsible for removing prayer from our schools. The Illuminati purposely suppressed the Lord's children from being led and taught Christian prayer in schools. The *Engel v. Vitale* decision was rendered on June 25, 1962. Then, one year later, on June 17, 1963, the Illuminati High Priest Supreme Court Justices rendered another decision to attach Christians. On June 17, 1963, the Illuminati High Priest Supreme Court Justices removed Bible reading from public schools in the *Abington School District v. Schempp* case. In the *Abington School District v. Schempp* case, the Illuminati Free Mason High Priest voted to remove public reading of the Holy Bible from public schools. And the same Illuminati Free Mason High Priest voted the same way. The four Illuminati High Priest Free Masons Supreme Court Justices who voted to remove Bible reading out of schools are Chief Justice Earl Warren, Justice Hugo L. Black, Justice Thomas C. Justice, and William O. Douglas. And again, the Illuminati Free Mason High Priest Potter C. Stewart voted against removing Bible reading from schools just to make it look good!

So, within a year, the Illuminati and its High Priest launched an all-out attack on Christians! And Christians sat back and did nothing! The main reason Christians have done nothing is because the Illuminati brainwashed Christians and the American people with the false belief that there should be a *separation of church and state*. But while the Illuminati was brainwashing you with the thought there should be a *separation between church and state*, the Illuminati has been using government resources to promote their satanic agenda! The Illuminati used government-appointed Judges who sat on the U.S. Supreme Court to attack Christianity when they removed prayer and Bible reading from schools. This means the ILLUMINATI never intended to have a *separation between church and state*. The Illuminati just wanted to use the argument there needs to be a *separation of church and state* as a foundation to deny those who believe in Jesus Christ the right to do so in public schools and government.

The Illuminati and their Free Mason High Priest worship Satan as a god. They use their position of power to lift their religion, which is Luciferin religion (Satanism), by destroying Christianity. This means they are using taxpayer's dollars as a servant of the court to promote the Luciferin religion (Satanism) by destroying Christianity. This means they never intended for there to be a *separation of church and state*! They just wanted to manipulate Christians to believe there should be a *separation of church and state*. And guess what? It worked! The Illuminati's true intentions were to **separate** the children from the Most High God Jehovah and the Lord Jesus Christ by removing prayer and Bible reading from schools so children who attend public schools wouldn't know the one and only true God Jehovah! And if you look at the decay of the moral fiber of the United States of America, it worked!

The Illuminati don't believe in *a separation of church and state* because they use taxpayer dollars to test children in the third grade to see who is gifted and who isn't gifted. Then, the Illuminati use taxpayer dollars to form these gifted programs in public schools to condition the minds of the gifted students for future recruitment into the Illuminati! If the Illuminati believe in *a separation of church and state,* they won't use taxpayers' dollars to target children to become a part of their cult! The Illuminati manipulated Christians to believe something they don't even believe! Many Christians are running around here talking about how there must be *a separation of church and state* while the same people that brainwashed them are using taxpayer dollars to recruit children into the Luciferin cult, the Illuminati! That doesn't sound like *a separation of church and state* to me because they are using government resources to recruit people into their cult to worship Satan as god! Once they test children in public taxpayer schools, the Illuminati recruit the people they tested at public Colleges and Universities that receive tax dollars. They hold these meetings at Colleges and Universities, which the taxpayers fund. So please tell me, how is that *separation between church and state* when they are using government money and government resources to recruit people into the Illuminati?

Now, if you look at the ruling of the Supreme Court on other cases like abortion, the Nativity Scene being used on government land, abortion, and gay marriage. Satan's will is projected in each decision the Supreme Court has rendered. And each decision goes against the will of the Most High God Jehovah. For example, the Lord said; Thou shall not kill. But the Illuminati-controlled Supreme Court ruled in the past the murder of millions of unborn children was legal. Then, the Illuminati-controlled Supreme Court ruled the Nativity Scene, which represents the birth of Jesus Christ, cannot be displayed on government land. But at the same time, the Illuminati displays the Great Seal of the United States of America on the U.S. One Dollar Bill, on government buildings, on government letterheads, etc. The Great Seal of the United States of America has a picture of an alien that the Illuminati worship as god. The Illuminati Supreme Court will allow the image of the beast (an alien) to be on the back of the U.S. One Dollar Bill, displayed as the official United States Seal on money, displayed on official letterheads and displayed on government buildings, but the Illuminati Supreme Court doesn't want to allow the Nativity Scene to be displayed on government land for one month. The Illuminati have their satanic beliefs posted year-round on money, government buildings, and letterheads but they want allow Christians to have the Nativity Scene up for one month! Wow! Do you see how the Illuminati made fools out of you?

Better yet, the Illuminati can display their god, an alien, in the Great Seal of the United States of America, but Judge Roy Moore couldn't display the Ten Commandments in his Courtroom! Do you see how the Illuminati is using the U.S. Government and State Government to practice their religion, but at the same time, the Illuminati is using the U.S. Government and State Government to suppress Christianity?

Then the Illuminati-controlled Supreme Court ruled marriage can be between two people of the same sex! When the word of God says a man shall become one with his wife, and wife refers to a woman, God meant for a man to unite with a natural-born woman. When God made Eve, he created Eve to be Adams's wife, which tells you God meant for marriage to be between a man and a woman! Then the Lord tells you in Leviticus 18:22 that people of the same sex shouldn't have sexual relations.

Leviticus 18:22 You shall not lie with a male as with a woman. It *is* an abomination. (NKJ, Biblegateway.com)

If the scriptures in the Holy Bible tell you people of the same sex shouldn't have sexual relations, why would the U.S. Supreme Court rule in favor of gay marriage? The answer to that question is this. The majority of the Justices on the U.S. Supreme Court are members of the Illuminati, and they worship Satan as a god. And Satan's people will always go against Biblical scriptures and the will of the Most High God Jehovah. Also, many of the power brokers in the Illuminati are homosexuals and pedophiles! It's the Illuminati power brokers who used the news media and media outlets to promote homosexuality! The Illuminati agenda is a Satanic agenda. Gay marriage, homosexuality, and transgender are Satanic agenda! The Illuminati use the news media to publicly scorn anybody who stands up against homosexuality, gay marriage, and transgender. Once they used the media to publicly scorn people who stands against homosexuality, gay marriage, and transgender, they condition your minds that you will be at risk of being publicly scorned and ridiculed for opposing they wicked ideology. This technique they use is called social engineering! The Illuminati has social-engineered the public by using the news media and other media outlets as a weapon against the people. And guess what, it worked!

In all the case decisions I just mentioned, the Illuminati-controlled U.S. Supreme Court ruled against the word of the Most High God Jehovah. The Illuminati agenda goes against the word of the Most High God Jehovah! It's not hard to see if you remove your personal feelings and emotions and just look at the truth! The Illuminati controlled the Judicial Branch, the Executive Office (Presidents), and the Legislative Branch (Congressmen, Senators) for many years! Many U.S. Presidents, Congressmen, and Federal Judges were and are Illuminati High Priest Free Masons. You will be astonished at what has been happening in front of your unsuspecting eyes.

Once your eyes are open to the absolute truth, you will begin to understand what they taught you about the founding fathers of this country. The history of the founding fathers was structured around teaching you about the Illuminati Free Mason High Priest like George Washington, Benjamin Franklin, John Hancock, and the other Free Masons. When we think about the United States' founding fathers, we only think about those who were Free Masons. And that was done by design because we were taught what the Illuminati wanted us to know. Most of the founding fathers were not Free Mason High Priest. Most of the founding fathers were Christian Pastors! But the founding fathers that were Christians Pastors are rarely mentioned in the history books and on television. The ones that were Illuminati High Priest are the ones that are mostly mentioned in the history books and on television.

The Illuminati have been teaching you the history they want you to know. For instance, nine out of the fifty-six signers of the Declaration of Independence were Free Masons, but **twenty-nine signers of the Declaration of Independence were Christian Pastors**. But you would be brainwashed by the Illuminati historians to believe the only people who signed the U.S. Constitution were Free Masons. And you would believe this by how they present the founding fathers to you. Whenever you hear anything about the signers of the Declaration of Independence, the media and history books only talk about the ones who were part of the Illuminati, those who were Illuminati High Priest Free Masons!

The history books and the media always talk about Benjamin Franklin as if he were a god. But did the history books tell you Benjamin Franklin was an Illuminati Free Mason High Priest, and he was also a member of other cults like the Hellfire Club? "News." *Worldview Weekend*,www.worldviewweekend.com/news/article/ben-franklin-hellfire-club-and-his-view-jesus-christ. Benjamin Franklin and his Hellfire Club members would practice satanic rituals and have orgies in underground caves. Then, on top of that, they found the remains of 10 humans buried under the house where Benjamin Franklin lived in London. There were six children's remains found, and four adult remains found under the house. The remains date back to when Benjamin Franklin lived at the house. "News." *Worldview Weekend*, www.worldviewweekend.com/news/article/ben-franklin-hellfire-club-and-his-view-jesus- christ.

Let's connect the dots. Benjamin Franklin was an Illuminati High Priest who worshiped Satan as a god. Then Benjamin Franklin was a member of other cults like the Hellfire Club that practiced satanic rituals and orgies. Then, the remains of 10 human beings were found under the house where Benjamin Franklin lived. The remains date back to when Benjamin Franklin lived in the house. With all that information, it would be very reasonable to believe Benjamin Franklin was murdering children and adults for satanic sacrifices! This is the absolute truth because the Lord revealed this to me! But the Illuminati control news media, and historians would have you believe Benjamin Franklin didn't do anything wrong! They want you to believe one of Benjamin Franklin's friends brought the bodies to the house so they could study the anatomy. Then they would also have you believe that after they studied the anatomy, they just conveniently disposed of the bodies by burying them under the house where Benjamin Franklin lived. The reason why Benjamin Franklin buried the bodies under the house was because he was trying to hide his crimes! Just like serial killers of today bury the remains of others on their property to hide the evidence of their crimes! Benjamin Franklin's acts are an example of how evil and sick the members of the Illuminati are!

People have been trying to warn you about the Illuminati and the satanic blood sacrifices they perform. They like to torture and eat babies; they have pedophilia rings where they sex traffic kids and teenagers. One of these sex traffickers were Jeffrey Epstein. He provided teens to his rich and powerful clients like Presidents, Senators, government officials, actors, etc. Jeffrey Epstein is a member of the Illuminati. The same people you praise in the public eye are some monsters behind closed doors! They do some of the most horrific satanic rituals and sacrifices! And if anything is ever leaked about them and their rituals, it will be covered up by the Illuminati control media.

Just like the Illuminati-controlled media covered up the teen sex slave ring Bill Clinton, U.S. Senators, and other Illuminati members like Jeffrey Epstein were part of. This story of the teen sex slave ring Bill Clinton participated in got little to no coverage by the Illuminati control news media. A U.S. President involved in a teen sex trafficking ring and having sex with teens is a major story and a felony crime. But since the Illuminati controls the mainstream media, you heard little to nothing about Bill Clinton and the teen sex slave ring he was a part of! Because Bill Clinton is Illuminati! But Donald Trump is not Illuminati. They are persecuting Donald Trump by Illuminati prosecutors and Illuminati judges but they don't even attempt to bring a case against Bill Clinton and others who were involved in the sec trafficking ring. This is the United States of America Book of Secrets! This is the Illuminati's Book of Secrets!

70. The Illuminati and Political Elections

The Illuminati has seized power in the United States of America and other nations by manipulating political elections. In this chapter, I will show you how they have manipulated political elections to ensure any vote cast is cast for an Illuminati candidate. So you can understand what I am about to explain, I will use a Presidential Election here in the United States of America as an example. But this election manipulation is not limited to Presidential elections, this is happening in most elections that is being held in the United States of America and other nations throughout the world. I will show you how the Illuminati has seized power through political elections.

The first thing the Illuminati does to seize power through an election is to line Illuminati candidates in both the Democratic Primaries and the Republican Primaries. Say you are having an election for President of the United States, and the Illuminati want to make sure they get an Illuminati member elected as President. They will load the Democratic primaries with Illuminati members and then load the Republican primaries with Illuminati members. For example, if you look at the 2016 Presidential Primaries, you will fully understand how the Illuminati rig the elections to ensure an Illuminati candidate would win.

By loading the Democratic primaries and the Republican primaries with Illuminati members, they all but guarantee they will have an Illuminati member elected as President. Many people registered to be candidates for the Democratic Party for President, but only three Illuminati candidates and one regular candidate were chosen to be in the debates. The three Illuminati Candidates chosen for the Democratic debates were Hillary Clinton, Bernie Sanders, and Robert O'Malley. Yes, Bernie Sanders is Illuminati! The one regular candidate was Senator Jim Webb from Virginia. And the only reason Jim Webb was allowed in the debates was because he was a Senator. Out of all the people who registered to be a Democratic Candidate for President, how were only those four chosen to be in the televised national debates? Who decides who is allowed in the debates? The Illuminati has been deciding on who is allowed in the national TV debates! You must remember the Illuminati has gain control over the television networks by placing their people in key positions and by controlling the financials of the networks through mergers and acquisitions.

In the 2016 Democratic Presidential Debates, you had three Illuminati candidates and one regular candidate in the nationally televised debates. That means the Illuminati had a 75% chance they would have an Illuminati member win the Democratic primaries because three out of the four Democratic candidates were in the nationally televised debates were Illuminati members. The Illuminati had a 75% chance the Democratic nominee would be an Illuminati member. Those were great odds, but the Illuminati had to ensure they made their odds even better. Senator Jim Webb was not a member of the Illuminati. So, the Illuminati had to make sure they marginalized Senator Jim Webb. Marginalize means treating a person, group, or concept as insignificant. Google, n.d. Web. 20 Dec. 2015. <http://www.google.com/#q=marginalized&*&spf=1>. Another definition of marginalization is putting or keeping someone in a powerless or unimportant position within a society or group. "Marginalize." *Merriam-Webster*. Merriam-Webster, n.d. Web. 20 Dec. 2015. <http://www.merriam-webster.com/dictionary/marginalize>.

The Illuminati had to make sure they marginalized Senator Jim Webb. The Illuminati control news media made Senator Jim Webb appear insignificant. In the Democratic debates Senator Jim Webb participated in, the news media made sure Senator Jim Webb rarely got time to talk during the debate, and when he did get time to talk, they cut his time short. But they gave the other Illuminati candidates plenty of opportunities to speak. By doing this, they marginalized Senator Jim Webb's importance in the Democratic debates.

They used the mediator in the debates to marginalize him so they could send a message to the viewing audience that Senator Jim Webb was an insignificant candidate. And once the mediator did that to Senator Jim Webb, they affected his campaign and his ability to raise money. I have witnessed mediators do this same strategy against other candidates who were not members of the Illuminati establishment. When you hear the word establishment in the news media, they are referring to the Illuminati.

As a child, my dad told me I needed to watch the news to know what was happening worldwide. So, as a child, I began watching the National news on ABC News, NBC News, and CBS News. We didn't have cable as a child, so those were my only options. I became a national news junkie as a child. I was just absorbing everything that was going on in the world. And if I didn't understand something, the Lord would be right there to explain it to me. And when the news media manipulates things or didn't tell the truth. The Lord would be right there to explain the truth to me.

As a child, the Lord explained to me the tactics the news media use to marginalize certain political candidates. I just didn't understand who the news media chose to marginalize and why. As of today, I understand how the news media chose the candidates to marginalize. The Illuminati control news media always marginalizes the non-Illuminati candidates (regular candidates), like Senator Jim Webb. I have seen the Illuminati-control news media use this tactic to marginalize non-Illuminati candidates by not giving them any media coverage in the prime-time news media and by not giving them any talking time during the debates. And this tactic normally runs the non-Illuminati candidates (regular candidates) off, just like they ran Senator Jim Webb off!

But say if the marginalization tactic doesn't work and the non-Illuminati candidate is still doing well. The Illuminati then deploys their weapon of mass destruction against the non-Illuminati candidate (regular candidate), and that weapon of mass destruction is the news media. To give you an example of a non-Illuminati candidate doing well until the Illuminati control media launch an all-out assault against them, let's look at the Republican candidate Ben Carson. Ben Carson and Donald Trump were non-Illuminati candidates in the Republican debates.

The Illuminati saw Ben Carson as a threat once he started to poll well. The Illuminati didn't expect Trump could win because they didn't think Trump would carry any of the black vote. But they were afraid that Ben Carson would carry the black vote if he received the Republican nomination. So the Illuminati released the Illuminati control news media on Dr. Ben Carson. Once the Illuminati deployed its weapon of mass destruction, they destroyed Dr. Ben Carson's campaign. The Illuminati control media started making attacks against Dr. Ben Carson's integrity, questioning whether he was telling the truth about his past. The Illuminati controlled news media attacked Dr. Caron's creditability. The attacks on Dr. Ben Carson were seven days a week, every hour on the hour. These attacks didn't stop until the Illuminati made Dr. Ben Carson lose many of his supporters. Once the Illuminati controlled news media got the desired result of stopping any type of momentum by Dr. Carson's campaign, they eased up, but the damage had already been done! The Illuminati controlled news media destroyed Dr. Carson's campaign.

The Illuminati controls all the major news organizations. It doesn't matter if it's CNN, NBC, ABC, CBS, MSNBC, FOX, etc. Whether it's the Washington Post, New York Times, Wall Street Journal, etc. The Illuminati control these media outlets by controlling the Corporations that own the media company and by having Illuminati members in positions of power within these news organizations. By being in positions of power within the news organization, the Illuminati controls what is being reported and how the story is being reported. This way, the Illuminati controls the flow of information. And since the Illuminati controls the flow of information, the Illuminati dictate what you know and what you don't know. These news organizations have Illuminati members as CEOs, Members of the Board, Editors, Contributors, commentators, and any other position of power within the news organization. News people are nothing more than actors. They are reading from a script that they didn't write. News commentators and reports read from a teleprompter. That means they are just acting out the words they are reading from the teleprompter. So basically, they are being told what to say and how to say it. Actors! The Illuminati figured out that if you want to control people, you must control four things: food, water, the money supply (Federal Reserve), and the flow of information (the news media).

When the governing body of the Illuminati gives an order to destroy a particular candidate, all the news organizations go on the attack at the same time. This is what happened to Dr. Ben Carson. All the news organizations attacked him simultaneously on the same subject matter! Doesn't that seem a little suspicious that every mainstream news organization attacked Dr. Ben Carson simultaneously and on the same subject matter? That is more than suspicious; that was a coordinated attack by the Illuminati to destroy the campaign of Dr. Ben Carson. President Franklin D. Roosevelt said, "In politics, nothing happens by accident. If it happens, you can bet it was planned that way."

"Franklin D. Roosevelt Quotes." *BrainyQuote*.Xplore, n.d. Web. 06 Apr. 2017. <http://www.brainyquote.com/quotes/quotes/f/franklind164126.html>.

It was a planned attack when the Illuminati controlled news media all attacked Dr. Ben Carson on the same subject matter at the same time! This is the method the Illuminati have used for years to marginalize and eliminate non-Illuminati candidates from the election process. The Illuminati and the Illuminati control media have deployed the same systematic attack that they used on Dr. Ben Carson on many other non-Illuminati candidates (regular candidates) throughout the years. It's a systematic attack because you can easily see the coordination and orchestration of the mainstream media deployed simultaneously. The method of launching the weapon of mass destruction, the news media against non-Illuminati candidates (regular candidates), has been an effective tool they have used for many years. The Illuminati constantly use their weapon of mass destruction against regular candidates (non-Illuminati Candidates) because the American people never wise up and understand what they (the Illuminati) are doing. And since the American people never wise up to the tactics the Illuminati is using, the Illuminati keep running the same play out of the same Illuminati playbook! The Illuminati constantly uses the same play out of the same Illuminati playbook. You will begin to understand this once you continue reading this book. You must also remember I am using the Presidential primaries as an example, but this is the method the Illuminati use in all political elections here in the United States of America and around the world.

The media is the main avenue the Illuminati use to destroy non-Illuminati candidates (regular candidates). And suppose the media and its political commentators or contributors don't deter you from voting for an ordinary candidate. In that case, the Illuminati will use these so-called "polls" to deter you from voting for a candidate. See, the Illuminati is going to use the media to deter you one way or the other from voting for the non-Illuminati candidate (regular candidate). The Illuminati have polls released to tell you what candidate you should vote for. They use polls to play mind games with the viewing audience! The Lord revealed this to me as a child and as an adult. The Illuminati can brainwash you to believe a candidate does not have a chance to win by releasing bad poll numbers on the non-Illuminati candidate (regular candidate). And once the Illuminati control media keep releasing bad poll numbers on a non–Illuminati candidate, then you decide in your mind the candidate you like can't win because they have bad poll numbers. So, you decide to choose another candidate to vote for, and that candidate just so happens to be a member of the Illuminati! And now the non-Illuminati candidate (regular candidate) lost your support because the Illuminati-controlled news media gave you some numbers telling you the non-Illuminati candidate can't win! And the numbers the Illuminati control media gave you were created and manipulated to persuade you not to support the non-Illuminati candidate (regular candidate)! And guess what, it worked!

So, between the mainstream media marginalizing non-Illuminati candidates (regular candidates), and then the Illuminati launching their weapon of mass destruction against non-Illuminati candidates (regular candidates) and then the Illuminati releasing bad poll numbers against the non-Illuminati candidates (regular candidates), you are persuaded not to vote for the non-Illuminati candidate (regular candidate). And once you decide not to vote for the non-Illuminati candidate (regular candidate) then you support and vote for the Illuminati candidate. So, the Illuminati and the Illuminati control media have manipulated you through the entire election process, and they manipulated you until they got the desired result they wanted, which was for you to elect an Illuminati candidate. This is why the Illuminati say, "It doesn't matter who the people voted for because they always vote for us". The Illuminati say this because a vote cast is almost always cast for the Illuminati.

So, the three stages I just showed you were designed to discourage ordinary people (non-Illuminati candidates) from running for political office. It was also designed to keep ordinary people (non-Illuminati candidates) from being elected to public office. And if the Illuminati can keep the ordinary people from being elected to public office, then who will hold positions of Federal and State elected officials? The answer is the members of the Illuminati will hold these positions as Federal and State elected officials! And that's what the Illuminati want! So they can make laws to enslave and ultimately destroy the American people.

One of the ways the Illuminati has been so successful at disguising their Illuminati members in elections is by having the Illuminati members go after each other and criticize each other in front of the national viewing audience. The Illuminati members are allowed to insult one another and do other dirty tricks on each other in political campaigns. The reason why the governing body of the Illuminati allows this infighting of their members during political campaigns is because it helps disguise what the Illuminati is doing during political elections. When an Illuminati member like Hillary Clinton and Bernie Sanders fight each other, insult each other, and attack each other in national debates and at political rallies, it gives a sense of realism to the election process. And it makes it hard for the citizens of the United States to understand the elections are rigged in favor of the Illuminati candidates. Also, when the Illuminati candidates attack each other, it makes you people get all emotional, and once you get emotional, you people fight each other.

Once the Illuminati candidates slander each other during debates and political rallies, it is hard for the citizens of the United States to see a conspiracy of an Illuminati-controlled election because the citizens of the United States see the politicians fighting each other on national television. So, it's hard for the American people to conceive the thought that these people who are fighting each other and slandering each other are all members of the same secret society (the Illuminati) because it appears the candidates don't like each other.

It was hard for you to understand Ted Cruz and John Kasich were both Illuminati members because they all fought each other on national television during debates and political rallies. In **most cases**, the Illuminati don't care which Illuminati candidate wins as long as one of the Illuminati candidates wins! Let me say that again so you can understand what I just said: in **most cases**, the Illuminati don't care which Illuminati candidate wins a political election as long as one of the Illuminati candidates wins! The key phrase is, **in most cases**. I say **most cases** because, in chapters to come, we will talk about a Presidential election designed for only one specific Illuminati candidate to win!

The fighting you see in the Democratic Presidential Primaries, Republican Presidential Primaries, and in the Presidential election was all by design. And the fighting between the Illuminati candidates makes the elections appear genuine. When, in fact, everything has been staged for an Illuminati candidate to win the Presidency! In most cases a vote for either a Republican Nominee or for a Democratic Nominee is a vote for the Illuminati! That's why the elections are rigged!

Since your vote will be cast for an Illuminati candidate, no matter if you voted for a Democratic Nominee or a Republican Nominee, does it matter if you vote Democrat or Republican? No, it does not matter because the Illuminati control the individual that is elected as President, Senator, etc. And that elected person will do whatever the Illuminati governing body wants them to do. The Illuminati want their people in office because the Illuminati knows they control the decisions that person will make.

It's never been about the political party itself. It's about having an Illuminati member elected! I know you have been brainwashed and indoctrinated to believe your political party is greater than the other. If you are a Republican, you have been brainwashed, and if you are a Democrat, you have been indoctrinated. Indoctrination means to teach someone to fully accept a particular group's ideas, opinions, and beliefs and **not consider other ideas, opinions, and beliefs**. "Indoctrinate." *Merriam-Webster*. Merriam-Webster, n.d. Web. May 4, 2017. <http://www.merriam-webster.com/dictionary/indoctrinate>.

If you look at the definition, I just gave you for indoctrination, you will see the beliefs of the American people. If you are a Democrat, you have been indoctrinated to believe the Democratic Party's ideas are better than the Republican Party's. Then, if you are a Republican, you have been indoctrinated to believe the Republican Party's ideas are better than the Democratic Party's. You must remember that indoctrination means to teach someone to fully accept a particular group's ideas, opinions, and beliefs and not to consider other groups' ideas, opinions, and beliefs.

So basically, the American citizens have been indoctrinated with these two beliefs. The Democrats believe the Republicans are wrong, and the Republicans believe the Democrats are wrong. And if you are a member of either party, you have been indoctrinated with those beliefs. The Illuminati controls media make sure you stay indoctrinated with those beliefs. This is why the mainstream news media were designed to feed into your indoctrination of the Democratic Party and the Republican Party. The mainstream news media is designed to make sure you never become un-indoctrinated. You were raised to be a part of this indoctrinated political system. You were raised as a child to be either Democrat or Republican. You were raised just like a cow is raised to go to the slaughterhouse to be killed! You were programmed either by family, friends, or the news media to be either Republican or Democrat. Once you were fed your political beliefs, then your TV-programmer took over and continued to indoctrinate you year after year through television until you became a fully indoctrinated member of your political party.

The Illuminati use National News Media companies like ABC News, CBS News, NBC News, MSNBC News, and CNN News to indoctrinate Democrats, while Fox News indoctrinate Republicans. The national news media outlets are responsible for indoctrinating people to be either Democrat or Republican to maintain a chaotic atmosphere so the Illuminati can seize power through CHAOS! Again, indoctrination means to teach someone to fully accept the ideas, opinions, and beliefs of a particular group and to not consider other ideas, opinions, and beliefs.

The Illuminati have indoctrinated you with this belief that your political party is superior to the other political party, so you can continue to fight each other! And while you are fighting each other, the Illuminati has been seizing power through CHAOS! Look at the CHAOS that is going on between the citizens of the United States of America because of the Democratic Party and the Republican Party! This CHAOS between the Democratic Gang and the Republican Gang was not done by accident. While the people have been fighting each other, the Illuminati are making moves for a total takeover behind closed doors. And the Illuminati makes sure the mainstream Illuminati-controlled news media keep you all distracted while the Illuminati secretly implement their plans! This is what's really happening!

This two-party political system was designed to indoctrinate you with certain beliefs so they can play the American people against each other. So basically, they indoctrinated the American people in a two-party political system so they could divide and conquer the American people! That's what the system was designed to do, and if you listen to yourselves and others, you will see it has been very successful at dividing the American people. The Illuminati used this system to divide Democrats against Republicans and Republicans against Democrats. While the Democrat citizens have been fighting the Republican citizens and the Republican citizens have been fighting the Democrat citizens, the Illuminati has used that constant diversion to seize political power by passing specific laws to enslave you. The Illuminati has total control of the Democratic Party, and they are trying to get total control of the Republican Party.

Now, let's look at the Hillary Clinton email scandal. Hillary Clinton used a private server to store Top-Secret Classified documents. She stored Highly Classified Government Documents on an unprotected server where anyone could have hacked into it and gotten top-secret classified information about the U.S. Government.

Once this was discovered, Hillary Clinton had Top Secret Classified information on this server, and there was a big media dog and pony show. This dog and pony show went on for some months. Then there was a hearing by a Senate Committee where Hillary Clinton had to answer questions. And the result was this: nothing! Absolutely nothing! What Hillary Clinton did as Secretary of State was a criminal act. It was a crime for her to have Top Secret Classified information on a private server. She should have been sentenced to prison for that criminal act. But since she is Illuminati, her fellow Illuminati members made sure she wasn't prosecuted, but they put on this dog and pony show for the American people so they could at least say, "We had a Senate hearing!" Even though the Senate hearing was so, they wouldn't do anything! This is how the Illuminati protects its people in Congress and other positions of power. And then the Illuminati members in the FBI also protected Hillary Clinton by not pressing any charges. Are you starting to understand this Illuminati game? The Illuminati protects its own, but they prosecute others for the least of crimes. Look at how they are prosecuting Donald Trump. Look how they tried to assassinate Donald Trump. Trump is not a member of the Illuminati.

Even though an Illuminati member is caught red-handed breaking laws or committing acts of treason, they are always protected by their fellow Illuminati members. And they are not prosecuted or even given a slap on the wrist. In Hillary Clinton's case, absolutely nothing happened! Even the Illuminati control FBI decided not to prosecute their Illuminati member, Hillary Clinton. This type of behavior has been going on for many years in this country and around the world. The Illuminati members who are caught doing any type of crime never get prosecuted for the crime, and if they do get prosecuted, they get a slap on the wrist. Like Oliver North got a slap on the wrist for the hundreds of crimes he committed in the cocaine trade in the Iran Contra Affair. Then, right after he was convicted, he was immediately pardoned by his Illuminati member, President George H. W. Bush. Are you starting to understand this Illuminati game? The Illuminati members never stand trial or are immediately pardoned if found guilty. When you see someone who is being prosecuted, and they are sentenced to long jail time, they are not Illuminati! The Illuminati does not allow their people to go to jail for long periods. If anything, the charges just disappear, or they disappear! Like Jeffrey Epstein. You all think he is dead. Epstein is lying low on an island somewhere, molesting other children. Jeffrey Epstein was Illuminati.

Since we are talking about Hillary Clinton and her emails, let me inform you why she put classified information on an unprotected server. What I am about to tell you was given to me by the Most High God Jehovah and the Lord Jesus Christ. Hillary Clinton purposely had classified information on an unprotected server as Secretary of State so she could purposely leak Top Secret Intelligence to foreign countries! Everyone has been looking at this thing from the wrong angle by assuming Hillary Clinton made a mistake by sending classified information on an unsecured server. But it was not a mistake; it was done on purpose! Hillary Clinton purposely sent Top Secret information on an unsecured server so she could leak information to other countries that knew to monitor any emails from that server! She was passing off Top Secret information to someone and some country! This is what the Lord revealed to me. Hillary Clinton committed acts of Treason! Hillary Clinton was purposely passing Top Secret Information to other countries by sending emails on an unsecured server. The country or countries who knew to monitor her emails on the unprotected server knew where to obtain the top-secret information they were looking for! Hillary Clinton could claim it was a mistake by passing information this way. When, in fact, it was not a mistake. It was done on purpose! It was an act of Treason! This is what the Most High God Jehovah revealed to me!

Also, you all need to understand that Donald Trump is not Illuminati. You must remember one thing: every time the Illuminati makes a move, it's by design. By design, all hell broke loose after Donald Trump was elected. All the protests you saw after the election of Donald Trump were paid for and financed by Illuminati members. Illuminati member George Soros spent millions of dollars to finance the marches you have seen across the United States of America. But the question is why? Why would the Illuminati finance march against the newly elected President, Donald Trump? Why would the Illuminati control news media launch an all-out attack against President Donald Trump? The reason an all-out attack was launched against Donald Trump is because Donald Trump is not Illuminati, and he was not supposed to win the 2016 election.

All the CHAOS you see in the news media with Donald Trump is by design! It is all designed to persuade the American people not to elect an ordinary person as President of the United States who's never been involved in politics before! This is the subliminal message they are sending you through the news media! See, Satan and the Illuminati understand the Most High God Jehovah is sending a spiritual man to become the President of the United States, and this spiritual man has never been involved in politics before. The Illuminati is afraid of this man. The Illuminati are using the news media and Donald Trump to discourage you from electing this man God is sending to be President of the United States. Everything you see on TV from 2016 to 2024 concerning Donald Trump as President of the United States was by design. All the CHAOS about Russia and everything else was a lie and by design. It has all been scripted like a movie is scripted! Never in the history of the United States have you witnessed any President charged with crimes like they are charging Donald Trump. You are watching the Illuminati at work when you see Donald Trump on trial. All the CHAOS you see on TV and the internet is by design by the Illuminati, and the Illuminati control news media! And it's all designed to discourage you, the American people, from electing the man the Most High God Jehovah is sending to be President of the United States of America! So don't get caught up in the emotional turmoil the Illuminati control news media is trying to get you caught up in! The Illuminati is playing mind games with you. In a chapter to come I will show how they played mind games with you in the 2008 stock market crash and the Covid-19 Pandemic!

Once the Lord revealed to me how the Illuminati crowd their candidates into the election process. I then understood the lady's meaning when she told my mom that people who attend this school become Presidents, Senators, and other high-ranking government officials. Because the elections are rigged in favor of the Illuminati candidates, and the hiring process is rigged for Illuminati candidates. And since the elections are rig for the Illuminati candidates, this is how so many Illuminati members become Presidents, Senators, and high-ranking government officials.

Another way the Illuminati rigged the Presidential elections was by setting up **super delegates** in the Democratic and Republican

Primaries. These super delegates are the last safeguard the Illuminati set up to prevent ordinary people from winning a Democratic or Republican primary. Let me show you what they did when they arranged these super delegates! Let's use the Democratic Presidential Primaries as an example.

Super delegates are awarded to Democratic governors, Democratic Senators, and Democratic congressional representatives, as well as certain Democratic big-city Mayors, Democratic state lawmakers, and Democratic Presidents and Vice Presidents. These super delegates can vote however they want in the primaries. They do not have to vote according to the people's popular vote. Since the super delegates are awarded to people in the hierarchy of the Democratic Party, this means these super delegates are awarded to people who will be seeking reelection as Democrats. And since they will be seeking reelection at some point, they can be pressured by the Democratic Party or by the Illuminati to vote a certain way with their super delegates or be ostracized by the Democratic Party and not receive financial backing in their next election. Many people who receive super delegates are members of the Illuminati anyway. After they are instructed to pledge their super delegates a certain way, the Illuminati members who were assigned super delegates vote the way the Illuminati instructed them to vote. The Illuminati set this super delegate system up as a safeguard to prevent non-Illuminati members from ever being nominated by either party! The super delegates were created in 1981. The system was rigged for only an Illuminati candidate to win the Democratic Nomination or the Republican Nomination! The system was rigged because the super delegates were enough to swing the election in favor of the Illuminati candidate!

For example, to win the Democratic nomination in 2016 a candidate must receive 2,382 delegates. In the Democratic Presidential primaries there were 712 super delegates awarded. If the Illuminati controls the people who award the super delegates, they can very much control the outcome of the election. By instructing those people they control to vote for a certain candidate! You watched it happen in the 2016 Democratic Primaries, but you didn't understand what you were watching.

In the Democratic primaries there were 712 super delegates awarded. And 609 of those super delegates went to Illuminati member Hillary Clinton, 47 super delegates went to Illuminati member Bernie Sanders and then there were the undeclared super delegates. You should ask why Hillary Clinton got 609 super delegates and Bernie Sanders only got 47 super delegates. The reason why Hillary Clinton got so many super delegates is because the "Order of the Quest," which is the governing body of the Illuminati, promised Hillary Clinton the Democratic Nomination back in 2008! Most of the super delegates went to Hillary Clinton because those who held super delegates were instructed to cast their super delegates for Hillary Clinton. But why were they instructed to cast their super delegates for Hillary Clinton?

In 2008, Hillary Clinton was in a heated Democratic Primary race against Barack Obama. But the Illuminati only wanted Barack Obama to win the 2008 Presidential election. The governing body of the Illuminati ordered Hillary Clinton to stand down in exchange for the Secretary of State position in the Barack Obama Administration, and they also promised her the Democratic Nomination for the 2016 Presidential election. This is how it went down in 2008.

On June 5, 2008, the governing body of the Illuminati held a secret meeting in Chantilly, Virginia. The "Order of the Quest" is the Board of Directors of the Illuminati that sets world policy and the Illuminati agenda. So, during this meeting on June 5, 2008, Barack Obama and Hillary Clinton met with the "Order of the Quest". In this meeting, the "Order of the Quest" commanded Hillary Clinton to stand down and suspend her campaign for the Democratic Nomination for Presidency and to support Barack Obama as President of the United States of America. In return, they guaranteed Hillary Clinton the Secretary of State position in Barack Obama's Administration, and they guaranteed her she would win the Democratic Nomination for 2016. They ensured Hillary Clinton would receive almost all the super delegates for the nomination, almost guaranteeing her the Democratic Nomination. On June 7, 2008, Hillary Clinton suspended her campaign for President, which was exactly two days after she and Barack Obama met with the heads of the Illuminati! This secret meeting was hidden from the press, and only the higher echelons of the Illuminati knew about it.

To keep the meeting a secret from any media source the Illuminati didn't control, the Illuminati leaked a cover story to the press. The cover story stated that Hillary Clinton and Barack Obama had a private meeting at Feinstein's house. Just to let you know Barack Obama and Hillary Clinton **didn't** meet at Feinstein's house. Barack Obama and Hillary Clinton meet with the "Order of the Quest" in Chantilly, Virginia. The "Order of the Quest" (Illuminati) was trying to keep their meeting with

Barack Obama and Hillary Clinton out of the media. So, it wouldn't look suspicious when Hillary Clinton immediately suspended her campaign within 48 hours after she met with the governing body of the Illuminati, the "Order of the Quest". Are you beginning to understand this Illuminati game? The reason why Hillary Clinton received 609 of the 712 super delegates is because the governing body of the Illuminati made those who were assigned super delegates pledge their super delegates to Hillary Clinton.

The super delegates for the Democratic Party and the Republican Party were set up as a safeguard to keep non-Illuminati members from winning a political party nomination! The super delegates were also designed to allow the Illuminati to choose what member they wanted to be elected to a certain party. If you look at the 2016 Democratic Primaries, both Hillary Clinton and Bernie Sanders are members of the Illuminati. But since the governing body of the Illuminati promised Hillary Clinton the Democratic Nomination, they made sure most of the super delegates went to her! They dictated what Illuminati member won the 2016 Democratic nomination!

The elections are rigged in favor of the Illuminati! Whether through marginalizing non-Illuminati candidates, the media releasing their weapons of mass destruction on non-Illuminati candidates, the Illuminati releasing false poll numbers against non-Illuminati candidates, or the super delegates being pledged for their fellow Illuminati members. The elections are rigged in favor of the Illuminati candidate! In the 2016 Presidential election, a non-Illuminati member won the Presidency. His name was Donald Trump. Donald Trump is not a member of the Illuminati. The reason Donald Trump won the Republican primary was because Super Delegates were suspended for the Republican Primaries for the 2016 election. This was very strange to me. And everything that happened in Donald Trump's Presidency was staged by the Illuminati! All of it is smoke and mirrors by the Illuminati to make CHAOS! You must remember this! The Illuminati always use chaos to gain power! I will explain this chaos method to you in the chapters to come!

71. My Theory Different From TV Evangelist

The year is 2001, and I have been watching different Evangelists on TV for several years. I remember many of them would teach different lessons about the end times. Many TV evangelists were teaching that the antichrist would be a white man out of Europe. After hearing that, I began saying to myself, "Lord, everybody is saying the antichrist is going to be a white man out of Europe, but things don't normally happen the way people expect them to happen." I then said, "Lord, Satan normally throws a curve ball in there somewhere. While everybody is looking for the antichrist to be a white man out of Europe, what if he is a Black man, a Chinese man or a Latino man, etc." My spirit felt like something different would happen than what they were predicting. My thinking was Satan always has a curve ball in their somewhere!

72. Hidden Messages In the Bible

As a new creature in Christ, I am studying my Bible daily. The more I read my Bible, the wiser I become. I started to notice I knew present and future events that would happen by simply reading my Bible. The more I read the Bible, the more I felt like there were hidden messages in the Bible that were being uploaded to my mind. I sensed the messages were hidden in a code in the Holy Bible that my naked eyes couldn't see. So you may understand what I am saying, let me explain to you what I was experiencing.

I am reading the Bible, but the scriptures are specific to today's time (or general time frame). After I read the scriptures, a code I can't see with my naked eye is uploaded to my mind. And the code tells me about present or future events. Then I would tell people what would happen in local or world events based on what I read in the Holy Bible. Then, within days or months, the event I said would happen in real life, happens. Then people would ask me, "How did you know that was going to happen?" I would then tell them, "I read it in the Bible!" Once I told a person I read it in the Bible, they would look at me like I was nuts! I would go back to my Bible to find the scriptures to prove I read it in the Bible. But it was not there once I returned to the exact place in the Holy Bible where I thought I read it. At first, this confused me. But then I realized the Holy Bible had coded messages that spoke of present and future events.

So I started telling my brother "W" and others there are hidden messages in the Holy Bible your necked eye cannot see. I told them it's a hidden code inside the scriptures. My brother thought I was crazy when I first told him this, so he laughed at me. But then the History Channel started to show a TV show called The Bible Codes, and my brother didn't think I was crazy anymore!

The Holy Bible has hidden codes in it. These codes tell you what will happen in the present day, the near future, and the distant future. But this code is only revealed to those who have received the Holy Spirit. Once you have received the Holy Spirit, the code can be accessed if you diligently study the Holy Bible. The Holy Spirit gave me access to God's mind, which in turn gave me access to the Bible Code. This is what the Apostle Paul was talking about in 1 Corinthians 2:10-11.

1 Corinthians 2:10-11 reads, [10] "These are the things God has revealed to us by his Spirit. The Spirit searches all things, even the deep things of God. [11] For who knows a person's thoughts except their own Spirit within them? In the same way no one knows the thoughts of God except the Spirit of God. (NIV, Biblegateway.com)

Once you receive the Spirit of God, you can search even the deep things of God. What is the Spirit of God that is mentioned in verse 10? The Spirit of God referred to in verse 10 is the Holy Spirit. The scripture says once you receive the Holy Spirit, you can search God's deep things! The depths of God's mind are the deep things the Apostle Paul refers to. Once you receive the Holy Spirit, you receive security clearance to search the mind of God. Now, the Holy Spirit gives you a free admission to God's mind. But based on who you are and the role the Lord wants you to play in this world depends on the security clearance you get. You can't go to the ULTRA ULTRA Secret Security Level of God's mind with only a top-secret security Clearance.

So those who have received the Holy Spirit have access to the Lord's mind. But your security clearance depends on how much information and what information God wants you to have. Once I received the Holy Spirit, God opened his mind to me. And God gave me a ULTRA ULTRA ULTRA Secret Security clearance. But God had to let me access the information at different times and not all at once because the vast amount of knowledge, wisdom, and understanding I received from God was overwhelming!

God revealed to me there are two codes in the Holy Bible. One code can only be accessed with the Holy Spirit, the First Bible Code (FBC). The other Bible Code is the "Second Bible Code" (SBC), which is right in front of your face every time you read the Bible! God gave me all the information to crack the "Second Bible Code"! The "Second Bible Code" (SBC) is in front of everyone's eyes, but everyone misunderstood what the Bible is trying to tell them. The Second Bible Code (SBC) will shock the world when I reveal it in this book! The Second Bible Code told us everything we wanted to know, but we missed it! Once I reveal the Second Bible Code, it is going to put Christians, Jews, Scientists, archeologists, and even transform nonbelievers into believers and put all of us on the same page for the first time in history! The Second Bible Code (SBC) was right in front of our eyes the entire time, but we missed it! Just continue reading, and this code will be revealed to you!

73. Fulfillment of The Prophesy of The World Trade Center

The date is September 11, 2001, and I am on jury duty at the Jefferson County Courthouse. I am in the jury holding area waiting to be called and assigned to a case. I remember it like it was just yesterday. Everyone was in the jury holding room watching "The Jerry Springer Show". I remember saying, "I am not about to watch that mess." So I got up and went to the drink machine. Once I got my soda, I walked back to my seat. At that very moment, this very distinct feeling came over me. This distinct feeling only occurs when I enter the physical place and time where my spirit has already been.

Once the distinct feeling came over me, I said, "Lord, what is going on?" As I began to look up, someone changed the channel on the television to one of the news stations. At that point I saw what the Lord showed me in a vision seven years prior. The news station showed a plane flying into the World Trade Center. Once I saw the plane flying into the World Trade Center, I said, "Lord, that's what you showed me when I was at JSU!"

I remember the year was 1994 when I was at Jacksonville State University at the car wash with my friends. My friends and I were talking about the 1993 bombing of the World Trade Center and one of my friends said, "They are going to attack the World Trade Center again." Once my friend said that, my spirit recognized it was a true statement. I then looked to the sky and said, "Lord, what is going to be the next terrorist attack on the World Trade Center?" At that moment, the Lord showed me a vision of planes flying into the World Trade Center. As the Lord showed me this vision, one of my friends shook me and interrupted the vision. I then turned to my friends and said, "The next terrorist attack on the World Trade Center, terrorists are going to fly planes into the World Trade Center on suicide missions like the Japanese pilots did in World War II." This is my testimony to the world; the Lord showed me the events of the World Trade Center and 9/11/2001, seven years before it happened.

They dismissed us from jury duty that day because of the terrorist attacks. I wanted to call my friends and ask them did they remembered what I said in college about planes flying into the World Trade Center. But the Lord kept telling me not to get on the phone talking about what I said seven years ago about planes flying into the World Trade Center. The Lord kept telling me every phone call in the U. S. was being recorded, and the FBI would be kicking in my door.

Once I got home, I turned on the TV watched the news. I watched everything play out on TV when they said the Pentagon had been attacked. They said a plane flew into the Pentagon. As I was sitting and watching this live on TV. They went to a live shot showing the hole in the Pentagon and the fire burning. As I was sitting there watching, the Lord said, "Where is the debris from the plane? There is no debris." Once the Lord said that to me. I noticed there was no debris from the plane. I started to wonder how a plane could strike the Pentagon if there were no debris left from the plane. So, I looked at the TV, and I tried to find any type of debris that would prove that a plane hit the Pentagon. I couldn't find any. Then the news person said he didn't see any debris and the plane must have disintegrated. After the news person said that they went to a commercial break and didn't return to the live shot for an hour or so. Once they returned to the live shot of the Pentagon, they showed airplane wheels to the right of the hole at the Pentagon. At that point, I realized they put airplane wheels there because they weren't there before. They placed airplane wheels at the Pentagon, where the hole was made. So, my question is this. What struck the Pentagon, and why didn't we see a video of a plane flying into the Pentagon like we saw a picture of planes flying into the World Trade Center? There are hundreds of security cameras outside the Pentagon and none of them caught a plane flying into it. This is my testimony to what happened and what I saw.

So, I waited about two or three months after the attacks on World Trade Center before I called this guy "M". When I called "M", he picked up the phone and recognized it was me. This is what he said, "Man, I know what you are calling about; I been waiting for you to call me ever since that day. You are calling about what you said in college." I then replied, "So you remember." "M" reply was "Yes, but do not say what we are talking about, you know they are recording all phone calls in the U.S." "M" then asked me, "How did you know that was going to happen?" I then told him, "The Lord showed it to me in a vision that day." Once I said this to "M" I remember the phone just went silent, because "M" couldn't grasp what I said. When I tell people the Lord told me something or showed me something, the average person cannot conceive that in their minds.

I then talked to "M" a little longer and then gave a guy named "T" a call. When I called "T," he said, "I know why you are calling." I replied, "Do you remember what I said to you in college about 9/11?" Tony said, "Yes, but don't talk over these phones. You know they are recording and listening to all the phone calls." So "T" and I talked on the phone in code for about fifteen more minutes, and then we hung up.

I want to explain the distinct feeling I had right before I saw the plane fly into the World Trade Center while I was at jury duty. After I have witnessed a vision in the spirit, a distinct feeling comes over me when I step into the physical place and time of what I witness in the spirit. This feeling is like merging my physical body with the portion of my spirit that has visited the future. It's like a holy energy is passing through me at that time. That's the best way I can describe it. I have this feeling because my spirit has already been to the place where my physical body is just arriving. This may sound crazy, but when the Lord takes me in the spirit to witness future events, it is the essence of time travel! Because the future events the Lord is showing me haven't occurred in the physical realm yet! The Lord is taking me to the future before the future has occurred!

It took me years to truly grasp this, but the Most High God Jehovah and the Lord Jesus Christ transcend time, space, and matter. Time has no limitations on the Most High God Jehovah. Time travel is nothing for the Lord. I know this because the Lord has taken me into the spirit to witness future events that haven't happened here on Earth yet. By doing this, I realize time does not limit the Most High God from seeing or showing me the real-life events that will occur years before they happen here in our physical realm. This means the Holy Father already knows everything that will happen in this world because he has already witnessed it. This is how the Holy Father gives us Prophets' Prophecies because he has already seen the future and tells us things to come in our lifetime. Or he takes us to the future to witness the events that have not yet occurred in the physical realm! And once he tells us and shows us things to come, those things he told us and showed us become prophecies. When the Lord showed me a vision of planes flying into the World Trade Center back in 1994, that was a prophecy given to me by the Lord!

Now, the question must be asked: who were the terrorists? We know who flew the planes, but who else was involved? Was this an inside job? Did the Illuminati want terrorists to attack the World Trade Center to get certain laws passed in the U.S. so they could do surveillance on U.S. citizens? And why did they have to put airplane wheels at the Pentagon after the attack was done on the Pentagon. Was it a plane that hit the Pentagon or one of our own missiles? I'm just asking the questions that you should be asking. Never be afraid to ask the tough questions.

74. Prophesy of New Orleans

It was February 2, 2002, and my brother "W" and I went to New Orleans to hang out for the Super Bowl. It was Super Bowl XXXVI (36), and the Saint Louis Rams were playing the New England Patriots. We had no intention of going into the game; we were just going to enjoy some of the festivities that were going on in New Orleans.

Upon arriving in New Orleans, we got situated and headed downtown. Once I exited the vehicle and started walking, this eerie feeling came over me! I tried to shrug it off, but the eerie feeling didn't leave me. I kept looking up at the sky and my surroundings, but I couldn't pinpoint what made me feel eerie. The sun began to set, and the feeling became more eerie and intense. I told my brother about it, but he told me to grab a beer and stop tripping.

Once it was nightfall, the eerie feeling was overbearing. I started looking up into the sky, but nothing was there. I felt like it was something in the sky, but I didn't see anything in the sky. So eventually, I said, "Lord, what is going on?" At that very moment of me completing my sentence, the Lord allowed me to look at the sky above and see into the spiritual realm. I instantly saw swarms of demons flying above us in the air. When I say swarms of demons, it was swarms of demons! These demons I saw swarming in the air were the most hideous creatures I had ever seen. Some of these demons looked like pterodactyls. I remember one of them was a large dragon. The large dragon demon swallowed up one of the smaller dragon demons. And then there were others that looked like aliens.

The demons were swarming above in the air, listening to the voices of mankind. And when they heard mankind speak words that went against the word of God, they came down to inhabit that person. The demons were always listening and paying attention to what people were saying. They were right above our heads, just listening and waiting for someone to say something or do something that went against the Most High God Jehovah, and the Lord Jesus Christ. And once the demons heard someone speak against the Lord and his word, one of the demons would quickly swoop down to enter that person to inhabit them. I was standing there in New Orleans, Louisiana, on Bourbon Street, witnessing all of this. I was watching the swarms and swarms of demons in the sky.

Then, in an instant, I wasn't allowed to see in the spiritual realm anymore. At this point, I recognized what I had been feeling all day. I felt the evil from the swarms of demons in the air. After I couldn't see into the spirit anymore, I said aloud, "Lord, it is so much evil in this city!" At that very moment of me completing my sentence, the voice of an Angel spoke to me in my left ear and said, "The Lord is going to destroy this city." At that moment, I knew what was said to me in my left ear was the absolute truth. I turned to my brother and said, "We need to leave this city now." My brother then told me to stop tripping! My brother's solution was for me to grab a beer and have fun. It was at that moment I felt like Lot. I felt like Lot because angels warned Lot they would destroy Sodom and Gomorrah. So Lot tried to warn his son-in-law to get out of the city. But his son-in-law thought Lot was joking, and they didn't listen to Lot, and they didn't leave the city. And once the angels destroyed Sodom, the son-in-law's died! The story of Lot can be read in the Book of Genesis Chapter 19.

My brother "W" wouldn't listen to me once I told him the Lord was going to destroy New Orleans. And it was at that moment I felt like Lot. So, I emphatically told him we must leave New Orleans. After I repeatedly and emphatically told him what the voice said, he finally listened to me, and we left New Orleans. My brother kept saying, "It may be a terrorist attack down there; terrorists may set off a nuclear bomb or a dirty bomb." After thinking about what my brother said, I told him, "A bomb is man-made; the voice told me the Lord is going to destroy that city."

The voice that spoke to me was the voice of an angel; I knew it was an angel because of what the voice said to me. The voice said, "The Lord is going to destroy this city." The key word was "The Lord." The voice didn't say, "I am going to destroy this city." So, it had to be the voice of an angel. I remember the day of the Super Bowl I was waiting and watching to see what would happen to New Orleans. But nothing happened! I remember keeping my eyes on New Orleans for at least a year after I received the message, but nothing happened! So, I said to myself, "Maybe I was tripping that night." Or was I?

The demons were swarming in the sky, listening to the words and actions of the people below. And they were waiting on people to speak against the Lord and his word. And they were waiting on people's actions to go against the Lord and his word. And if any person spoke words that went against the Lord and his word. The demons would swoop down from the air and enter that person to dwell in. The demons are looking for a suitable place to live. Just like the demon in the nightclub was moving from person to person, looking for a place to live. These demons listen to men speak because out of the mouth flows the thoughts of the heart. So, if a person is speaking against the Lord and his word, that means that person's heart is against the Lord and his word! And if their hearts are against the Lord, that means their spirits are against the Lord. And if a person's spirit is against the Lord, that means they belong to Satan. And since the demons are followers of Satan, they need a person to dwell in who goes against the Lord and his word. The demons are looking for a host they can occupy. I used the word "host" because that word means more than what you were taught!

So Jesus said what comes out of a person's mouth is what makes them unclean because out of the mouth, the hearts speak. Let's look at what Jesus said in Matthew 18-20.

Matthew 15:18-20 Jesus said, [18] **But the things that come out of a person's mouth come from the heart**, and these defile them. [19] For out of the heart come evil thoughts—murder, adultery, sexual immorality, theft, false testimony, slander. [20] These are what defile a person;..." (NIV, BibleGateway.com)

Ephesians 6:12 reads, [12] For our struggle is not against flesh and blood, but against the rulers, against the authorities, **against the powers of this dark world and against the spiritual forces of evil in the heavenly realms.** (NIV BibleGateway.com)

Now, the Apostle Paul said, our war is not against each other but against the authorities, against the power of this dark world, and against the spiritual forces of evil in the air (heavenly realm). Those demons I witness in the air in New Orleans are the spiritual authorities and powers of this dark world that the Apostle Paul was talking about. The Apostle Paul had already warned us of these demons in the air. This was the third time I had seen a demon in the air. The first time I saw a demon in the air (the spiritual realm), I was in the third grade. Remember, I saw the three demons standing behind the three kids. Then I saw a demon in the club moving through the air. Then, I saw demons in the air over New Orleans. This proves that demons are all around us! They are in the air!

75. Who Is That Guy?

One evening in February of 2002, I played basketball at the YMCA gym in downtown Birmingham located at 2101 4th Avenue North. I often played basketball at the YMCA and was familiar with all the guys I shot ball with. On this day, this guy none of us knew came into the gym and wanted to play ball with us. It wasn't a big deal because we needed one more player. But there was something strange about this guy. He looked kind of odd to me, and he had a very strange demeanor. Then he had these long sweatpants on. I waited for him to remove his sweatpants, but he didn't.

When it came time to decide who was guarding whom, this strange guy was very emphatic about checking me. This guy wanted to check me and no one else. He made that very clear! I didn't check him during the game like I normally did other guys. I would normally play real physical defense with anybody I was guarding. But with this guy, I didn't even get close to him. For some reason, I didn't want to brush up against him. For some reason, I didn't want to touch him. It was strange because it's hard to play a game of basketball without touching the person you are guarding. That's virtually impossible!

This guy would always stare at me with this strange look during the game. As we ran up and down the floor, he ran beside me, **staring** at me. I remember thinking, "Why is this guy staring at me?" And I also thought, "Who is this guy?" I didn't say anything to anybody the entire time this guy was in the gym. I didn't open my mouth to say one word! I didn't know why; I just didn't say a word!

Once the game was over, the same guy prioritized approaching me and trying to befriend me! As he was walking towards me talking, I was listening to him talk. Then, once he was about five feet away from me, he stretched out his arm and attempted to place his hand on my shoulder. At that moment, the Lord Jesus Christ yelled at me and said, "Don't let him touch you!" Once, I heard the Lord say that. I quickly pulled away from him and started backing away. Once I pulled away from him, he had this look on his face as though he knew I was no ordinary man. Then he stared at me again as if he was trying to see who I was. I remember thinking, "What is going on?" By this time, some guy entered the gym door and said to the guy, "Barack, come on, man, we have to go." When the guy called his name, I remember thinking, "Barack is an odd name." As he walked out the door, he turned around and stared at me again. And again, it was like he was trying to see who I was. His persona was so weird that the other guys in the gym huddled around me after he left; they started making jokes about the guy staring at me. Then somebody asks, "Who is that guy?" Someone in the gym replied, "He is some kind of city official from Chicago."

The man I am referring to with the long sweatpants and strange demeanor would later become President of the United States of America, and his name is Barack Obama! But you must remember, this was before Barack Obama appeared on the national scene. All of this happened in the year of 2002. And you must remember that Barack Obama didn't appear on the national scene until the 2004 Democratic National Convention. During this time, Barack Obama was not recognized as a celebrity or public figure! You must also remember I didn't realize I was the Prophet Elisha during this time. When I was saying he was looking at me as though he was trying to see who I was. I didn't fully understand that he was truly trying to see who I was.

After that basketball game, I didn't play anymore because I was trying to figure out what had just happened. I was confused about who the man was and why he was staring at me. And I was confused about why the Lord Jesus Christ yelled at me, "Don't let him touch you!" I was confused because I was trying to figure out what had just happened! Once I left the gym, I jumped into my car and started driving.

76. The Voice Reveals Himself

After the basketball game with the guy named Barack, I left the gym because I was trying to figure out what had just happened. I walked out of the gym, jumped into my car, and began driving. While driving, the voice spoke to me in my left ear and said, "Do you know who I am?" Once I heard the voice, I didn't reply. I said to myself, "Just ignore it and keep driving." Then the voice said again, "Do you know who I am?" At that point, I knew I couldn't deny him any longer! I responded, "Yes, it is you, Jesus." Then Jesus said to me, "Yes." Then I said, "Lord, who am I?" Jesus said, "It is not your time yet. I must hide you." I said, "Hide me, hide me from what my Lord?" Jesus then responded, "It is not your time yet. I must hide you." I said, "What are you hiding me from, my Lord." Jesus then responded, "The evil one." I didn't understand when the Lord said, "The evil one." I kept thinking, "Who is the evil one?" I knew Jesus was talking about Satan. But I felt like Jesus was referring to some man in this world as the evil one!

After Jesus spoke those words to me, I was baffled and confused. I wanted to know more and the complete details of what was going on. The Lord told me things that had me very curious. Things like, "It is not your time yet. I must hide you." and what he was hiding me from, "The evil one." At the time, I was trying to figure out who I was and why the Lord was telling me these things. I didn't remember the Lord told me I was Elisha in college.

So, when Jesus Christ told me, "It is not your time yet. I must hide you." I wanted to know: who was I, when would it be my time, and why did the Lord just tell me these things? Then, I wanted to know who the evil one was. When the Lord referred to the evil one, I had a feeling that the Lord was talking about an actual living, breathing man who was Satan in the flesh.

Also, why did the Lord tell me that information at that moment? The moment the Lord told me that information is just as important as the information itself. Many years later, it was revealed why the Lord said those things to me at that exact moment. It was because of what transpired in the gym. While I was at the gym, something mysterious happened, and I asked the Lord what was happening. The Lord answered me, but I didn't understand it because I didn't put the pieces together. It was not time to understand who I had just encountered at the gym and why he was truly there. It was a reason why the Lord didn't want that guy in the long sweatpants name Barack to touch me. It was a reason why I played an entire basketball game without touching or brushing up against that guy. It was a reason I didn't speak one word to anybody while he was in the gym (so the spirits in that man wouldn't recognize my voice). It was a reason why the Lord Jesus Christ yelled at me and said, **"Don't let him touch you!"** It was a reason why the Lord Jesus Christ said to me, **"It is not your time yet. I must hide you."** And it was a reason why I asked the Lord, "What are you hiding me from my Lord." And then Jesus responded, **"The evil one."**

77. The Lord Moves Me

So this is what happened after I had an encounter with a man named Barack Obama in the gym. I was fired from my job and moved to Huntsville, Alabama. The Lord took me out of Birmingham and placed me in Huntsville, Alabama to hide me. Through some peculiar circumstances, I landed in Huntsville. How did I land in Huntsville? I will show you.

I was living in Birmingham, Alabama, and teaching at Saint Paul Cathedral, a Catholic School in downtown Birmingham. There was a child in my 6th grade Math and Social Studies class who I will call "C". After observing this child's work assignments and handwriting, I saw this child had a learning disability. From my observation, he was either extremely slow or he had dyslexia. The child was reading on a 1st-grade level and writing on a K5 level. His letters and numbers were always backward, and you couldn't make them out. So, being the concerned man that I am, I went to the principal and said, "Mr. B, I have a child in my class who has a learning disability." Then I said, "This kid needs to be tested." Mr. B replied, "Mr. Brown, you know we need all the kids we can get, we can't afford to lose any students."

After Mr. B said that I stood there and looked at him like, "Are you serious!" I saw Mr. B wouldn't do anything about this, so I went one step further and called the child's mother. That was a big help! The mother insisted "C" didn't have a learning disability and he was ok. So, after going to the principal and talking to the child's mother, I was still at point zero. So I went one step further and went to the principal again and said, "Mr. B, we need to get "C" tested so we can get him some help. If he gets help now, he can catch up and be fine in the future." But Mr. B replied, "Mr. Brown, you are not qualified or certified to say if a child has a learning disability." I replied, "Well, let's get someone up here to test the child!" Once I said that, Mr. B stormed away mad. Mr. B had just retired as a Principal from the Birmingham City Schools, so he was getting a retirement check and a check for being the principal at Saint Paul. Mr. B didn't care about educating the kids at Saint Paul; he worked there just to get a paycheck with his retirement check.

A couple of days after I talked to "C's" mom, a man began coming to the school to see Mr. B. This man went into Mr. B's office daily to sit down with him. Day after day, Mr. B and this man would sit and talk in Mr. B's office, laughing and joking. They had become the best of friends overnight. I found out later that the man was "C's" grandfather. After I called "C's" mother, "C's" grandfather started coming to the school and mingling with Mr. B.

It was time for grades to come out, so I told Mr. B I did everything possible to help "C." I gave him so much extra credit work, but there was no way he would pass either of my classes. Mr. B responded, "You give him whatever he needs to pass." I told Mr. B. I wasn't going to change my grades, and there was no way "C" would pass either of my classes. Mr. B saw I wasn't going to change my grades, so he fired me and changed the grades himself!

So, I challenged the firing with the Diocese of Birmingham and had a hearing. This hearing consists of Mr. B, a man on Saint Paul's PTA board (he later became a member of the Birmingham City Council), a nun, and one other guy. They said, "We will remove the termination from our records, but we think it's better you and Mr. B should not work together." So, they decided to remove the termination and make it appear like I resigned. So basically, they wanted to push the matter of passing students alone under the rug.

So, what happened to student "C"? I cannot testify to this information because two other people close to the situation passed this information on to me. The school was closed down within a year or so after I left Saint Paul. So, "C's" mother tried to enroll "C" at another Catholic School. At the new school every person had to be tested before being admitted into the school. So they tested "C," and after they tested him, they wouldn't allow him to enroll because he was too far behind for the grade he was supposed to be in. So the mother either sued or threatened to sue the Diocese of Birmingham because the child had been in the Catholic School system since Kindergarten, and the school just passed him along. What was the outcome of this situation? Common sense tells me the Diocese settled with the parent before it went to court. But money didn't help "C" circumstances because "C" was left behind!

If Mr. B had listened to me, everything would have worked out perfectly. The child would have gotten tested, and we could have helped the child overcome his learning disability. But since Mr. B didn't listen to me, the Diocese paid out money, and the child was still left behind!! But the parents were as much to blame as the school! Because when I called the mother, I heard in her voice that she knew her child had a learning disability, but she was planning the lawsuit the entire time. She wanted money instead of a good education for her child! To the mother and grandfather of "C," I must say, "You are pathetic!!" You put money before the well-being of your child! Ridiculous!

So, I got fired from Saint Paul within a month after the Lord said, "It is not your time yet. I **must hide you."** So, after I had left St. Paul, I was unemployed, and I needed a job. So, I did what unemployed people do. I looked for a job and sat around the house! After I had been unemployed for about 30 days, my two sisters decided they wanted to buy two brand new Infiniti's. So they asked me to negotiate the deal for them. I called an Infiniti car dealership in Huntsville, Alabama. I started negotiating with the salesman, and a few days later, I got great deals on the two brand-new Infiniti. I worked the salesperson and the manager so hard in the negotiations that the Finance Manager asked me did I want to come and work for them. So, I asked the Lord if I should take the job and move to Huntsville. At that moment, the Lord said to me, "Go!" After the Lord spoke to me and told me to go, I went! At that time, I didn't understand the Lord was moving me for a purpose. The Lord was guiding my footsteps! The Lord was placing me where he needed me to be so he could hide me and reveal some very important information!

I didn't understand my peculiar firing, and my peculiar job opportunity came right after my encounter in the gym with that strange guy named Barack Obama. I also didn't realize the Lord had already told me he had to hide me. I didn't understand the Lord wanted to physically hide me. Once I was fired, I was taken out of public view and sitting at home looking for a job. Then, the Lord moved me from Birmingham to Huntsville. When the Lord moved me from Birmingham to Huntsville, the Lord was hiding me! The man named Barack knew how I looked but he didn't know my name. Once I got fired, I stopped going to the YMCA because I didn't have gas money, and I didn't have money for the monthly dues. Once I stopped going to the YMCA, Barack could not find me because he didn't know my name. My firing was divine providence. Divine providence is when God works behind the scenes to accomplish his works. And God's work was to hide me. For God to hide me, God needed to move me from my job as a teacher. Because the school I taught at was next door to the YMCA, where I shot basketball at.

So, I received the job at Huntsville Autoplex in Huntsville, Alabama. Huntsville Autoplex was made up of three car dealerships. There was an Infiniti dealership, a Lexus dealership, and a Dodge dealership. An African American woman name Elena owned all three dealerships. I remember the first time I saw Elena; I fell in love with her time I saw her. It was something very special about her, but I didn't know what it was. It was something very special about her, but I couldn't place my finger on it. I fell in love with her when I saw her. I remember the first time she walked by me; she had a smile on her face and just stared at me. It was something about her! But I couldn't place my finger on it. I just instantly fell in love with her when I saw her. I mean, I fell in love with her instantly! She was beautiful, classy, and sexy. I was drawn to her and instantly fell in love with her! I was in love with Elena! The high point of my day was when I saw Elena walking by! My God! I wanted to make a move on her, but I didn't want to risk my job! I was in love.

78. How Did Black People Become Perceived as Evil

It's 2002, and I was filled with the Holy Spirit, and the Holy Spirit walked and talked with me daily. So, one day, I was reading something that references black as evil. Once I read whatever it was, I questioned the Lord. I said, "Lord, why do white people and other groups of people think black people are evil?" At that very moment the Lord said, Then the Lord said to me, "A prophecy was given in ancient times to one of my prophets. In the prophecy, I stated, "The evil one will come as a black person. This prophecy was handed down from generation to generation until man had changed the meaning of the original prophecy from "**the evil one will come as a black person**" **to** "**black people are evil.**" So, with the changing of the original prophesy to "black people are evil." Black people have been demonized as evil by other races throughout the ages."

So once the prophecy of "The evil one will come as a black person" was passed down from generation to generation, the meaning was accidentally changed to "Black people are evil." From that little slip-up, Satan exploited the feelings of white people and other races through slavery, death, and the mistreatment of black people throughout the ages. Satan twisted someone's mind to twist the original prophecy, which caused millions of people to suffer! But many years later, the Lord would teach me other things that were twisted throughout the ages!

79. The Holy Spirit Councils Me About Race

I am a new creature in Christ because I am submitting to the Lord and the Holy Spirit. My thoughts and my ways are being changed. The more I search for the Lord, the more he reveals himself to me. The Holy Spirit possesses me! As soon as I move to Huntsville, Alabama, the Holy Spirit starts to counsel me on race. I have never been a racist, but I was no fan of white people. I was born and raised in the South of the United

States of America. Just say I have seen some white people do some things to black people that weren't called for.

I grew up in Birmingham, Alabama, watching all kinds of blatant racial behavior. For example, one day, I was in the car with my dad, and we were leaving his job at Kirkpatrick Sand and Cement Company. I was about six or seven years old. My dad was driving, and this car with three white men pulled beside us and started screaming at us, "Fucking Niggers!!". They screamed "Fucking Niggers" at us over and over! Then they forced us off the road. Luckily, it was a small gas station when they forced us off the road. So my dad pulled into the gas station, and the white men immediately jumped out of their car and walked towards our car. My dad jumped out of the car, grabbed his hammer, and met the three white men halfway.

I don't know what those white men were thinking. I guess they thought they were going to intimidate or punk my daddy. My dad met the three white men about halfway with his hammer in his hand. The three white men tried to use words to scare my daddy by screaming, "Nigger!! You Fucking Nigger!!" But my daddy didn't flinch nor budge! My dad just stood there and gave it right back to them verbally. The men didn't want a piece of my daddy because they hurried back to their car and sped off. I guess it wasn't enough of them; I guess they needed the numbers to be more in their favor! Also, do you think them three white men cared that my dad had his six-year-old son in the car with him? The answer is no! So I guess you can call them white men "terrorists"! Because they were trying to terrorize my dad and me!

So after my daddy got back into the car, my dad said these very important words to me. My dad said, "There is no white, there is no black, there are just people!" Then my dad said again, "There is no white, there is no black, there are just people!" What my dad was saying was one's race does not matter! My daddy used that saying up to his death. My dad was a smart man! My dad only had a third-grade education, but he was smarter and wiser than most people with Bachelor's Degrees, Master's Degrees, and PhD's because he saw that one's race didn't matter!

I saw so much blatant racism being done to my parents and other black people that I couldn't tolerate it, like when my mother took me down to Jefferson County Courthouse in downtown Birmingham in the late 70s. My mother was going to get her car tags; she had all the documentation. So we waited in line until it was our turn. Once we reached the counter to get car tags, this white lady grabbed the paper from my mother's hands, looked at it for about three seconds, and then gave it back to my mother and said, "You need to go over there and wait." My mother asked the white lady what was wrong. The white lady said with a nasty attitude, "You need to wait over there until I call you." So we went and sat in some chairs and waited. The white lady continued to see other customers who were white. After waiting about an hour, my mother returned to the window, and the woman told my mother she had to wait. When my mother came to sit down, I saw how furious my mother was. She then turned to me and said, "You are just as good as anyone else. Don't let anybody make you feel like you are less than them. No matter what color they are." After sitting there for another thirty minutes, the white lady called us to the counter and processed my mother's paperwork. My mother had all of the required paperwork, and the white lady gave my mom her car tags. The white lady had a smirk on her face like she had done something great! The racist white lady wanted us to wait while she served all the other white people.

So after that day and many other days like that day, I was no fan of white people. I didn't hate white people, but I was no fan of white people either. What I couldn't understand is how a human being could treat another human being the way white people treated black people! It didn't make sense to me! The cruelty that white people treated black people was pure evil, and it was of Satan! But then those same racist white people would call themselves Christians! How could you even call yourself a Christian when you purposely hate and try to demean your fellow man because of the color of his skin? That is not of Christ; the behavior white people display towards black people is from Satan! That type of racial hate is from Satan! And I, the Prophet Elisha, said it!

There was no hate in my heart towards white people, but there was "something" that wanted me to hate white people. See, I could never allow hate into my heart for white people because I didn't agree with hate. But something tried its best to get me to hate white people. But every time something tried to get me to hate white people, I always heard my dad's voice saying, "There is no white, there is no black, there are just people!"

So once the Lord moved me to Huntsville, Alabama, the Holy Spirit started to counsel me on race. Day after day the Holy Spirit would show me that one's race didn't matter. The Holy Spirit would reveal to me in the Bible that one's race should never be an issue. The Holy Spirit showed me that the only thing that mattered was the Lord's word! After the Holy Spirit council me daily, I was cleansed from that "something" that wanted me to dislike and hate white people. I never disliked anyone else on the basics of race again. My thinking became different! My thinking was what my daddy said years ago. "There is no white, there is no black, there are just people!" Many years later, while studying the Lord's word, I came across the Apostle Paul's teachings in the Book of Galatians, and it reminded me of what my dad said many years ago.

Galatians 3:26-28 reads, [26] So in Christ Jesus you are all children of God through faith, [27] for all of you who were baptized into Christ have clothed yourselves with Christ. [28] **There is neither Jew nor Gentile, neither slave nor free, nor is there male and female, for you are all one in Christ Jesus.** (NIV, BibleGateway.com)

When I first read those words of the Apostle Paul, I thought about my dad saying, "There is no white, there is no black, there are just people." If you are a part of the body of Christ, you can't stand on the side of racism. There is neither black nor white because you all are one in Christ Jesus!

80. You Can Never Be Judged

The closer I grew to God, the more I wanted to confess to him. I remember praying and confessing to the Lord that I would never fear no man, woman, or child alive, and I would only fear him. In this confession of faith, I would also confess to the Lord that I would never bow down to no man, woman, or child alive, and I would only bow down to him. I began saying this because my spirit wanted to confess these things.

One day, after I gave my confession, the Lord said, "You can never be judged by no man, no woman, nor no child alive." Once, I heard the Lord say that I didn't understand, but I accepted the Lord's words as the absolute truth and thanked the Lord. So the Lord said I can never be judged! Then, the Lord revealed to me in the Bible how I could never be judged. In 1 Corinthians 2:15 tells you that a spiritual man cannot be judged.

1 Corinthians 2:15 reads, [15] "The spiritual man makes judgments about all things, But he himself is not subject to any man's judgment:" (NIV, BibleGateway.com)

81. I Decipher The Meaning of 666

It is 2002, and I was studying the Book of Revelation when I ran across Revelation 13:18.

Revelation 13:18 This calls for wisdom. If anyone has insight, let him **calculate** the number of the beast, for it is man's number. His number is 666. (NIV, BibleGateway.com)

Once I read Revelation 13:18, I kept reading the scripture over and over. The word "calculate" just jumped out at me. I said, "Lord, you want us to apply the rules of mathematics to this." So I took the scripture line by line, and this is what I came up with.

Step 1: **"This calls for wisdom"**. The only way a person obtains true wisdom is from the Lord. No matter what this world has taught you. True wisdom comes from the Lord.

Step 2: **"If anyone has insight, let him calculate the number of the beast..."** The scripture told us to calculate, meaning we are to perform mathematical calculations on the numbers. Once I realized the Lord wanted us to perform some type of mathematical computation, the Lord then reminded me of a basic rule of math I learned in the third grade. In basic math, we learned that any numbers line up side by side, with nothing between them (this means no commas, decimals, or any other sign in between them). The rule of math is to multiply.

If we have 5,875 can we multiply these numbers? The answer is no because there is a comma in between the numbers. If we have 587, can we multiply? The answer is yes; we can multiply because there is nothing between the numbers. The way we would do this is to multiply. 5 x 8 = 40   40 x 7 = 280. So 587 = 280 So, let's do the same thing for 666. 6 x 6 = 36 and 36 x 6 = **216.** So, the answer is 216. So 666 = 216

Step 3: "**...for it is man's number**". The number you will look for that represents Satan is 216 because the scripture says, **"...for it is man's number"**. We are looking for a man's number that will represent Satan. This means something a man will create that equals 216 that represents Satan! So, the number we should be looking for is 216, not 666. So, man will create something that equals 216, but it represents Satan.

Step 4: **"...His number is 666"**. The number 666 has been assigned to Satan by the Most High God Jehovah. We are looking for a number that is equivalent to 666. Once we use the rule of math because the Lord told us to calculate, 666 is equivalent to 216. Once I discovered 216, I thought about what the scripture said in Revelation 13:16.

Revelation 13:16-17 ¹⁶ He also forced everyone, small and great, rich and poor, free and slave, to receive a mark on his right hand or on his forehead, ¹⁷ so that no one could buy or sell unless he had the mark, which is the name of the beast or the number of his name. (NIV, BibleGateway.com)

Once I read Revelation 13:16 I ask myself this question. What could they produce that a person couldn't buy, sell, or trade without this? When I looked at the number 216, I said, "This sounds like a computer chip. This sounds like a 216 Megabyte computer chip." Then I said, "A megabyte chip needs a CPU to operate." I don't think a megabyte chip can work in the human body. I knew I was on to something, but I had to make sense of it. So, I thought about it occasionally, and I kept running into the same roadblock. You must remember all of this took place in 2002. Some of the devices we have today, we didn't have back in 2002. We all know and understand the capabilities of a computer chip in today's time! The most important thing was I discovered that 666 truly means 216!

82. Warning From The Holy Spirit

After receiving the Holy Spirit, I talked to anyone who would listen to me about my Lord and Savior, Jesus Christ. No matter where I was, I would talk to people about having a relationship with Christ. And many people didn't realize they could have a relationship with Christ. I was neither a minister nor a pastor; I was just a guy teaching people about the Lord. Whenever I spoke to anyone about the word of God, they would say, "You speak as though you have authority!" And what they didn't truly understand is that I do have authority! The authority I spoke with was from the Holy Spirit. The Holy Spirit was speaking through me to share the good news of Christ and give my testimony. I was witnessing to everyone I encountered. I was doing what Jesus said we would do when we received the Holy Spirit.

In Acts 1:8, Jesus said, "But you will receive power when the Holy Spirit comes on you, and you will be my witness in Jerusalem, and in all Judea and Samaria and to the ends of the earth." (NIV, BibleGateway.com)

So now it's January 2003; I am still living in Huntsville. One day, the Holy Spirit said to me, "Satan is sending someone to throw you off of your path." When I heard this, I knew it was true. I began to be very cautious of everyone I hung around. I immediately thought, "I got to watch all the guys around me and not let them lead me the wrong way." This was the first warning the Lord gave me, but it wouldn't be the last.

Once I received the Holy Spirit, I was witnessing to all I encountered! And because I was witnessing to people about the great news of Jesus Christ, Satan was sending someone to throw me off my path!

83. Vision of Two Women In Wedding Dresses

It's March of 2003. One night, after I prayed, I fell into a deep sleep. After I fell into a deep sleep, the Lord took me into the Spirit, and this is what the Lord showed me and told me. He showed me two women standing at a distance. And both women were wearing wedding dresses. The women were standing side by side. I then said, "Lord, who are these women?" The Lord then said to me, "These are your wives." I then said to the Lord, "Wives!" I was shocked because it was two of them!

The two women looked identical; both women had wedding dresses on, and they both had veils over their faces. I couldn't distinguish one from the other except for one distinct characteristic. One of the women had long hair. The one with long hair approached me like she was to be first. Then, the woman with the long hair grabbed her hair and placed it over her shoulder. She took a brush and started stroking her hair in front of me while she was chanting words out of her mouth (witchcraft). I immediately became confused by the vision. I was instantly placed in a state of confusion. Flashes of my future started passing by me very fast. I saw very hard and depressing times go by really fast. Suddenly, numbers began to appear; the first number was $10,000; then $10,000 turned into $100,000, and then $100,000 turned into $1,000,000. Then $1,000,000 turned into $10,000,000; then $10,000,000 turned into $100,000,000; then $100,000,000 turned into $1,000,000,000; then the numbers kept growing. The numbers got so large I couldn't even count them, and then I woke up. I woke up with the impression the woman did something to me that made my mind very confused. I woke up saying, "This woman took $1,000,000 from me. This woman took $1,000,000 from me." I kept saying this over and over and over!

When I woke up, misery clung to me. The Lord showed me years filled with turmoil and anguish in the vision. Then I thought about everything the Lord showed me and told me. The Lord showed me two women in wedding dresses, and then the Lord said, "These are your wives." When the Lord said those words, the Lord was telling me I was going to be married twice. Both women had veils over their faces, so I couldn't see their faces, but there was one distinguished characteristic between the two women. One had long hair, and the other had short hair. The woman with long hair approached me first because she was to be my first wife. She then took her long hair, placed it over her shoulder, and brushed it in front of me while chanting something from her lips. I then instantly became confused. I became confused because she was using witchcraft on me! Then, I started seeing glimpses of events that were filled with pain and anguish. But unlike other visions the Lord had given me, these glimpses into the future went by extremely fast, so I couldn't distinguish details about future events. I just knew it was a time that was full of pain and anguish. Then these numbers appeared; $10,000 appeared first, then $10,000 turned into $100,000, then $100,000 turned into a $1,000,000, $1,000,000 turned into $10,000,000 and then $10,000,000 turned into $100,000,000 then a $100,000,000 turned into $1,000,000,000 and then the numbers got so large with so many zeros I couldn't even begin to count them.

The first three numbers represented money Satan had taken from me, but the next numbers represented what the Lord gave back to me to restore me. So once the Lord restored me, the Lord made me a multimillionaire!

84. The Gift Of Hearing People Thoughts

The time was around March 2003, and I was becoming one with Christ. The Holy Spirit that was in me was teaching everyone I met about the Lord. While living in Huntsville, I remember some supernatural things began to happen to me. While working at Huntsville Autoplex my coworkers would always approach me to ask me questions. Each time they approached me to ask me a question, I would look at the ground and I thought I heard my coworker ask me a question. I would always respond to them by saying, "To answer your question," and then I proceeded to answer their question. Each time, my coworkers would walk away with this puzzling look on their faces after I answered their questions.

As time passed, I noticed the people at my job started to look at me strangely, and they would always get into a circle and whisper something about me. One day, while talking to my buddy "T,". I was looking down at the ground, and I thought "T" had asked me a question, so I said, "To answer your question," and I proceeded to answer his question. "T" then said, "I didn't ask you that question, but I was thinking that." I then said to "T," What do you mean you didn't ask me that question? I just heard you ask me that question." "T" then said, "Nope, I didn't ask you that question, but I was thinking that." "T" then said, "Everybody else has been noticing you always know what somebody else is thinking." I immediately got mad with "T" because I thought he was trying to make me look crazy. So, I stormed off from "T" because I thought he was trying to make it seem like I was crazy. After I had calmed down, I thought about what "T" had said. So, I started to pay close attention to everyone I talked to.

So, later that day, this guy approached me to ask me a question. When the guy approached me, I looked at the ground but then glanced up at his lips to see if his lips were moving. At that very moment, I glanced up at his lips. His lips didn't move, but I heard the exact words he was thinking in his mind in my mind. Once I heard his thoughts, I then asked him, "Did you want to know___?" The young man replied, "Yes." Once he replied yes, I was astonished at what had just happened! I heard his exact thoughts in my mind; I heard his thoughts word for word.

Once I realized I had heard his thoughts, I had to try it out on other people before I was fully convinced. So, I approached others to see if I could hear their thoughts. Each time I approach someone, I heard their exact thoughts in my mind before they open their mouths. Once I realized I was hearing people's thoughts. I wanted to know how this was possible. At the time I didn't understand I received a supernatural power once I received the Holy Spirit. In Acts 1:8, Jesus told us we would receive power once we received the Holy Spirit.

In Acts 1:8, Jesus said, "But you will receive power when the Holy Spirit comes on you;..." (NIV, BibleGateway.com)

I received the power to hear people's thoughts, and I was astonished! So, I was eager to read my Bible because I wanted to know how I was able to hear people's thoughts. I mistakenly left my Bible at home that day so I was eager to get off work to go home and read my Bible.

Once I got home, I picked up my Bible to understand what was happening to me. I scanned the Book of Matthew, looking for the passage where Jesus knew all the trap questions of the Pharisees and Teachers of the Law. That chapter showed how Jesus knew their thoughts before the Pharisees asked him any questions. But instead of me finding that scripture, I ran across Matthew 17:20. In Matthew 17:20 Jesus Christ talks about having faith the size of a mustard seed.

Matthew 17:20 reads, [20] "...if you have faith as small as a mustard seed, you can say to this mountain, move from here to there, and it will move. Nothing will be impossible for you". (NIV, BibleGateway.com)

85. Walk By Faith and Not By Sight

After reading Matthew 17:20, I immediately said, "Lord, I have that kind of faith, Lord, I have that kind of faith." I immediately grabbed a cup of water and placed it on the table, and then I said, "In the name of Jesus Christ, whom I have faith in, I command you cup to move from here to over there." Guess what happened after I said that? Absolutely nothing! The cup didn't move! Once the cup didn't move, I got more authoritative with my voice. So I said, "In the name of Jesus Christ, I command you cup to move from here to over there!" Guess what happened after I said that? Absolutely nothing! The cup still didn't move! Once the cup didn't move, I screamed at the top of my lungs. Screaming at the top of my lungs, I said, "In the name of Jesus Christ, whom I have faith in, I command you cup to move from here to over there!!!" And then, guess what happened? Absolutely nothing! The cup still didn't move! I finally said, "I better stop screaming because people outside may think I lost my mind." I laughed at myself while thinking, "Boy, you are in here talking to a cup."

At that very moment I had to use the restroom, so I went and used the restroom. Once I finished using the restroom, I walked through my bedroom to return to the kitchen area. As I walked through the bedroom, the Holy Spirit spoke into my left ear and said, "Walk by faith and not by sight." I said, "Ok Lord, I read that before I understand." When I didn't understand, I didn't understand why the Holy Spirit had just said that to me. As soon as I got to the kitchen area, I saw the cup was on the opposite side of the table. I immediately became startled because the cup had moved to the opposite side of the table! Then I said, "How did the cup get from here to over there?" Then the Holy Spirit said again, "Walk by faith and not by sight." I said, "Yes Lord, I understand." But truly, I didn't understand. I didn't understand why the Holy Spirit was saying this to me at that very moment. So I said again, "Lord, how did the cup get from here to there?" Again, the Holy Spirit said, "Walk by faith and not by sight." I started saying, "Yes, I". At that moment, a great revelation hit me, and I stopped speaking. The great revelation was this. Since I didn't see the cup move with my eyes, I didn't believe the cup would move. And once the cup did move, my mind didn't believe what my eyes didn't see. I had enough faith to speak to the cup to tell the cup to move, and I expected the cup to move. But on the other hand, I didn't have enough faith once I didn't see the cup move with my own eyes. The Holy Spirit was trying to tell me to walk by faith and not by sight. That's why the Holy Spirit came to me three times saying, "Walk by faith and not by sight." Once you speak by faith you must believe by faith and not believe based on what your eyes see! Believe it, and you will receive it!

I was able to speak to the cup, and it moved because I received power when the Holy Spirit entered me. The Lord said this would happen once a person received the Holy Spirit. In Acts 1:8 Jesus said we will receive power when the Holy Spirit comes on us. Then, the Apostle Paul talked about the gifts of the Holy Spirit in 1 Corinthians 12:4-11.

1 Corinthians 12:7-11 reads, [7] Now to each one the manifestation of the Spirit is given for the common good. [8] To one there is given through the Spirit a message of wisdom, to another a message of knowledge by means of the same Spirit, [9] to another faith by the same Spirit, to another gift of healing by that one Spirit, [10] **to another miraculous powers, to another prophecy**, to another distinguishing between spirits, to another speaking in different kinds of tongues, and to still another the interpretation of tongues. [11] All these are the work of one and the same Spirit, and he distributes them to each one, just as he determines. (NIV, BibleGateway.com)

When the Holy Spirit comes on a person, that person may be able to do supernatural things. If you read throughout the New Testament in the Holy Bible, it explains some of the supernatural things the people could do when they received the Holy Spirit. I had received the Holy Spirit, and I was able to do supernatural things. I was able to hear other people's thoughts. I was able to tell a cup to move, and the cup moved. I was able to do these things because the Holy Spirit was in me.

Once you receive the Holy Spirit, some form of 1 Corinthians 12:7-11 will be manifested. But many people don't understand that because many people today equate receiving the Holy Spirit with having a happy feeling in church. When you receive the Holy Spirit, supernatural things happen, like the supernatural things that was happening to me and the supernatural things happening to the Disciples and Apostles in the New Testament.

86. A Specific Prophesy About Me In The Bible

So, immediately after the cup moved across the table, I pressed the Lord for answers. I started asking the Lord the same question I have been asking him since childhood, "Lord, who am I?" I asked the Lord this question many times, but I needed an answer this time. I didn't remember the Lord had already told me I was Elisha when I was in college. That memory was blotted out by the traumatic experience of being blinded in my left eye. The same day the Lord revealed to me I was Elisha is the same day I was blinded in my left eye by this guy named Elisha.

So here I was again, pressing the Lord for answers he had already given me. So I kept asking the Lord, "Lord, who am I?" Too many supernatural things were happening to me in my life that I didn't understand. So that day, I pressed the Lord for answers again by asking him repeatedly, "Lord, who am I?" On my final plea, the Holy Spirit said to me in my left ear, "There are specific prophesies about you in the Bible." Once I heard this, I didn't understand. I wondered how there could be specific prophesies about me in the Bible. Then I opened my Bible; it opened on a specific page. Then, the Lord took my eyes to a specific scripture. In the scriptures the Lord showed me the specific Prophesy about me. I was astonished at what I was reading. As I read the scriptures, the Holy Spirit said to me in my left ear, "This is about you." I was blown away by what I read. Then the Holy Spirit said to me in my left ear, "It's not time yet for you to do these things."

As I read the scriptures, I couldn't believe it, but at the same time, I did believe it! I was astonished! The scripture I read discussed a man who will do great wonders and lead the Lord's people during the end times. I was in awe at what I read and heard the Holy Spirit say to me.

I was in awe when the Holy Spirit led me to the scriptures talking about me doing great wonders and leading people through the end times! I didn't know what to say! How often does a person find a scripture in the Holy Bible that is thousands of years old talking about them specifically? A scripture that was prophesying the great miracles and wonders I would do! This is why I was so astonished, and I was in awe! After the Holy Spirit revealed all that to me, I sat in awe for the rest of that day! I am a manifestation of God's word. The word of God had become flesh, and I dwelled among them.

John 1:14 The Word became flesh and made his dwelling among us. (NIV, Biblegateway.com)

After the Lord showed me the scriptures in the Holy Bible that were about me, the Lord wouldn't allow me to find that scripture again. I looked and looked and looked for the scriptures. And for some reason, I couldn't find the scriptures again. The Lord wiped my memory concerning where I could find the scriptures. The Lord will not allow me to remember because it's not time yet for me to do those things.

87. The Lord Reveals To Pastor

The year is 2003, and I am 32 years old. I was still attending the same Church I received the Holy Spirit. So, I was commuting from Huntsville to Birmingham to attend Church. One Sunday, I was at Church ready to receive the word. After praise and worship were over, the Pastor began to speak. Before the Pastor could start the sermon, something forced him to say, "The Lord has already revealed to me who is going to take over this church after me." Pastor said this over and over. While Pastor is saying this, he stares at me the entire time. But Pastor was kind of angry and upset when he was saying this. It was like he wasn't happy.

So, Pastor said the Lord revealed to him that I would take over the Church after him. Once I thought about the message, I said to the Lord, "Lord, if it is your will for me to teach your word, I will teach your word. But Lord, please allow me to be financially set before I start teaching your word because I don't want to get caught up in the money game like some pastors." I then said, "Lord, I don't want to be sleeping with different women like some pastors do." "Lord, I want to teach your word the way you meant for it to be taught."

For years, I ran from teaching the word of God. But now I was a man surrendering to the word of the Lord. I was willing to do whatever the Lord asked of me. I was like the Prophet Jonah. At first, I ran from the Lord as the Prophet Jonah ran from the Lord, but then I submitted to the Lord's will by teaching his word as the Prophet Jonah submitted to the Lord's will by teaching the Lord's word.

88. Satan is Sending Someone

This is the point in my life the Lord is about to allow me to be put to the test. It has been about three years since the Holy Spirit entered me, walked with me, and counseled me. Now, it was time for me to be put to the test. At the time, I didn't know this, but the Lord was about to teach me a lot about the spiritual side of this world while allowing Satan to have complete access to me! God was about to give me ten PhDs, in his word, and teach me about this world spiritually and physically. This PhD coursework the Lord was about to give me would last over a decade!

It is the beginning of May 2003; I live in Huntsville, Alabama. One Sunday night, I got a phone call from my brother "C". In his phone call, my brother said, "L" wants you to call her." I then responded by saying, "Who?" Then he went into detail on who "L" is. Then he gave me her phone number and like a person without good sense I gave her a call. See my brother "C" is to me as Cain was to his brother Abel. Just in case you don't know, Cain killed his brother Abel because Cain was jealous of Abel.

So, I called "L" that Sunday night, and after talking to her for a while, I asked her did she have any kids, and her response was, "No". So, on Monday night, I was talking to her again and heard "L" talking to a child. I asked her, "Who was that you are talking to?" She then said, "My son." I then said to her, "You told me you didn't have any kids!" Then she quickly denied saying that! That was the first sign I was dealing with a psychopath! And I should have hung up the phone right then and there! But like a person without good sense, I continue to talk to her!

At the end of the conversation, she asked if she could come to Huntsville and visit me. She then said, "I can come up there on Friday!" And like a person without good sense, I said, "Yes." This is an example of Satan putting himself in your lap without you making any effort. After I said yes, she could come to Huntsville on Friday to visit me. These are the events that happened to me from Tuesday morning to when she arrived on Friday evening. I locked my keys in the car five times between Tuesday morning and Friday evening. I locked myself out of my apartment twice between Tuesday and Friday. For a total of seven times, I locked myself out of my apartment and my car. I didn't understand why I was suddenly locking myself out of my apartment and car. Do you think the Lord was trying to tell me something? You must also remember the Lord gave me a warning four months prior, in January of 2003, that Satan was sending someone to throw me off my path. I want you to remember that because that is very important! I locked myself out of my car and out of my apartment a total of seven times once I agreed to allow "L" to come to Huntsville to visit me. The Lord tried to stop me from getting with "L", but I didn't understand the message. I want you to watch what happens to me and my life from this point on!

On Friday, May 9, 2003, "L" and her son visited my apartment in Huntsville, Alabama, and spent the night. When she first got there, I had the strangest feeling about her. I felt like something was not right about her! I didn't sleep well that night because I felt something was not right about her!

Saturday morning, she gets up and cooks breakfast for me. After eating one-third of my breakfast, I suddenly began to vomit everywhere. I was just vomiting all over the place. This was the strangest thing I had ever seen in my life! Immediately after I was done vomiting, I said, "My Lord, what just happened?" At that moment, the Holy Spirit said to me in my left ear, "Your spirit rejected the food." After I heard the Holy Spirit speak, I was trying to understand, "How could my spirit reject the food?" I didn't know this at the time, but "L" had placed a spell on my food because she was trying to use witchcraft on me! That's why the Holy Spirit said to me, "Your spirit rejected the food." My spirit rejected the food because my spirit was filled with the Holy Spirit. My spirit and the Holy Spirit rejected the food because "L" had placed a spell on the food!

After I threw up and the Holy Spirit said that to me, I was confused! I should have run from that woman and never looked back. But instead, I continued to see her. I kept having this feeling something wasn't right about her. After being involved with her for about a month or two, I kept trying to leave her, but I couldn't break free from her. I tried to stop seeing her, but some supernatural force kept bringing me back to her. Just to let you know, I have had many women in my life, but I have never experienced anything like this before. I also noticed one other thing: the gift of hearing people's thoughts had left me. So once I hooked up with "L", the gift of hearing people's thoughts left me! I didn't realize this then, but the gift left me because the Holy Spirit had left me! Something strange was going on with this woman, but I couldn't place my finger on it! I didn't know this at the time, but the warning God gave me was being fulfilled with "L". Remember, in January 2003, the Holy Spirit said to me, "Satan is sending someone to throw you off of your path." Well, "L" was that someone God was warning me about!

89. Something Appears Out of The Darkness

It's July of 2003; I am in Birmingham for the weekend. I decided to spend the night at "L's" apartment. That night, I slept with "L" beside me. My eyes were closed, and I was dozing off; then something appeared out of the darkness. My eyes are closed, but I see it in the spiritual realm. Whatever it was, it was pure evil. It came towards me, trying to sneak up on me. It was at this point that I opened my eyes so I could rebuke the evil spirit. Once I opened my eyes, I saw the spirit of a lady rushing towards me. I sat up in bed and immediately said, "I rebuke you in the name...." Before I could finish the phrase and rebuke the evil spirit in the name of Jesus Christ, the spirit slammed into my head causing me to be dazed in this misty haze, and I was instantly put to sleep.

The very next morning, when I woke up, I remembered the entire event that had happened that night. But one detail eluded me; I thought I had finished my sentence and rebuked the evil spirit in the name of Jesus Christ. That was the thought that was given to me, and that was the thought I carried for a very long time. Out of all my encounters with supernatural things, this one was the strangest because the details of what happened after I saw the evil spirit were hidden from me.

90. You Must Be Talking About That Book

Once the Lord removed the blinders from my eyes and removed the chain of bondage from my mind, the Lord downloaded my mind with so much information that I never looked at this world the same. Do you remember Chapter 63 titled, "My Eyes Were Open"? In that chapter, I told you how I was driving on Highway 280 and felt that something was wrong with this world. Then, at that very moment, the Lord freed me and downloaded my mind with so much information! Then, the Lord opened my eyes so I could see this world was nothing more than an **illusion**. An illusion that appears to be real! A system built upon a lie! An illusion of lies built upon other lies. The Lord revealed to me **this system** we live in and what it was truly designed for!

After that day, I started telling everyone who would listen to me who the group the Illuminati was and how they were trying to seize control over the world system. And how they had plans to crash the economy. I also told people many other things concerning future events in this country. Whenever I told people these things, they always said, "You must have read that book. You are saying everything this book had said." I would then respond, "No, I am just telling you what was revealed to me." Then they would respond, "Everything you said was in that book that talks about the end times." After hearing them say the words end time, I assumed they were referring to the Bible and talking about the Book of Revelations. I never asked them the name of the book.

Once I had been living in Huntsville for a while, I continued talking to people about what the Lord had revealed to me. Each time, people would always have the same reply: "You must have read that book. You are saying everything this book had said." I then would respond "No, I am just telling you what was revealed to me." Then they would insist I had read the book!

One day, this guy made the same statement, and I asked him, "What is the name of this book you are talking about?" The guy said, "Behold A Pale Horse" by Milton William Cooper! After he told me this, I said to myself, "I wonder if that's the same book everyone else was talking about?"

After talking to other people about the things the Lord revealed to me. The name of that book came up again. So, I went out and purchased the book, and once I started to read it. I was blown away! I was blown away because most of the things the Lord downloaded my mind with and revealed to me were in the book, "Behold The Pale Horse." It was like reading something I had already read four and five times before. Because everything I was telling people was in that book! I understood why people told me, "You must have read that book!" Because to them, it sounded like I was taking information from that book and repeating it! After I read that book, I saw how real everything was.

Milton William Cooper wrote the book Behold a Pale Horse. He was a Navy Intelligence Officer who worked at the Pentagon. One day, while at work, he found some papers on a copy machine. These papers outlined the plans of the Illuminati. Cooper eventually published some of those papers in his book. This book was Copy written in 1991, and it gives the plans of the Illuminati for the New World Order! Just to let you know, many of the things Cooper said the Illuminati would do. They have already done it! And they did it right in front of your face! They have been making slaves out of all of you, and they are doing it right in front of your face! Because they think you are so stupid you don't have the mind to do anything to stop them!

Also, Milton William Cooper found these papers on a copy machine at the Pentagon. That means there must be people at the Pentagon who are members of the Illuminati! That's how Milton William Cooper stumbled upon the papers. Not too long after Milton William Cooper published the book Behold the Pale Horse, he was gunned down and assassinated by Sheriffs! I told you the Illuminati like to use public executions to place fear into people. I told you Police Officers and Sheriffs are members of the Illuminati, too. And when you have Policemen, Sheriffs, and other law enforcement officers who are members of the Illuminati, they are legalized hitmen who can perform public executions by gunning a person down in broad daylight (Milton William Cooper). Or they have police officers or other law enforcement officers choke people to death in broad daylight because that person spoke out against the Illuminati. But when the mainstream media reports the killing of citizens by an Illuminati Police Officer, it's never mentioned in the story that the individual that was murdered was talking about the Illuminati! And the Illuminati Police Officers are never convicted of murder, and they rarely stand trial. Someone needs to go back and check all the police shootings and chokings to see if the victim had been talking about the Illuminati to others! Suppose the victims had been talking to others about the Illuminati. In that case, there is a very good chance the Illuminati used their members, who are Police Officers and Sheriffs, to silence them by killing them! Like the Illuminati used the Sheriffs to kill Milton William Cooper!

The Illuminati use their members, who are Police Officers, Sheriffs, State Troopers, and other law enforcement officers, to kill citizens who are publicly speaking out against the Illuminati! These law enforcement officers are nothing more than legalized hitmen for the Illuminati! You must remember the Illuminati is a Luciferian Religion. Anyone who wants to worship Satan join. Law enforcement officers are recruited and paid extra money from outside sources to join! Because the Illuminati must have Police Officers and other Law Enforcement to harass or assassinate civilians who may cause problems for the Illuminati!

91. The Lord Places Me At The Right Place

The year is 2003, and I am at work at Huntsville Autoplex, when I suddenly got into my car and left work for no reason. It was very peculiar because I didn't know where I was going or why. I was in the driver's seat, my hands were on the steering wheel but I wasn't in control of the steering wheel. I wasn't steering the car, the Lord was steering the car for me. My hands turned the steering wheel but I didn't make the decision to turn the steering wheel, the Lord did. The Lord drove me to downtown Huntsville. Then the Lord parked the car in the parking spot that was next to a park. After the car was parked, I got out of the car and sat on the park bench that was right next to my parking spot. I knew what was happening but I kept asking myself, "What are you doing, and why am I here?" I wasn't in control; God was in control.

After sitting on the bench for about 45 seconds, this white guy came and sat next to me. After he sat down, we immediately started talking to each other. The guy explained that he was in Huntsville on Federal Government business and was helping to restructure and realign the voting maps across the country. He then went on to say how this change would be for the 2008 Presidential Election. He then explained to me how the changes they were making didn't make sense and what they were doing was wrong. At the end of the conversation, the guy gave me the "stare" then he said, "Look, I am not prejudiced, but what I am about to say may sound prejudiced. What they are doing with this realigning of the voting maps is wrong because they are giving more voting power to the inner cities across the country, and they are taking away voting power from citizens in suburban and rural areas." **Then he said, "It's like they are intentionally setting this thing up for a black man to become President**." Then the guy looked at me again and said, "I know how this sounds, but I am not racist. What they are doing is wrong." Then, the guy got up and walked away.

When the guy said these things, he had the same stare that my mother had when she revealed my Jewish heritage; he also had the same stare that I have seen on many occasions when the Lord speaks through a person. As I sat there, my spirit knew what he said was the absolute truth, but I didn't understand what it all meant at the time. I knew it was very important, but I couldn't see what it was leading to. So I said, "Lord, what do you want me to do with this information?" I knew I had to do something with the information, but at the time, I didn't know what to do with it.

After sitting there for a moment, I got in my car and drove back to work. While driving, I kept thinking, "Lord, what do you want me to do with this information?" My spirit knew what I heard was very important, but I didn't fully understand how important. At the time, I didn't realize the things the man said were of Biblical proportion! Also, when the man said, "they." He was referring to the Illuminati! This is the group that has acquired so much power that it has the power to manipulate an election through redistribution of voting power by giving more voting power to inner cities where large populations of minorities live and then taking away voting power from suburban and rural areas where whites live.

So, the voting maps were being manipulated for the 2008 Presidential election! Who was the voting map being manipulated for? The voting maps were set up to give more delegates to the inner city and remove delegates from the suburban and rural areas. This meant whoever carried the inner city votes, which is largely minority, would win more delegates in a Democratic or Republican Primary! Even if one person carried more of the popular vote, the delegates would weigh in favor of the person who won the minority vote, which was the inner city areas! This is why the guy said, **"It's like they are intentionally setting this thing up for a black man to become President."** This rule change was set up for the 2008 Presidential election! Who was elected President in 2008? The answer is Barack Obama was elected President in 2008! This is the United States of America's Book of Secrets! This is the Illuminati's Book of Secrets!

After receiving all that information from that man, I realized why I jumped into my car, and the Lord drove me to downtown Huntsville. The Lord made me jump into my car, and then the Lord drove me to downtown Huntsville. Then, the Lord had a parking space open for me right in front of this park bench. Then, the Lord made me get out of the car and sit down on the bench. Then, within 45 seconds, a man came and sat down and gave me important and valuable information. This is a prime example of the Lord guiding my footsteps!

Now, let's look at what is happening today. Many white Americans understood what happened in 2008 and the change made by redistricting the voting maps. Since many white Americans understand this change, there has been a Nationwide push for White Americans to repopulate the inner cities.

92. Engineer Reveals Plan For A Black Project

It is 2003, and I am still living in Huntsville. I am still a car salesman at the Huntsville Autoplex. One day for lunch I jumped in my car and started driving. I had no idea where I was going; I was just in the driver's seat. Then suddenly, something made me pull into this Hotel parking lot. It was this bar lounge located in the Hotel Parking Lot. I exited my car, went inside, and sat at the bar. This was very peculiar because I had never been to this bar lounge. I wasn't eating or drinking; I was just sitting at the bar.

While I was sitting at the bar, this guy walked up to the bar and stood beside me. So, the gentleman and I started talking. During the conversation, I noticed he had some ID cards hanging around his neck. So I asked him what type of work he did. The guy told me he was a computer engineer. Then the guy tells me he works for a government defense contractor in Huntsville. The guy was just talking, and then he gave me **the stare** and he said, "I don't know why I am telling you this because I can lose my security clearance and my job." He said, "We are working on a Black Project with Army Intelligence." Then he said, "We are all most finish developing a computer mainframe that can track every transaction in the world in real time." Then, after the guy tells me this Ultra Ultra Ultra Top Secret Information, he gets this look on his face like, "Oh my God, what have I done!" He then rushes out of the bar lounge with this look that says, "Am I crazy? Why did I reveal that top-secret information to this man? I can lose everything!" I tell you the absolute truth; that was the look on his face after he realized he had given me HIGHLY CLASSIFIED INFORMATION! That man was scared to death after he gave me that information about the Black Project he was working on!

My spirit knew the information was the absolute truth once I heard it and when I saw the "stare". Once I saw the "stare," I knew the Lord made the man tell me what he told me. The man didn't know or understand why he revealed that information to me. After the man left, I said, "Lord, what am I supposed to do with all this information you are giving me?" I knew what I was hearing was very important, but I didn't know what to do with the information. I didn't realize the Lord was giving me all this information so I could release it in this book one day!

For you all who don't understand what a Black Project is, let me explain to you what a Black Project is. A Black Project is a Project the United States Government has classified ULTRA, ULTRA, ULTRA, ULTRA TOP SECRET. Black Projects are so secret that the United States Congress doesn't even know the project exists. Only a few Senators on a particular subcommittee may know of the project's existence. But as far as Congress and the rest of the world, the project doesn't exist. A Black Project is far above a Top-Secret Security Clearance. Top Secret is not the highest security clearance the U.S. Government has. There are various levels of security clearance. When you get into Black Projects, they are at the top of Security Clearance. Information on a Black Project should never be made known to the public. When the Engineer told me about the Black Project he was working on, he jeopardized his life. They kill people for revealing anything about a Black Project because the project is not supposed to exist, so the public should never have any knowledge of the program's existence.

Let's look at what the guy said and what it all means. The guy said, "We are working on a Black Project with Army Intelligence." Then he said, "We are almost finished developing a computer mainframe that can track every transaction in the world in real-time." The first question you must ask yourself is, why does the U.S. Government want to track every transaction in the world in real-time? What are they planning to use this technology for? And why didn't they want the American people and the people in this world to know they were working on this type of technology? If you notice, the Engineer said they could track every transaction in the world in real-time. So that means they didn't just make this technology for people in the United States of America. But they made it for everyone in the world. What do they have planned for everyone in this world that they want to track every transaction in the world in real time?

So you can begin to see the big picture of what they have planned for everyone in this world; you must think about this: Why would the U.S. Government want to track every transaction in the world? The only way it would be beneficial is if they had a way of connecting every transaction to a specific individual.

Many years after that incident in Huntsville, I started to think more and more about what the Engineer said. And all the pieces came together and made sense to me. Since that day in 2003, a lot has happened: a lot of technology has hit the scene, and a lot of ways we do business have changed. We use the Internet to conduct most of our business. Every time you buy something on the Internet, it is a transaction. Every time you buy something in the store with your debit or credit card, it's a transaction. Every time you make a phone call, it's a transaction. It doesn't matter if the call is from your cell phone or landline; it's a transaction. Every time you send an email, it's a transaction. Every time you text someone, it's a transaction. Whenever you post something on the Internet or a social media site, it's a transaction. Every time you chat online, that's a transaction. Every time you acquire credit, that's a transaction. Every monetary purchase used with a debit card, PayPal, credit card, or electronic device is a transaction.

The first thing you should know is that everything you do electronically is stored in your very own digital file. The U.S. Government has created a file on everyone in the U.S. and the world. All your emails, social media posts, phone calls, text messages, financial information, credit information, and purchases are all stored on a platform within this mainframe. You have a real-time file stored on this platform within the mainframe. All this I am telling you was proven when Edward Snowden former contract worker with the NSA (National Security Agency), released information to The Guardian Newspaper that the U.S. Government and the United Kingdom were gathering personal information, including phone calls on U.S. citizens and people in other nations and storing it in a digital file. The U.S. Government has had a supercomputer mainframe since 2003 that could track every transaction in the world in real-time. And they have been collecting data on everyone in the world.

The United States government is keeping secret files on everyone, just like Nazi Germany kept secret files on everyone right before they took over Germany! And these files will be used against you if you ever try to challenge the Illuminati and the powers that be. The information in those digital transactions can be used against you if you attempt to challenge them. They know your secrets! They know all the phone calls you made and to whom. They have recordings of all your phone calls! They have every text message you ever sent! They have all the naked pictures you texted! They have every online post you ever posted! They have all your sexting texts! This is one of the reasons they created a mainframe that can track every transaction in the world in real-time. They can use this information against you publicly if you ever try to oppose the Illuminati, or the Illuminati agenda, or one of their members that is in the Illuminati!

This is how the Illuminati uses the information that they store on you. The Illuminati sees you are becoming a problem! The Illuminati within the government access the supercomputer mainframe and search all your digital transactions that are located in your digital file so they can find some information to use against you! They first threaten you with this information. And if you don't back off, they proceed with this public smear campaign against you. Once they find some dirt on you in your digital file, they release this information to the public, and the Illuminati control news media so they can shame you and discredit you before the world! They will make your secrets known to shame you and to put fear into you until you surrender to them or to the Illuminati member you opposed!

You have witnessed the Illuminati media and government do this to many people! You just didn't understand how and from whom the news media got their information. The personal text information and recorded phone call the media uses to destroy people are coming from the U.S. Government supercomputer mainframe that is tracking every transaction in the world in real time! The media always claim their information comes from a confidential source or a hack done on a person's email, computer, or phone. Well, I am here to give you the absolute truth: the confidential source the news media gets its information from is the Illuminati within the government, which has access to the supercomputer mainframe that stores every digital transaction you do!

You must remember the Engineer told me the computer mainframe could track every transaction in the world in real-time. If a person uses cash, the computer mainframe cannot track that person's transaction. They have no way of connecting a cash transaction to a specific person. It seems to me they must have plans on removing cash from circulation. But if they do away with cash, what will they replace it with? They will replace cash with the Central Bank Digital Currency connected to the chip implant. The Central Bank Digital Currency will be the One World Currency under a One World Government ruled by a One World Leader!

So once the Engineer revealed to me they were almost finished with the computer mainframe that could track every transaction in the world in real-time. I immediately began to think about what I discovered concerning 666 equals 216. And 216 stood for a 216-computer chip. At this point I realized they had plans to give everyone a chip so they could track every financial transaction to a specific person. At that point, I realized they had plans to remove cash from the U.S. and world economies. To remove cash from the world system, they had to crash the U.S. Economy and World Economy a couple of times to pull this off! This is the United States of America's Book of Secrets! This is the Illuminati's Book of Secrets!

93. Confirmation Of Black Project

After the Engineer revealed to me the information about the supercomputer mainframe the U.S. Government was building, the Lord came to me a couple of weeks later to confirm what the Engineer had told me. One night, I was lying in bed asleep when the Lord said to me in my left ear, "Get up and turn to CNN." I immediately woke up, got out of bed, walked into the living room, and turned on the TV to CNN within five minutes of sitting there watching the news. The CNN anchor said, "This is just in. CNN has just confirmed that Army Intelligence has almost completed working on a supercomputer that can track every transaction in the world in real-time. We will have this story after this break." When I heard the anchor lady say that I was like, wow!

So, I sat there watching the TV, waiting for the story. It was about 4:00 in the morning when this happened. So, they returned from the commercial break and said nothing about the supercomputer story. They covered a couple of other stories and went into another commercial break. Once they returned from that commercial break, they still didn't say anything about the supercomputer story. It's now about 4:30 in the morning, and not a word about the supercomputer story. It's five in the morning, and they still haven't said anything about the supercomputer story. It's now six in the morning, and they still haven't said anything about the supercomputer story. It's seven in the morning, and they still haven't said anything about the supercomputer story. It's now eight in the morning and nothing about the story. It's now nine in the morning, and there's still nothing about the supercomputer story. I was thinking, what in the world happened to the report about the supercomputer? I sat there for five hours waiting on CNN to report on how army intelligence was almost finished with a supercomputer that could track every transaction in the world in real time. And they never aired the story!

It was at that point I realized the U.S. Government, or the Illuminati, made CNN not run the story. I guarantee you the Pentagon or someone else in the U.S. Government or the Illuminati made sure CNN didn't break that story. That's why they never came back with the story. You must remember, the Engineer told me it was a Black Project, which means the project doesn't exist! So, neither Congress nor the world is supposed to know about the project. That's why the U.S. Government or high-ranking members of the Illuminati made sure the story didn't air on CNN.

This was the second time I witnessed the U.S. Government ensure the news media didn't air a story. The first time I witnessed the U.S. Government make sure the news media didn't air a story was when I witnessed the spaceship in Twentynine Palms, California. The news media said nothing about the spaceship, like the event never happened! And now the U.S. Government made sure CNN pulled the story of the supercomputer that can track every transaction in the world in real time. The government can make sure any story they don't want to air on TV doesn't air on TV. This means all the news you are watching on TV about the government is what they want you to see and know. This also means you are living in a matrix where you are being fed information, they want you to know to distract you from the truth! This is the United States of America Book of Secrets! This is the Illuminati Book of Secrets.

94. The Lord Reveals To Me The President For 2009

It's July 2004; I'm at a friend's apartment watching the Democratic National Convention. When this man got up and started to speak (Barack Obama), upon seeing this man, I immediately recognized this man. I recognized the man, but I didn't remember I played a game of basketball with him. Once he began to speak, my spirit immediately recognized him. I said out loud, "Lord, my spirit recognizes this man!" I then start saying, "Lord, I know this man! Lord, I know this man!" I said this over and over and over. Then I said, "Lord, my spirit recognizes this man!" I watched part of the speech Barack Obama gave. Then I said, "Lord, something is not right about this man." I then said, "Lord, he is the antichrist!" I then said, "Lord, who is this man?" And at that very moment the Holy Spirit said to me, "He will become the next President of the United States."

I knew it was the absolute truth once I heard the Holy Spirit say that. I started rationalizing what the Holy Spirit had just said to me. I sat down and started counting the years on my fingers. I said aloud, "He cannot become the President this term because this election is between George W. Bush and Senator Carrie." For Barack Obama to become the next President, he would have to run for President in 2008, and he would take office in 2009.

Once I realized that Barack Obama would take office in 2009, I immediately thought about the vision the Lord gave me in Chapter 45, titled "I Witness The Second Coming of The Lord". Remember, the Lord gave me a vision while I was at Jacksonville State University, and the Lord warned me that some event would bring about the Great Tribulation and the second coming of the Lord Jesus Christ. In that vision I sensed the Lord was pointing me to the year of 2009 because the vision showed me at my twentieth-year high school reunion. And since I graduated high school in 1989; my twentieth reunion would occur in 2009. The overall vision left me with the impression that the Lord was telling me some significant event would happen in 2009.

After thinking about that vision, I said, "Lord, he is the antichrist." My spirit just knew Barack Obama was the antichrist. So, I asked the

Lord, "Lord, is he the antichrist?" I asked the Lord this several times, but the Lord didn't answer me. Then I said, "Lord, My spirit recognizes this man. He has to be the antichrist." At that time the Lord didn't answer the question for me. I didn't realize I was using the wrong term at the time. I used the term antichrist because that is what the world taught me. The world had taught me, and you, the wrong term on purpose, but I didn't know this at the time. The Lord didn't answer my question because I asked him the wrong question. As a society, we use the word antichrist out of term. 1 John 2:22 gives you the true definition of what antichrist means.

1 John 2:22 reads, [22] "Who is the liar? It is whoever denies that Jesus is the Christ. Such a person is the antichrist—denying the Father and the Son." (NIV, BibleGateway.com)

So anyone who denies Jesus is not the Son of God is an antichrist. So if your friends or neighbors deny Jesus is the Christ, they are antichrists. So when we as a society have been looking for the one who will come and be the son of Satan, we use the term antichrist. And that is the wrong term to use! I will teach you the proper term like the Lord taught me! I will give you the proper term to use for the son of Satan because the Holy Bible uses a specific name for the son of Satan.

When I asked the Lord was Barack Obama the antichrist, the Lord didn't answer me because I was using the wrong term. Even though the Lord didn't answer me, I knew I was right; I knew that Barack Obama was the evil one. My spirit felt like the man I was watching on TV was the evil one. I felt that way because the Lord had already told me that about Barack Obama, I just didn't remember. Remember what the Lord told me after I finished playing a game of basketball with Barack Obama? Remember the Lord told me he had to hide me from the evil one.

Also, I eventually understood what the man in Huntsville told me that day I was sitting on the bench. Remember, Chapter 91 is titled "The Lord Places Me at the Right Place". Remember, the Lord had driven me to downtown Huntsville, and the Lord made me park my car. And then the Lord made me get out of the car and sit on this park bench. Then, this man came and sat beside me and explained that he was in Huntsville on Federal Government business, and they were restructuring and realigning the voting maps across the country. He then went on to say how this change would be for the **2008 Presidential Election**. He then explained to me how the changes they made didn't make sense and what they were doing was wrong. At the end of the conversation, the guy gave me the "stare." Then he said, "Look, I am not prejudiced, but what I am about to say may sound prejudiced. What they are doing with this realigning of the voting maps is wrong because they are giving more voting power to the inner cities across the country, and they are taking away voting power from citizens in suburban and rural areas." Then he said, "It's like they are intentionally setting this thing up for **a black man to become President**." Then the guy looked at me again and said, "I know how this sound, but I am not racist. What they are doing is wrong." Then, the guy got up and walked away.

The change for the redistricting and realigning the voting maps would occur for the 2008 Presidential election. Who was the black man elected President in the 2008 Presidential election? Barack Obama was the black man elected President in the 2008 Presidential election. It seems to me the man on the park bench spoke the truth. The Illuminati within the U.S. Government manipulated the 2008 Presidential election by redistricting the voting maps! You still don't believe the Illuminati is real? The Illuminati is as real as it gets. And they have been manipulating you for years!

The man told me about this voting manipulation in 2003, 5 years before the 2008 Presidential Election. And it just so happened that in 2004, Barack Obama gave the Keynote Speech at the Democratic National Convention! That Keynote Speech put him on a National stage for a Presidential Candidate for the 2008 election. The Illuminati planned for Barack Obama to become President well before the 2004 Democratic National Convention. Do you understand why the Lord drove me to that location and made me sit on that bench? The Lord placed me there so he could give me pieces of the puzzle so I could connect the dots and explain all of this to you. This is the United States of America's Book of Secrets! This is the Illuminati Book of Secrets.

95. The Hate In Birmingham, AL Is Revealed

It is 2004, and I'm traveling back and forward between Birmingham and Huntsville. I'm traveling back and forward because my mom has been in the hospital for more than several months now. I am on I-65 South in the Gardendale, Fultondale area.

As I was driving, the Lord said, "Look into the sky." While driving, I looked into the sky and saw something in the clouds. Then I said, "Lord, what is that?" Then, the Lord allowed me to see into the spiritual realm. Then I saw it as clear as day. The huge face of a demonic spirit was in the sky, hovering over the City of Birmingham, Alabama. Upon seeing it, I was astonished! I couldn't believe my eyes! Then the Lord told me, "This is the demon that causes men to hate each other." After the Lord said this to me, I continued to look into the sky into the face of the demon. The face of the demon was not human. I am unsure what type of being it was, but its face was not human.

I could see the demon in the spiritual realm for a few minutes. Then suddenly, I wasn't allowed to see into the spiritual realm anymore, and the demon blended in amongst the clouds. I still could see the demon's face amongst the clouds, but it wasn't as clear as it was before. So, I thought about what the Lord said to me about the demon. The Lord said, "This is the demon that causes men to hate each other." After analyzing the Lord's statement, I immediately thought about Birmingham, Alabama's reputation with black-and-white relations. Then, I also thought about the reputation Birmingham had for black-on-black crime. And why the murder rate is so high in Birmingham. This demon that hovers above Birmingham is making or influencing men to hate each other.

The Lord showed me the demon above Birmingham, but that doesn't mean the demon is not in your town, city, county, parish, state, or country. If you notice, the Lord said, "This is the demon that causes men to hate each other." The Lord didn't say the demon was isolated to Birmingham. This confirms what the Apostle Paul told us in Ephesians 6:12. Our war is not against flesh and blood (not against each other) but against the authorities of dark forces in the heavenly realm (dark forces in the air) that make us hate one another.

96. The Birth of My Daughter

The day is September 13, 2004, and I am in the delivery room at Brookwood Hospital waiting for my daughter to be born. Once the doctor delivered my daughter, the doctor handed my daughter over to me. At that very moment, something very powerful and genuine overtook me. I instantly felt something I had never felt before. It was the strongest kind of love I had ever felt. It was a kind of love that I can't explain. It was a love I had never known before that moment. I was overtaken by love.

I immediately took my daughter, lifted her up, and offered her to the Lord. I prayed and offered her up to the Lord and asked the Lord to watch over her, protect her, and bless her. My exact words were, "Lord, I give you this child. This child belongs to you, my Lord. You are her Father, Lord, and I am just her daddy. Bless this child with your spirit, my Lord. There may come a time when I cannot protect or care for her. But Lord, you can always be there to protect her and take care of her. I give this child up to you as an offering, my Lord. I ask these things in the name of Jesus Christ. Amen."

97. The Lord Answers My Prayer

I remember when I was about sixteen years old, my mother became ill and she went to the hospital. I became very concerned for my mother at that time. I thought my mother was going to die. From that point on, I prayed every night for years that my mother wouldn't die until she met my wife and my child. When my daughter was born, my mother was in the hospital.

On September 13, 2004, my daughter was born to "L" and me. On September 15, 2004, I took my daughter to Baptist Medical Center Montclair so my mom could see her. When my mom saw my daughter, her face showed an expression of astonishment. One of the reasons I think she was astonished is because my daughter looked identical to my mother. Then my mother grabbed my hand and said, "No matter what happens, you protect that baby and take care of her. You don't realize what you got yourself into, but you must protect that baby."

My mom went into the Hospital in February 2004 and stayed there until September 18, 2004. She had been suffering for many months, lying in that hospital bed. I prayed for many months for my mother to be healed, but for some reason, she never was healed. I prayed and prayed for her healing, and I had faith and expectation of her healing, but nothing happened. I couldn't figure out why my mother wasn't being healed because I had faith that she would be healed. I expected supernatural healing because supernatural things always happen to me. You must remember that I told a cup to move across a table, and the cup moved! Speaking by faith that my mother be healed was easy because I had great faith in the name of the Lord.

On Saturday morning, September 18, 2004, my mother, Dannie Mae Brown, passed away at Baptist Medical Center Montclair. I was in Huntsville when my mother died because my manager made it mandatory for me to work that Saturday morning. So I got a call at work, and I was informed that my mother had passed away. And I didn't understand why the Lord didn't heal my mother. And I didn't understand why the Lord let my mother die!

After I had calmed down, I immediately thought about my prayers and how the Lord granted me what I had asked for. So I thought, "What if I had been more specific with my prayers? Would my mother still be alive if I asked the Lord to let my mother live long enough to help raise my child?"

But some years after my mom passed, I thought about something my mom used to say. My mom always said, "The Lord has only given me seventy years to live." She said this as far back as I can remember. Then, after my mom turned seventy, she said, "The Lord gave me a couple more years because he only guaranteed me seventy years to live." Two years later, my mom died. My mom had just turned seventy-two when she died. After using hindsight and looking back at the entire situation, my mom was right when she said, "The Lord gave me a couple more years because he only guaranteed me seventy."

My mom was the only person that came close to understanding me. My mom was always my crutch; whenever I had any type of problem, I would always go to my mom. So, I thought, maybe that's why the Lord took her. So, I would have no choice but to turn to the Lord to be my crutch and rock. So, I thought the Lord wanted me to take this walk of faith without my mother! But some years later, I would learn it wasn't the Lord who took my mother's life. It was Satan who took my mother's life. It was Satan who brought that sickness upon my mother. It was Satan who had my mother in that Hospital bed for eight months. It was Satan who wanted to take my crutch from me. Satan knew he was about to launch an all-out assault against me, and Satan didn't want me to have no one I could turn to for help! Satan knew my mother would stand by me through hell and hot water. Satan took that one person in this world that would stand by me.

It was Satan who brought sickness and death to my mother. But Satan wanted me to blame the Lord for my mother's death. And Satan wanted me to blame the Lord for not allowing my mother to be healed when I prayed for healing. Satan was trying to turn me against the Most High God, and I didn't even know it! Satan was playing the same trick on me that he played on many others. Satan took the one person I truly love, and he brought sickness and suffering to her. Satan did this because Satan hoped I would lose faith in God once she wasn't healed. Satan wanted me to be angry with God and to question the Lord for not healing my mother. Satan wanted me to act like many others in this world when they lose a loved one. Satan wanted me to be an accuser of the Most High God. When I was going through all these things, I didn't know this but once I had come out, the Lord gave me insight into these things. Satan had declared war against me since I was a child, but now Satan was taking his final stand against me, and he was waging an all-out assault against me, and my mother was the first causality of this all-out assault.

98. Vision of A Woman Who Face Changed

The time is April 2005, and I live in Nashville, Tennessee. One night, after praying, I fell into a deep sleep. The Lord then took me into the spirit, and this is what I witnessed. The Lord showed me a woman standing alone in a desolate place. I asked the Lord, "Lord, who is that woman?" Then, the Lord took me closer to see the woman more clearly. When I got closer to the woman, I saw it was "Li". "Li" is "L's" sister. "L" is the girl that came to visit me in Huntsville.

I then said, "Lord, that is "Li"." At that moment, "Li" head turned to the left, and another woman's face appeared on her body. This face that appeared was one of pure evil. Then, that woman's face turned to the left, and another woman's face appeared. Again, the face was that of pure evil. And like before, the woman's face turns to the left again, and another woman's face appears. Like the other two faces, this one was pure evil. I said, "Lord, these are the faces of witches." At that very moment, I awoke from my sleep. After I awakened from my sleep, I said again, "My Lord, those were faces of witches."

This was the second vision the Lord had given me that referred to witchcraft, identifying "L" or "L's" family members. Remember, "L" is the woman who came and visited me in Huntsville. She is the same woman who cooked me breakfast, and while I was eating the breakfast, I threw up everywhere. That's when the Holy Spirit told me, "Your spirit rejected the food."

The vision told me that multiple witches' spirits possessed "Li". We must look at real life to understand the vision about "Li". "Li" suffers from seizures. And based on what the Lord taught me through scriptures, people who have seizures are possessed by demons or spirits. Matthew 17:14-18 tells the story of Jesus healing the boy with seizures. The scripture also tells you that it was a demon in the boy causing the seizures.

Matthew 17:14-18 reads, [14] When they came to the crowd, a man approached Jesus and knelt before him. [15] "Lord, have mercy on my son," he said. "He has **seizures** and is suffering greatly. He often falls into the fire or into the water. [16] I brought him to your disciples, but they could not heal him." [17] "You unbelieving and perverse generation," Jesus replied, "how long shall I stay with you? How long shall I put up with you? Bring the boy here to me." [18] Jesus rebuked the **demon**, and it came out of the boy, and he was healed at that moment. (NIV, BibleGateway.com)

If you noticed, the scripture said the demon came out of the boy, and the boy was healed from having seizures. I know the world has taught you seizures are a medical condition. That is a lie! The scriptures said the boy had seizures, and then Jesus rebuked the demon, and the demon came out of the boy. And the boy didn't have seizures anymore. The boy was having seizures because of the demon that was in him. Just to let you know. Every demon has a characteristic. This demon characteristic was making the boy have seizures.

The world has taught you seizures happen because of a medical condition. I once believed that because I was taught the same thing until the Lord taught me differently. So why do you people always accept the world's explanation and reject the Lord's word! Just to let you know, the world offers you lies, fantasies, and fairy tales, but the Lord gives you the absolute truth! If the scripture said, Jesus rebuked the demon, and the demon came out of the boy and the boy was healed from having seizures. That means the demon was the cause of the boy having seizures.

The Lord was letting you know that if a person has seizures, then they have a demon or evil spirits in them that need to be cast out of them. So if one of your family members has seizures, take them to a priest or to a prophet who has the spiritual authority to cast out the demon!

In the vision the Lord gave me, he showed "Li's" face, and then he showed me three faces of witches. Remember, each face represented the spirit of a witch. So, the vision was telling me two things. The first thing it was telling me is that witchcraft is going on in "L's" family. The second thing it told me is that "Li" has three spirits of witches in her. These three different spirits are what is causing "Li" to have seizures. Also, the Lord showed "Li" in a desolate place! The Lord was telling me "Li" would be sent to a desolate place because she was doing witchcraft while she was here on earth.

99. Something Appears Out Of The Darkness 2

It is the beginning of 2005, and I live in Nashville, Tennessee, but I came home to Birmingham for the weekend. So I went to the apartment I had gotten for "L". "L" is the young lady that fixed me breakfast, and after I ate some of it, I started throwing up everywhere. So that night, I went to sleep, and "L" was lying beside me. My eyes were closed and out of the darkness appeared this entity. My spirit immediately saw the entity and recognized it was pure evil! While my eyes were still closed, the entity approached me like it was trying to see who I was. It was trying to get as close as possible to me to see who I truly was. I saw the entity was a man who was pure evil! I then said, "I rebuke you in the name of Jesus Christ." Once I said those words, it immediately fled away into the darkness. I know one thing about the evil man I saw: he fears the name of Jesus Christ! Because once I rebuked it in the name of Jesus Christ, it became fearful, and he fled away in fear!

100. The Prophesy of the Destruction of New Orleans

It's August 2005 and I had moved back to my hometown of Birmingham, Alabama. It was the night Hurricane Katrina hit New Orleans. I was up most of the night because I felt something stirring in my spirit, but eventually, I went to sleep. The next day, I woke up and began watching something on TV, but then I decided to change the station to CNN. Just about the time I was changing the channel, this intense feeling came across me, and I said, "Lord, what is going on?" At that moment, I looked at the TV, and CNN showed all the devastation in New Orleans. Once I saw the devastation, I instantly thought about what the angel of the Lord said to me on February 2, 2002. When I was in New Orleans on February 2, 2002, for Super Bowl 36, an angel of the Lord said, "The Lord is going to destroy this city." **The** Lord did what the angel of the Lord told me he would do. The Lord destroyed New Orleans. What you all call Hurricane Katrina, I call the breath of God! This was the second prophecy the Lord gave me that had come true nationally. The first one was 911! And the second was the destruction of New Orleans. From the time the angel told me the Lord was going destroy New Orleans, to the point that the prophecy was fulfilled was three years and six months!

101. "Save my people"

The Lord took me into the spirit a day after Hurricane Katrina hit, and this is what I witnessed. The Lord showed me a sea of people that covered different colors, ethnicities, and nationalities, but most were people of color. These people were too numerous to count. The Lord showed me millions upon millions of people during times of great cataclysm on the earth. Then the Lord spoke to me and said, "Save my people!"

After the Lord said that to me, I immediately woke up. My first thought was, "The Lord must want me to help the people of New Orleans." So that morning, I started to call different bus companies, trying to see if they were willing to go to New Orleans and assist the people in getting them out. I told the bus companies I would pay for all the buses and supply food and water for them. After talking to one bus company and discussing the price and everything, we decided I needed to coordinate this with the Red Cross first.

I immediately went to the Birmingham Jefferson Civic Center because the Red Cross had set up their headquarters for Hurricane Katrina there. To make a long story short, that day, I got into a group meeting where I and ten others met with this individual who identified himself as being over the relief efforts for Hurricane Katrina for the Red Cross in Birmingham. I sat in a meeting with him and others; I told him I would pay for some buses to go to New Orleans and help the stranded people get out. He responded, "We don't need any buses to go down there, but you can give us some money." I then explained to him the people didn't have a way out. He said, "I could donate some money to the Red Cross because they didn't want to bring those people here to Birmingham!" It bothered me when he made that comment because his concerns weren't about getting the people out. After I heard his comments, I saw I wasn't going to be able to coordinate anything with the Red Cross, so I got up and walked out of the meeting. I was very upset and angry because no buses had been sent to New Orleans to get the people out.

Days later I felt I let the Lord down because I didn't save the Lord's people. But then the Lord gave me a great revelation. The people the Lord wanted me to save are you! You are the people who need to be saved from the Illuminati! When the Lord said to me, "Save my people!" The Lord wanted me to save his people by warning his people about the Illuminati. The Lord wants me to wake you up so you will know what the Illuminati have been doing to you. The Lord wants me to open your eyes so you will know the absolute truth about the Illuminati and their plans for you! The Illuminati have plans on killing 200 million of you in the United States and another 7.3 billion of you in the world. The Illuminati want to decrease the population to 500 million by 2030. The Illuminati are trying to cut off the food supply. When I say they are trying to kill you, they are literally trying to kill you. The Illuminati are real, and their plans to kill you are real! If you think the Illuminati does not exist, then ask yourself, why did the Illuminati put the hidden message and the picture of the alien (image of the beast) on the back of the U.S. One Dollar Bill? You are the people the Lord wants me to save.

The Lord also told me worldwide disasters like Hurricane Katrina will happen worldwide at one time! So one of the things God wanted me to do is to save his people during the times of great cataclysm during the Great Tribulation. This is the same thing the Lord revealed to me in the scripture that talked about me in the Holy Bible. In Chapter 86, titled "A Specific Prophesy About Me In The Bible," I told you how the Holy Spirit spoke into my left ear and said, "There are specific prophesies about you in the Bible." Then, when I opened the Bible, the Bible opened to a specific page, then the Holy Spirit took my eyes directly to the scripture. Once I read the scripture, the Holy Spirit spoke to me again and said, "This is about you." The scripture was telling how I would do great miracles during a time of great despair on this earth.

When God said, "Save my people," God gave me my mission! And the mission is the same thing God showed me in the fourth grade. Do you remember what I told you in chapter 23, "I Repeated The Words The Lord Spoke"? In that chapter, I told how I was in the fourth grade, and the teacher saw some kids picking on me, and the teacher said to the kids, "You all need to stop picking on him because you don't know who the Lord is going to raise him to be. And one day, you may have to ask him for help!" Then, at that very moment, the Lord showed me a vision of how a massive amount of people had to come to me for food and provisions. They had to come to me for food and provisions because it was a time of great cataclysm on earth. It was a time of great trials and tribulation. There was a great cataclysm, and the world was in great distress. And I was given authority by the Lord to oversee billions of his people.

The vision the Lord gave me while I was in the fourth grade, where a mass amount people had to come to me for food and provision, matches the vision the Lord gave me when he showed me millions upon millions of people from every color, ethnicities and nationality needed my help. When the Lord said to me, "Save my people," it matched the vision he gave me in the fourth grade. Jesus revealed to me that he references the vision he showed me in Matthew 24:45-47.

Jesus said in Mathew 24:45-47, [45] "Who then is a faithful and wise servant, whom his master made ruler over his household, **to give them food in due season?** [46] Blessed *is* that servant whom his master, when he comes, will find so doing. [47] Assuredly; I say to you that he will make him ruler over all his goods. (NIV, BibleGateway.com)

My mission is to save the Lord's people, and my mission is too Big to Fail! Now that you know my mission is to save the Lord's people, watch how Satan tries to stop me from fulfilling my mission by trying to destroy me at every turn so I can never reach my divine destiny.

102. The Holy Spirit Speaks To My Daughter

It's February 2006, and I'm on the way to get my taxes done. My daughter is now 18 months old, and she is in the back seat. The windows are rolled up because it is cold outside, and the radio is turned off because I have a lot of things on my mind. I was driving down the road and it was very quiet in the car. Then suddenly, my daughter began screaming, "Daddy, did you hear that?" My mind was on other things, so I replied, "No, Kennedy, I don't hear anything." So, a few seconds later, my daughter said again, "Daddy, did you hear that?" Again, my mind was preoccupied with things I had to do, so I replied, "No, Kennedy, I don't hear anything."

At this point, I started thinking to myself, what did she hear? I looked around and said, "The radio is off, and the windows are rolled up. What in the world is she hearing?" Then, with so much excitement, she said it again, "Daddy, did you hear that?" I turned around and said, "Kennedy, what do you hear?" She said, "Daddy, the Voice said God is good, and so is your daddy!" When my daughter said, **"The Voice,"** I knew the Holy Spirit was speaking to her. I was overwhelmed with joy because the Holy Spirit talked to my child. At that very moment, I praised God's name while driving. I shouted, "Thank You, Lord! Thank You Jesus, for speaking to my child that I offered up to You when she was born." That day was one of the happiest days of my life! I was overwhelmed with joy! I don't know if there is any greater feeling when you know that the Lord Jesus Christ and the Holy Spirit are speaking to your child. Because when the Holy Spirit speaks to your child, you know your child is one of the chosen ones!

If you noticed, I offered my child to the Lord when she was born. Then, I ask the Lord to bless my child with his spirit. As a result of me saying that prayer, the Holy Spirit or the Lord Jesus Christ was speaking to her. The voice my daughter heard was the same voice I have heard on many occasions. It is the voice of the Holy Spirit or the Lord Jesus Christ. My daughter belongs to the Lord because she heard his voice. This was the first time I realized the Holy Spirit was speaking to my daughter. But it wouldn't be the last time the Lord spoke to her. My daughter has told me of visions she had. The visions referred to things that would occur after the Great Tribulations. She described a great memorial that took place after the Great Tribulation was over.

103. All Warning Signs Ignored And I Get Married

The years are 2005 and 2006. I remember going to church every Sunday, and the Bishop would stand before the congregation and say, "Don't marry that woman if the Lord hasn't told you to marry her!" When I heard Bishop say this, I knew the message was for me, but something was clouding my thoughts at the time, and it was trying to stop me from seeing or hearing the truth. Ever since I got with "L" something was trying to stop me from recognizing the truth!

The Holy Spirit spoke through Bishop, saying, "Don't marry that woman if the Lord hasn't told you to marry her!" During the same time Bishop was saying this. I remember praying, asking the Lord if I should marry "L". The Lord was giving me the answer through Bishop, but I was looking for the answer to come directly from the Lord to me. I was accustomed to the Lord telling me things directly. I wasn't used to getting information from a third party on something I asked the Lord. The Lord never told me yes or no, which was very odd because the Lord would always tell me something. So once I didn't get a direct answer from God, I decided to marry "L". Even though the Holy Spirit had warned me not to marry her through Bishop, I married her anyway! And I would pay the price for not listening to the warning!

So, in real life, this is what happened. The woman I decided to marry was "L," who was the same woman who came to Huntsville to visit me. "L" was the woman that cooked breakfast for me, and I threw up everywhere. Then the Holy Spirit told me, "Your spirit rejected the food." From that day on, I started becoming confused. Well, "L" had placed a spell on me, and I didn't realize it (witchcraft). So, when I decided to marry "L," I was under a spell she had placed on me. She would always come and stand in front of me and brush her hair. Then, I would instantly become confused about everything, and I would have some type of memory loss.

So, before I married "L," I tallied up all the wedding and reception receipts. The cost of the wedding and the reception was exactly $10,000 on the dot. There were no cents! It was $10,000 on the dot! I was amazed when I saw the exact cost of the wedding and the reception was $10,000! Once I saw the cost of the wedding and reception was $10,000, I started to call off the wedding. The reason I started to call off the wedding is because everything was matching up with the vision the Lord showed me.

Do you remember Chapter 83, "Vision of Two Women in Wedding Dresses"? In that chapter, I told you how the Lord took me into the spirit and showed me two women in wedding dresses standing side by side. In that vision, the Lord said, "These are your wives." Remember, both women had veils covering their faces, so I couldn't distinguish one from the other. Remember how there was only one distinct characteristic between the two women? One had long hair, and one had short hair. Then, the one with long hair approached me as though she was first. Well, in that vision, it showed me I was going through hell because of the woman I married. Then, at the end of the vision, numbers started to appear. The first number was $10,000.00 and then $10,000 turned into $100,000.00 then $100,000 turned into a $1,000,000 then $1,000,000 turned into $10,000,000 the $10,000,000 turned into $100,000,000 then $100,000,000 turned into $1,000,000,000... Then I woke up saying, "This woman took a million dollars from me."

Once I saw I paid $10,000 out of my pocket for the wedding and reception. I realized that was the first number I saw in the vision. Then I realized the woman in the vision had long hair. And the woman in the vision with the long hair approached me as though I married her first. Then I realized "L" had long hair like the woman in the vision. Everything in real life matched the vision. But I didn't realize "L" was doing witchcraft on me.

I remember I was about to run for the hills the day of the wedding. I knew I was making a huge mistake by marrying "L". I should have left her standing at the altar and ran out of the church. But I was not just thinking about myself; I was thinking of my daughter. I went ahead and married "L," and then I entered the abyss.

104. Holy Spirit Warns Me of Satan's Plan

It's August 2006, and I have been married to "L" for three months. I am standing in my driveway, thinking about my wife. I was trying to put some pieces together about her that didn't make sense to me. I then said, "Lord, I believe my wife was a trap sent to me by Satan." At that very moment, the Lord said to me in my left ear, "Your wife was a trap sent by Satan for you, Bishop, and the Church." When the Lord said this, I didn't understand. I knew it was true, but I didn't understand. I started asking myself questions. I wanted to know how "L" could be a trap for me, Bishop, and the Church. How can she be a trap for Bishop? How can she be a trap for the Church?

105. Go and Get Baptize Part II

It's the summer of 2006, and I am at GL CHURCH. During this time, the Lord came to me and said, "Go and get baptized". When I heard the Lord say that I didn't question it. I just did what the Lord told me to do, and I got baptized for a second time. I had already been baptized once as a child because the Lord spoke to me and told me to get baptized (Chapter 7).

I am thirty-five years old, and the Lord said, "Go and get baptized". Once the Lord told me to get baptized, I did just that. I went and got baptized again. When I was baptized for the second time, I was submerged under water, and I was baptized in the name of the Holy Father, in the name of the Son Jesus Christ, and in the name of the Holy Spirit. So, that day, I was baptized for the second time in my life. I was baptized as a child, and I was baptized as an adult. The Lord told me to go and get baptized on both occasions.

As the years passed, I wondered why the Lord wanted me to be baptized twice. The more I thought about it, the more it didn't make sense. It was not until I was fasting during the week of January 19, 2016, that the Lord revealed why he had me get baptized twice. During my fast, the Lord revealed to me that when I was baptized as a child, water was sprinkled on my head, and I was baptized in the name of the Holy Father, the Son Jesus Christ, and the Holy Spirit. Then the Lord revealed to me that during my second baptism as an adult, I was submerged under the water, and I was baptized in the name of the Holy Father, in the name of the Son Jesus Christ, and in the name of the Holy Spirit. Then the Lord revealed to me he had me get baptized twice to show the world that sprinkling water on the head or submerging the entire body underwater is sufficient for baptism.

Once the Lord revealed that to me, the Lord revealed he was settling a dispute that had been going on for almost a thousand years in the Church! Many religious sects have been battling and quarreling over which type of baptism is correct. Some believe you can only be properly baptized if submerged under the water. And then some believe you can be properly baptized by just sprinkling water on one's head. And this difference of opinion has caused many disputes in the Church.

The Lord had me, the Prophet Elisha, get baptized twice to settle the dispute. The Lord told me to, "Go and get baptize" as a child. And that day I got baptized as a child; water was sprinkled on my head. And since the Lord told me to go and get baptized, the Lord must accept the sprinkling of water on one's head as an acceptable form of baptism. Because that day, water was sprinkled on my head, and I was baptized.

Then, when I was 35 years old, the Lord told me again, "Go and get baptized". So, I went and got baptized again, and I was submerged underwater as I was baptized. And again, the Lord told me to go and get baptized when I was submerged under water, which means being submerged under water is an acceptable form of baptism. The Lord was using me as an example to prove both methods of baptism are sufficient! One is not greater than the other. And one is not lesser than the other. But both methods of baptism are sufficient! Stop quarreling over which form of baptism is correct!

Satan followers, the Illuminati has crafted a super complex scheme to take over the entire world, but you Christians are quarreling over which method of baptism is acceptable! Some of you should feel stupid because Satan's people, the Illuminati, have united under one cause to have the entire world worship the image of the beast as a god, but you people in the Church are divided by your church denominations, and which form of baptism is correct? It doesn't matter about the Church denomination if your Church worships the Most High God Jehovah as God, and they believe Jesus Christ is the son of the living God! Some of you should feel stupid because Satan's people, the Illuminati, are working together to destroy Christians while Christians are working together to divide themselves based on denominations and which form of baptism is acceptable! A house that is divided cannot stand strong! And Christians are divided! We must stop being divided and we must unite as one!

106. Satan Tries To Chase Me Out Of The Lords Word

Since 1999, I constantly read my Bible to keep a close relationship with Christ. But once I married "L", whenever I opened my Bible to read, some craziness would always start with "L" and her family. At first, I didn't recognize the pattern, but as time passed, I noticed all the mayhem would break loose whenever I tried to read the Bible. So, one night, I said, "It's quiet; I can get some studying done now." So I opened my Bible and started studying the Lord's word, and as soon as I began to study, "L" came to me with all the mess that was going on in her family over something I supposedly had done. So, instead of studying the Lord's word, I defended myself from all kinds of lies.

After that happened, I said, "Every time I open my Bible, all hell breaks loose with her and her family." As time progressed, I wasn't studying the word as frequently because I didn't want to deal with all the craziness. It wasn't until a year later I recognized Satan was trying to chase me out of the Lord's word by making all hell break loose every time I attempted to read the Bible. To study the Bible while I was with "L" was hell on earth.

107. The Lord Reveals To Me Partly Who I Am

It's November 2006, and one night after dealing with my wife, her family, and all the evilness that came with them. My heart became heavy. My heart was so heavy the only thing I could do was pray. I kneeled beside my bed, and I began to pray. The only thing that would come out of my mouth was, "Lord, how long must I endure this?" Over and over, I asked the Lord, "Lord, how long must I endure this?" Immediately after praying, I fell into a deep sleep, and the Lord took me into the Spirit, and this is what the Lord showed me.

The Lord took me into the Spirit and showed me the new GL Church completed. Then, the Lord took me into the sanctuary. Here, I witness the Bishop giving a Sermon in the new Church. During Bishop's sermon, I witnessed him going off into a rage that was not of God but a rage of boastfulness that came from Satan. Then the Lord said, "I am sending three angels to get Bishop." I then looked over my left shoulder and saw three angels of the Lord." Then the Lord said to me, "You are the only one in the church that has the authority to speak to the three angels."

Once I saw the three angels, I turned around to look at Bishop; at that point, the Lord showed me another man with a shaved ball head who was kind of muscular. At first, I didn't recognize this man because he was muscular and had a shaved head. This man was preaching in the Church. This man was Bishop, but his appearance had changed because he had lost weight and shaved his head. Some of the things Bishop was preaching weren't right at all! Then, the Lord took me through the Church, showing me different things that were going on in the Church. The Lord showed me things teenagers were doing in the Church that they shouldn't have done. Then, the Lord took me throughout the Church. Then, the Lord showed me a woman standing behind what looked like a kitchen table, and the Lord said to me, "This is your wife." The woman he showed me was not the woman I was married to. And then the Lord said to me, "You are my Prophet."

Once I woke up, I thought about everything the Lord showed me and told me. The Lord showed me those things to tell me I must endure the hell I was in until those things he showed me in the vision were fulfilled. At the end of the vision, the Lord showed me this woman who would be my wife. And that woman kind of looked like "L," but she had short hair. This meant that "L" was sent to look like the real thing. This also meant the woman I had married was a decoy sent by Satan! You must remember the rule! Satan always sends a decoy that looks like the real thing before God sends the real thing!

If you remember, Chapter 83 is titled "Vision of Two Women In Wedding Dresses". In that vision, the Lord told me I would be married twice because he showed me two women in wedding dresses. When the Lord showed me and told me the woman in the Church was my wife. The Lord was basically telling me, "This is going to be your second wife, whom I, the Lord, have chosen for you." This meant the Lord would be sending me my second wife. This also meant Satan sent me my first wife! This meant Satan sent a decoy to me, and I married the decoy! This is why my life was a living hell! This is why I was in a living nightmare: because I fell for Satan's decoy! Satan always sends a decoy that initially looks, acts, and even sounds like the real thing. But the decoys are far from the real thing. Decoys are nothing but demons in sheep's clothing. Decoys always physically look like the authentic person. Satan always sends the decoy to look and act like the authentic person. The decoy looks and acts like the real thing that it tricks one's senses and Spirit. But one thing always follows a decoy! Destruction and hell! The decoy is sent to kill, steal, and destroy. The decoy connects itself to you so it can destroy you! You must remember that if there is a decoy, there must be an authentic person from the Lord. The authentic person is sent from the Lord to bless you. But the decoy is sent to destroy you! Based on what I just told you, I want you to pay attention to what happens in my life because of the decoy I married!

After the Lord showed me the vision, I thought about the other things the Lord showed me and told me. I thought about what the Lord had told me about Bishop and the rage Bishop displayed in my vision. The Lord said, "I am sending three angels to get Bishop, and you are the only one in the church that has authority to speak to the three angels."

When the Lord told me I was the only one who could speak to the three angels. He was telling me I had authority over Bishop's life. To the average individual, it looks like it meant I could intercede for Bishop. But the question I had to ask was, why did the Lord give me authority to intercede on the Bishop's behalf? I ask this question because the Lord said, "I am sending three angels to get Bishop." The next question that came to mind was, why would the Lord tell me he is sending three angels to get Bishop just for me to intercede? That didn't make sense to me. Did the Lord want me to stop the three angels? If so, why would the Lord send three angels if the Lord wanted me to stop the three angels?

I had many questions and was trying to understand what the Lord told me concerning the Bishop. I felt like there was more to it than just normal prayer intercession! As of today, I know why the Lord told me, "You are the only one in the church that has the authority to speak to the three angels." The Lord was telling me I have the authority to tell the angels when to take Bishop, which means I have authority over Bishop's life. As you continue to read, you will understand why the Lord gave me such authority over the Bishop's life.

In the vision, the Lord said I was his Prophet. This was the very first time the Lord called me his Prophet! But you must remember, the Lord told me I was Elisha while in college. Now, the Lord just told me I was his Prophet! If you put the two things together, the Lord told me I am the **Prophet Elisha.** But at this time, I still didn't remember the Lord telling me I was Elisha.

108. Satan Tries To Kill Me But God's Grace Saves Me

So "L" and I got married on April 29, 2006. Right after we got back from our honeymoon in Cancun, I noticed a huge change in her and her attitude. I remember thinking, "This woman just changed into somebody else overnight." I started to think "L" was either strictly evil or she had multiple personality disorder.

In May 2006, my wife, "L," discussed getting life insurance policies. We were married for about a week, and she was discussing getting life insurance policies! That entire month, she insisted on getting life insurance policies. Whenever she would ask about getting life insurance policies, I would always tell her, "I don't need a policy because I know for a fact I am not going anywhere."

One day in May of 2006, I walked downstairs from my bedroom, and my wife met me at the bottom of the stairs; she said, "Mrs. so and so is here, and she has our life insurance policies ready for us to sign!" I looked at her like, "What!" I looked at my wife like she was crazy because I never agreed to get a life insurance policy, but she had an insurance agent show up at my house with life insurance policies for me to sign. The insurance lady was also a coworker of my wife. I didn't want to make a scene, so I just went ahead and signed the life insurance policy.

One night in either August or September of 2006, I came home after watching a boxing match on TV at my neighbor's house. So, I went upstairs and told my wife I was home. She then responded, "OK, are you coming to bed?" I said, "No, I am going to catch some highlights on Sports Center first." I went back downstairs to my den in the basement. After watching Sports Center for about ten minutes, I had to get something out of my car in the garage. I walked into the garage and saw someone run past the window in the garage door. I thought, "Who is sneaking past my garage late at night?" Once I saw the person sneak past my garage door, I turned around and went back into the den. I was about to grab my gun off the entertainment center, but the Lord said, "No!" Once, I heard the Lord say, "No!" I didn't grab my gun. I turned around and walked back into the garage, and then there was a hard, forceful knock on the garage door. Then I heard, "Police, open up!!" I said to myself, "Police, what the police are doing here?"

Then I opened the garage door, and outside were four Birmingham Police Officers with guns in their hand. They said, "We got a call saying a burglary was in process." I told them I live there. I immediately scream out "L", "L", "L". She then came running down the stairs saying, "Ken, I didn't know you were here!" I then said to her, "Girl, I just came upstairs and told you I was here, and I am going back downstairs to watch Sports Center." She then said, "I was asleep." The Officers stood there looking at me like, "Man, you don't see what is going on!"

This was the very first time she set me up to be shot by the Police. And I probably would have gotten shot by the Police if I had grabbed my gun once I saw someone run past my garage door! If the Lord hadn't told me no, I would have grabbed my gun and walked into the garage with a gun in my hand. Then there's no telling what would have happened because Birmingham Police might have shot me because they were told that a burglary was taking place! And there I was downstairs in the garage with a gun! So that was the first time my wife "L" set me up to be shot by the Police, but it wouldn't be the last time she set me up to be shot by the Police.

The night is December 4, 2006, and I have just finished watching SportsCenter. After watching SportsCenter, I decided to go to bed. Once I reached the bedroom, I noticed my wife was still up. I thought it was very strange she was still awake because it was 11:30 PM, and she normally was asleep by 9:00 or, at the latest, 9:30 PM. I normally stay up late, but she is still awake and out of bed for some reason. So I went to bed. Once I started to doze off, my wife said, "Ken, somebody broke into the house." I replied, "L," nobody has broken into the house." She then insists over and over that someone has broken into the house. She wouldn't leave me alone, and she wouldn't let me go to sleep.

Once she saw I wasn't going to get up, she said, "You know your daughter is in the house too! What if somebody broke into the house and they do something to your daughter." My wife knew I would do anything for my daughter, so she mentioned my daughter so I would get up and check the house. Then my wife "L" said, "Get your gun and go check the house." I told her I didn't need my gun, but she insisted. So, I got out of bed and grabbed my .40 caliber so she would leave me alone (the .40 caliber gun was one of the two guns she insisted on buying me in December 2005). So, I walked down to the first floor and then to the basement with my gun in my hand. As soon as my foot hit the last step in the basement, the Lord said to me in my left ear, "Go back upstairs!"

Once I heard the Lord speak, I immediately turned around and went back upstairs. I was walking softly, so I guess "L" didn't hear me coming back up the stairs. Once I reached the top of the steps, I saw "L" in our bedroom on the phone. I said, "L", who are you talking to on the phone?" Before I got the third or fourth word out of my mouth, she immediately placed her hand over the mic on the phone. She covered up the mic because she didn't want whoever she was talking to, to hear my voice. She then started acting frantic while covering the mic on the phone. She screamed, "Go back downstairs and check the house; someone broke into the house!!" She was screaming, acting like she was out of her mind! I then said to myself, "This girl is crazy." I just wanted to get away from her.

So, I walked back down to the basement and checked the doors. Then, I walked back to the first floor and checked all the windows. While on the first floor, I was walking towards the front door when I saw someone run across the front yard through the glass on the front door. I said, "This girl may have been right, someone probably did break into the house." I opened the door and walked onto the front porch with my .40-caliber semi-automatic gun in my hand. Once I got onto the porch, there were about five Birmingham Police Officers in my front yard with their weapons pointed at me. They started screaming, "Drop the gun. Drop the gun!" I stood there thinking, "What in the world is going on!"

I didn't understand what was going on. I was trying to assess the situation! I was trying to understand where all these Police Officers came from and why these Police Officers had guns pointed at me. Not only was I caught off guard, but I was not thinking clearly! You, the reader, must remember "L" had a spell on me, and the spell wasn't allowing me to think clearly. So, I stood there on my front porch with a gun in my hand, and I didn't drop the gun when the Police Officers instructed me to do so. I wasn't thinking clearly like I normally do. Something was clouding my thoughts. I was battling something, but I had no idea what I was battling.

So, the Police Officers continued to yell at me to drop the gun. Then, the Lord said to me, "Put the gun in your pocket!" "Put the gun in your pocket!" "Put the gun in your pocket!" So, I eased the gun in my pocket. The Police Officer walked towards me and asked me some questions; I told him I lived there. Then one of the officers said, "A woman called 911 and said there was a burglar in her house, and there was **no one here but her and her two children.** And she and her two children are upstairs in the bedroom." The Police Officers were looking at me like, "Do you understand what we are saying." I heard what the officer said but it wasn't registering in my mind. I heard the officer clearly, but something clouded my thoughts and mind. I was lost in a mist of confusion. I was not thinking clearly like I normally do. Then my wife "L" came onto the front porch yelling "Ken", "Ken" as if she was so surprised about everything. The officers just stared at me like, do you understand what we are saying? And I stood there caught in a mist of confusion. The officers were trying to tell me my wife was setting me up to be killed by the Police. But it was not registering with me because of the spell she placed on me. You, the reader, must understand that I didn't realize she had a spell on me. Something was clouding my thoughts, and I wasn't processing information like I normally do. Again, I tell you I was not thinking clearly.

Now, what I am about to reveal to you is all hindsight because I didn't see her plan at first. I didn't realize my wife at the time was trying to kill me! Do you remember when my wife covered up the mic on the phone when I returned upstairs? My wife was on the phone with 911 operators. She covered up the mic on the phone so the 911 operator wouldn't hear my voice because she had told the 911 operator the only people in the house **were her and her two children**. She covered up the mic so the 911 operator wouldn't hear a man's voice, my voice! She also told the 911 operator they were in the upstairs bedroom. So that meant, when the officers saw a man carrying a gun downstairs, that man had to be the burglar! This meant the Police Officers had the right to shoot me! This also means my wife was trying to kill me! Also, my wife begged me to carry my gun with me when I went to check the house. She wanted me to have my gun so it would give the Police Officers a reason to shoot me! Because the Police Officers would have perceived me as an armed burglar!

The question is, how long was she planning to kill me? After I went back and started thinking about everything she did before this date, I could see how she had planned this out since December 2005 before we married. This was her plan from the beginning! How do I know this? Let's go through a timeline and look at the evidence.

In December 2005, before Christmas, "L" insisted I needed a gun in the house. She kept insisting this day after day. I told her I wasn't about to spend money on a gun. I told her I had a gun before, and I sold it. She then said, "I will buy it for you." To discourage her from buying me a gun, I said, "If you buy me one gun, you might as well buy me two guns." I told her I wanted one gun to keep in my car and one for the house! She said, "OK," and then we went to the gun store, and she brought me two guns.

In the year of 2006 before we got married, I remember times when I would leave the house and go somewhere. Then, when I returned, my neighbor would always be standing outside in his yard. Then my neighbor would say, "Brown, what was the Police doing at your house?" I would then respond, "I didn't know the Police were at my house!" I would then ask my wife, "What was the Police doing here?" Her response would always be, "There was no Police here!" Or she would say, "They had the wrong house." I would always walk away with the thought that something wasn't right.

I think "L" was calling the Police like there was a burglar at the house while I was not at home. The police officers would respond to the call and be accustomed to only seeing her and the kids at the house. When they responded to a burglary call in the future and saw me, they would remember only a woman and her two kids lived there. When she called 911 and reported a burglar in the house, they would perceive me as the burglar! She was also setting up her defense so she couldn't be charged with murder. She had set me up from the very beginning! For the Police to shoot me as a burglar, I had to have a weapon like a gun. So, she made sure I had a weapon; that's why she brought me the two guns for Christmas!

A couple of years later, I realized what "L" was up to. So, I went and got a printout of the 911 calls that were placed from my house. Once I saw the printout, I saw a list of 911 calls that were placed from my house that I didn't even know about! There were 911 calls placed before we got married and afterwards. Once I saw the 911 calls from my house, I understood why the neighbor always asked me, "Brown, what was the Police doing at your house?"

She planned to have me shot by the Police and receive the life insurance policy she had on me. The life insurance policy would have doubled for accidental death! The same life insurance policy she had her coworker placed on me a month after we were married. Once the officers shot and killed me, she was going to file a wrongful death suit against the Birmingham Police Department. My wife, "L," was trying to kill me so she could get paid! The night of December 4, 2006, was the second time she set me up to be shot and killed by the Birmingham Police Department.

Now, let's address one other subject. On December 4, 2006, the Police were called to my house for a burglary in process. Unknowingly, I stepped onto my front porch with a loaded .40-caliber pistol. Birmingham Police had their guns pointed at me. The officers instructed me to drop my gun, and I failed to do so! The officers didn't shoot me when I failed to drop the gun. The officers properly assessed the situation and eventually allowed me to put the gun in my pocket! This was a job well done by those Birmingham Police Officers who responded to the call; now if Birmingham Police Officers didn't shoot me when they responded to a call that a burglary was in process! How in the world are all these Police Officers across America shooting and killing unarmed people?

109. The Apocrypha

One day, I was at Brooms Barber Shop on Arkadelphia Road waiting for a haircut. While I was waiting, we were discussing the Holy Bible. In the midst of the discussion, this guy said things about the word of God I never read before in the Bible. I was thinking to myself where is he getting this information from because what he is saying isn't in the Holy Bible. I was thinking since the things he was saying weren't in the Holy Bible, it couldn't be true! The guy began to name some books that didn't appear in the Holy Bible. I rejected the information because the books he mentioned didn't appear in the Holy Bible. I thought the only accurate word of God was in the Holy Bible. That's what I was taught, so that's what I thought! Just because you were taught something doesn't mean it's the truth.

I immediately rejected what the guy was saying because the things he was saying didn't appear in the Holy Bible. I walked out of the barbershop upset. I thought the guy was trying to discredit the Holy Bible. So, as a man of God, I was getting ready to go off! I walked outside to the parking lot, angry and upset. As I walked into the parking lot, this man appeared behind me and called my name. I didn't know this man and had never seen him before, but he knew my name. This man appeared out of nowhere! The man started talking to me about the Apocrypha and how these books are God's word. And he explained to me how I should read them. After the guy encouraged me to read the Books of the Apocrypha, I told the man, "The Holy Bible doesn't mention the things the man in the Barber Shop was mentioning!" Then the man said, "Things had been removed from the Holy Bible by man! The Holy Bible had things removed by man to stop man from knowing the truth, and certain things were changed to hide the truth!"

I didn't understand what this man was saying or what he was trying to say! Once I got curious about who this man was, I was distracted from him for a brief second. At that very moment, I heard some car tires making skid noises like a car was about to crash into something, so I turned my head away from the man for a brief second to see what was happening. Then, once I turned my head back to the man, he was gone! I looked for the man, but he was nowhere to be found. I only took my eyes off him for two seconds, and he was gone. It was like he disappeared into thin air. I didn't understand it; one second he was there, and the next second, he was gone. I went into the barbershop, but the man was not there. One of the barbers asked me, "Where did that man go to that you was talking to?" I shrugged my shoulders and said, "I don't know." The man had disappeared into thin air, and I never saw him again.

I didn't realize the man was not a man at all. The man that appeared before me was an angel of the Lord. The angel was sent to me to plant the seed in my mind to read the Books of the Apocrypha and other books that don't appear in the Holy Bible. At the time I didn't understand the importance of those books, but the Lord had plans on giving me proof of what he was getting ready to reveal about this world and the true history of mankind. And what a history it is! This is not the history they taught you in elementary school or parts of the history they taught you in Church, but this is the true history of mankind! God wanted me to read the books of the Apocrypha because God was preparing to tell me everything about the true history of mankind!

So, some years after, the angel visited me at the barbershop. I began to read the Books of the Apocrypha, and the Lord showed me how this was his word. I read the Book of Jasher and the Book of Enoch, and they opened my eyes to things that weren't in the Bible. Also, the Lord showed me what happened during the two thousand years from Adam to the Great Flood of Noah. The Lord gave me details that aren't in the Holy Bible and explained why the Lord had to destroy the earth. Then, the Lord revealed to me the absolute truth of how some things were purposely removed from the Holy Bible to hide the absolute truth about the history of mankind. Then the Lord revealed to me how certain things were changed in the Holy Bible to hide the truth! The Holy Bible is the true word of the Most High God Jehovah, and the Lord Jesus Christ, but certain things were kept out of the Bible by man, so man wouldn't know the absolute truth about the true history of mankind! As you continue to read this book, the things removed from the Holy Bible will be revealed to you as the Lord revealed it to me!

110. The Holy Spirit Makes Bishop Speak

The year is 2007, and I am at church with my wife. Bishop walks on stage and begins to speak. The first thing that came out of his mouth was, **"Why do a man of God sleep with a whore, night after night!"** Everyone at church was astonished when Bishop said this, but I had a feeling the message was meant for me. I knew the Lord was sending me a strong message to stop sleeping with my wife. But my wife was using witchcraft on me, and I was under a spell, and it was clouding my thoughts. I heard the Lord's message through Bishop, but it didn't fully register in my mind.

After Bishop said that, he had a look on his face that said, "My God, why did I say that?" Bishop said that because the Lord made him say it. When the Lord takes control over you, you must yield to the Lord and say what the Lord has you to say. I have often been in that situation when the Lord would have me say things to people I didn't understand.

111. The Lord Reveals To Me Who My Wife Truly Is

It is February 2007, and one night, my wife comes home, and she begins to give me an explanation of where she has been. I was watching her tell lie after lie. I remember thinking, "Lord, who is this woman?" After our conversation, my heart became so heavy that I fell to my knees and began praying. The only words that came out of my mouth were, "Lord, reveal to me the absolute truth of who this woman "L" truly is. Lord, reveal to me the absolute truth of who this woman "L" truly is," I said those words repeatedly. Immediately after praying, I jumped into bed and fell into a deep sleep. The Lord took me in the spirit, and this is what the Lord showed me.

The Lord showed me walking in green pastures on a beautiful day! There wasn't a cloud in the sky, and the temperature was perfect; it was just a perfect day. On this beautiful day, I was walking in green pastures. The grass was so green; it was the prettiest green grass I had ever seen. There wasn't one blemish on the grass. Green pastures surrounded me! Then, the Lord showed my sisters standing to my right at a distance. They were standing off the green pastures, looking at me on the green pastures. The Lord wouldn't allow my sisters to enter the green pastures. Then, this beautiful white and tan creature appeared and crawled all over me. This beautiful creature wasn't of this world. And nothing in this world resembles this beautiful creature. But just for description purposes, I will say it reminded me of a small koala bear with two small horns on its head. I had an emotion of so much love for that little creature, and it had so much love for me.

I played with the little koala bear-looking creature until it had to leave me for a little while. When the little koala bear-looking creature had to leave me, I became sad, and the koala bear-looking creature became sad, too. The koala bear-looking creature then left me and stood off in the distance. Once the little koala bear-looking creature left, I began to walk through the green pastures. As I was walking through the green pastures, I stepped over a baby snake. It was not a full-grown snake. It was like a child snake. Then, I continued to walk through the green pastures when a Giant King Cobra appeared out of nowhere and rose above me. The Giant King Cobra was a **cream color with burgundy colored spots on it**. It was still a beautiful day when the Giant King Cobra appeared on the green pastures. Then the Giant King Cobra tried to bite me again and again. Then suddenly, that beautiful day turned into total darkness! It went from a beautiful day to total darkness! There was no sunlight. So, the Giant King Cobra continued to try to bite me again and again, so I ran. While I was running, I stumbled and fell. Then, the Lord spoke to me while I was still on the ground. The Lord said to me, "Satan has no authority to do any harm to you."

I had no fear once the Lord spoke; my fear was gone. I got up and faced the Giant King Cobra as it towered over me. It tried to bite me, but I didn't flinch. It tried to bite me again, but I didn't move or waver. The Giant King Cobra knew it had no authority to harm me! It wanted to cause fear in me! But I had no fear because of the words the Lord had spoken to me. I stood up to the giant snake because I knew what the Lord had spoken was the absolute truth. Then I rebuked the Giant King Cobra in the name of Jesus Christ! Upon my rebuking, the Giant King Cobra, in the name of Jesus Christ, the Giant King Cobra fled away into the darkness in fear! Then the Lord spoke to me again and said, "You are my Prophet!"

Once I woke up, I knew exactly what the vision was telling me. I knew the vision was telling me my wife was a servant of Satan! I laid in the bed in a fetal position, praying. I said to the Lord, "Please Lord, don't let "L" put on the colors of that King Cobra." I prayed this prayer over and over. By the time I was finished praying, "L" began to wake up and she started getting ready for work. She entered the closet and put on a **cream turtleneck and some burgundy wine-colored pants**. The exact same colors as the Giant King Cobra! I knew at that very moment that "L" didn't represent my Lord in heaven, but she represented Satan. I was sleeping with the enemy!

The Giant King Cobra represents my wife "L", Satan, and the image of the beast. This is not the first time the Lord has shown me my enemy as a snake in a vision; he has done this on many occasions. That's how I knew the meaning of the vision once I woke up. I wonder why the Lord showed "L" as a King Cobra snake rather than a regular snake. Years later, I realized the Lord was telling me more than just my wife represented Satan. The Lord was telling me more about the anatomy of Satan. That's why the Lord used symbolism in that vision. If you noticed, this was the first vision in this book in which the Lord used symbolism to show or tell me something. The reason is that a symbolic vision can tell you two, three, or more messages simultaneously. But each message is not revealed until the appropriate time comes.

The King Cobra is called the King of the Snakes, which means "L" is the King of manipulation, the King of deception, and the King of misdirection. "L" has all the characteristics of her father, Satan. She presents herself as a quiet lamb, but she is nothing but a snake in lamb clothing. I have met plenty of people in my lifetime, and I have never witnessed anyone who could deceive and manipulate any situation as she can.

In the vision, the Lord showed me walking across green pastures. The green pastures represent my life in Christ and the abundance of blessings he has given me. The green pastures are blessings bestowed upon me by the Lord. It was not until I looked back over my life and examined it that I realized how blessed I truly am.

The beautiful koala bear-looking creature represented my daughter. The koala bear-looking creature had so much love for me, and I had so much love for it. I have so much love for my daughter, and my daughter has so much love for me. When we were separated, she became sad, and I became sad, too. This represented a time to come.

In the vision my sisters weren't allowed onto the green pastures. They had to watch from a distance because of what they had done, and they weren't allowed to enter the green pastures. Which means they could not share in the abundance of blessings the Lord had given me.

The child snake represents someone who is related to my daughter. When I stumbled and fell, it represented the time I had to go through. I didn't realize what was to come soon, was going test my strength in Christ. When the King Cobra towered above me, it was a Giant, something that was too big for me to take on by myself. But once the Lord said, "Satan has no authority to do any harm to you." That Giant King Cobra didn't look so big anymore because I had the promise of God. But that promise from God was not just a promise but a spiritual reality! This meant Satan could never do any harm to me! That's why every attempt made in my life failed! The murder attempts always failed because Satan had no authority to do any harm to me!

When my wife "L" set me up to be shot by the Police in my own house on two separate occasions, the murder attempts failed. When the guys led me into the abandoned building, and they tried to shoot me, the murder attempt failed. When this guy named Keith pointed the gun at me and pulled the trigger three times, the gun didn't fire a shot, the murder attempt failed! When people in high school wanted me dead, no harm came to me. When Flood pulled up on me and pointed a gun at me, no harm came to me. I took all of this guy named Dope money while gambling in his apartment at JSU. While leaving his apartment with two thousand dollars of his money I turned my back to Dope and he pointed a gun at me but no harm came to me. When this guy named Jacarr hid in the bushes to shot me in the back at JSU, the murder attempt failed and I only got a few scratches on me. But the same guy who shot me in the back at JSU eventually got shot in his back in his hometown of Phoenix City, and he became paralyzed from the neck down and eventually died. So he reaped what he tried to sow on me! The Lord enacted a spiritual law that affects all people in this world. You will always reap what you have sown!

Galatians 6:7 Do not be deceived; God cannot be mocked. A man reaps what he sows. (NIV, Biblegateway.com)

No harm ever came to me when Satan sent people to kill me because the Lord said, "Satan has no authority to do any harm to you." The promises of God's words will always manifest as the absolute truth! Thank you, Jesus!

Once I rebuked King Cobra in the name of Jesus Christ, the Giant King Cobra became small, and it was the one who fled away in fear! Don't let Satan intimidate you with his so-called Giants! Because Satan will try to cause fear in you in so many ways! Satan has no authority over you! Not unless you surrender your God-given authority to him! Also, at the end of the vision, the Lord gave me confirmation for a second time that I am his Prophet!

112. My Wife Is Jezebel

A few days after the Lord revealed my wife to me as being the King Cobra in the vision, I was walking through the house thinking about the vision. I kept thinking, "My Lord, who is this woman I am sleeping next to every night?" I knew she was from Satan, but I felt like there was more to it. As I kept thinking this over and over, my wife "L" came and stood in front of me. Then, at that very moment, I said out loud, "My Lord, who is this woman?" At that moment, the Lord said to me, "Jezebel!" I then said to my wife, "You are Jezebel!" Then, for a brief second, I saw the spirit of Jezebel inside of my wife. And the spirit of Jezebel looked at me and smiled. Then my wife "L" walked off smiling. I said, "My God, she is Jezebel in the flesh!!!" I then realized I had married a decoy, and that decoy was Jezebel from the Old Testament!

Jezebel was a Sidonian woman who worshiped the false god Baal. Baal was once a high-ranking being in Satan's army who walked the face of this earth. Once Baal died, he became a high-ranking demonic spirit in Satan's Army. Baal once lived as a living being who was once flesh, but upon his death, it transcended into a demonic spirit.

So Jezebel worshiped the false god Baal, and Jezebel also did witchcraft. Jezebel married the King of Israel, whose name was Ahab. Jezebel also got Ahab, the King of Israel, to worship the false God Baal. Since Jezebel was married to the King of Israel, she had authority in the land of Israel. Since Jezebel worshiped Baal, she started killing off the Lord's true Prophets. This is shown to you in 1 Kings 18:4.

1 Kings 18:4 reads, [4] "While Jezebel was killing off the Lord's prophets, Obadiah had taken a hundred prophets and hidden them in two caves..." (NIV, BibleGateway.com)

Jezebel was killing off the Lord's Prophets. Now, during Jezebel's time, there was a prophet of the Lord who lived in Israel, and his name was Elijah! Elijah was one of the Lord's true Prophets. Since the people in Israel were following Jezebel's false prophets, Elijah challenged all of Jezebel's false prophets to a miracle test. And when they couldn't perform any miracles like the Prophet Elijah did, Elijah had all of Jezebel's false prophets put to death. Once word got back to Jezebel that the Prophet Elijah had all her false prophets killed, Jezebel sent this message to Elijah, "May the gods deal with me, be it ever so severely, if by this time tomorrow I do not make your life like that of one of them (1Kings 19:2, NIV Biblegateway.com).

So basically, Jezebel wanted the Prophet Elijah dead! So Jezebel tormented the Prophet Elijah. Jezebel had the Prophet Elijah fearful of her! Jezebel was tormenting the Prophet Elijah with fear!

Now we understand the relationship between the Prophet Elijah and Jezebel. Let's look at the relationship between my wife "L," who is Jezebel, and I, the Prophet Elisha. During Biblical times, Jezebel wanted the Prophet Elijah dead. During my time, my wife "L," who is Jezebel, wanted me, the Prophet Elisha, dead! That's why my wife Jezebel set me up to be shot by Birmingham Police on two separate occasions. Do you think that is a coincidence? No, it's not!

Jezebel, in the Old Testament, practiced witchcraft and sorcery. Jezebel worshiped the false God Baal, and to worship Baal is to worship Satan! My wife "L" (Jezebel) practiced witchcraft! And to practice witchcraft is to worship Satan! Remember, the Lord had been warning me about witchcraft with my wife "L" and her sister "Li"! Remember the vision the Lord gave me about two women in wedding dresses? In that vision, the Lord warned me that the first woman I married was going to do witchcraft on me! And the first woman I married was Jezebel! In Biblical times, Jezebel worshiped Baal; to worship Baal was to worship Satan. And Jezebel, in the Biblical time, practice witchcraft! Jezebel, in my time, practiced witchcraft, and to practice witchcraft is to worship Satan.

Satan sent Jezebel to destroy and distract me. Do you remember the Lord gave me warnings in January of 2003, when the Lord said to me, "Satan is sending someone to throw you off of your path?" Then, four months later, I hooked up with "L" and eventually married her. So "L" is Jezebel, and Satan sent Jezebel to throw me off my path! Chapter 104 is titled "Holy Spirit Warns Me of Satan's Plan". In that chapter, the Lord said to me, "Your wife was a trap set by Satan for you, Bishop, and the Church." Jezebel was the trap Satan had set for me, Bishop, and the Church! Jezebel was sent to me by Satan so Satan could attempt to stop god's plan! Jezebel had a spell on me, which caused me to marry her! And since Jezebel had a spell on me, the Lord tried to get me to open my eyes so I could see what was happening. That's why in Chapter 109 that is titled, "The Holy Spirit Makes Bishop Speaks," the Holy Spirit made Bishop say, "Why does a man of God sleep with a whore night after night." That whore the Lord was talking about was my wife Jezebel ("L")! I was sleeping with the whore Jezebel night after night. And I was being tormented by Jezebel just like she was tormenting the Prophet Elijah!

Now, you should start to notice a pattern here! The pattern is this! You noticed the Prophet Elijah return as John the Baptist. Then I, the Prophet Elisha, returned as Kennedy K. Brown. Then Jezebel from the Old Testament returns to this world as my wife "L"! If you noticed, just like the Lord sent me and the Prophet Elijah back into this world, Satan also sent his best weapon against the Prophet Elijah back into this world, and her name is Jezebel! Was it just a coincidence Jezebel crossed my path here in this world? The answer is no; it was not a coincidence. Satan intentionally sent Jezebel into my life so Jezebel could do the same to me that she did to the Prophet Elijah during the times of the Old Testament. Jezebel had the Prophet Elijah fearful.

It couldn't be a coincidence that my wife was Jezebel, and our paths just happened to cross! To understand what is happening. You must look at this world as a battlefield in a major war between the Most High God Jehovah, and Satan. In this war, there are rules the Most High God must follow, and there are rules Satan must follow. And say one of the rules is that each side can use certain key pieces on multiple occasions! So, say the Most High God Jehovah chose to use the Prophet Elijah, the Prophet Elisha, and the Lord Jesus Christ for his key pieces that can come into this world on two occasions! The Prophet Elijah and I (Elisha) have entered this world twice. And Jesus will return towards the end for his second coming. Since God Jehovah got to use his key pieces on multiple occasions, that means Satan also gets a chance to use his key pieces like Jezebel and others on multiple occasions!

God sent me, the Prophet Elisha, back into this world for a second time, and Satan sent his best weapon against the Lord's Prophets back into this world for a second time, and her name is Jezebel. Jezebel, in the Old Testament, killed many of God's Prophets. My wife, "L" Jezebel of today, tried to kill me, the Prophet Elisha, on multiple occasions.

Satan was trying to either have me killed or have me to flee in fear! And if I would have fled in fear of Jezebel, then I would have aborted all the promises god made me, and I would have forfeited my destiny as the Prophet Elisha! If you remember the story of the Prophet

Elijah and Jezebel after Jezebel put fear into the Prophet Elijah by threatening to kill him. The Lord had to come and get Elijah and bring him into the heavens. The Lord revealed to me he came to get Elijah because Elijah allowed Jezebel to put fear into him. The story of the Prophet Elijah fleeing can be found in 1 Kings 19:1-18.

Satan made sure Jezebel was intentionally placed in my life so Jezebel could place fear into me and try to chase me out of the Lord's word so I would abort and forfeit my destiny as the Prophet Elisha. It was not a coincidence that my path crossed with Jezebel. Jezebel was Satan's plan for me from the very beginning. How do I know? I will show you what the Lord showed me in the next chapter.

113. The Anatomy of Satan Part 6

This chapter of The Anatomy of Satan will examine how Satan plans his attack years in advance. While many people think the actions of Satan are random, that is not true. Satan is a highly intelligent being who has god-like characteristics, and he plans his attacks years in advance. The anatomy of Satan is to plan a long-term strategic attack to destroy God's people.

So, you can understand how Satan plans his attack over many years; let me show you what the Lord showed me. Satan had a plan to use Jezebel to destroy me since I was a child, and I didn't even see it. These things that were happening in my life didn't happen by chance. They were a systematic, sophisticated trap set by Satan. Satan was waging an all-out war against me, so I couldn't fulfill the mission the Lord had planned for me. The war that Satan waged against me was designed to either destroy me or discourage me so I wouldn't want or even desire to fulfill the Lord's mission. Satan is a thinking being that plans his attacks years in advance.

After the Lord revealed to me my wife "L" was Jezebel. The Lord allowed me to remember my first encounter with Jezebel when I was ten years old. In Chapter 19 titled "Who is that little girl?" I told you about my encounter with this six-year-old girl when visiting my grandmother in Lavaca, Alabama. Well, that same six-year-old girl I encountered at my grandmother's house when I was ten years old was Jezebel! I didn't know or understand this when I married "L", but she was the same girl the Lord warned me about when I was ten years old.

I was playing with this strange girl at my grandmother's house. Then this girl's mother screamed at me, "Ken, she is too young for you. Ken, you are ten, and she is only six. She is too young for you. Leave her alone, Ken." Once her mother said those words, I was about to walk away from the little girl, but the Lord stopped me. I then turned and looked at the little girl, and at that very moment, the Lord said to me, "One day, this little girl is going to make your life hell. She is going to bring many problems into your life!" Once I heard those words, I was puzzled and confused. I just looked at that girl and stared at her. I was so confused I went and sat on my grandmother's porch steps. I was trying to sort through everything that was said to me. But I couldn't. I just knew there was something very peculiar about that little girl. I kept thinking, "Who is that little girl?"

The same little girl I saw that day when I was ten years old was the same woman I married. "L" (Jezebel) was the peculiar little girl I had seen that day when I was ten years old. And I didn't know this until the Lord reminded me of this. And the Lord didn't remind me of that day until after he revealed my wife "L" is Jezebel.

Satan had planned for my paths to cross with Jezebel since I was a child. This also means Satan knew I was the Prophet Elisha since I was a child! Did you understand what I just said? Satan knew I was the Prophet Elisha since I was a child. That's why Satan planted Jezebel so close to me. That's why demons were sent out to make people hate me as a child and as a man. That's why so many people tried to kill me when I was younger because Satan knew I was the return of the Prophet Elisha from the Old Testament. And since Satan knows who I am, he planted Jezebel so close to me to guarantee our paths cross. Let me show you how Satan planted Jezebel so close to me.

I have a first cousin who I will call "B". "B" married this woman named "G". My cousin "B" had two girls by this woman name "G". So after they had two daughters together, "B" and the woman "G" got a divorce. Then the woman "G" goes out and has another child by another man. This child was "L", the woman I married. I saw "L" on one occasion growing up, and that was at my grandmother's house when I was ten years old. I didn't see her again until about twenty-two years later. And when I saw her twenty-two years later, I didn't know who she was or who she was related to. And then one night, my brother "C," who acts like Cain, the son of Adam, tells me "L" wanted me to give her a call. Jezebel stalked me by initiating contact with me through my brother "C"! Then, after talking to her on the phone twice, she offered to come and visit me in Huntsville that same week. That was the same week I locked myself out of my car and apartment seven times.

So once the Lord showed me all the events that happened, it was easy to see it wasn't a coincidence that Jezebel was placed in my path. Satan planned all of that from the very beginning. Satan's plan was to make sure I didn't get with the girl named Sandra when I was at JSU. Remember I told you how Satan was trying to keep me and this girl name Sandra apart when I was in college? Satan had placed people in my life and people in Sandra's life to make sure we didn't get together. See, if I would have gotten with Sandra in college. It was a 99.9% probability that we would have gotten married. And if I had married Sandra, that would have canceled out Satan's plan for me to marry Jezebel. This is why Satan had to make sure me and Sandra never hooked up because his plans to destroy me involved his best weapon against the Lord's Prophets, which is Jezebel!

Since Satan planted Jezebel so close to me and my family, this proves that Satan knows I am the Prophet Elisha from the Old Testament! The anatomy of Satan is to plan a long-term strategic attack to destroy God's people. Satan has been attacking all of us with long-term strategic attacks. We just didn't realize it!

114. Something Appears Out Of The Darkness 3

The year is 2007, and I am lying in bed asleep with the woman I am married to (Jezebel). This time, we are in the house I purchased in 2005. I am lying in bed asleep, but then this entity comes out of the darkness. I woke up once I sensed the entity's presence, but my eyes remained closed. Like before, this entity appeared out of the darkness and was pure evil. My eyes are closed but I see it more clearly this time. It approached me, trying to see "Who I am." The face of the figure is that of a man. It's a red and blue silhouette of a face I have seen before. Before the evil could come any closer, I said, "I rebuke you in the name of Jesus Christ!" The evil man feared the name of Jesus Christ, and he fled into the darkness.

When I opened my eyes, I said, "I know that face and facial structure." The red and blue silhouette face and facial structure I saw was that of Barack Obama. The way I saw his face would be later made into pictures and posters throughout the U. S. and the world. Do you know the pictures of Barack Obama with his face in a sketch with a red and blue print? That's exactly how I saw the evil man who appeared out of the darkness that night. I saw him in that red blueprint well before those pictures came out.

Once I realized that face was Barack Obama, I also realized he was the evil that appeared out of the darkness on the other occasion. In Chapter 99, titled "Something Appears Out of the Darkness 2," I told you how this evil spirit approached me when I was asleep. And the evil spirit was a man. The evil spirit that approached me on both occasions was Barack Obama. So, what does this mean? Just continue to read, and you will find out!

115. The Lord Delivers Me And Open My Eyes

I remember the days the Holy Spirit walked with me daily. The Holy Spirit walked and counseled me for three years and ministered the gospel to me. Those were the most incredible days of my life. The Holy Spirit was building my spirit up in the word of God daily. But then I decided to enter a relationship with "L," who was Jezebel in the flesh! And the Holy Spirit left me.

Once the Holy Spirit left me, I felt something trying to chip away at my spiritual armor! Slowly but surely, day by day, something was trying to put thoughts in my head that went against the word of God. I found myself regularly rebuking the thoughts in the name of Jesus Christ. Then, after I rebuke the thoughts in the name of Jesus Christ, those thoughts would stop for a while, but then they would slowly return. This became a daily battle I was going through, but I didn't understand why! Before I met "L," the Holy Spirit was with me, but now I am being tormented by something every day. Then, whatever it was that was tormenting me was also trying to make me fearful! It tried to make me fear everything. I didn't understand it! What I was experiencing was unlike anything I had experienced before!

It was December 2007, and I was standing in the restroom. As I got ready to exit the restroom, the woman I am married to (Jezebel) stood in front of me, placed her hair on her shoulder, and started brushing it in my direction. Instantly, I went into a trance like a zombie. Something like magical sprinkles dropped down from above and landed on my head. It had a tingly sensation. I couldn't move, nor did I know what was happening. I was in a mist of nothingness. In some kind of way, I started calling on the Lord in my mind. I kept saying, "Lord, what is going on." I said this several times in my mind. Finally, the Lord heard my cry, and the Lord brought me out of the trance. My wife "L" (Jezebel) was standing directly in front of me, chanting something from her mouth. So I immediately pushed her out of my way and said, "What are you doing?" She was shocked when she saw me come out of the trance. I then immediately ran out of the room and went into the basement and started repeating, "No weapon formed against me shall prosper in the name of the Lord Jesus Christ." I repeated this about twenty times.

It finally came to me that she (Jezebel) had been doing witchcraft on me since 2003. She was using witchcraft to control me!! Jezebel was casting a spell upon spell on me. That's why I was always confused. That's why I couldn't break away from her. That's why I was not seeing things clearly like I usually do. That's why I couldn't understand what the police officer was trying to tell me on the nights she set me up to be shot by the police. It was the spell she had on me that was clouding my mind.

So just like the Lord revealed to me in Chapter 83 that is titled "Vision of Two Women In Wedding Dresses", I married a woman with long hair who was doing witchcraft on me! As I reflect on my past, it was so many times that "L" came in front of me and brushed her hair while chanting something from her mouth. Each time, I would go into a trance, and I wouldn't remember anything when I came through. That's why I couldn't make the connection between what the Lord was telling me and her doing witchcraft on me. Because each time the Lord revealed something to me, Satan would use Jezebel and her witchcraft to steal it away from me. No matter what the Lord tried to do to open my eyes, the spell was keeping me in a mist of confusion.

116. My Disobedience To The Lord

After Christmas in December 2007, I told Jezebel she had to leave, so I put her out of the house! I would have done it sooner, but I had to think about my daughter being left with Jezebel. So, I sent Jezebel on her way! It's April 2008, and I have decided to file for a divorce against Jezebel. I said to myself, "I need to find a really good Lawyer." At that very moment, the Lord said to me, "You are to handle this case yourself." So, I decided to handle the case myself because the Lord told me to.

After the Lord told me to handle my divorce case myself, I went to my sisters and brothers and told them I decided to file for a divorce and I was going to handle the case myself. Immediately, they all began to tell me, "You don't need to handle the case yourself; you need to hire an attorney." Then, they began to give me a bunch of reasons, which were nothing but Satan's fear tactics. But I didn't recognize it for what it was! The advice my sisters and brothers were giving me was a Satanic Contradiction. The reason their advice was a Satanic Contradiction is because they were telling me to go against what the Lord told me to do. The Lord told me to handle the case myself, but my siblings told me to hire an attorney and not handle the case myself. Just to let you know, Satan will always tell you to do the opposite of what the Lord tells you to do because Satan wants to steal the blessing God has for you! So Satan always sends a Satanic Contradiction so he can steal the blessing the Lord has for you.

After listening to my siblings for many days, I disobeyed the Lord. I decided to hire an attorney. Once I hired an attorney, everything in the hearings went against me, and things weren't handled how I wanted them to be handled. So, I fired that attorney and hired another attorney. To make a long story short, everything went against me as long as I had an attorney. So, after I had gotten fed up with everything, I fired the second attorney and represented myself. Once I represented myself, everything immediately turned in my favor. The only thing I had to do was to show up to court. How did it happen? You must remember the promise the Lord made me. Remember, the Lord told me, "You can never be judged by no man, no woman, nor no child alive". I didn't need an attorney; I needed obedience and faith! The power of the Lord never fails when you are obedient to him. Obedience is better than sacrifice!

You must also remember that I went to law school for a year during the late 90's. In Chapter 58, titled "Transition From My Past To My Present In Christ," when I decided to leave law school in the late '90s, the Lord said, "You will only need to be a Lawyer for one case anyway." And then, the Lord showed me standing in a courtroom standing before a judge in a divorce proceeding. I'm about to live out what the Lord already showed me years in advance. I am living out the divorce case and representing myself the same way the Lord had shown me years prior.

117. The Lord Reveals to Me the True Meaning Of 666

While reading the Book of Revelations in 2002, I discovered scriptures that gave me insight into what 666 truly means. Since the scriptures told us to calculate, I multiplied the number 666 and came up with 216 (6x6=36, 36x6=216). Then I had this feeling the mark of the beast was a computer chip that was 216 megabytes. But I concluded a

216-megabyte chip wouldn't work in the human body. I wasn't sure about a megabyte chip. I continued to think about my answer occasionally, but I always got stuck. Until one day, I pleaded with the Lord to tell me what 666 truly meant.

It's August 17, 2007, and I am standing in my driveway thinking. Then suddenly, I began to plead with the Lord to tell me what 666 truly means! I said to the Lord, "Lord, tell me what 666 truly means, oh Lord." Again, I said, "Lord, tell me what 666 truly means, oh Lord." I repeated this over and over. Then I finally said, "Lord, I need you to reveal to me the absolute truth of what 666 truly means." When I finished my plea, the wind began to blow the trees. Then, the leaves on the trees started to flap like a bird flapping its wings. Then I felt the presence of the Lord. I then said to myself, "The Lord is here!" Then, at that very moment, the Lord said to me, "216-Megahertz Chip." Once, I heard the Lord say, "216-Megahertz Chip." I immediately thought about how I discovered 666 to mean 216. After I realized I was right about the 216, I realized I was thinking about megabyte chips instead of a megahertz chip.

Then I ran inside, jumped on the computer, and searched for a 216-megahertz human chip. Then, this article was pulled up on the MSNBC website. The article shows a picture of the 216-megahertz chip and explains how it will be used in humans. The article's title was "FDA approves computer chip for humans." FDA stands for Food Drug Administration which is a United States of America government agency. The chip is 216 MHz! In the MSNBC article, it shows you how small this chip is compared to a penny. The article does not tell you everything they plan on using this chip for. They just gave you some general information about the chip. I am putting the first two pages of the article I printed on August 17, 2007, in this book. The same article I pulled up the day the Lord told me 666 stands for "216-Megahertz Chip".

Web MSNBC   Make MSNBC Your Homepage | MSN Home | Hotmail | Sign In

Home » Health » Health Care

FDA approves computer chip for humans

Devices could help doctors with stored medical information

- Health
- Diet & Nutrition
- Fitness
- Women's Health
- Kids & Parenting
- Men's Health
- Sexual Health
- Aging
- Heart Health
- Cancer
- Pregnancy
- Infectious Diseases
- Mental Health
- More Health News
- Pet Health
- Skin & Beauty
- Health Library
- Health Columns
- BabyQuest
- **Video**
- **U.S. News**
- **Politics**
- **World News**
- **Business**
- **Sports**
- **Entertainment**
- **Health**
- **Tech / Science**
- **Travel**
- **Weather**
- **Blogs Etc.**

Associated Press
Updated: 5:38 p.m. CT Oct 13, 2004

WASHINGTON - Medical milestone or privacy invasion? A tiny computer chip approved Wednesday for implantation in a patient's arm can speed vital information about a patient's medical history to doctors and hospitals. But critics warn that it could open new ways to imperil the confidentiality of medical records.

The Food and Drug Administration said Wednesday that Applied Digital Solutions of Delray Beach, Fla., could market the VeriChip, an implantable computer chip about the size of a grain of rice, for medical purposes.

With the pinch of a syringe, the microchip is inserted under the skin in a procedure that takes less than 20 minutes and leaves no stitches. Silently and invisibly, the dormant chip stores a code that releases patient-specific information when a scanner passes over it.

Story continues below ↓

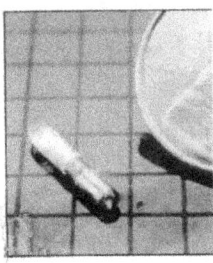

The VeriChip, the size of a grain of under the skin with a needle in a p takes less than 20 minutes to com

Most Popular

Most Viewed · Top Rated

Cave-in at Utah mine kills 3 resc
Canadian woman delivers identi
For Giuliani, Ground Zero is linc
Smile ... Or Else
Is universal health insuranc horizon?

Most viewed on MSNBC.com

http://www.msnbc.msn.com/ID/6237364   8/17/2007

Chip's dual uses raise alarm

The VeriChip itself contains no medical records, just codes that can be scanned, and revealed, in a doctor's office or hospital. With that code, the health providers can unlock that portion of a secure database that holds that person's medical information, including allergies and prior treatment. The electronic database, not the chip, would be updated with each medical visit.

The microchips have already been implanted in 1 million pets. But the chip's possible dual use for tracking people's movements — as well as speeding delivery of their medical information to emergency rooms — has raised alarm.

"If privacy protections aren't built in at the outset, there could be harmful consequences for patients," said Emily Stewart, a policy analyst at the Health Privacy Project.

To protect patient privacy, the devices should reveal only vital medical information, like blood type and allergic reactions, needed for health care workers to do their jobs, Stewart said.

An information technology guru at Detroit Medical Center, however, sees the benefits of the devices and will lobby for his center's inclusion in a VeriChip pilot program.

"One of the big problems in health care has been the medical records situation. So much of it is still on paper," said David Ellis, the center's chief futurist and co-founder of the Michigan Electronic Medical Records Initiative.

Revelation 13:16 "He also forced everyone, small and great, rich and poor, free and slave, to receive a mark on his right hand or on his forehead, **so that no one could buy or sell unless he had the mark, which is the name of the beast or the number of his name**".

The Chip shown on the previous page is the mark of the beast they will use, so no one can buy or sell unless they have the Chip. The Chip is half the size of a grain of rice. I need you to think about that. The Chip is so small it can be injected into you without you even noticing it is there. The Chip will be injected right under the skin with a simple device. This Chip is 216 MHz (Megahertz), and it was specifically designed for human beings. The Chip transmits a signal in Megahertz frequency like an FM car radio. This means scanners in stores, cell towers, and satellites can read the signal. They call this Chip the RFID chip. RFID stands for radio frequency identification.

The Illuminati has plans to remove cash from the financial system and replace it with the Central Bank Digital Currency (CBDC) and the Chip. The Illuminati can remove cash easily from our society. You must remember the Illuminati owns the Federal Reserve, and the Federal Reserve owns the currency that's in your pockets. The Illuminati control government and media will try to convince you that you do not need money if you take the CBDC and the Chip. The Illuminati and its people are going to try to convince you that you need the Chip to prevent identity theft. They're going to use identity theft as one of their main reasons why everyone should have to get a chip. This leads me to believe that all these security breaches of governmental databases and corporate databases are sponsored by those who are upper-level members of the Illuminati in the U.S. Government. They will persuade you to take the 216 MHz chip so no one can steal your identity.

Also, they will use the excuse of the U.S. Dollar being counterfeited as another reason why the U.S. is going to the Chip. They will even create a problem by purposely devaluing the dollar by causing banks to collapse and crashing the economy to manipulate you into taking the Chip. The Chip ties in with the new digital currency they plan to use. The CBDC, which is the Central Bank Digital Currency. You must remember who owns the Central Banks around the world, the Illuminati! The Illuminati own the Federal Reserve, and the Federal Reserve is the Central Bank for the United States of America.

The 216 MHz chip will be connected to the supercomputer mainframe that can track every transaction in the world in real time. The 216 MHz chip was designed to be connected to the supercomputer mainframe the Engineer told me about. In 2003, the Engineer told me they were almost finished constructing a computer mainframe that could track every transaction in the world in real time. The 216 MHz human chip will be online with the same supercomputer mainframe that can track every transaction worldwide. They want to track every transaction in the world in real time because they can control who can buy or sell.

Those who don't take the Chip or CBDC will be locked out of the financial system. This means you cannot buy food, water, or medicine, nor can you work if you don't take the Chip! This also means if you don't take the Chip, you reject the beast, which is Satan, and you reject the **image of the beast**. All those who do accept the Chip will worship Satan and the image of the beast. It has been well prophesied in the last days that we will go to a one-world monetary system, one-world government, and a one-world system. What better way to go to a one-world monetary system than to have everyone use the Central Bank Digital Currency (CBDC) with a chip that's online on the same supercomputer mainframe? The CBDC is the one world currency, and the Chip is connected to the CBDC and the supercomputer mainframe! The 216-megahertz Chip, called the RFID chip, will be linked to the supercomputer mainframe that can track every transaction in the world in real time.

The Chip will hold everything from medical records to financial information on you. The Chip will hold your social credit score. They can control what you can and cannot buy based on your social credit score. The Chip has already been mass-produced. The production of the Chip has been funded and paid for by the U. S. Government under a bill passed in Congress in 2004. And guess what department name they passed this Bill under? The Department of U.S. Health Administration! The Department of the U. S. Health Administration oversees **HEALTH CARE!** And since Health Care and the Chip is in the medical field. That means the Illuminati Medical Department, which is called the Brotherhood of the Snake, will oversee the injection of the Chip. This means the medical industry will be responsible for implanting the Chip into people. The Chip will be used to maintain all medical records and financial records, and it will be your identification. This Chip will be your Passport and Driver's License.

This Chip is described as a Class II medical device in the laws they passed for the mandatory use of the Chip. The law they passed that made this Chip mandatory for every American to receive is Bill HR 4872. What is Bill HR 4872, you ask? Bill HR 4872 is the Affordable Care Act (Obama Care)! You thought the Obama Care was about getting poor people health insurance, didn't you? The Obama Care Health Care Bill was never about getting poor people Health Care. It was about manipulating you into supporting a law that would make it mandatory for you to take **the Chip, which is the mark of the beast.**

Pages 1013 through 1020 of the Affordable Care Act (Obama Care) are under the heading of Subtitle C, **"National Medical Device Registry"**. It tells you how everyone will be required to have this Class II medical device implant. This Class II medical device is the same as the 216 MHz chip (RFID chip) I have been telling you about. They classified the device as a Class II medical device in the Health Care Bill to help disguise their intentions. They classified the device as a Class II medical device in the Health Care Bill, but it does not give you the definition of what a Class II medical device is. To understand a Class II medical device, you must look it up on the FDA (Food Drug Administration) website. The FDA classified the 216 MHz chip as a Class II medical device. The FDA states a Class II medical device is an "Implantable Radiofrequency transponder system for patient identification and health information." If you noticed, the FDA used the term radiofrequency. They used the term radiofrequency because the Chip is 216 Megahertz, and **Megahertz is a radio frequency**! This Class II medical device is the same Chip the FDA approved for humans in the MSNBC article I just showed you.

Also, the FDA used the term Implantable Radiofrequency. This means the Chip will be implanted into the human body, giving off a radiofrequency. Also, the FDA states the Chip will be used for identification. This Chip will be your identification and passport. If you look at the title, they label the Chip under the **"National Medical Device Registry"**. It is called the "National Medical Device Registry" because they plan to ensure everyone in the United States registers to receive this Chip! They plan to inject this Chip into the American citizens and people in other countries.

Also, I want you to take notice of something else: a bill was passed by Congress back in 2004 to provide funding to mass produce this Chip (mark of the beast). And then a law was passed on March 23, 2010, to make it mandatory for you to take this Chip. They secured the funding for the mass production of the Chip in 2004. Once they secured funding for the mass production of the Chip in 2004, they came back and passed a law six years later (March 23, 2010) to make it mandatory for you to take this Chip. They spaced out the timing so no one would truly understand what they were doing and so no one would understand when they planned on doing this mass injection of the chip!

Do you think it was a coincidence that both laws were passed under the Department of U.S. Health Administration? No, it was not a coincidence! Things don't just happen; they are planned! Again, President Franklin D. Roosevelt said, "In politics, nothing happens by accident. If it happens, you can bet it was planned that way." "Franklin D. Roosevelt Quotes." *BrainyQuote*. Xplore, n.d. Web. 06 Apr. 2017. <http://www.brainyquote.com/quotes/quotes/f/franklind164126.html>.

Also, I want to make sure you understand this: the Affordable Care Act makes it mandatory for everyone to receive the chip implant. The law was not just for those who signed up for Obama Care. The law is for everyone in the United States of America to receive the mark of the beast, the 216-Megahertz Chip (RFID chip)! When you people were supporting Barack Obama and Obama Care, you were supporting the law to make it mandatory for everyone to receive the mark of the beast (chip implant)! The Illuminati made fools out of you again! I will put the five pages of the Affordable Care Act that make it mandatory for you to take the Mark of the Beast in this book, but you need to read 1013-1020 of the law. Here are pages 1013 through 1017 of the Affordable Care Act. Start reading under the heading of Subtitle C – National Medical Device Registry.

"(F) a program administered by the Indian Health Service or the Bureau of Indian Affairs or operated by an Indian tribe or a tribal organization under the Indian Self-Determination and Education Assistance Act, a Native Hawaiian entity, or an urban Indian program under title V of the Indian Health Care Improvement Act.

"(m) AUTHORIZATION OF APPROPRIATIONS.—For purposes of carrying out this section, there are authorized to be appropriated $50,000,000 for fiscal year 2010 and such sums as may be necessary for each of the fiscal years 2011 through 2014.".

(b) EFFECTIVE DATE.—The Secretary of Health and Human Services shall begin awarding grants under section 399Z–1 of the Public Health Service Act, as added by subsection (b), not later than July 1, 2010, without regard to whether or not final regulations have been issued under section 399Z–1(h) of such Act.

Subtitle C—National Medical Device Registry

SEC. 2521. NATIONAL MEDICAL DEVICE REGISTRY.

(a) REGISTRY.—

(1) IN GENERAL.—Section 519 of the Federal Food, Drug, and Cosmetic Act (21 U.S.C. 360i) is amended—

 (A) by redesignating subsection (g) as subsection (h); and

 (B) by inserting after subsection (f) the following:

 "National Medical Device Registry

 "(g)(1) The Secretary shall establish a national medical device registry (in this subsection referred to as the 'registry') to facilitate analysis of postmarket safety and outcomes data on each device that—

  "(A) is or has been used in or on a patient; and

  "(B) is—

   "(i) a class III device; or

   "(ii) a class II device that is implantable, life-supporting, or life-sustaining.

 "(2) In developing the registry, the Secretary shall, in consultation with the Commissioner of Food and Drugs, the Administrator of the Centers for Medicare & Medicaid Services, the head of the Office of the National Coordinator for Health Information Technology, and the Secretary of Veterans Affairs, determine the best methods for—

"(A) including in the registry, in a manner consistent with subsection (f), appropriate information to identify each device described in paragraph (1) by type, model, and serial number or other unique identifier;

"(B) validating methods for analyzing patient safety and outcomes data from multiple sources and for linking such data with the information included in the registry as described in subparagraph (A), including, to the extent feasible, use of—

"(i) data provided to the Secretary under other provisions of this chapter; and

"(ii) information from public and private sources identified under paragraph (3);

"(C) integrating the activities described in this subsection with—

"(i) activities under paragraph (3) of section 505(k) (relating to active postmarket risk identification);

"(ii) activities under paragraph (4) of section 505(k) (relating to advanced analysis of drug safety data); and

"(iii) other postmarket device surveillance activities of the Secretary authorized by this chapter; and

"(D) providing public access to the data and analysis collected or developed through the registry in a manner and form that protects patient privacy and proprietary information and is comprehensive, useful, and not misleading to patients, physicians, and scientists.

"(3)(A) To facilitate analyses of postmarket safety and patient outcomes for devices described in paragraph (1), the Secretary shall, in collaboration with public, academic, and private entities, develop methods to—

    "(i) obtain access to disparate sources of patient safety and outcomes data, including—

        "(I) Federal health-related electronic data (such as data from the Medicare program under title XVIII of the Social Security Act or from the health systems of the Department of Veterans Affairs);

        "(II) private sector health-related electronic data (such as pharmaceutical purchase data and health insurance claims data); and

        "(III) other data as the Secretary deems necessary to permit postmarket assessment of device safety and effectiveness; and "(ii) link data obtained under clause (i) with information in the registry.

"(B) In this paragraph, the term 'data' refers to information respecting a device described in paragraph (1), including claims data, patient survey data, standardized analytic files that allow for the pooling and analysis of data from disparate data environments, electronic health records, and any other data deemed appropriate by the Secretary.

"(4) Not later than 36 months after the date of the enactment of this subsection, the Secretary shall promulgate regulations for establishment and operation of the registry under paragraph (1). Such regulations—

"(A)(i) in the case of devices that are described in paragraph (1) and sold on or after the date of the enactment of this subsection, shall require manufacturers of such devices to submit information to the registry, including, for each such device, the type, model, and serial number or, if required under subsection (f), other unique device identifier; and

"(ii) in the case of devices that are described in paragraph (1) and sold before such date, may require manufacturers of such devices to submit such information to the registry, if deemed necessary by the Secretary to protect the public health;

Now, if you notice, the Affordable Care Act seems like it's not saying much if you read it. It's written in the ways old English laws were written. The Illuminati's preferred method of writing laws in this old English format because the average person can't understand what they are truly saying. And when the average person can't understand what they are truly saying in laws like this, they can pass a law to enslave you without you knowing what's in the law. Also, you must remember in Chapter 16, titled "A Word Hidden in a Picture", I told you how we were tested in the third grade when I and three other people in my class were labeled as Gifted once we saw the Illuminati steganography. And since my dad and mother won't let me join the Gifted program the three other people who did join were being pulled out of class and taught how to read and understand old English. The reason why they were taught old English is because some of the people who join the Illuminati become high ranking government officials. The three other kids labeled as Gifted were being trained as children to read and understand old English so that one day, they could either write the laws or interpret them. And all three of them now work for the Federal Government in some capacity? Is that a coincidence?

The Affordable Care Act is written so the average individual can't understand it. The Affordable Care Act tells you that it will be mandatory for you to take a chip implant! If you noticed, in the Affordable Care Act, they constantly use the term "Secretary". I want to make sure you understand who they are referring to when they use the term "Secretary". They are referring to the Secretary of Health and Human Services or the Secretary of the World Health Organization (WHO). They plan to let the World Health Organization take over all countries during a Health Pandemic. They will try to give the World Health Organization unlimited power.

To sum it up, the Affordable Care Act (Obama Care) made it mandatory for every individual in the United States to have this chip implanted in them. I want to make this very clear: Obama Care made it mandatory for everyone in the United States of America to get the chip implanted in them. And the chip is the mark of the beast! It doesn't matter if you signed up for Obama Care or if you didn't sign up for Obama Care! Everyone in the United States must take the mark of the beast (the chip). You must ask yourself why Barack Obama made sure his health care law, the Affordable Care Act, made it mandatory for every citizen in the United States of America to receive the mark of the beast (216-

Megahertz chip, RFID chip)! You need to ask yourself, who is Barack Obama? Once you ask yourself those questions, the next thing you need to do is look at the Illuminati control Supreme Court! The Illuminati-controlled U.S. Supreme Court upheld a law that mandates you, the American people, to receive a chip in your hand (the mark of the beast). And again, the Illuminati-controlled U.S. Supreme Court passes another law that goes against the word of the Most High God Jehovah!

The U.S. Supreme Court supports a law that will enslave the American people to take the mark of the beast and to worship Satan as god! This is another example of how the Illuminati are using Government resources (Supreme Court, Congress, Presidency) to push their religious agenda to get you to worship Satan. At the same time, they convince Christians there should be a separation between church and state! And many of you fools believe this lie they taught you! If the Illuminati believe there should be a separation of church and state. Why are the Illuminati constantly using Government resources and laws to make sure you follow them and worship Satan as god? The Illuminati is using the U.S. Government and taxpayer's dollars to recruit members into the Illuminati, and then they are using their positions in Federal government agencies to manipulate you to receive the Mark of the Beast so you can worship Satan as god. They made it a law for you to take the Mark of the Beast (the chip)! Is that a separation of church and state? No!

You thought Barack Obama wanted the Affordable Care Act passed into law because he wanted poor people to have insurance, didn't you? It was never about poor people! They just distracted you with the emotionally sympathetic talking point of "poor people need insurance" to get you all emotional! Because the Illuminati know once you get emotional, you won't listen when people try to tell you what they are doing! And the Illuminati love it when you don't listen to the truth! Because when you don't listen to the truth, you will accept any lie the Illuminati tells you through the news media! And when you don't listen to the truth, you make slaves out of yourselves! Obama Care was never about getting insurance for poor people! It was about passing a law that will mandate everyone to take the chip which is the Mark of the Beast! They mask or hid their true agenda of mandating everyone to get a chip, with the sympathetic talking point that poor people need insurance.

So, since we know the 216 MHz Chip is the Class II and Class III medical device and that the chip is the Mark of the Beast. You must ask yourself two questions. Why did Barack Obama make sure his Affordable Care Act, Bill HR 4872 (Obama Care), made it mandatory for you to receive this chip, which is the Mark of the Beast? Why? Jesus Christ would never ask you to take a chip in your hand. Only a man of Satan wants you to take a chip implant in your hand or body. You must start asking yourself, who is Barack Obama? Barack Obama is for homosexuality and he is a homosexual. Yes, Barack Obama is a homosexual! Just a little insight, Barack Obama Chef was murdered at Barack Obama's home. He didn't accidentally drown. Their Chef Tafari Campbell was about to release a tell all book. But he mysteriously drowned right before the book came out. Sounds suspicious to me. Was he about to release information on how Michelle Obama is a transgender woman, and how her real name is Michael Robinson. Was he about to tell how he witnessed Michelle Obama standing up urinating, because Michelle Obama has a penis.

Just to let you know, Michelle Obama is a man pretending to be a woman. They have pulled off one of the greatest scams ever portrayed on the American people. This is the first biggest hoax ever pulled by Barack Obama. But this want be the last hoax he tries to pull on the American people and people of this world. Barack Obama presented a man as a woman and all of yawl believe him. Barack Obama told you Michelle was a woman, and you believed him. Michelle Obama presented himself as a woman and you believe him. Michelle Obama is a man dressed up as a woman. My information comes from the Most High God Jehovah and the Lord Jesus Christ. Where does your information come from, TV? Don't believe what you think your eyes and ears hear. Your thinking process is this; if Michelle Obama was a man that would have been all over the news and the internet. I can understand your thinking process. But what you don't understand is how much control the Illuminati have over the news media and the internet. The Illuminati made sure the mainstream media never exposed Michelle Obama is a man.

Barack Obama is a homosexual, and Michelle Obama is a man pretending to be a woman. Michelle Obama real name is Michael Robinson. The truth shall set you free. And just to tell you the absolute truth. God came to me in 2007 and told me Barack Obama was not born in the United States of America. That's what the Most High God Jehovah told me! Now call that a conspiracy theory! The Obama's and the news media have lied and lied and lied to the American people about everything. And you believe their lies because you are a Democrat! Stop being an idiot and a fool for these people! But they couldn't have pulled off this scam without the American media being complicity in the scam. The news organizations that you trust lied to you: ABC, CBS, NBC, CNN, and MSNBC. One thing I can tell you is that Fox News did attempt to tell you the truth! Michelle Obama is a man!

Jesus Christ would never be for homosexuality or transgender because it is wickedness! So, who is Barack Obama? Why does he want you to take the Mark of the Beast, and he wants you and your children to be gay and transgender? Homosexuality and transgender are from Satan. Satan and the Illuminati are the ones who are behind the scenes promoting homosexuality and transgender.

The year is 2012, and I was thinking about the 216-Megahertz chip being the Mark of the Beast (Class II medical device, RFID chip). I was also thinking about how Satan owns that person once they take the chip. So, as I was thinking about the chip being the Mark of the Beast, the Lord spoke to me and said, "Besides the chip being the Mark of the Beast and all who take the chip are owned by Satan. What else can this chip do? Why do the Illuminati, the son of Satan and the image of the beast, want you to take this chip in your hand or on your forehead? What else happens once that chip is injected into your hand?"

Once the Lord said those things to me, I began to think about what he had said. After pondering the questions, I couldn't come up with an answer. So, I thought about the questions some more. Once the questions were given to me, I thought about it for many days. The Lord asked me those questions so my mind could conceive what he was about to reveal to me. So, after thinking about the questions for many days without coming up with an answer, I posed the same question to the Lord.

So, one day, I asked the Lord the exact same questions he had asked me. I said to the Lord, "Lord, besides the chip being the Mark of the Beast and all who take the chip are owned by Satan. What else can this chip do? Why do the Illuminati, the son of Satan and the image of the beast, want us to take this chip in our hand or on our forehead? What else happens once that chip is injected into our hand?" Then, at that very moment of me finishing my sentence, the Lord answered me.

The Lord said, "The human body is full of neurotransmitters; these transmitters relay messages to the brain. The brain then responds to the messages transmitted by the neurotransmitters with a course of action. Once the chip is injected into the human hand, it can relay messages to the neurotransmitters in your body. Then, the neurotransmitters will relay whatever message was received by the chip to the brain. So basically whatever message is sent to the chip, the neurotransmitters in your body will deliver that message to the brain, and the brain will act upon that message."

Once the Lord said that to me, I was astonished and in total disbelief! Once I heard the Lord say those things, I was shocked! I didn't know what to do or say because I understood what the Lord told me. The Lord was telling me they can control you and your actions once you take the chip. They can control you and your actions because your thoughts won't be your thoughts anymore because they can give you a thought by relaying a message to the chip in your hand.

Once a message has been relayed to your chip, the chip will relay that message to the neurotransmitters in your body. Then, the neurotransmitters act as a chemical messenger in your body and relay the message to your brain. Then, you would act on any messages sent to your brain by the chip. This means once a person takes the chip, they can be controlled! Their thoughts are not their thoughts anymore. They can program your brain to be like a robot. The Lord revealed that they can take away your memories and replace them with false memories. They can wipe your mind free of the memories you collected over your lifetime and then inject your mind with the memories they want you to have. For example, they can take your child away from you and then send your chip a message, making you forget you ever had a child. Oh my God! Does this sound like the **neuralink chip** that this man named **Elon** supposedly invented? You all are being played. You better wake up.

The Lord revealed to me messages would be sent from the supercomputer mainframe that can track every transaction in the world in real time to your chip. These messages sent from the supercomputer mainframe to your chip are transactions! This is another reason they want to track every transaction worldwide. The message they send to your chip is a transaction! So basically, they have found a way to take away free will from mankind! Did you hear what I just said? They have found a way to take away free will from mankind! See, the Most High God gave every man free will when he created man. Now, Satan's people the Illuminati and the image of the beast have found a way to take away man's free will by giving them a chip that will send messages to their brain.

So, the message your chip receives will be a transaction. And you will do anything the message tells you to do! If the message tells you to go into a school and start shooting little kids, you will do that! Or if they send a message to your chip and tell you to shoot people at a concert in Las Vegas, then you would do that. This makes this chip different from any other computer chip in this world! The Mark of the Beast chip was designed to control the human brain! So, whoever controls the supercomputer mainframe controls you. This means you will receive instructions from those who control the supercomputer mainframe. So if they send you a message not to eat, you will stop eating. This means you will be like a walking zombie once you take the chip! The Walking Dead! And as long as the chip is receiving and delivering the message to the brain, the body will continue to follow its instructions! The Walking Dead! And the only way to kill a person who takes the chip is to shoot them in the head. A shot to the head is the only way to sever the connection from the chip relaying messages to the brain! These people have found a way to take away free will!

So, say they wanted to test this chip to ensure it works. The Illuminati would then inject a person with a chip without that person knowing. Then, they would input a command into the supercomputer mainframe for that person to go into a movie theater and shoot up the movie theater. Then that person's chip would receive the message, and then that person would go into a movie theater and start shooting people. Or they may send a person a message to go into a school and start shooting people. You must understand they must ensure the chip is fully operational before they make everybody get one. So they had to test the chip on ordinary people doing extreme acts! Is this the cause of so many mass shootings and other hellacious acts?

So you may fully understand this process, let's look at how the message will be relayed to the chip. The message will be relayed from this supercomputer mainframe to the 5G network to the chip in your hand. This supercomputer mainframe is the same mainframe the Government has created to track every transaction in the world in real time. This makes this supercomputer mainframe the Government created different from any other mainframe in the world. They can relay messages to the chip in your hand and then the chip will relay messages to your brain. And all of this is done in real time, which means no delay. The people who have the power to send messages to your chip are nothing more than your programmer or your god! If you take the chip, you will be nothing more than a slave to do whatever message or command the Illuminati or the image of the beast sends you.

So, whoever receives the chip is a slave. The programmer at the supercomputer mainframe can either send a specific message to a specific person or the programmer can send out a mass message or group message to everyone. A mass message will give everyone a hive mentality like worker ants. This is the big reason why they want everyone to take the chip. So they can control everyone!

Everything the Lord said to me made sense and made me understand some questions I had asked in my twenties. Many years ago, I was reading the Book of Revelations, and I saw scriptures referring to people being killed and beheaded because of their testimony of Christ. Then I wondered how they could pull off killing and beheading people in the U.S. and get away with it without a public outcry taking place. This question came to mind because here in the U.S., our country was formed on the thought of freedom and liberty for all! So, I couldn't perceive or even imagine people being killed or beheaded because of their testimony of Jesus Christ. So once the Government starts enforcing the law and making everyone get the Class II medical device implant (the chip), the Government will use their supercomputer mainframe to send out a mass message to all those people who did get the chip to turn in or murder all family members and friends who didn't get the chip. When this message goes out, nobody will know it. Only those people who got the chip will receive the mental message. So the people who received the chip will be turning in those who didn't receive the chip.

Once the Government decides, everyone who intends to get the chip has gotten one. Then, the Government will send out another mass message for parents to kill their family members and friends who didn't receive the chip. Or they can send out a message to the children to kill their parents and friends who haven't received the chip. So then they can "Purge" everyone out of society who has not received the chip! The Illuminati refer to this mass murder (Purge) as *the Great Cleansing*! *The Great Cleansing* (The Purge) is designed to murder everyone who believes in Jesus Christ and opposes the Illuminati and their agenda! They will turn people against each other the same way they turned the people who took the COVID-19 vaccine against those who refused to take the COVID-19 vaccine!

This means the children who receive the Mark of the Beast (the chip) will have their parents put to death who didn't receive the Mark of the Beast (the chip). The father who receives the Mark of the Beast will have his son put to death who didn't receive the Mark of the Beast (the chip). The mother who receives the Mark of the Beast will have her daughter put to death who didn't receive the Mark of the Beast (the chip). The brother who receives the Mark of the Beast will have his brother put to death who didn't receive the Mark. The Illuminati refers to this as *The Great Cleansing*. This *Great Cleansing* is meant to kill anyone who doesn't want to go alone with the Illuminati's plan. Anyone who opposes the Illuminati and their plan will be killed!

Jesus warned you of this *Great Cleansing (The Purge)* in Mark 13:12-13, [12] "Brother will betray brother to death, and a father his child. Children will rebel against their parents and have them put to death. [13] Everyone will hate you because of me, but the one who stands firm to the end will be saved."

Many of you think these things cannot and will not happen in the United States of America and other nations. This Great Cleansing is when the Illuminati plans to kill 7.5 billion people worldwide. This may be how they plan to reduce the population to 500 million so the earth will be more sustainable. When you hear them use the word sustainable, that means to reduce the population, and the only way they can make this world more sustainable is to reduce the population by killing off a mass amount of people.

Also, Jesus said in Mathew 13:13, [13] "Everyone will hate you because of me, but the one who stands firm to the end will be saved." This means if you believe in Jesus Christ, the world is going to hate you like Hitler hated the Christians and Jews in Nazi Germany! Don't expect your treatment to be any different than how the Christians and Jews were treated in Nazi Germany! Once people take the chip, they belong to Satan, and they are not your friends!

Once Jesus died for our sins, the devil was defeated because men could accept Jesus Christ as their Lord and Savior and ask for his forgiveness, and all would be forgiven, and they would receive eternal life. But just like in any war, the enemy came up with a battle plan to defeat Jesus Christ, going to the cross and dying for our sins! There are three things that can defeat a true believer of Jesus Christ and strip them of all the promises and spiritual realities Jesus Christ promised. These three things were designed by Satan to steal the souls of all believers of the Lord Jesus Christ and to shift this war in Satan's favor! These three things were designed to even defeat Jesus Christ, going to the cross for mankind. These three things are listed in the Bible, but many people don't truly understand their significance!

You will never enter the Kingdom of Heaven if you do any of the three things I am about to mention. If you take the chip, you will never enter the Kingdom of Heaven, and the Lord will not forgive you! You will be tormented forever and ever if you take the chip. If you worship Satan or the son of Satan (Barack Obama), you will never enter the Kingdom of Heaven. You will be tormented forever and ever. If you worship the image of the beast, you will never enter the Kingdom of Heaven. You will be tormented forever and ever. If you do any of those three things I mentioned above, you will never enter the Kingdom of Heaven, and your sins won't be forgiven! How do I know this for a fact? Because this is told to you in the Book of Revelations! Revelations 14:9-11 tells you what will happen to those who take the mark of the beast, who worship the beast or the image of the beast!

Revelation 14:9-11 reads, [9] "A third angel followed them and said in a loud voice: "If anyone **worships the beast** and **its image and receives its mark on their forehead or on their hand**, [10] they, too, will drink the wine of God's fury, which has been poured full strength into the cup of his wrath. They will be tormented with burning sulfur in the presence of the holy angels and of the Lamb. [11] And **the smoke of their torment will rise for ever and ever.** There will be no rest day or night for those who worship the beast and its image, or for anyone who receives the mark of its name." (NIV, BibleGateway.com)

It doesn't get any plainer than that! The Lord told you in the scripture that if anyone worships the beast (the Son of Satan or Satan), or worships the image of the beast or receives the mark of the beast (the chip), then they will be tormented with burning sulfur forever and ever! So if you think your sins will be forgiven if you take the mark of the beast, the chip. You are one thousand percent wrong! I just told you what the mark of the beast is. The mark of the beast is a 216-megahertz computer chip called the RFID chip for humans or the Class II or III medical device! You must remember the Lord told me that 666 meant 216 Megahertz Chip! That 216-megahertz chip is the same as the RFID chip for humans and the Class II or Class III medical device the FDA refers to. If you take that chip, you will be sentenced to hell for an eternity.

Do you remember the coded message I showed you on the back of the U.S. One Dollar Bill? Let's connect the dots of the coded message on the back of the U.S. One Dollar Bill with what the Lord revealed to me about the chip (mark of the beast). The coded message was this; "Annuit Coeptis Novus Ordo Seclorum In God we Trust." And we translated that to mean, "He favors our undertaking of a New Order of the Ages in God we Trust." Then the Illuminati hid the alien within the Great Seal of the United States! So, the decoded version of the phrase means this. "Satan favors the Illuminati undertaking of ushering in a New Order of the Ages where all mankind will trust in Satan's image of the beast as god!"

The Lord revealed to me how the Illuminati planned on ushering this "New Order of the Ages where all mankind will trust in Satan's image as god!" The Illuminati plan to have everyone in the world take the chip in their hand. Then they will send out a mass message to everyone's chip saying, "Satan is god, now worship him as god!" Or the message may say, "Worship the image of the beast as god!" And all who receive the chip will do it because the neurotransmitters in the human body will relay the message it receives from the chip to the human brain! And once the message is relayed to the brain that message becomes that person's thoughts. And that person's thought becomes that person's reality! This is how the Illuminati plan on ushering in the New Order of the Ages, where all mankind will trust in Satan and his image of the beast as god! The Illuminati is going to plant the thought into your head to worship Satan as a god or worship the image of the beast as a god! This is what everything is leading to! But many of you don't think these things could happen in the United States of America. If only your eyes were open and the chain of bondage was removed from your mind, you would understand they just took another step to prepare you to take the Mark of the Beast. And they did it right in front of your face, for you and the world to see.

It's March 2020, and the COVID-19 Pandemic (Plandemic) is happening. Once this outbreak started in the United States, I felt like something wasn't right! I felt like something wasn't right about this COVID-19 Pandemic; the news coverage and everything seemed like a military Psyops operation! So, I asked the Lord what was really going on with this Coronavirus Pandemic (COVID-19). At that moment, the Lord said to me, "It has to do with the chip!" Once the Lord said that to me, I didn't understand. So I asked the Lord, "Lord, what does the Coronavirus have to do with the chip." Then I said, "Lord, I need some proof." Then, at that very moment of asking the Lord for proof. A video of an Anthony Patch interview was sent to my inbox, but there was no sender. It was strange because there was no sender! The interview was done back in January 2014 by a man named Anthony Patch.

Anthony Patch does research into the secret projects the Government is working on. Back in January 2014, Anthony Patch did an interview telling how the Government would release the Coronavirus on the world population and cause a pandemic. So the people would demand a vaccine for the Coronavirus! In 2014, Anthony Patch said the Government (the Illuminati within all Governments) would purposely release the Coronavirus. And they were going to release the Coronavirus to cause a pandemic so the people would demand a vaccine. Anthony Patch said the Government knew they couldn't force anyone to take this vaccine, so they had to manipulate people into demanding a vaccine. And that's exactly what happened. They use the Illuminati control news media to manipulate people to take the vaccine. They also use the news media to manipulate people against each other by scorning those who refuse to take the vaccine. They use psychological warfare on you.

Just to let you know the Coronavirus vaccine had been created well before they released the COVID-19 virus. The vaccine had been stockpiled years in advance! In Anthony Patch's interview, he said the vaccine had something to do with mind control. Once I heard the words mind control, I understood what the Lord told me. The Lord told me the Coronavirus had to do with the chip. And the chip has to do with mind control, so the vaccine work with the 216 Megabyte chip. The vaccine is a primer for the human body to receive the chip. This vaccine was created to help information flow from the chip to the human brain more efficiently. The Coronavirus vaccine has small nanotechnology and gold particles that the human eye cannot see! The vaccine was designed to pair a super advanced communication technology with a 216-Megahertz computer chip. The graphene oxide (nanotechnology) is self-assembled and will attach itself to the molecular structure of one's DNA. Once the vaccine connects itself to the molecular structure, a third strand of DNA is formed. Now this vaccine will be use as a weapon to connect you to 5G towers and send messages to your chip implant. If they tell you to kill, you will kill. If they tell you to stop eating, you will stop eating. If they tell you to turn yourself over to them and be decommission then you will turn yourself over to them and be decommission (meaning put to death).

The other reason why they needed you to take the vaccine is so they could infect you with a disease they call Disease X, which is a deadly form of the Marburg disease. Once you voluntarily took the vaccine, the vaccine has microscopic couplets in it that's enclosed in a hydrogel. The couplets contain what they call Disease X, which is the Marburg virus. The couplets won't burst open until a very high frequency from the 5G towers hits either your body or the chip causing the couplets to burst open and infecting you with Disease X, which is the Marburg virus. That is the most effective way to kill 7.5 billion people. They gave you a biological weapon! And if you haven't noticed, people have been dying left and right from that Coronavirus vaccine. Some are saying the death rate has increased to 18% worldwide because of the Coronavirus vaccine. And they are expecting the death rate to go even higher. But you wouldn't know this because they keep it out of the mainstream media. Not everyone received the same vaccine. The people they want to DIE got one vaccine and the people they want to control got another.

The Coronavirus vaccine also contains mRNA. The mRNA shuts down your immune system. Once your immune system shuts down, your body can't fight diseases, viruses, or bacteria. Once your immune system is compromised, the Marburg virus which is Disease X will have almost a 100% kill rate. Also, the Coronavirus vaccine is said to produce cancer cells in people. And this cancer is what they call super cancer. It's a super cancer because your immune system has been turned off. It seems to me they created the perfect biological weapon to kill 7.5 billion people. To kill 7.5 billion people, they had to get creative in multiple ways.

The Illuminati is currently reducing the food supply by having farmers produce less food and killing off livestock around the world because they are about to starve you to death. Food processing plants are being burned to the ground and closed at alarming rates. They are using Global Warming and CO_2 to cover why they want farmers to produce less food. This is part of the plan to kill off 7.5 billion people to starve people to death. The cost of food skyrocketing is just a ploy to condition your mind to food scarcity.

They have multiple plans to kill you, including injecting the ones they call "the useless eaters" with a biological weapon. That's what they call you, "the useless eaters". They want cows to be killed off because they said when cows defecate, they are causing CO_2 to rise. This is how stupid they think you are. They are telling you cows are part of the problem with climate change. Cows have been on this planet for thousands of years, and this planet has been fine, but suddenly, the food supply (cows) is harmful to the planet. The CO_2 level is fine; to be honest, the higher the CO_2 level, the more plant and animals thrive. See, plants use CO_2 for food, and then plants take that CO_2 and turn it into oxygen for us to breathe. Without CO_2, there would be no oxygen for us to breathe.

It seems to me if they want to lower CO_2 levels, they are trying to kill off people because lower levels of CO_2 mean less oxygen plants and trees can produce, and less oxygen means you die. This well-known man who owns a computer software company whose name starts with "Ga" said we need to burn and kill all the trees because they are bad for CO_2 levels. That's just the opposite, trees are great for the planet because trees create oxygen for you to breathe. They have been lying to you about climate change. This planet's climate has always changed from spring to summer, summer to fall, fall to winter, and winter to spring. The climate has always changed since this earth was created. They think that you are stupid so they make up things to tell you and you believe them. The Illuminati truly believe you are stupid! Stop listening to these evil people who are trying to kill you!

Can I prove this Coronavirus was released on purpose? Yes, I can! See, the only thing you must do is to follow the evidence. There is always a clue or clues that will lead you to the absolute truth. I told you earlier that the Illuminati controls Congress; well, here is your proof. The CARES Act, which stands for the Coronavirus Aid, Relief, and Economic Security Act, is the one clue that tells the truth about everything and is your proof. The CARES Act is where the money came from for the Stimulus Checks and the Small Business Payroll Protection Plan passed for the Coronavirus Pandemic. Congress passed this on March 25, 2020 (3/25/2020) and then signed into law by President Donald Trump on March 27, 2020 (3/27/2020). Now follow this timeline and pay attention to the dates and you will see how the Coronavirus Pandemic was planned to be released on the world.

On December 31, 2019, Chinese authorities treated dozens of cases of pneumonia of unknown cause (Coronavirus) in Wuhan, China. On January 23, 2020, Chinese Authorities Closed off Wuhan, China, because of the Coronavirus. On January 30, 2020, the W.H.O. (World Health Organization) declared a global health emergency. On March 13, 2020, President Trump declared a National Emergency because of the Coronavirus. On March 27, 2020, Trump signed the CARES Act stimulus bill into law; that Bill is known as H.R. 748, passed by the 116th Congress 2019-2020. And one other thing, do you know where the two trillion dollars came from to fund the CARES Act stimulus package? It was loaned to us by the Federal Reserve. Also, the Federal Reserve put one trillion dollars into the stock market during this Coronavirus pandemic they caused. Now we have to pay back the Federal Reserve even more money for a Pandemic they purposely caused!

Now, since we see the timeline, let me show you what the Lord showed me. Whenever a bill is presented to the U.S. House of Representatives, it shows the date the Bill was presented. It also shows what phase the Bill is in and the date. The public can see this info on **www.Congress.gov.** This website shows you what is going on with any Bill introduced to Congress in the United States. For the CARES Act the Bill was first introduced on January 24, 2019 (1/24/2019). Yes, the CARES Act was introduced into the U.S. House of Representatives on January 24, 2019 (1/24/2019), a full year before China closed off Wuhan China because of the Coronavirus. Remember, China did not close off Wuhan China until January 23, 2020. The U.S. House of Representatives introduced the CARES Act on January 24, 2019, a full year and almost two months before President Donald Trump declared a National Emergency because of the Coronavirus! Donald Trump declared a National Emergency on March 13, 2020. Wow!

The outbreak of COVID-19 originated in Wuhan, China, and China closed off Wuhan China on January 23, 2020. The United States President Donald Trump declared a National State of Emergency on March 13, 2020; why did the U.S. House of Representatives introduce an emergency financial aid stimulus package called the CARES Act **(H.R. 748) one year before anything was known about a Coronavirus Pandemic?** So, the CARES Act was introduced in the U.S. House of Representatives on January 24, 2019 (1/24/2019), one year before anything was known about the Coronavirus Pandemic. The CARES Act went from the U.S. House to the U.S. Senate on July 18, 2019. Then it stayed in the Senate, and nothing else was done on the CARES Act until they were ready to push it through the Senate during an emergency Pandemic on March 20, 2020 (3/20/2020).

So basically, they had the CARES Act already worked out by July 18, 2019. So when the Illuminati released the Coronavirus, the U.S. House of Representatives and the U.S. Senate acted like they just drafted the CARES Act to help the American people. When, in fact, the CARES

ACT was drafted many years in advance. See, they introduced the legislation for the CARES Act on January 24, 2019, but when was the legislation drafted? It was probably drafted ten to fifteen years before the 2020 Pandemic. Do you remember the Illuminati think tank groups I told you about in Chapter 66 titled, "The Illuminati Corporation Structure"? They are the ones who drafted the CARES Act. And it was introduced into Congress on January 24, 2019.

It was like Congress knew it would be a Coronavirus Pandemic because they named the legislation the Coronavirus Aide Relief Emergency Security Act a full year and two months before the Pandemic occurred. Yes, Congress knew about the planned Pandemic just like the media knew about the planned Pandemic (Pandemic). The media had all the talking points ready for you when the planned Pandemic (Pandemic) occurred. The media, along with people within Congress, the Pentagon, and the CIA, had the entire thing planned out. It's time for you to face the absolute truth: Our Government has been overthrown by a secret society called the Illuminati. A secret society that worships Satan as a god. Remember the Bill was introduced to the House of Representatives on January 24, 2019, and then it went to the Senate on July 18, 2019, where it just sat there until March 20, 2020, when it was passed in the Senate and then President Trump signed it into law on March 27, 2020, during the Pandemic (Pandemic).

All the things the media was reporting about Democrats and the Republicans fighting over certain things they wanted the CARES Act to include or not include was just another lie; it was just another dog and pony show for the people! They always do dog and pony shows for you because you always fall for it! I hope you are angry because you need to be angry. So, how many people did the Illuminati kill by releasing the Coronavirus? Just to let you know, the Illuminati don't care about how many of you die. If it takes them killing a hundred million of you or more, they will do it! Remember, the Illuminati worship Satan as god! The Illuminati only cares about achieving their goals, which is putting a chip in your hand (mark of the beast), getting you to worship Satan and his image of the beast as a god, getting the Son of Satan appointed as a One World Leader, having a One World Government, and having a One World Monetary System. And guess what? They are close to making all this happen in the next two to six years, if not sooner! I have watched their moves and they are at the gate of accomplishing everything I just mentioned! You just don't understand how close they are! They have been waiting on the 5G or 6G Network technology to pair it with the chip!

If they already had this CARES Act Bill introduced to Congress on January 24, 2019, a full year before the W.H.O. (World Health Organization) declared the Coronavirus a Pandemic, this entire Coronavirus Pandemic was planned! And since Coronavirus was planned that means the virus was manmade! The virus was created in a laboratory! The virus was constructed by Dr. Fau and his team in the 80's and 90's. Dr. Fau is the so-called expert because he helped create the Coronavirus by weaponizing it with payloads of mRNA and Malburg disease.

On the next two pages, you can see when the law was introduced into the House of Representatives, moved through the Senate, and then signed by President Donald Trump. Look at where I have the arrows located.

CONGRESS.GOV

H.R.748 - CARES Act
116th Congress (2019-2020) | Get alerts

Sponsor: Rep. Courtney, Joe [D-CT-2] (Introduced 01/24/2019)
Committees: House - Ways and Means
Latest Action (modified): 03/27/2020 Became Public Law No: 116-136 (All Actions)
Roll Call Votes: There have been 5 roll call votes
Tracker: Introduced Passed House Passed Senate Resolving Differences To President Became Law

Summary(5) Text(5) **Actions(45)** Titles(24) Amendments(15) Cosponsors(369) Committees(1) Related Bills(48)

Bill History – Congressional Record References

45 results for All Actions |
Compact View

Date	Chamber	All Actions
03/31/2020-3:03pm	House	POSITION STATEMENTS FOR THE RECORD - The Chair announced that all Members may have five legislative days in which to include their stated position on the voice vote on the motion to concur in the Senate amendment to H.R. 748, and those statements will appear in the appropriate point in the Record. Agreed to without objection.
03/27/2020		Became Public Law No: 116-136.
03/27/2020		Signed by President.
03/27/2020	House	Presented to President.
03/27/2020-1:27pm	House	Motion to reconsider laid on the table Agreed to without objection.
03/27/2020-1:26pm	House	OBJECTION TO VOTE - At the conclusion of debate on the motion to concur in the Senate amendment to H.R. 748, the Chair put the question on the motion and by voice vote, announced that the ayes had prevailed. Mr. Massie demanded a recorded vote, and the Chair determined that an insufficient number of Members having arisen, the demand for a recorded vote was refused. Mr. Massie made a point of order that a quorum was not present and the Chair counted for a quorum. Subsequently, the Chair announced that a quorum was present.
03/27/2020-1:25pm	House	On motion that the House agree to the Senate amendment Agreed to by voice vote. (text: CR H1732-1818)
03/27/2020-1:25pm	House	The previous question was ordered pursuant to H.Res. 911.
03/27/2020-9:06am	House	DEBATE - Pursuant to the provisions of H. Res. 911, the House proceeded with 3 hours of debate on the motion that the House concur in the Senate amendment to H.R. 748.
03/27/2020-9:05am	House	Pursuant to the provisions of H. Res. 911, Mr. Hoyer moved that the House concur in the Senate amendment to H.R. 748. (consideration: CR H1732-1864)
03/26/2020	Senate	Message on Senate action sent to the House.
03/25/2020	Senate	Passed Senate, under the order of 3/25/20, having achieved 60 votes in the affirmative, with an amendment by Yea-Nay Vote. 96 - 0. Record Vote Number: 80.
03/25/2020	Senate	S.Amdt.1578 Amendment SA 1578 agreed to in Senate by Unanimous Consent.
03/25/2020	Senate	S.Amdt.1577 Amendment SA 1577, under the order of 3/25/20, not having achieved 60 votes in the affirmative, was not agreed to in Senate by Yea-Nay Vote. 48 - 48. Record Vote Number: 79.
03/25/2020	Senate	S.Amdt.1577 Amendment SA 1577 proposed by Senator Sasse to Amendment SA 1578. (consideration: CR S2059-2060; text: CR S2060) To ensure that additional unemployment benefits do not result in an individual receiving unemployment compensation that is more than the amount of wages the individual was earning prior to becoming unemployed.
03/25/2020	Senate	S.Amdt.1578 Amendment SA 1578 proposed by Senator McConnell. (consideration: CR S2059, S2060; text: CR S2063-2156) Providing emergency assistance and health care response for individuals, families, and businesses affected by the 2020 coronavirus pandemic.

7/10/2020

On the next page it will show that the CARES Act was introduced to U.S. on January 24, 2019.

Date	Chamber	All Actions
03/25/2020	Senate	Measure laid before Senate by unanimous consent. (consideration: CR S2059-2060)
03/25/2020	Senate	Second cloture motion on the motion to proceed to the measure withdrawn by unanimous consent in Senate. (CR S2059)
03/25/2020	Senate	Motion to proceed to measure considered in Senate. (CR S2022)
03/24/2020	Senate	Motion to proceed to measure considered in Senate. (CR S1976)
03/23/2020	Senate	Second cloture motion on the motion to proceed to the measure presented in Senate. (CR S1957)
03/23/2020	Senate	Motion to proceed to measure considered in Senate. (CR S1929)
03/23/2020	Senate	Upon reconsideration, cloture on the motion to proceed to the measure not invoked in Senate by Yea-Nay Vote. 49 - 46. Record Vote Number: 78. (CR S1928)
03/23/2020	Senate	Motion by Senator McConnell to reconsider the vote by which cloture on the motion to proceed to the measure was not invoked (Record Vote No. 77) agreed to in Senate by Voice Vote.
03/23/2020	Senate	Motion to proceed to consideration of the motion to reconsider the vote by which cloture on the motion to proceed to the measure was not invoked (Record Vote No. 77) agreed to in Senate by Voice Vote. (CR S1921)
03/22/2020	Senate	Motion by Senator McConnell to reconsider the vote by which cloture on the motion to proceed to the measure was not invoked (Record Vote No. 77) entered in Senate.
03/22/2020	Senate	Cloture on the motion to proceed to the measure not invoked in Senate by Yea-Nay Vote. 47 - 47. Record Vote Number: 77. (CR S1901)
03/22/2020	Senate	Motion to proceed to measure considered in Senate. (CR S1895, S1897, S1913)
03/21/2020	Senate	Motion to proceed to measure considered in Senate. (CR S1882)
03/20/2020	Senate	Cloture motion on the motion to proceed to the measure presented in Senate. (CR S1876)
03/20/2020	Senate	Motion to proceed to consideration of measure made in Senate. (CR S1876)
07/22/2019	Senate	Read the second time. Placed on Senate Legislative Calendar under General Orders. Calendar No. 157.
07/18/2019	Senate	Received in the Senate. Read the first time. Placed on Senate Legislative Calendar under Read the First Time.
07/17/2019-6:57pm	House	Motion to reconsider laid on the table Agreed to without objection.
07/17/2019-6:57pm	House	On motion to suspend the rules and pass the bill, as amended Agreed to by the Yeas and Nays: (2/3 required): 419 - 6 (Roll no. 493). (text: CR H5958-5959)
07/17/2019-6:44pm	House	Considered as unfinished business. (consideration: CR H5980-5981)
07/17/2019-5:03pm	House	At the conclusion of debate, the Yeas and Nays were demanded and ordered. Pursuant to the provisions of clause 8, rule XX, the Chair announced that further proceedings on the motion would be postponed.
07/17/2019-4:24pm	House	DEBATE - The House proceeded with forty minutes of debate on H.R. 748.
07/17/2019-4:23pm	House	Considered under suspension of the rules. (consideration: CR H5958-5973)
07/17/2019-4:23pm	House	Mr. Neal moved to suspend the rules and pass the bill, as amended.
07/17/2019-4:23pm	House	The Chair announced the Speaker's designation, pursuant to clause 7(a)(1) of rule 15, of H.R. 748 as the measure on the Consensus Calendar to be considered this week.
07/17/2019	House	Assigned to the Consensus Calendar, Calendar No. 2.
05/21/2019	House	Motion to place bill on Consensus Calendar filed by Mr. Courtney.
01/24/2019	House	Referred to the House Committee on Ways and Means.
01/24/2019	House	Introduced in House

Now, let me state something for you. I originally printed some copies of this book on November 7, 2018, because I thought it was ready when it was not! It was still a work in progress! In November 2019, the Lord told me I had released this book too early! Then, the Lord clarified something he had told me some years ago.

In the year of 2012, the Lord started telling me the Illuminati released a worldwide virus on this world. My interpretation was that the virus the

Illuminati released on the world was Mortgage Derivatives. In Chapter 118, titled "Prophesy of Derivatives and the Stock Market Crash," I thought the Lord only meant the virus of Mortgage Derivatives was released on the world. But the Lord was telling the Illuminati released a worldwide virus! The Illuminati released the Coronavirus worldwide! The Illuminati don't care who they kill or what possession they make you lose! It's all about accomplishing their goals! And the Illuminati goals are to steal, kill and destroy. I admit I missed it when the Lord told me the Illuminati released a worldwide virus! The Lord wasn't just talking about Mortgage Derivatives. He was also talking about the Coronavirus!

Also, just to let you know all those people with Coronavirus didn't die from the virus! Some were killed on purpose by the Illuminati doctors! The Illuminati wanted the death toll to rise quickly so they could cause panic! The medical field falls under the Illuminati Medical Department called The Brotherhood of the Snake! So, the Illuminati had to make sure they caused a lot of fear in the citizens of the United States, and they had to do it fast! You must remember this Pandemic was planned, so the Illuminati doctors had to follow the orders that were passed down to them by the hierarchy of the Illuminati! They had to kill as many people as possible to cause fear and panic in the United States! A lot of people had to die fast! And the Illuminati doctors did what they were ordered to do! Kill!

Also, many people who were buried in those mass graves in New York didn't die from the Coronavirus! Some people were killed, and they didn't even have Coronavirus! And those who may have died from natural deaths were labeled as Coronavirus deaths! The Hospitals put pressure on Corners to list the Cause of Death as Coronavirus because the government purposely placed financial incentives on people dying from the Coronavirus! This meant the Hospitals got large checks for everyone listed as a Coronavirus death! This guaranteed the Hospitals were going to over-inflate the Coronavirus deaths by either killing people or letting people die or labeling natural deaths as Coronavirus deaths! You understand why they prepared the CARES Act one year ahead of time! There was no need for the Illuminati to go through all the trouble of planning the Coronavirus pandemic and submitting the CARES Act if large amounts of people didn't die fast in the United States! They needed fear, and they needed it fast! So they had their Illuminati doctors killing people!

Also, do you remember all those people who were buried in mass graves in New York? I think they were buried in mass graves to cover up the crimes! It's hard to legally exhume a body from a mass grave versus an individual grave! So, a lot of the people were murdered in New York Hospitals to cause the Coronavirus death toll to rise fast! So, the Illuminati knew they needed one major City to have a full-blown outbreak of the Coronavirus, and that City was New York! The Illuminati needed to make the American people fearful and the people of the world fearful! The quick way to feed fear is death! They needed many deaths in New York City, and they needed it fast! The Illuminati doctors were ordered to kill! And the decision was made well ahead of time to bury the bodies in mass graves to cover up the crimes! When I told you the Illuminati don't care about who they kill, you thought I was joking! The Illuminati worship Satan as a god! And just to let you know, Satan and his people come to kill, steal, and destroy! Everything I am explaining to you is not just happening in the U.S. This thing is happening the same way worldwide! You must remember the Illuminati is on every continent and is in every nation's government throughout the world! They did the same thing in your country! They operate the same way everywhere! The Illuminati is so organized and efficient at what they do. They have been around for thousands of years and they have been working behind the scenes.

The Republican and Democratic Congressmen didn't warn you, nor did they tell you the Affordable Care Act made it mandatory for you to receive this chip implant in your hand, which is the mark of the beast. The news media didn't warn you either, did they? The Democratic Congressmen, Republican Congressmen, and the news media didn't want you to know the Affordable Care Act (Obamacare) made it mandatory for you to get a chip implant (mark of the beast). I thought you could trust the news media to tell you the truth! I thought the news media was your friend and would always tell you the truth. I thought you Democrats could trust your Democratic Congressmen because they are the good guys, and the Republican Congressmen are the bad guys. I thought you Republicans could trust your Republican Congressmen because the Republican Congressmen are the good guys, and the Democratic Congressmen are the bad guys!

Since you Democrats and you Republicans can trust your political party so much, why didn't your political party warn you the Affordable Care Act (Obamacare) made it mandatory for you to receive an implantable chip (mark of the beast) in your hand? They didn't tell you because many of your Republican and Democratic Congressmen are members of the Illuminati, and they are helping the Illuminati and their agenda. The news media didn't tell you nor warn you the Affordable Care Act made it mandatory for you to take the Mark of the Beast (chip implant) because most of the people in the news media are members of the Illuminati, and the Illuminati control the mainstream news media like ABC, CBS, NBC, FOX, CNN, MSNBC, and many others. The Affordable Care Act was passed into law on March 23, 2010. So why haven't they (your political party and the news media) warned you all these years? Is it because your Democratic lawmakers and your Republican lawmakers are members of the Illuminati?

Also, why didn't your Democratic Congressmen and your Republican Congressmen warn you that they were going to release the Coronavirus in the U.S.? I thought you could trust them! Why didn't the media tell you the truth about how the U.S. started the CARES Act one full year before the Pandemic? If I found that information on www.Congress.gov are you saying none of the mainstream news organizations saw it? The news organizations are used as a tool by the Illuminati to control the thinking process of the masses! They pump you full of fear, don't they? They feed you fear of the Pandemic day, noon, and night on television! Then, when it was time for them to change the station in your minds. They started a war! Then they pumped you full of fear on World War III. Then you forgot all about the Coronavirus! They changed the station in your mind! Like they always do!

118.   Prophesy of Derivatives and Stock Market Crash Fulfilled

In 2002, I told everyone who would listen to me that the stock market would crash. Each passing year, my intensity grew in telling people the stop market would crash. The Holy Spirit was speaking through me to warn everyone who would listen. Everyone I talked to thought I was losing my mind because no one else could foresee the stock market crashing. Everyone's understanding was how could the stock market crash when the stock market was reaching new record highs. I remember as time grew closer and closer to 2007 my intensity grew in telling people the stock market would crash.

One person was my sister "V"; "V" was the one who joined the Illuminati while at Auburn. I knew "V" had some stocks and a nice 401K account. In 2007, I advised her to take everything out of her 401K and take whatever she had out of the stock market. I told my sister to take whatever penalty they would access to her. At the time, she thought I was crazy for giving her that financial advice. I knew the stock market would crash because the Holy Spirit was speaking through me to warn everyone who would listen.

Now it's 2008, and I am watching the stock market fall off a cliff with my own eyes. While everyone was in full panic, I saw in the physical realm what I already knew in the spiritual realm. While everyone was panicking, I sat back with an attitude of "I told you so!" I knew the stock market was about to crash because it had already been revealed to me by the Holy Spirit in 1994. Do you remember what the Holy Spirit told me in 1994 concerning the stock market? The Holy Spirit told me derivatives would cause the stock market to crash.

In Chapter 51, titled "The Prophesy of Derivatives and Stock Market Crash," I told you how my professor, Dr. Scroggins, walked into class and said, "We are going to start on derivatives today." I then turned to the page with the formula for mortgage derivatives. Once I saw the formula for mortgage derivatives, I just stared at the formula. While I was staring at the formula, I kept thinking to myself, something isn't right about this formula. I kept having this thought the formula was violating the rule of mathematics. I then said, "Lord, something is not right about this formula." Then, at that very moment, the Holy Spirit said, "This formula is going to cause the stock market to crash." Once I heard the Holy Spirit say that, I raised my hand and said, "Dr. Scroggins, Dr. Scroggins, Dr. Scroggins." Then Dr. Scroggins said, "What Kennedy!" I said, "Dr. Scroggins, this formula for derivatives is wrong." Dr. Scroggins said, "Kennedy, what are you talking about!" I said, "This formula for mortgage derivatives is set up wrong; this is going to cause the stock market to crash!!!" After I said that, the professor and everyone else started laughing at me.

Since you remember that chapter, I am about to reveal the truth about the 2008 stock market crash. And how derivatives were designed to go off like a nuclear bomb in 2008 and you will understand why the stock market crashed in 2008. Because the Illuminati, the Illuminati-controlled U.S. Government, and the Illuminati-controlled news media purposely mislead you with a bunch of lies and deception! And most of the U.S. population and the world population bought into the lies of the Illuminati!

What if I tell you they intentionally crashed the stock market? Could you handle the truth, or will you plug your ears up like a little child and scream, "Conspiracy theory, Conspiracy theory!" While the average person was losing their money and their property value was decreasing, the rich Illuminati members didn't lose anything during the 2008 market crash because their money was ensured against the stock market crash in special insurance funds that were designated just for them for the 2008 stock market crash. The rich Illuminati members didn't lose any of their money, but instead of losing money, they made billions of dollars!

It was the Illuminati that orchestrated the stock market crash in 2008. It was neither by accident nor by coincidence that the stock market crashed in 2008. It was a well-calculated plan to crash the U.S. economy. The question you should be asking is: why? Why would the Illuminati want to crash the U.S. Stock Market? What would the Illuminati gain by crashing the U.S. Stock Market? The final question is how the Illuminati could pull off such a daunting task of crashing the U.S. Stock Markets and other stock markets in the world.

To understand what truly happened in 2008, you must understand that derivatives were engineered to do exactly what they did. Derivatives were created and designed to crash the U.S. and world stock markets. Financial engineers created derivatives. Financial engineers create and design financial products! You have engineers in every aspect of our society, like automotive, computer, and electrical engineers. There are also financial engineers who create and design financial products. Financial products are created by using mathematical equations to represent the financial product. Derivatives are nothing but a mathematical equation! And like any mathematical equation, the equation can be manipulated to give you a desired response or a desired reaction. Derivatives are financial products that were engineered for the specific purpose of crashing the financial markets.

The formula was designed to explode like a nuclear bomb once certain trigger points ignited. The formula for derivatives was purposely violating some of the rules of mathematics. It was not possible they made a mistake without them catching it. Because every formula for a financial product is run through a computer simulation module and the **error** would have been caught immediately by the computer simulation module. Also, these formulas are checked and double checked by many people. Now, if I saw something was wrong with the formula just by looking at it. Are you telling me no one else knew something was wrong with the formula before it was introduced to the U.S. Financial Markets and the world financial markets?

The first thing you need to understand is that the U. S. Government and the news media sold the American people and people around the world on one of the biggest lies ever told! They told you the market collapsed because poor people bought houses they couldn't afford! The government used the media to control the thoughts of its citizens as to what was going on and why. But like everything else in our country and worldwide, if you control the news media, you control the citizens' thinking process. Whoever controls the flow of information to the masses (the news media) controls the people of this world!

The first thing they did was create derivatives by creating a formula for them! Derivatives were introduced in the 1970s, around the same time 401 K's was introduced into society. That was not a coincidence both financial products were introduced into society about the same time! Just to let you know, if they introduced Derivatives in the 1970s, that means the formula may have been created in the 1950s or 1960s because everything the Illuminati does is planned years in advance!

What are Mortgage Derivatives? Mortgage Derivatives are a financial product that was created from a mathematical formula. Mortgage Derivatives are mortgage-back securities. Once a mortgage is created on a house, that mortgage is bundled with other mortgages. And once mortgages are bundled together, they are taken to Wall Street and sold. Bundling mortgages helps the lender and investors minimize risk while generating higher returns on investment.

When mortgages are bundled, a derivative is attached to them as a financial instrument. Once these derivatives are attached to bundled mortgages, investors like Bear Stearns, Leahman Brothers, and many other companies buy them to receive income streams from bundled mortgages when homeowners make their monthly mortgage payments. These monthly mortgage payments being made by homeowners are considered an income stream or cash flow for investors. Investors cherish a cash flow even if investors must make a significant investment into mortgage derivatives to obtain a piece of that cash flow. Let's look at some numbers to understand how large this cash flow is. These numbers we are about to look at are very small compared to the real transactions that were taking place. All the numbers I am about to give you are fictitious. I am using these numbers to give an average individual insight into what transpired with Mortgage Derivatives. So, let's begin.

Say, Bank "W" did home loans for One Billion dollars' worth of mortgages in January 2005. Bank "W" would bundle all those mortgages and take them to Wall Street. So, Bank "W" had One Billion dollars' worth of mortgages. Let's assume each loan is valued at $200,000 per mortgage. That will give you a total of 5000 mortgages outstanding. One Billion divided by $200,000 = 5000, so we have 5000 mortgages outstanding. Then, we will assume each loan was on a thirty-year mortgage with an interest rate of 7%.

The monthly principal and interest payment per mortgage is $1,330.60. Multiply the monthly mortgage payment of $1330.60 times five thousand mortgages per month, which equals $6,653,000 per month. $6,653,000 was the monthly mortgage income stream based on the One Billion dollars worth of mortgages. I'm trying to keep this simple.

Suppose you take $6,653,000 and multiply it by 12 months in a year, which will equal $79,836,000 a year. Just for this scenario we will say that $79,836,000 was the yearly cash flow. Other things must be considered when calculating cash flow but we are going to keep this simple. So the $79,836,000 is very enticing to investment bankers and other investors. One Billion dollars worth of mortgages gave them a monthly income stream of $6,653,000 per month and $79,836,000 per year. In a 30-year mortgage, most of the payment goes directly to the interest in the first seven years. Most of the $79,836,000 was interest payments made on the mortgage loans. These numbers I am using to paint a picture for you are very small compared to the real numbers!

Bank "W" would like to diversify their risk on the One Billion dollar worth of mortgages while maintaining some income streams from the mortgage payments. So bank "W" takes their One Billion dollar worth of residential mortgages to Wall Street; then Wall Street invested in derivatives on top of derivatives to an amount that was twenty times the initial investment of One Billion dollars. Which means Wall Street invested Twenty billion dollars worth of derivatives for the One Billion in mortgages. There were derivatives on top of derivatives on top of derivatives on top of other derivatives. Basically look at derivatives on top of derivatives as a side bet to the original bet. The derivatives themselves are not real property but a financial instruments. The mortgage derivatives have been attached to the bundled mortgages and sold to different investors. The investors who bought the Twenty Billion worth of derivatives plan to gain some of the income stream or cash flow generated when homeowners pay their monthly mortgage payments on the One Billion dollars worth of mortgages.

The initial investment made by Bank "W" was One Billion dollars worth of mortgages, and Bank "W" wanted to diversify its risk by taking them to Wall Street to be sold. Then Investors invested an additional Twenty Billion to get some of the income stream. On One Billion dollars' worth of real property as collateral (Your Homes), there were Twenty Billion dollars' worth of investments made. WOW!!! The thinking was everybody would make money on the deal! But the derivatives were only good if the economic conditions stayed the same. Property value had to stay the same or increase, and the number of foreclosures couldn't rise above a certain rate. All the things I mentioned in the previous sentence are variables that ignited the derivative bomb! Since we see the general understanding of derivatives let's look at the trigger points that had to be in place before derivatives exploded.

Derivatives were engineered and then introduced to the U.S. Financial Markets in the 1970's. So, we know creating derivatives was the first step that had to be done. The second step was implemented in the 1980s and 1990s to ensure the derivative VIRUS infected the U.S. stock markets and foreign markets worldwide simultaneously. The second step was the deregulation under Ronald Regan, George H. W. Bush, Secretary of Treasury Allan Greenspan, and Bill Clinton. During the 1980s and 1990s, Regan, Bush, Clinton, and Greenspan started deregulating Wall Street. Just to let you know, Bush, Clinton, and Greenspan are all members of the Illuminati!

When Ronald Regan saw he was going to win the Republican Primaries, Ronald Regan was asked if he was going to choose George H.W. Bush as his Vice President. Ronald Regan said, he would never choose a man who was part of a secret society to be his Vice President. Ronald Regan was very emphatic when he made that statement. But some kind of way the Illuminati forced Ronald Regan to change his mind. So Ronald Reagan went back on his word and choose George H.W. Bush to be his Vice President. While Ronald Regan was President, Vice President George H.W. Bush was undermining him. Ronald Regan was not Illuminati. And since Ronald Regan was not Illuminati, they attempted to assassinate President Ronald Regan! The first shooter in the Ronald Regan assassination attempt was John Hinkley Jr.. John Hinkley

Jr. was close friends with George W. Bush, who was the son of Vice President George H.W. Bush. John Hinkley Jr. visited George W. Bush and Vice President George H.W. Bush at their home on many occasions. So if John Hinkley Jr. was visiting the Vice President George H.W. Bush who was an ex-CIA Director and Vice President of the United States, do you think it just so happened that John Hinkley Jr. tried to assassinate Ronald Regan. Come on, you all are smarted than that. John Hinkley Jr. was just a decoy for the assassination attempt. There was a second shooter present when Ronald Regan got shoot, but the Illuminati control news media purposely kept that out of the news because that would have given an appearance of a coup d'etat, which means a regime change by force. The regime change was orchestrated by the Illuminati, and ex-CIA Director who was Vice President George H.W. Bush, who just so happened to be a member of the Illuminati! Ronald Regan was supposed to be assassinated so the Illuminati would have one of their own as President George H. W. Bush. Do you see a pattern here? If you are President and you are not Illuminati, you either get killed (Abraham Lincoln, John F. Kennedy), or they attempt to kill you (Ronald Regan), or they try to kill you or throw you in jail (Donald Trump). Remember this one rule, there is always a second shooter! One shooter is a decoy to take the fall, and the other shooter is to take the kill shot. Thomas Matthew Crook was a decoy, there was a second shooter present. The second shooter fired the shot that scraped President Trump ear.

Deregulation began with Reagan and Bush. Then, under the Bush administration, this deregulation continued. Under the Clinton administration, President Bill Clinton signed into law The Gramm-Leach-Bliley Act. The Gramm-Leach-Bliley Act **removed Great Depression Era laws that separated banking, insurance, and brokerage activities.** After the Great Depression in the 1930s, laws were implemented to prevent another Great Depression from happening. Those laws were in place because economists and lawmakers saw what caused the Great Depression in the 1930s. So Great Depression laws were in place to separate banking, insurance, and brokerage activities. But once the Illuminati members deregulated Wall Street, they removed the Great Depression Era laws that separated banking, insurance, and brokerage activities! This allowed the mortgage derivatives VIRUS to be released worldwide; derivatives had little to no oversight by the government.

George H. W. Bush, Bill Clinton, and their Illuminati buddies purposely removed Great Depression Era laws to make sure they created another collapse of the stock market, like the collapse of the stock market in the 1930s. They knew the exact laws to remove to ensure another stock market collapse. So when they deregulated Wall Street and removed the laws that were in place to prevent another Great Depression from happening, they purposely set the stage for another depression or recession. Because once they remove the laws to separate banking, insurance, and brokerage activities; financial institutions begin to combine those different markets. And once they combined those different markets, those institutions became **"Two Big to Fail"**. In 2008 and 2009, you heard the phrase **"Too Big to Fail"** a lot. Those "Two Big to Fail" institutions had combined banking, insurance, and brokerage activities!

By removing Great Depression Era laws, derivatives were free to roam the U.S. and foreign financial markets without regulation. Now, you should take notice that it was Republican Presidents and a Democratic President signed bills into law that helped derivatives roam free in the United States financial markets and the world financial markets! Two Presidents of two different political parties signed the critical bills into law! Even though the Presidents belong to two different political parties, they both are members of the Skull and Bones, which means they both are members of the Illuminati. George H. W. Bush is a member of Skull and Bones, and Bill Clinton is a member of Skull and Bones, so they are both members of the Illuminati.

George H. W. Bush was the CIA director before becoming Vice President. George H.W. Bush was a member of the Illuminati WAR Department, which is called Skull and Bones. Bill Clinton is also a member of the Illuminati WAR Department, the Skull and Bones! Do you think it is a coincidence that both Presidents were members of the Illuminati? When Bill Clinton was running for President, he ran against his Illuminati brother, George H.W. Bush. It didn't matter if you voted for the Democrats or the Republicans. A vote for Bill Clinton was a vote for the Illuminati, and a vote for George H.W. Bush was a vote for the Illuminati. When Al Gore ran for President against George W. Bush, Al Gore was Illuminati, and George W. Bush was Illuminati, so did it matter if you voted for Democratic or Republican? A vote for either candidate is a vote for the Illuminati. Do you see how they rig the elections for the Illuminati?

The third step was to export American jobs overseas to different countries. American jobs were being shipped overseas to other countries at an alarming rate starting in the '80s, 90s, and 2000s. This was not a coincidence; American jobs were being shipped overseas while laws were passed to unleash derivatives on the U.S. and world financial markets. So, at the same time, they started deregulation, they started selling Mortgage Derivatives, and they started a mass exportation of American jobs! American jobs were intentionally being exported to countries around the world to set the stage for a future financial collapse! Manufacturing, textile, customer service, high-tech, and other jobs were being shipped overseas at an alarming rate.

The Illuminati got their Skull and Bones President Bill Clinton to push for certain laws and trade agreements to be passed! And Clinton stayed loyal to the Illuminati and did what was asked of him, which was an act of HIGH TREASON against the people of the United States of America! The Illuminati and Bill Clinton push for NAFTA to become law. NAFTA stands for the North American Free Trade Agreement! This law guaranteed millions of American jobs would be lost to other nations. This is what NAFTA was designed to do! And that is what NAFTA did! NAFTA killed over 30 million American jobs! And that's exactly why the Illuminati wanted NAFTA signed into law! So, a mass exodus of American jobs could take place over a short period of time! And it just so happened to be Illuminati President Bill Clinton who pushed for NAFTA to become law!

Who was in power in the 80s, 90s, and 2000s when all the jobs were shipped overseas? The Illuminati had the people in power when all the major laws had to be changed and when all the jobs were being shipped overseas! Bush was Vice President and President in the 80's and 90's. Then Bill Clinton was President in the '90s when he helped push the NAFTA agenda! Then Illuminati member George W. Bush was President in the 2000s when there was a mass exodus of U.S. jobs!

President Franklin D. Roosevelt said, "In politics, nothing happens by accident. If it happens, you can bet it was planned that way." *Franklin D. Roosevelt Quotes." BrainyQuote. Xplore, n.d. Web. 06 Apr. 2017. <http://www.brainyquote.com/quotes/quotes/f/franklind164126.html>.*

So once the Illuminati Presidents and Congressmen passed the laws, the Illuminati CEOs and the Illuminati Board members of major Corporations started shipping jobs to other countries. The way the Illuminati pulled this office is by having their people in positions of power years in advance. The Illuminati recruits the smartest and the brightest. Those people who are highly intelligent. Once they recruit these people the Illuminati put them in positions of power. And they keep moving that person up into higher positions of power. These positions of power are in the private sector as well as the government sector. They have people in all walks of life in key positions of power. Like many CEOs and Board members of major corporations are members of the Illuminati. When the governing body of the Illuminati, "The Order of the Quest," has an agenda to crash the U.S. stock market with Derivatives. The governing body knows they must set the conditions right first. The governing body of the Illuminati gives orders to the CEOs and Board Members of Corporations to ship jobs overseas to foreign countries. The Illuminati already had the Trilateral Commission and the Council of Foreign Relations making deals with other nations years in advance so the transition of U.S. jobs to foreign nations would go smoothly. This is what happens: other nations get U.S. jobs while the Illuminati uses the Trilateral Commission and the Council of Foreign Relations to get concessions from other nations to become a part of this Global Economy by rewriting their constitutions to allow for a One World Government. Everything the Illuminati is doing is working together to help their agenda and their cause. The Illuminati needed to crash the U.S. economy and weaken the United States, so the Illuminati ship jobs overseas, but the Illuminati also needs other nations to rewrite their constitutions to allow for a One World Government under a One World Leader. They were able to kill two birds with one stone. These people are so organized and smart.

The Illuminati CEOs and the Illuminati Board Members do what they were ordered to do and ship American jobs overseas to foreign countries. Even though the Illuminati CEOs and the Illuminati Board Members are following orders, they are aware they will receive multimillion-dollar bonuses and larger salaries once they ship the American jobs overseas. The Illuminati CEOs and the Illuminati Board Members got larger bonuses for shipping jobs overseas because they were now paying cheaper labor costs. Cheaper labor cost means higher profit margins, and higher profit margins mean the CEOs and Board Members get larger salaries and bonuses. It just so happened that most of these CEOs and Board Members are members of the Illuminati! Keep the money in the family.

So, jobs were being lost at an alarming rate in the United States of America. So, fewer American jobs in the private sector meant less money consumers could spend on things they don't need and on things they do need. So fewer American jobs in the private sector means less money being spent by consumers, less money being spent means less income for businesses, and less tax revenue being collected by local, state, and federal governments. Less income for businesses means less government tax revenues, which meant higher deficits by local, state, and federal governments. Less tax revenue by local, state, and federal government means hiring freezes and eventually layoffs in the government. Layoffs mean fewer jobs. Fewer jobs mean more people out of work. Fewer jobs mean fewer mortgage payments being made on time. Fewer jobs mean fewer interest payments being collected on mortgage loans, credit cards, car loans, installment loans, and other loans.

There was a mass exodus of jobs! But they deceived you by saying, "fewer jobs meant cheaper prices for you in the store." They told the American people that products would be cheaper for them and their families if things were made in other countries. I have one question for you. Have the products been cheaper for you yet? The answer is "no"! But they promise you the products would be cheaper if they moved those jobs overseas! Are you telling me they lied to you again? I am not surprised because they lie to you all the time.

Step four was to expose the accounting fraud that was going on in many corporations in the late 90's and early 2000's. This was a very important step. The accounting frauds had to be exposed publicly with lots of media attention. They needed to place fear in every corporation that no accounting fraud could occur because they needed all corporations to report accurate numbers in 2007, 2008, and 2009. The accounting frauds were exposed to ensure no company cooked the books during the 2008 stock market crash. This would ensure true numbers were reported to Wall Street in 2008 each quarter. If all the corporations reported true numbers in 2007, 2008, and 2009, they knew it would cause more panic in the stock market and more panic among Americans. The more panic they could produce, the more power they could gain! They had to expose the accounting frauds in the late 1990s and early 2000s so no corporations wouldn't dare cook the books during the 2008 stock market crash!

The fifth and most important step was shutting down the subprime housing market in 2007 and manipulating people into foreclosure! See, before and during the 2008 stock market crash, I was a mortgage broker! I saw the events that were taking place firsthand in the subprime market! Before I go into detail, let me ask you a question. Do you think it was a coincidence the Lord had me major in Finance and I was working as a mortgage broker, or was it divine providence and divine purpose for me to major in Finance and be a mortgage broker? The Lord had me major in Finance and worked as a mortgage broker so I could watch the collapse of derivatives, the subprime housing industry, and the stock market simultaneously! I could truly see and understand how they manipulated the entire system! As a mortgage broker and someone who knew the stock market would crash ahead of time, I understood everything and how it happened in the subprime housing market! And that "B.S." they told you on television was just that, "B.S.".

First, let's get some understanding of what the subprime market was. The subprime market was created as a secondary financing market to provide some homeowners with financing options for purchasing or refinancing their homes! One would apply for a subprime loan if they had some credit issues, like low credit scores, or unconventional income etc. Normally, a person would choose to go subprime if they couldn't meet the requirements of government loan programs or conventional loans. First, you must understand that the lenders and the investors determine the loan programs! This means that lenders like "City Lenders" or "Trust Bank" would determine what loan programs they would offer! And lenders only offered loan programs they could sell to the investors. Lenders never offered loan programs the investors wouldn't buy because the lender would be stuck with those loans! The lenders only offered loan programs the investors would buy from them. The investors on Wall Street normally dictated the loan programs the lenders and the banks offered!

So, say investors like "Towns and Towns" tell Wells Lenders we will only buy subprime loans from you. If Towns and Towns is the only investor Wells Lender has, then Well Lenders will offer only Subprime Loans. It wouldn't make sense for Wells Lenders to offer "A Paper Loans" if they didn't have an investor to buy their "A Paper Loans". Because if Wells Lenders didn't have anyone to buy their "A Paper Loans" from them, they would be stuck with the loans, which would tie up their revenue, and they wouldn't be able to make new loans. And if they couldn't make new loans, they might as well go out of business. So, lenders only made loans they could sell to investors. The Lenders, the Investors, and Wall Street are solely responsible for the type of loans offered to customers.

The mortgage broker didn't dictate what loan programs were available to customers! The lenders, the investors, and Wall Street determine what loan programs are available to the customers. I had to make that clear to you because, in 2008 and 2009, the media made it appear like it was the Mortgage broker's fault for the subprime crisis! When the Mortgage Broker had no power to determine what loans the banks or lenders were offering. The power was with Alan Greenspan, Wall Street Investors, and the Lenders. The Mortgage Brokers were the small men on the totem pole. The Mortgage Brokers were not responsible for the subprime crisis. But like always, the U.S. Government and the Illuminati-controlled news media lied to the American people and told them that it was the Mortgage Brokers' fault for the subprime crisis. And the American people believed them!

The subprime market was set up to steer people with poor credit and special financing needs into adjustable-rate mortgages (ARMs). Now, before we go any further, let's think about something! Who normally has poor credit, the rich or the poor? Just to let you know, the poor and the lower middle class normally have bad credit! The subprime market was designed for the poor and lower-middle-class people!

The subprime market was set up to steer people into an Adjustable-Rate Mortgage (ARM) by setting the interest rate low on ARMs and the fixed-rate loan interest rates extremely high. This was done intentionally so the customer would look at the teaser rate on the Adjustable-Rate Mortgage (ARM), and it would be low compared to the interest rate on the fixed-rate loan. The borrower would always choose the teaser rate on the adjustable-rate mortgage because the interest rate on the ARM was significantly lower than the subprime fixed-rate mortgage.

For example, say I had a customer who wanted a thirty-year loan, and they had a 520 credit score. The lenders would then offer them an adjustable-rate mortgage for a 6.5% interest rate that would be fixed for two years, but after the two years are up, the interest rate would adjust for the remainder of the loan. Or the customer would be given the option to take a 30-year fixed rate mortgage, where their interest rate would be fixed for the entire loan duration! But there is a catch: the interest rate would be fixed at about 12% or even higher for 30 years. When the customers saw a 6.5% interest rate on an Adjustable Rate Mortgage (ARM) and saw the 12% interest rate on a subprime 30-year fixed rate mortgage, the customers were steered to the 6.5% Adjustable-Rate Mortgage because a lower interest rate meant lower house payment!

So many people chose to take Adjustable-Rate Mortgages with the hopes they could get their credit repaired before the teaser rate of 6.5% expired in two years. So they were hoping to refinance their house before the two years were up. And that's exactly how the Illuminati wanted them to think. Because the governing body of the Illuminati, which is called "The Order of the Quest," had planned on shutting down the subprime market. Once they shut down the subprime market, those who needed to refinance their mortgage before their teaser rate expired couldn't do so! And that's exactly what the Illuminate made sure happened. The Illuminati intentionally shut down the Subprime market in 2007. And once they shut down the Subprime Market, those who had expiring teaser rates couldn't refinance their mortgages. And that meant their mortgage payments would increase because their interest rate increased. And since their interest rate had increased, their house payments would also increase. And in many cases, their mortgage payment doubled once the interest rate increased because the stock market was crashing. And once their house payment doubled, many people couldn't make their house payments, so their houses went into foreclosure!

The Subprime Market was intentionally shut down to cause the housing market to produce a flood of foreclosures simultaneously! Remember that the derivative formula didn't compensate for a higher-than-normal foreclosure rate! That meant they needed a flood of houses to go into foreclosure all at once! And that's exactly what happened when they shut down the Subprime Market!

This is why the Lord told me to return to Jacksonville State University and major in Finance! So I could be exposed to mortgage derivatives and understand what happened in 2007, 2008, and 2009. I was a Mortgage Broker in 2007, and I noticed how they suddenly shut down the subprime market. When they shut down the subprime market, no problems were being caused by the subprime market! The subprime markets were intentionally shut down to cause all the problems in the 2008 subprime market crash. Do you understand what I am telling you? If the Illuminati hadn't shut down the subprime market, then no major problems would have ever arisen from the subprime market. But when they shut down the subprime market, they created a multi-trillion-dollar problem because trillions of dollars invested in derivatives were connected to subprime mortgages!

In 2007, I noticed many people who had subprime loans with expiring teaser rates on their Adjustable-Rate Mortgages (ARMs) couldn't refinance because the subprime market had been shut down suddenly in 2007. Once those people couldn't find anyone to refinance them because the subprime market was intentionally shut down, their interest rate adjusted, and their house payments almost doubled! And once their house payments almost doubled, they couldn't make their mortgage payments, so their houses went into foreclosure! This is what caused foreclosures to take place all at once!

By shutting down the subprime markets, they took the money out of the economy for people to refinance their Adjustable-Rate Mortgages. And once they shut down the subprime market, they caused trillions of dollars worth of derivatives to be deemed worthless! And once they shut down the subprime market and took the money out of the economy, the subprime housing market was flooded with foreclosures all at one time! And that's exactly what the Illuminati wanted! The subprime housing market wouldn't have crashed if they didn't purpose shut down the subprime financing! It's a very easy concept to understand. They purposely cause a flood of foreclosures by shutting down the subprime financing market. By shutting down the subprime market, they pulled the rug from under all those who had Adjustable-Rate Mortgages. They shut down the subprime market to cause the foreclosures in 2007, 2008, 2009, and 2010.

Now, some derivatives were worthless because they shut down the subprime market, and other derivatives were deemed worthless once the market was flooded with foreclosures! Once the market was flooded with foreclosures, many of the derivatives decreased in value because the derivative formula didn't compensate for a higher-than-normal foreclosure rate and a decrease in property value. Derivatives, along with subprime mortgages, were being labeled as toxic assets.

Property value began to decrease once foreclosures occurred above the normal rate. Property value decreased because the foreclosures pushed down the price of houses that were being sold. Houses were being dumped for pennies on the dollar. So, houses were losing their value. Once the foreclosure rate was well above average and property value fell, the derivatives attached to mortgages became highly toxic assets.

After they shut down the subprime market, the Illuminati went to the news media and told the news media the economy was crashing because poor people bought houses they couldn't afford! And once the Illuminati had its people say these "lies" to the news media, all you people brought into their lies, and then you repeated their lies to all your friends and all your co-workers! Because according to you; it had to be true because they said it on TV! This is a prime example of how the media tells you what to think! Stop listening to the corrupt news media and their lies! Pray over whatever these people on television try to tell you, and let the Lord Jesus Christ lead you to the absolute truth!

Now, since you are getting a picture of what happened in 2008, let's go to step six, which was for the high-ranking Illuminati members to place their bets that the housing prices were going to fall and that people were going to default on their loans. Once the Illuminati members who were privileged to the Illuminati plan of crashing the economy placed their bets on Wall Street, they made millions and billions of dollars because they had inside information that the Subprime financing markets were going to be shut down to cause a flood of foreclosures.

The Illuminati made money during the crash by betting that housing prices would fall. The Illuminati members knew housing prices were going to fall because they knew they were about to cause a flood of foreclosures to take place. They placed their bets housing prices were going to fall. And once the housing prices did fall, they made millions and billions of dollars on Wall Street! They also made millions and billions when they shorted the market. When those members of the Illuminati were privileged to plans of crashing the stock markets, they shorted stocks. And when they shorted the stocks, they made millions and billions of dollars! They were betting that the price of the shares would go down. And they made billions each time the stock decreased in value. Then some sold their shares high right before the market crash because they knew the markets would crash. Once the stock declined greatly in value during the stock market crash, they turned around and bought the same shares at a much cheaper price. They made millions and billions because they knew arrange the collapse of the subprime housing market. I guess Donald Trump was right when he said the system is rigged!

Another way the Illuminati made millions and billions was by placing their bets through Credit Default Swaps (CDS). Credit Default Swaps (CDS) is a credit derivative contract. Credit Default Swaps allow people to bet on the solvency of local municipalities like Jefferson County, Alabama, or bet on people losing their houses or companies defaulting on loans. For example, Jefferson County, Alabama, eventually had to file for Bankruptcy because it invested heavily in derivatives. Of course, this was not what they released to the public. They use a scandal involving politicians to cover up the true reason why Jefferson County had to file Bankruptcy.

When Jefferson County had to file for Bankruptcy, whoever bet Jefferson County wouldn't be able to pay its bills or whoever bet that Jefferson County would have a credit downgrade, or whoever insured any bonds that Jefferson County, Alabama was holding, with Credit Default Swaps, they made millions and billions of dollars by Jefferson County just filing Bankruptcy. And guess what, I live in Birmingham, Alabama which is in Jefferson County, Alabama. Do you think that is another coincidence, or was it meant for me to see this firsthand?

So, step six was for the upper-level Illuminati members to make millions and billions of dollars by placing their bets that the value of houses would fall and people and companies would default on their loans. And when all these things happened as planned, they made millions and billions of dollars from those bets they placed on Wall Street. And those bets they placed on Wall Street were nothing more than the largest insider trader scheme in the history of the world! The high-ranking Illuminati members knew for a fact the stock market and the housing market were going to crash in 2008 because they were the ones who put all the variables to crash the housing market and the stock market into play! If you want to know who was in on it, follow the bets placed on Wall Street, and the bets will lead you to the money! And the money will lead you to the people on the inside!

Mathematics is the most precise tool and dangerous weapon known to man! And if you don't think mathematics is the most dangerous weapon and precise tool known to man. You don't realize they created nuclear and atomic bombs from mathematical formulas. Derivatives are made from a mathematical formula. The Illuminati want average people to be subpar in mathematics because if you don't understand mathematics, then you will never see what they are doing to you! The Illuminati used mathematics as a weapon to cause massive causalities to the poor, middle class, and the unsuspecting by creating a mathematical formula called mortgage derivatives to crash the stock market! Not only did they crash the stock and housing markets, but none of you knew what they were doing or what they did! I must give credit where credit is due! The moves they made were ingenious! Because none of you saw it coming! Just like none of you saw them injecting you with nanotechnology and a biological weapon and calling it a cure for COVID-19.

Once they ignited all the trigger points to crash the economy with mortgage derivatives, the Illuminati sent a shock wave through the economy. This shock wave is the seventh step! The Illuminati made sure oil prices skyrocketed on Wall Street! The oil price went from $30.00 to $145.00 a barrel for no reason! Once oil prices more than quadrupled, it sent a chain reaction through the markets because the average individual thought higher oil prices meant higher prices for gas, goods, and services. But the average person doesn't understand that today's gas price is based on the price of oil we bought five or more years ago! But the Illuminati saw they could manipulate society because the average individual doesn't understand if a barrel of oil triples today in price. The gas at the pump should not reflect that increase in oil until about five or more years from now! Because oil is purchased on futures contracts! This is why the Lord told me to major in Finance at Jacksonville State University! So I could understand Future contracts.

Futures contracts are financial contracts that obligate the buyer to purchase or seller to sell a physical commodity or a financial instrument at a predetermined quantity at a predetermined future date and at a predetermined price. Staff, Investopedia. "Futures Contract." *Investopedia*. N.p., 23 Nov. 2003. Web. 22 Sept. 2014. <http://www.investopedia.com/terms/f/futurescontract.asp>.

A futures contract means this: today, I am purchasing oil on contract for oil that will be delivered to me in the future. The future maybe two, three, four, five years, etc. Suppose I purchased barrels of oil for $15.00 a barrel on a three-year futures contract three years ago. Then, the price of gas per gallon at the pump today should represent what I paid for that oil three years ago. This means no matter what happens with the economy, gas prices should remain a $1.50 a gallon, because I purchased that oil three years ago for $15.00 a barrel on futures contracts. But what they did to you all in 2008 was just the opposite. The Illuminati made sure a shockwave was sent through the economy. What they did was quadruple the price of oil on Wall Street. And many of you thought since oil on Wall Street quadrupled, the gas price at the pump should double and triple also. But that is not true!

The Illuminati knew the average person didn't understand futures contracts, so they played mind games with the American people. The price of gas in 2008 should have reflected what they paid for the price of oil in 2000, 2001, and 2002 or whenever the future contract was purchased. If the oil was purchased on a future contract for $15.00 a barrel back in 2000, the gas price at the pump in 2008 should reflect what the oil was purchased for back in 2000; this means the price of gas should have been $1.50 a gallon because the oil was purchased on future contracts years before oil prices quadrupled in 2008. I am using hypothetical numbers that represent the truth.

Once you understand futures, you should understand that oil prices on Wall Street today do not reflect gas prices at the pump today! Once you understand that, you should understand why BP, Exxon, Chevron, Shell, and all the other oil companies were reporting record profits in the billions of dollars each quarter in 2008 and 2009! They could report these record profits in the billions of dollars each quarter because they doubled and tripled the price of gasoline at the pumps. They charged you $5.00 for a gallon of gas when they paid $15.00 a barrel of oil on future contracts five years prior! This is why the oil companies made record profits in the billions of dollars each quarter! And they are doing the same thing to you in 2022!

The Illuminati took advantage of the American people's ignorance of the future, and they immediately raised gas prices! They double the price of gasoline at the pumps. And the financial markets reacted to the hike in gasoline prices! This was designed to send a shockwave through the American economy! And it did just that! So, they raised the price of gasoline two and three times the average price. The immediate hike in gasoline prices meant higher food prices and higher goods and services prices. They had to raise the price of gasoline so ordinary people would feel and immediate impact in their wallets! They also had to raise gas prices so that ordinary people would assume they increased because the stock market and the economy were crashing! And that was not the case! Sending a shockwave through the economy was designed to psychologically affect the American people! They wanted a mass amount of fear from the American people. They love to have you fearful and unknowledgeable because the more fear you are in and the less knowledge, wisdom, and understanding you have, the more power they have over you. For example, you were in fear of COVID-19, and you allowed them to inject you with a biological weapon and nanotechnology. Fear and chaos mean more power for them.

So, you went from paying $30 to fill your car up to spending $75, $85, and even $90 to fill your car up. To the average individual, that hurt! And to the average individual, they thought the price of gas increase was due to the stock market crashing! And that was so far from the truth! So, the increase in gas prices sent a shockwave throughout the economy! This shock wave was meant to suck any excess money out of the economy that ordinary citizens had. Instead of spending money at retail stores people had to furnish their cars with gas. And once people stopped shopping at the retail stores, these retail corporations had to report bad numbers to Wall Street for that quarter. Once people stopped shopping at retail stores, the retail stores had to stop ordering goods from the manufacturers, so the manufacturers had to report bad numbers to Wall Street also. By tripling the price of gasoline at the pumps, they sent an immediate shockwave through the economy that sent ripples through every industry! The shipping cost almost triples when you triple the price of gasoline. And once the shipping price goes up that means the merchandise goes up. This caused the stock market to crash even faster. And that's exactly what they wanted. The one common denominator that affects everyone is the price of gasoline! If you triple the price of gasoline, you send a shockwave through every industry! And this was the Illuminati's plan. Now, you should see how deep this Illuminati agenda goes! They manipulated the price of oil on Wall Street, and then these Illuminati-controlled oil companies manipulated oil prices at the pump!

When Milton William Cooper found the Illuminati papers on the copy machine at the Pentagon, those papers talked about crashing the economy by sending a shockwave through the economy by doubling the price of a natural resource! That natural resource was oil! And just like the Illuminati papers said, the Illuminati made sure a shockwave was sent through the U.S. economy by doubling and tripling the price of gasoline at the pumps. Just like they are sending a shockwave through the economy by raising the price for gas at the pump and food today.

So Milton William Cooper warned us of the Illuminati's plan years in advance in his book, Behold A Pale Horse! Milton William Cooper's book was published in 1991. So, the book was published with all the plans of the Illuminati seventeen years before the Illuminati did them in 2008. This proves that the Illuminati papers that Milton William Cooper found had the true plans of the Illuminati. It also gives you insight into how the Illuminati used their people in the Sheriff's Department to kill Milton William Cooper. Milton William Cooper was publicly executed by the Illuminati members who were Sheriffs! These Police Officers, Sheriffs, and State Troopers who are members of the Illuminati are nothing more than legalized hitmen for the Illuminati!

So, they sent a shock wave through the economy by raising the oil price to $145.00 a barrel. So once gas prices more than doubled, the market crash and foreclosures were happening at an alarming rate, and house values decreased, the $500 million investment made in Mortgage Derivatives by the investment bank is now becoming more and more worthless each day. During this time, derivatives were no longer viewed as valuable assets. They were being seen as Toxic Assets. So banks, investment banks, corporations, your local municipalities (Jefferson County, Alabama, where I live), and pension funds were buying and selling derivatives all started to take hits simultaneously. A lot of companies and municipalities were tied into the Derivative VIRUS.

In the same way, the U.S. markets were highly invested in the Derivative VIRUS; the world financial markets were highly invested in the Derivatives VIRUS! That's why all the markets in the world started to crash simultaneously! The derivative virus is what caused the markets around the world to collapse simultaneously! The Illuminati released a worldwide virus on the world! Was it a coincidence that all the world financial markets crashed simultaneously, or was it a plan? It was planned!

So the Illuminati unleashed Derivatives into the world financial markets! So the amount of money lost in derivatives caused some Investment Banks to go under, making all the companies invested in derivatives report terrible numbers to Wall Street. Once the numbers were reported, stock prices fell dramatically. Remember, they had already placed fear in corporations from cooking the books, so no corporation dared cook the books in 2008. Once stock prices began to drop, banks and corporations had to find additional income because of the worthless derivatives (Toxic Assets).

So they start selling off stocks for income and cutting jobs. So, a massive sell-off occurred at one time, and then the unemployment rate grew simultaneously. Then, banks had to hold on to any cash they had because they needed a safety net. After all, no one knew how fast and far the economy would fall! The Banks didn't know how bad the crash would be! So, the entire credit market (lending institutions) stopped lending simultaneously. With the credit markets frozen, banks, corporations, and everyone else had a raid on your 401K accounts!!! One day they told you your 401K was worth $200,000.00. Then, the next day, they said you only had $15,000.00 in your 401K account. So, $185,000 of your money disappeared into thin air! I guarantee you your money just didn't disappear into thin air! The corporations and the investment companies raided your 401K accounts! See, they made you a lot of promises, but when it came time for them to pay on their promises. They saw it was cheaper to renege on their promise and raid your 401K accounts! To put it plainly, you didn't lose your 401K money; they stole it from you!

When your money went missing out from your 401K accounts in 2007, 2008, 2009, and 2010, that fulfilled what I heard my daddy say in the late 1970s when I was a little boy. In Chapter 47, titled "My Father Speaking of Future Events," I told you that one day in the late 1970s, my daddy was angry and walked into the house and slammed the door. Then my mother said, "What is wrong, Brown?" Then my dad said, "When the people get ready to retire, the money will not be there for them!" My mother said, "Brown, how do you know the money will not be there for them to retire with?" My dad then replied, "Because the Lord told me." When your 401K money disappeared in 2007, 2008, 2009, and 2010, that's what my dad was referring to when he said, "When the people get ready to retire, the money will not be there for them!"

So the corporations, the investment companies, raided your 401K accounts! And I mean, they raided your accounts! This raid was planned before the market collapsed! 401 K's were introduced in the 1970s, around the same time mortgage derivatives were introduced! Do you think it was a coincidence that both financial products were introduced around the same time? Do you think it was a coincidence that millions of people's retirement money was being taken from them at the same time when the market collapsed? Do you think it was a coincidence the Lord told my dad people 401K money was not going to be there when people got ready to retire! It's time you people wake up from this unconscious state of mind! Watch the video about the 401K fallout on 60 Minutes to understand how they raided your 401K accounts with fees they didn't have to disclose to you. They use the financial crisis as an excuse to take all your money out of your 401K and place your money into their accounts! This was planned when they created and introduced 401 K's to the public! Things don't just happen; they are planned!

So after they raided your accounts, they sent you a letter saying you lost money in your 401K account! So they took all the money you had in your 401K accounts and transferred it back into their accounts! And then they told you, you lost your money in your 401K account because of the stock market crash! And then you said, "They said I lost my money in my 401K account!" Lord have mercy! I hope your eyes are opened to the absolute truth! Aren't you tired of these people making fools out of you? Please wake up and stand up!

So why did the stock market crash? The formula for derivatives was engineered to crash the U.S. stock market and the world's stock markets. Without the worthless derivatives, it was mathematically impossible for the number of mortgages that went into foreclosures to cause the economy to crash! Let me say that again. Without the worthless derivatives, it was mathematically impossible for the number of mortgages that went into foreclosures to cause the United States economy to crash!

You heard people on TV say, "Toxic Assets." You also heard them say, "No one knows how deep the bottom goes." The "Toxic Assets" were derivatives, and no one knew the exact dollar amount of the derivatives because the number was too high. No one knew because derivatives have been free to roam the world's financial markets since the late 80s without any regulation or oversight. There are derivatives on top of the original derivatives. So there are derivatives on top of derivatives on top of other derivatives on top of other derivatives! Derivatives were in all the major stock exchanges around the world. So, no one could grasp how deep the bottom was because the number was so high. I think there are hundreds and hundreds of trillions of dollars worth of Derivatives in U.S. and Foreign Markets. And when I say trillions, we are talking about hundreds and hundreds of trillions of dollars! No, I didn't make a mistake. I said I think there are hundreds and hundreds of trillions of dollars worth of Derivatives out there. Do you understand why they kept telling you on Television that nobody knows how deep the bottom is? Do you see why all the markets worldwide started to collapse at one time? Derivatives were the cause of the collapse of U.S. and foreign markets in 2008 and 2009. But you must remember derivatives were engineered and designed to crash the stock markets!

Remember what the Holy Spirit told me at Jacksonville State University in 1994? When I saw something was wrong with the derivative formula, I said aloud, "Lord, something is not right about this formula." At that moment, the Holy Spirit said to me, "This formula is going to cause the stock market to crash." And just like the Holy Spirit told me in 1994, mortgage derivatives crashed the stock market in 2008!

But some knew this formula was wrong when it was engineered because derivatives were engineered and designed to do exactly what it did: to crash the U.S. and foreign stock markets! But why? Why did the Illuminati go through all of that to crash the stock market? The entire reason this plan was set into play well before the 1970s was so the Illuminati could get Barack Obama elected as President of the United States of America and give all of the financial power to one man. The stock market had to crash in 2008! Gas prices had to double in 2008! You had to lose your 401K money in 2008! The subprime market had to be shut down in 2007, so it would affect foreclosures and the stock market in 2008, which would be just in time for the 2008 Presidential election! These things were done so the people in the United States would want "**Change!**"

Remember what President Franklin D. Roosevelt said, "In politics, nothing happens by accident. If it happens, you can bet it was planned that way." All these things were put in motion as a systematic plan to help sway the emotions of a nation to elect the first black President, Barack Obama, and to hand over all the financial authority to one man. Things don't just happen; they are planned!

So the question you must ask yourself is, who is Barack Obama? And what makes Barack Obama so special that a worldwide organization that worships Satan as god (the Illuminati) would go through all the planning and years of prep work to make all those things I just mentioned happen? Who is Barack Obama? Or you might want to ask, who is Barack Obama to the Illuminati? And why did the Illuminati go through all the trouble I just mentioned to make sure Barack Obama was elected in the 2008 Presidential Election? I know you don't understand this now, but the Illuminati is setting Barack Obama up to be a One World Leader! And making Barack Obama President of the United States of America was just the first step in positioning Barack Obama as a One World Leader. The reason why Barack Obama was chosen as this One World Leader is because Barack Obama is the

Illuminati's messiah! And the Illuminati's messiah is what you call the antichrist!

The reason the Illuminati went through all that trouble to get Barack Obama elected is because Barack Obama is the son of Satan! Barack Obama is the fulfillment of the Illuminati Prophecy that was placed on the back of the U.S. One Dollar Bill. Do you remember the phrase "E Pluribus Unum"? "E Pluribus Unum" means "Out of many, one." And I told you that was a prophecy for the Illuminati. The phrase should read, "Out of many comes one." And the Lord revealed to me that phrase truly means, out of many of the Illuminati will come the one who is the son of Satan! Barack Obama is the Illuminati's messiah! That's why all these things were done to crash the U.S. economy, so the Illuminati could get their messiah Barack Obama elected as President of the United States of America. The Illuminati used the Presidency to introduce their messiah to the world as this great savior!

The Presidency set the stage for Barack Obama to be a One World Leader under a One World Government! But before they can do this, they must start World War III so Barack Obama can usher in a peace agreement, and then Illuminati news media will crown him as the Prince of Peace! Do you think I am making this stuff up? The Illuminati plans on crowning Barack Obama the Prince of Peace. The term Prince of Peace refers to the son of the Most High God Jehovah, and his name is Jesus Christ. The term Prince of Peace was given to the Prophet Isaiah. The Prophet Isaiah prophesied about the coming of Jesus Christ as the Prince of Peace.

Isaiah 9:6 For to us a child is born, to us a son is given, and the government will be on his shoulders. And he will be called Wonderful Counselor, Mighty God, Everlasting Father, **Prince of Peace**. (NIV, Biblegateway.com)

So once the Illuminati start World War III then they will usher in Barack Obama to negotiate a peace agreement. And once Barack Obama negotiates this prearranged peace agreement, the Illuminati plan on ushering in Barack Obama as the Prince of Peace. You don't believe me? Well let me show you what they have done to start laying the groundwork to give Barack Obama the title Prince of Peace. In 2009, Barack Obama was awarded the Nobel Peace Prize for no reason! Barack Obama never did anything to receive that award! He didn't do anything to receive the Nobel Peace Prize! But the Illuminati ensured he received it because it would lay the groundwork for him to be called the Prince of Peace! The Most High God, Jehovah, told me all of this!

The Illuminati had 2008 marked as the target date to elect Barack Obama as President. This plan goes back well into the early 60's to elect there so call messiah as President. All the confusion and turmoil of 2008 was designed to creep the son of Satan, Barack Obama, into office amid all the chaos in 2008! Now that I told you Barack Obama is the son of Satan, do you understand why Barack Obama made sure his Affordable Health Care Plan (Obama Care) made it mandatory for you to receive the Mark of the Beast, the chip?

Many of you call the son of Satan the antichrist, but that is not the proper title for him. In chapters to come, I will give you the proper title for the son of Satan. I will give you the proper title for the son of Satan just like the Holy Father in Heaven gave it to me! In the Bible, the Lord uses another title to refer to the son of Satan. In the coming chapters, I will give you concrete Biblical proof that Jesus Christ said he saw Satan come as Barack Obama! This is in the Biblical scriptures for all to see! But it was lost in translation to many of us who don't speak the Hebrew language. I will translate words for you from English to Hebrew so you can see with your own eyes how Jesus Christ said he saw Satan come as Barack Obama! Many of you cannot handle what I said about Barack Obama! But I will give you concrete evidence: Jesus Christ said he saw Satan come as Barack Obama!

Derivatives were designed to crash the stock market in 2008 for the 2008 Presidential election. Also you must remember in 2003, they realigned the voting maps to manipulate the 2008 Presidential election. They gave more voting power to urban areas where more minorities live. They gave more delegates to the inner city, where a large population of minorities live, and then took away delegates from the suburban and rural areas. Whoever carried the minority vote in the Democratic Primaries carried the election! This voting alignment didn't go into effect until the 2008 Presidential election. The year Barack Obama was elected! The Illuminati got Barack Obama into power!

The Illuminati is using the same play out of the same Illuminati playbook they use in Germany, but they are just using it in a different country! I know this is the first time you have heard the absolute truth about the Illuminati being involved in the rise of Adolf Hitler! The Illuminati taught you the history they wanted you to know. The Illuminati taught you the Nazi's was responsible for helping Hitler, which is true to a certain extinct. The Nazi's was a political party like the Republican Party and the Democratic Party. It was the Illuminati who planned and orchestrated the takeover of Germany, and it was the Illuminati who supported and financed Adolf Hitler! Who do you think financed Hitler's war machine? It was the Illuminati who financed him. The thirteen families of the Illuminati financed Hitler's war machine! People like President George H. W. Bush's daddy, Prescott Bush, and other Illuminati members; Illuminati control corporations and Illuminati bankers. The Illuminati in America, along with the Illuminati in England and other countries, financed Hitler's war machine. The Illuminati was secretly financing Hitler's war machine. The Lord revealed to me the Illuminati was using Adolph Hitler and Nazi Germany as a test run to plan a future takeover of a nation like the United States of America! This explains why the United States brought all the top Nazi intelligence agents to America after World War II, Operation Paperclip. And once they brought the top Nazi intelligence agents here to the United States, they set up the same system here in the United States of America that they had set up in Nazi Germany.

One of the things Hitler did before he placed the Jews into Concentration Camps was to pass a law making it illegal for Jews to have guns. Does this sound familiar? Currently, in the United States, the Illuminati is pushing the same agenda. It is the Illuminati who is pushing laws to ban guns! The Illuminati want to disarm Americans so they can take over America like they took over Nazi Germany.

It was the Illuminati who helped Hitler rise to power! It was the Illuminati who financed Hitler's war machine! If you listen to these so-called historians, they will tell you Fritz Thyssen financed Adolf Hitler. But what the historians forgot to tell you is this: Illuminati members like Prescott Bush and others were sourcing the money to Fritz Thyssen through banks and institutions run and operated by Prescott Bush and other Illuminati members.

Just to let you know I am not making this up. Vesting Order 248 was signed by Leo T. Crowley, who was President Franklin Roosevelt's Alien Property Custodian. Seized the property of Prescott Bush under the Trading with the Enemy Act. Prescott Bush is the father of the 41st President George H.W. Bush. Tarpley, Webster "George Bush: The Unauthorized Biography" Tarpley.Net http://tarpley.net/online-books/george-bush-the-unauthorized-biography/ Accessed on 8 June 2014. Wow! The things that you don't know!

Prescott Bush was helping to finance the Illuminati and Adolf Hitler, so Prescott Bush was Illuminati. I already told you his son, the 41st President George H.W. Bush, is a Skull and Bones, which is Illuminati, and his grandson, the 43rd President George W. Bush, is also Skull and Bones Illuminati! Are you taking notice of how this Illuminati game is being played in American politics? I say American politics, but this Illuminati game is being played in every nation and every country. It was truly the Illuminati who helped Hitler rise to power! The Nazi's was just a political party like the Democrats and Republicans. And Hitler was a Nazi! Like Barack Obama is a Democrat!

Also, Germany's financial markets collapsed when Adolf Hitler seized power! Just like the U.S. stock market was on the verge of a collapse when Barack Obama got elected! Do you think those were coincidences? It's not a coincidence! The Illuminati is using the same play from the same Illuminati playbook they used for the takeover of Germany, but now they are using it in the United States of America!

In the Illuminati papers, Milton William Cooper found the Illuminati said they wanted to have long employment lines after they crashed the economy. The Illuminati wanted to use these long unemployment lines to place fear into people about unemployment. They also wanted to make it appear that Barack Obama came and saved them when he turned around the economy. And just like the Illuminati papers stated in Milton William Cooper's book, "Behold the Pale Horse," that is exactly what I witnessed in 2009, 2010, and 2011. I noticed here in Birmingham, Alabama there were extremely long lines for companies that advertised applications would be taken on certain days. I then realized the Illuminati recruiters for many major companies purposely set it up like that, so it would be long employment lines.

I noticed how the news media made sure they advertised these long lines on the news. It was at that point I realized this is what the Illuminati wanted. The Illuminati wanted the long employment lines and to use the media to broadcast it. This was not just happening here in Birmingham. This is what was happening across the nation! And those long employment lines were just another one of the Illuminati plans put into action! Just to let you know, the Illuminati always use CHAOS as a distraction, so you will never see what they are truly doing! And this CHAOS is always played out in the news media! The news media is the delivery system for the Illuminati's weapon of mass destruction, which is fear and CHAOS! The Illuminati pushes all your emotional buttons to make you want **Change in 2008**!

So once Barack Obama was elected President, they needed to show him as this great savior to the United States. They put all the stabilization techniques into action. The stimulus package was one stabilization technique they had planned. Then, they isolated the derivatives by removing them from the stock market and placing them in their own market. So basically, they quarantine the worldwide virus. Then I noticed they had all these new mortgage programs ready to stop foreclosures. Once these stabilization techniques were placed into action, they stopped the U.S. stock market from crashing, which, in terms, stopped the economy from bleeding. Well, these stabilizing techniques were already prepared before the economy crashed because the Illuminati knew their plans of crashing the economy and then having Barack Obama come in and stabilize the economy!

The Illuminati did all these things to usher in their false messiah, Barack Obama. But why would the Illuminati go through all the trouble of crashing the economy and rigging the elections so Barack Obama could stay in office just for just eight years? They plan is to usher in Barack Obama as a One World Leader for a One World Government. Once Barack Obama is appointed as a One World Leader, the Lord told me he will be like an Emperor! He will have total control. No one will be able to oppose him! To set Barack Obama up as an Emperor, they first had to use the Presidency of the United States as an introductory platform for Barack Obama!

To get Barack Obama in place as a One World Leader or Emperor, they must first create CHAOS by manipulating another World War! This potential War with North Korea, China, Russia, and Iran is being played out in the news media right now! And out of the ashes of World War III will rise the so-called savior, the false messiah Barack Obama, to lead the world to peace! Once Barack Obama brokers a prearranged peace agreement, the Illuminati and the Illuminati news media will deem him the Prince of Peace! But there is only one Prince of Peace, and his name is Jesus Christ the Messiah! And Barack Obama **is not** Jesus Christ the Messiah!

These things the Illuminati have been doing just didn't happen overnight. They have been very busy for many centuries and decades! So you can understand the things they have been doing to accomplish their goals. Let's look at the current economic situation of the United States of America! The national debt is 34 trillion dollars and climbing every day. The deficit was designed to be even higher. The Illuminati purposely led this nation into debt. But you must ask why? Why do the Illuminati want the U.S. national debt so high? The answer surrounds the word **sovereignty!** The United States was formed on the fundamental belief we are a sovereign nation! This means the citizens of this great nation answer to no other nation and no other government! The United States of America is and is supposed to be a sovereign nation! And this belief is a problem for the Illuminati! It's a problem for the Illuminati because the Illuminati want the citizens of this great nation to come under a One World Leader (Barack Obama) by way of the One World Government by way of the United Nations. And the citizens of this great nation of the United States of America would never agree to that because the United States would then lose its sovereignty!

The problem the Illuminati had to answer was how do you break a country's sovereignty? The answer they came up with is this. A nation's sovereignty is based on that nation's wealth! The United States' sovereignty is based on the United States' wealth. Suppose you strip the wealth of the United States and give it an enormous national debt that we can no longer afford. Its citizens will agree to relinquish its sovereignty to save itself from financial collapse! This is the true reason why the Illuminati made sure we, the United States of America, have a 34 trillion-dollar national debt and counting. They are trying to strip the United States of America of its sovereignty by taking away our nation's wealth! This plan to attack a nation's sovereignty by stripping them of their wealth and increasing their debt to a point they can no longer afford the debt is something the Illuminati has been using against many nations by way of the World Bank and World Trade Organization (WTO).

The Illuminati used their members in Congress in both the Democratic Party and the Republican Party to make sure the United States of America had an enormous debt load! The plan to overload the United States with debt so they can take away the United States' sovereignty has been in effect for many years! The Illuminati is not just using debt to strip America of its sovereignty. The strategy also includes a mass exodus of United States jobs. The Illuminati needed a mass exodus of jobs because a nation's wealth is also tied to the ability of a nation to employ its citizens. If you take away a large portion of jobs, you will eventually strip a nation of its wealth! Because the wealth of the people is the wealth of a nation! Also, to strip the United States of its sovereignty, you must strip the United States of its borders. The mass migration by illegal aliens from Mexico and other nations into the United States was planned by the Illuminati by way of the United Nations to strip the United States of its sovereignty by taking away its borders. No borders between the United States and Mexico strip the United States of its sovereignty. What happens when you crash the U.S. economy and you have millions of illegal immigrants in the U.S. I will tell you what happens. Chaos!

The Illuminati has also been social engineering the minds of U.S. citizens. They start this social engineering or brainwashing the people with terms like Global Economy and referring to other nations as "states". If you go back into your memory banks, you will remember how they had the news media program you to think the United States of America was no longer a sovereign nation! They did this by referring to other nations as "states"! These nations were no longer nations to the United States; overnight, they became "states" to us! The news media was referring to these other nations as "states" as though those nations were a part of the United States of America! And the news media was referring to these other nations as "states" as thou we were all governed by the same Constitution, rule of law, or ruler! As though we were under a One World Government! The news media was instructed to refer to other nations as states so the news media could condition the minds of their viewing audience. This was key in getting you, the American people, to stop seeing the United States as a sovereign nation! See, if the Illuminati can conform your thinking through the media, then 90% of their job has been done! Another phrase they use to get America to accept losing their sovereignty is the phrase "Global Economy!" They want people here in the United States to stop thinking about the U.S. economy, and they want you to start thinking about the Global Economy! Our elected officials should only be concerned about the U.S. economy because they were elected to do the will of the citizens of the United States of America and not the will of foreign nations, Global Economy!

Now you should clearly understand what happened in the year 2008 and what is happening now. The amazing thing is, in 1994, I told everyone in my Finance class that derivatives would cause the stock market to crash! But they all laughed at me! I wonder if they are laughing now! I covered a lot in this chapter and the previous chapter. It would be wise to read both twice.

119. The Chants of a Presidential Candidate Is Not Holy

It's 2008; I am watching the Democratic primaries very closely. I am watching every political rally Barack Obama had. He was a man of intrigue! Just like the Prophet Daniel prophesied in the Book of Daniel.

Daniel 8:23 read, [23] "...A stern faced King, a master of intrigue will, will arise. He will become very strong but not by his own power." (NIV, BibleGateway.com)

The Prophet Daniel prophesied about the coming of Barack Obama! In chapters to come, I will prove the Prophet Daniel was prophesying about Barack Obama in Daniel 8:23! The Prophet Daniel prophesied about many things that would happen before and during the Great Tribulation in the Book of Daniel. The Prophet Daniel said a stern face King, a master of intrigue would arise; Barack Obama is the master of intrigue, and the stern face King the Prophet Daniel was talking about! Every time Barack Obama was on TV in 2007, 2008, and 2009, I had to watch him, just like you had to watch him. It's like your spirit was captivated by this man! Something just captivated your spirit, didn't it? The Prophet Daniel also said this man will become very strong but not by his own power. Barack Obama became very strong by the power of Satan and the Illuminati!

Everything the Lord had told me was falling into place. I already knew the election's outcome because the Lord told me in 2004, while I watched the Democratic National Convention, that Barack Obama would be the next President. All of the events that happened before the 2008 election were staged like a theatrical event. All the drama that took place between 2000 to 2008 wore down the American people and pushed them towards "Change" in the 2008 election. The need for change was heightened once the 2008 stock market crash took place. So once the stock market began to crash, I watched the media pump the nation full of fear, which in terms assisted the mood of the American people to think about having "Change" and having a black president. The 2008 stock market crash was icing on the cake; Americans wanted "Change!"

Then Barack Obama started the chants, "Yes We Can". When I first heard the chant, I said to myself, "That means something." Then, once I heard Barack Obama say the chant, my spirit instantly recognized he was saying more than "Yes We Can". My spirit sensed something else was being said out of his mouth. Even though my ears heard Barack say, "Yes We Can", my spirit heard him saying something else, but I couldn't decipher it. I eventually concluded that Barack Obama was saying something satanic, but I couldn't recognize what he was saying! I knew whatever it was; it captivated people by the masses and was pure evil!

In January 2010, I heard a copy of Barack Obama's "Yes We Can" speech played backward, and every time Barack Obama said, "Yes We Can," he was truly saying, "Thank You Satan!" When I heard the recording played backward, I knew it was the absolute truth and not a scam. In 2008, my spirit recognized that the chant "Yes We Can" was unholy, but I could never decipher it. You must understand what is said physically differs from what a person's spirit is screaming out. Every time Barack Obama said, "Yes We Can," he was truly saying, "Thank You Satan!" and glorifying his father, Satan! And you were right there cheering him on!

120. The Holy Spirit Warns Me

It's November 4, 2008, and I just left home to go and vote for the Presidential election. As I was driving to the polling station, something tried to get me to vote for Barack Obama for President. Something in my mind kept trying to get me to vote for Barack Obama for President. I kept thinking the Lord didn't tell me Barack Obama was the evil one. Even though the Lord didn't tell me, my spirit knew that Barack Obama was the evil one. I thought I could be wrong, even though I knew I wasn't wrong. It was something in my mind that was trying to use race as a deciding factor for me! Something that was in my mind was trying its best to get me to vote for Barack Obama. Something in my mind kept saying, "You know this will be your only chance to help elect the first black President." That something that gave me that thought was trying to use race to override what my spirit knew. That something in my mind was playing the race card against me! So, a war was raging in my mind and my spirit. I knew not to vote for Barack Obama for President because I knew he was the evil one, but something in my mind was trying everything it could to get me to go against what my spirit knew. It was an intruder in my mind!

Once I got into the polling area and got ready to vote. This war was still raging in me. To settle this dispute, I said to myself, "Let me ask the Lord if I should vote for Barack Obama for President." I said, "Lord, can I vote for Barack Obama?" At that moment, the Holy Spirit yelled at me and said, "NO!" Once, I heard the voice of the Holy Spirit yell at me, saying, "NO!" That was my confirmation: Barack Obama was the evil one! So, I cast my vote for John McCain.

121. My Daughters Gift Is Revealed

It's December 2008, and I have my daughter for Christmas break. The date is between the 27th and the 30th of December 2008. My nephew and I planned on shooting some basketball at Briarwood Gym. I dropped my four-year-old daughter off at my nephew's house with his wife and daughter. Then, I met my nephew at the gym. After we played several games of basketball, I sprained my right ankle. This is an injury that has plagued me since High School. The slightest tweak of my right ankle would often result in a severe high-angle sprain. So when I twisted my ankle in the gym that night, I knew exactly what it was: a severe high ankle sprain.

Once I twisted my ankle, I couldn't put any pressure on it. Since I couldn't put any pressure on my ankle, my nephew and his friend helped me to the car. I chose not to go to the Hospital because they would only wrap it up and give me some crutches. I already had the wrap and the crutches at home from my previous visits to the Hospital. I went and picked up my daughter from my nephew's house, and I proceeded home. All the way home I had one concern, which was, how was I going to take care of my daughter? I had this recurring thought because my daughter was only four years old, and I had so many steps in my house.

Once my daughter and I reached home, I asked the Lord, "Lord, how am I going to take care of Madison when I can't walk." I asked the Lord this several times. Once we got home, I struggled to walk. I had a lot of steps I had to climb from the basement to the first floor and then up the steps to my bedroom. My daughter was used to me picking her up and carrying her up the steps. But that night, I told her she had to climb the steps by herself because I didn't want to risk the chance of falling with her in my arms. Once we reached the bedroom, I immediately put my daughter to bed, and I went to bed.

The next morning, my daughter woke me up, and I was in so much pain! Then I looked at my ankle; it had swelled to the size of a grapefruit! And my ankle was in so much pain! I had to use the restroom, but my ankle was in so much pain. So I hopped on one leg to the restroom. As I was trying to get to the restroom, I said, "Lord, how am I going to take care of Madison when I can't walk?"

After I finished using the restroom, I asked the Lord again, "Lord, how am I going to take care of Madison when I can't walk?" As I was making my way back to the bed, the Holy Spirit spoke into my left ear and said to me, "Have Madison lay her hands on your ankle." When I heard the Holy Spirit say that, I didn't understand, but I did what the Holy Spirit told me to do. I then told my daughter to place her hands on my ankle. I then placed my hand on my daughter's head and told her to repeat after me. I started to pray very slowly so she could repeat after me. I started praying a prayer of healing, and my daughter repeated every word I said.

Once I had finished praying, I opened my eyes and looked at my ankle, the swelling was gone, and the pain was gone! I didn't believe it! I placed my foot on the floor, and there was no pain when I started to walk. The pain was completely gone, and it didn't return. I went to the steps, walked down some of the steps, and went back up some of the steps. Once I returned up the steps, I instantly remembered what my mother told me about my great-grandfather Edgar Brown. Years ago, my mother told me my great-grandfather could lay hands on the sick, and no matter what their sickness, illness, disease, or medical problem was, it would be instantly healed. Once I remembered what my mother said about my great-grandfather, I realized my daughter had the same gift!

I blessed the Lord's Holy name that morning! I praised the Lord for blessing my daughter with a wonderful gift. Then, later that day, I remember a young lady told me her migraines disappeared instantly once my daughter placed her hands on her head. Then, after I realized my daughter's gifts were healing. I thought about how my father had just passed away the month before, in November 2008. And if my dad had just lived another month or so, I could have had my daughter lay hands on my dad, and all his medical problems would have been healed. This is why Satan took my dad's life in November 2008 because he knew my daughter's gift of healing was going to be revealed to me in December 2008.

Then, a couple of years later, I had a sister suffering from these reoccurring headaches daily. I had my daughter lay her hands on my sister's head while I had my daughter repeat after me, and my sister's headaches went away. Then, in 2012, my Aunt Evelyn, who is my dad's sister, was in the Hospital, and she was on her deathbed. I went to see her because everyone was visiting the Hospital to pay their respects. The day I went to the Hospital, I just so happened to have my daughter with me. My daughter, Aunt Ernestine, and others were in the room with my Aunt Evelyn. Everyone in the room was talking about how she had been unresponsive for days, and everyone just knew she was about to die. As I was standing there observing my Aunt, I could tell she was on her deathbed. I told my daughter to pray for my Aunt Evelyn. I had my daughter touch my Aunt Evelyn, then I placed my hand on my daughter's head and had my daughter repeat after me. Immediately after we finished praying for my Aunt, she immediately came to consciousness, and then she called out my name and said, "Ken!" I mean, immediately after we finished praying for her, she called out my name and came to consciousness. No one else in the Hospital room didn't truly grasp what they had just witnessed, but I understood! My Aunt was healed. My daughter has a gift of healing!

This is a word that was given to me by the Lord. The measure by which one believes is the measure by which one shall receive. If your faith believes Jesus Christ came for your **salvation**, you will receive **salvation**. But if your faith believes Jesus Christ came for your **salvation and prosperity,** you will receive salvation and prosperity. The measure by which one believes is the measure by which one receives. But if you believe Jesus Christ came so you can receive salvation, prosperity, and miraculous healing, then you will receive salvation, prosperity, and miraculous healing. The measure by which you believe is the measure by which you will receive.

Jesus promises healing to us, but most Christians never walk in the promise because their lack of faith won't allow them to receive the promise. Faith is the substance that drives God to move on our behalf. Confess this over your medical condition and believe you have received it, and you will receive your healing. I know this works because I have used this for any medical condition that tried to come my way. And I was instantly healed. So confess this.

By Jesus Stripes, I were healed! By Jesus Stripes (state your medical condition) I were healed. For example, By Jesus Stripes, my kidneys were healed. This which I give you comes from 1 Peter 2:24.

1 Peter 2:24 Who **his** own self bare our sins in **his** own body on the tree, that we, being dead to sins, should live unto righteousness: **by whose stripes ye were healed. (King James, Biblegateway.com)**

If you notice, the SCRIPTURE uses the word "were," which refers to past tense. It uses the word "were" because the belief is that it has already been done. See, when Jesus went to the cross, it was done! But many Christians don't believe it has already been done when Jesus went to the cross, so they don't receive this belief. And since they don't believe it, they can't receive it! This is why believing it has already been done is so important.

You need to confess your medical condition by saying. By Jesus Stripes (state your medical condition), I were healed. For example, By Jesus Stripes, my kidneys were healed! You may need to confess this numerous times before you receive your healing, so you must stand on it and believe it until you receive it. Trust me, it works!

The key to it is this. The measure by which one believes is the measure by which one shall receive. **If you don't believe it, you want receive it!** Doubt cancels our faith. Jesus said if one has the faith the size of a grain of mustard seed, nothing will be impossible for them. But the flip side is this: if you have doubted the size of a grain of mustard seed, it cancels your faith. This is why the phrase, the measure by which one believes is the measure by which one shall receive is so important. Because if you are confessing your healing with your tongue but you are doubting in your mind. You can't receive anything from God because your doubt canceled your faith! The measure by which one believes is the measure by which one shall receive. Faith is the substance that drives God to move on our behalf. Look at what Jesus said in Matthew 17:20.

Matthew 17:20 He replied, "Because you have so little **faith**. Truly I tell you, if you have **faith** as small as a **mustard seed**, you can say to this mountain, 'Move from here to there,' and it will move. Nothing will be impossible for you." (NIV, Biblegateway.com)

122. The Abomination that Cause Desolation Revealed

It's late January 2009, and I am in my car driving to Georgia to handle some business. Barack Obama has already been sworn in as the President of the United States. While I was driving, I was listening to some gospel music and praising the name of the Lord. Amidst me praising the Lord, I turned down the volume on the radio so I could ask the Lord a question. I said, "Lord, you never did tell me who Barack Obama truly is; I know who I think he is Lord, but I need for you to tell me who he truly is?" I kept asking the Lord this question repeatedly, and I kept pressing the Lord for the answer. Then, at the end of my plea, the Lord said, "He is the abomination that causes desolation." Once, I heard the Lord say that. I said, "What?" Then the Lord said it again, "He is the abomination that causes desolation." When the Lord said, "He is the abomination that causes desolation", the phrase threw me off for a moment because I was accustomed to the word "antichrist." Just like many of you were taught the word "antichrist" was referring to the son of Satan, I was taught the same thing. But the Lord used the phrase, "the abomination that causes desolation."

I then thought about what the Lord had just said to me, and then I said to myself, "The Prophet Daniel spoke of the abomination that causes desolation in the Book of Daniel, and Jesus Christ warned us of the abomination that causes desolation in Matthew 24:15." Then a great revelation hit me! The revelation was this: the Lord told us who the son of Satan was from the beginning. The word "abomination" was used as a descriptive term for the son of Satan's name and to also signify he would be a leader of a nation.

Let's look at the word Abomination broken down into two words and then compare it to President Obama's name. Abomination and Obamanation have almost the same pronunciation. In the word Abomination, the Lord was telling us his name would be **Obama**, and he would be a leader of a **nation** (Abomination) (Obamanation).

Once I heard the Lord say, Barack Obama is the Abomination that causes desolation, I knew it was the absolute truth! After the Lord answered my question, I thought about how this world taught us the wrong meaning of the word "antichrist". The world taught us the word antichrist refers to the son of Satan, and that's not correct. The word antichrist means anyone who denies Jesus Christ is the son of God. So whoever denies the son also denies the Father. This is reflected in scripture in 1 John 2:22.

1 John 2: 22 "Who is the liar? It is whoever denies that Jesus is the Christ. Such a person is the antichrist—denying the Father and the Son." (NIV, BibleGateway.com)

Anyone who denies Jesus is not the son of God is an antichrist. If your friends or neighbors deny Jesus is the Christ, they are antichrists. You must understand the word "antichrist" and the phrase "the abomination that causes desolation" are two different things. Instead of using the word "antichrist" to mean the son of Satan, the phrase "the abomination that causes desolation" should be used. The Prophet Daniel prophesied many things about the Abomination that would cause desolation in the Book of Daniel. The Book of Daniel talks about the end times, which refer to the Great Tribulation. In the Book of Daniel we get our first glimpse at the son of Satan and the things he will do during the Great Tribulation. In the Book of Daniel, the Prophet Daniel spoke of the stern face King who would appear.

Daniel 8:23 read, [23] "...A stern faced King, a master of intrigue will, will arise. He will become very strong but not by his own power." (NIV, BibleGateway.com)

The stern faced King mentioned in Daniel 8:23 and the Abomination that causes desolation are the same person. This was revealed to me by the Most High God Jehovah, and the Lord Jesus Christ.

So once the Lord revealed to me Barack Obama was the Abomination that causes desolation, I thought about something I said years prior. In Chapter 71 that is titled "My Theory Different From TV Evangelist," I talked about how TV Evangelists were teaching people the antichrist would be a white man out of Europe. Then, one day, I began to question the theory, and I said to myself, "Lord, everybody is saying the antichrist is going to be a white man out of Europe, but things don't normally happen the way people think they will." I then said, "Lord, Satan normally throws a curve ball in there somewhere. While everybody is looking for the antichrist to be a white man out of Europe, what if he is a Black man, Chinese man, Latino man, or even a woman come as the antichrist." I had the feeling something different would happen than what they were predicting.

So once the Lord finally revealed to me Barack Obama was the Abomination that causes desolation, I saw that my feeling was right. The son of Satan came as someone other than a white man. Also, the Lord revealed to me it was the Illuminati who released that false doctrine into the churches. The Illuminati wanted everyone to be brainwashed that a white man from Europe was going to appear and be the antichrist! So when the Illuminati snuck this black man into power that is the Abomination that causes desolation, then no one would be the wiser! The Illuminati is very good at playing mind games with you! They always put out false information ahead of time to throw you off track. You would be looking for one thing to happen, but then they come back at you with something totally different. This is a classic example of misdirection and misinformation! The Lord revealed to me the Illuminati were the ones who released the false doctrine into churches that the antichrist would be a white man out of Europe! The Illuminati had been releasing some false doctrines to some Pastors without the Pastors knowing it.

As time passed, I thought about other things the Lord told me and connected the dots to the phrase "the abomination that causes desolation." In Chapter 78, titled "How Did Black People Become

Perceived as Evil?" I asked the Lord, "Why were black people always perceived as evil?" Then the Lord said, "A prophecy was given in ancient times to one of my prophets. In the prophecy, I stated, "The evil one will come as a black person. This prophecy was handed down from generation to generation until man had changed the meaning of the original prophecy from **"the evil one will come as a black person" to "black people are evil."** So, with the changing of the original prophesy to "black people are evil." Black people have been demonized as evil by other races throughout the ages." So God told me that the evil one would come as a black man.

Also, you must remember what the Lord said to me after I shot a game of basketball with Barack Obama back in 2002. The Lord said he had to hide me from the evil one. The Lord was referring to Barack Obama as the evil one.

When the Lord spoke this to me, the Lord told me all I needed to know about the color of the Abomination that causes desolation. The Lord told me the color of the Abomination that causes desolation in the phrase, "The evil one will come as a black person." Before the Lord used the phrase "the abomination that causes desolation," the Lord had been using the phrase "the evil one". When the Lord told me Barack Obama "…is the abomination that causes desolation," that means the same thing as "the evil one". When the Lord used the phrase "the evil one will come as a black person," the Lord was also saying, "the abomination that causes desolation will come as a black person." And Barack Obama is the black person who is the evil one!

In the Book of Daniel, the Book of Matthew, and the Book of Mark, some scriptures refer to the Abomination that causes desolation in the Bible. I listed a few scriptures so you may read them for yourself. These scriptures talk about future events that the Abomination that causes desolation will do during the time of the Great Tribulation!

Matthew 24:15 "So when you see standing in the holy place 'the **abomination** that **causes desolation**,' spoken of through the Prophet Daniel—let the reader understand— (NIV, BibleGateway.com)

Mark 13:14 "When you see 'the **abomination that causes desolation**' standing where it does not belong—let the reader understand—then let those who are in Judea flee to the mountains. (NIV, BibleGateway.com)

Daniel 11:31 "His armed forces will rise up to desecrate the temple fortress and will abolish the daily sacrifice. Then they will set up the Abomination that causes desolation. (NIV, BibleGateway.com)

Daniel 12:11 "From the time that the daily sacrifice is abolished and the abomination that causes desolation is set up, there will be 1,290 days." (NIV, BibleGateway.com)

Daniel 9:27 **He will confirm a covenant with many for one 'seven.' In the middle of the 'seven' he will put an end to sacrifice and offering.** And at the temple he will set up an abomination that causes desolation, until the end that is decreed is poured out on him. (NIV, BibleGateway.com)

If you noticed in Daniel 9:27 says, **He will confirm a covenant with many for one 'seven.'** The "He" in Daniel 9:27 is referring to the Abomination that causes desolation.

So the first part of Daniel 9:27 says **the Abomination that causes desolation will confirm a covenant with many for seven years.**

This covenant spoken of in Daniel 9:27 is the peace agreement Barack Obama will broker during World War III. So Daniel 9:27 tells you that Obama made a peace agreement with many nations for seven years! And then the next sentence in Daniel 9:27 tells you how Barack Obama will break that peace treaty, and he will try to put an end to prayer, offerings, praise, and worship to the Most High God Jehovah and the Lord Jesus Christ. The second sentence in Daniel 9:27 read, **In the middle of the 'seven' he will put an end to sacrifice and offering.** The Illuminati had already made its first attempt to stop people from going to Church when they tried to make it mandatory to close churches during the Coronavirus pandemic! This is something Satan's people have been trying to do for years! The Illuminati want you to lose faith in God and the Church! This is one reason they keep repeating on television, "Believe in Science!"

Also, the scripture says the Abomination that causes desolation will put an end to sacrifice and offerings. The sacrifice is prayer, praise, tithes, and offerings! Once they go to a Central Bank Digital Currency (CBDC) and remove cash from the system, the CBDC will be programmed so that no tithes or any payments can go to churches. Remember what I taught you, they removed Automated Clearing House (ACH) payments and replaced it with FedNow, which means the Federal Reserve controls all digital transactions. This means the Federal Reserve will own the Central Bank Digital Currency

(CBDC). And who owns the Federal Reserve, the 13 families of the Illuminati who worship Satan as god and worship Barack Obama as the son of Satan. Barack Obama, who is the Abomination that causes desolation, will put an end to prayer, praise, tithes, and offerings. Cash will be removed from the system, and the order will be given that no Central Bank Digital Currency (CBDC) can be made to churches, which will end tithes and offerings and shut down the churches because they won't have money to operate. And no money for power, lights, water, or mortgage payments.

The phrase **the Abomination that causes desolation**, is telling you this. The word abomination is used to describe something that is exceptionally wicked, sinful, disgusting, hateful, and very vile to God. The word desolation is used to describe being spiritually empty, where you will be cut off from God and his love. Desolation also means you will be in an empty place without hope, where you will be destroyed. So, the Abomination will cause people to become desolate.

All who follow Barack Obama (the Abomination that causes desolation) will be following a man who is exceptionally wicked, sinful, disgusting, hateful, and very vile to God. And those who follow Barack Obama will become desolate, which means they will become spiritually empty and will be cut off from God and his love. And then they will be sentenced to an empty place without hope where they will be destroyed (hell). So basically, if you follow Barack Obama, you will be rebelling against the Most High God Jehovah, and the Lord Jesus Christ. That's what the phrase the Abomination that causes desolation is telling you.

123. The Lord Leaves the Name Of Satan In the Bible

One day while studying the Bible in the early 2000's I ran across a scripture that puzzled me. The scripture puzzled me because I felt like the scripture was telling me more than what my mind could conceive and more than what my eyes saw in words. I knew the scripture was very important, but at the time, I couldn't decipher what the scripture was truly telling me. Some years later, I came across the same scripture again. I read the scripture over and over and over. My spirit kept telling me there was more to the scripture than my eyes could see. As I looked at the scripture, I kept asking myself, "Why did Jesus reply like that in the scripture?" I am referring to Luke 10:18. I remember reading the scripture and felt Jesus was trying to tell us something. Then, the Lord told me to translate some English words into Hebrew. Once I translated the words into Hebrew, I saw what Jesus told us! And I understood what was in plain sight and why I felt the scripture was telling me more than the words my eyes saw.

So you may understand what I saw, I will discuss the scriptures in Luke 10:17-18. In Luke Chapter 10, Jesus sends out seventy-two people to teach the gospel, cast out demons, and heal the sick. Upon the seventy-two people returning to Jesus, they made a statement to Jesus in verse 17. And then Jesus replied to them in verses 18 through 20. The verse that stands out is Jesus' reply in verse 18. In the English translation, Jesus' reply in verse 18 isn't an appropriate response to the statement made by the seventy-two in verse 17. Jesus's response in verse 18 doesn't answer the statement made by the seventy-two in verse 17. Jesus' reply in verse 18 appears to be an off-the-wall reply! Jesus did this purposefully to ensure verse 18 stood out to the reader! I need you to read the scriptures carefully and look at the statement made to Jesus in verse 17. Then, look at Jesus' reply in verse 18.

Luke 10:17-18 reads, [17] The seventy-two returned with joy and said, "Lord, even the demons submit to us in your name." [18] He (Jesus) replied, "I saw Satan fall like lightning from heaven." (NIV, BibleGateway.com)

Did you see that? Did you see the statement the seventy-two made in verse 17? And did you see how Jesus started talking about seeing Satan fall like lightning from heaven in verse 18? What does Jesus's statement of seeing lighting falling from heaven have to do with the seventy-two statement? Jesus's response in verse 18 had nothing to do with answering the seventy-two statement. Jesus' reply in verse 18 was totally off the wall when you compare it to the comment made to him in verse 17. Jesus did that on purpose! The reason Jesus wanted his response to stand out is because Jesus knew me and others like me were going to be reading this text almost 2000 years later in an English translation. Jesus knew he had to make verse 18 stand out so it would catch my attention and others' attention because Jesus planned to reveal to us the name of the man who would appear as Satan in this world. And Jesus wanted me to have definitive proof to give you that Barack Obama is the son of Satan!

After I read Luke 10:17-18 over and over, my spirit knew it was something there in verse 18. The Lord told me to translate the two words into the Hebrew language. The translations were done by using Strong's Concordance Hebrew and Greek Lexicon.

In the English translation, it doesn't appear verse 18 was saying much, but when you translate the English word "lightning" into the Hebrew word, the word lighting translates to the word "Baraq," which is pronounced Baw-rak' (Barack). Baraq means lightning or to cast forth. Baraq is Strong's word 1299 and 1300 in Strong's Concordance Hebrew and Greek Lexicon.

The Lord told me the context in which the word heaven is used in Luke 10:18 was wrong. The Lord told me that the word heaven in Luke 10:18 refers to a high place, elevation, or height. The Lord told me the word heaven in verse 18 does not refer to God's dwelling place in heaven, but heaven references a high place, elevation, or height in verse 18. The Lord told me heaven was never supposed to be in the scripture. Someone changed the word from high place to the word heaven! So Luke 10:18 was supposed to read, I saw Satan fall from a high place. The word heaven is truly referring to a high place or heights like the Prophet Isaiah describes in Isaiah 14:12:14

Isaiah 14:12-14 reads, [12] "How you are fallen from heaven, **O Lucifer**, son of the morning! *How* you are cut down to the ground, You who weakened the nations! [13] For you have said in your heart: 'I will **ascend into heaven**, I will exalt my throne above the stars of God; I will also sit on the mount of the congregation. On the farthest sides of the north; [14] **I will ascend above the heights of the clouds, I will be like the Most High**.' (NKJ, Biblegateway.com)

The Lord told me that the term heaven used in Luke 10:18 describes a high place, elevation, or height among the clouds. Heaven was not used in the context of the place where the Most High God dwells. So, we are looking for the word in Hebrew that means high place, heights, or elevation. The Hebrew word for a high place, height, or elevation is "Bamah", pronounced Bam-maw (Bama). Bamah means high place, elevation, height, or high. Bamah is Strong's word 1116. The word lighting translates to the Hebrew word Baraq (Barack), and the word heaven, which refers to a high place, height, or elevation, translates to the Hebrew word Bamah (Bama). So basically, the words lighting and high place translated into the Hebrew words are Baraq Bamah, which is pronounced Barack Bama.

So you can understand why there is an O in the word Obama, you must understand that the letter O is a conjunctive letter used to join words together in the English language. In Hebrew, the letter U is used as a conjunctive letter to join words together. Since the Hebrew language does not have the letter O, the Hebrew language uses the letter U as a conjunctive letter, and the letter U in Hebrew is pronounced as the letter O in English.

So I placed the letter U in the word Ubamah (Obama), and it's pronounced the same as Obama. So basically, I am telling you that the translation for "lightning and high place" to the Hebrew language is Baraq Ubamah (Barack Obama). And Baraq Ubamah is the same name as Barack Obama! If we go back to Luke 10:18 and substitute the English word for lightning with the Hebrew word Baraq (Barack) and substitute the word heaven with the Hebrew word for high place with Ubamah (Obama), then we will see what Jesus Christ was telling us in Luke 10:18.

Luke 10:18 He (Jesus) replied, "I saw Satan fall like lightning from heaven." (NIV, BibleGateway.com)

Luke 10:18 He (Jesus) replied, "I saw Satan fall as Baraq Ubamah (Barack Obama)."

In Luke 10:18, Jesus Christ revealed to us he saw Satan fall to this earth as Barack Obama (Baraq Ubamah). You cannot say I am making this stuff up because I didn't create the Hebrew language, nor did I create the English language, and I didn't write the Bible! You can't say I am making this stuff up! Since you understand I didn't create the Bible, the English language, or the Hebrew language, you must accept the truth for what it is. Jesus Christ named Barack Obama as being Satan in the Holy Bible! This means Barack Obama is the evil one and the son of Satan in the flesh! Barack Obama is the abomination that causes desolation!

Luke 10:18 reads, [18] "He (Jesus) replied, I saw Satan fall as Baraq Ubamah (Barack Obama)."

This is why Jesus made verse 18 stand out: He wanted us to notice what he was revealing to us in verse 18. Jesus made sure he made verse 18 stand out because he was revealing to us that Satan would come to this world as Barack Obama.

Luke 10:18 He (Jesus) replied, "I saw Satan fall like lightning from heaven." (NIV, BibleGateway.com)

Luke 10:18 He (Jesus) replied, "I saw Satan fall as Baraq Ubamah (Barack Obama)."

Since I have shown you Jesus Christ's name, Barack Obama, as Satan in the Bible, now you should understand why the Illuminati did all they did to rig the election for Barack Obama to win the 2008 Presidential election.

So, with Barack Obama being elected as President and him being the son of Satan, it is leading to the fulfillment of the Illuminati High Priest Free Mason prophesy that is on the back of the U.S. One Dollar Bill. Remember the phrase "E Pluribus Unum" on back of the U.S. One Dollar Bill. The Latin phrase "E Pluribus Unum" says "Out of many, one". The phrase "Out of many, one" really is a coded message meaning "Out of many, comes one!" And "Out of many, comes one" truly means that out of many of the Illuminati will come the one who is the son of Satan.

So out of many of the Illuminati came the one son of Satan who name is Barack Obama. This is the true reason why the Illuminati Free Mason High Priest placed the prophecy of "E Pluribus Unum" on the back of the U.S. One Dollar Bill. It was a prophecy given by the Illuminati in plain sight! Now, every Christian should understand how Satan is using the Illuminati to duplicate what God did with Israel. You must remember, out of Israel came the son of God, the Lord Jesus Christ. Now, out of the Illuminati came the son of Satan, Barack Obama. Do you see how Satan is duplicating what God did?

So Jesus Christ confirms Satan will come as Barack Obama in Luke 10:18. Now you should understand why Barack Obama pushed for the Affordable Care Act, Bill HR 4872 (Obama Care), to be passed. Barack Obama and the Illuminati pushed for the Affordable Care Act, Bill HR 4872 (Obama Care), so they could make it mandatory for you to receive the chip, which is the mark of the beast.

The Affordable Care Act, Bill HR 4872 (Obama Care), made it mandatory by law for all American citizens to receive the Mark of the Beast (the chip). The same 216 chip I discovered from reading Biblical scripture and the same 216 MHz chip the Lord revealed to me is the same chip the Affordable Care Act, Bill HR 4872 (Obama Care) is mandating you get implanted into your hand or forehead. They haven't enforced the law yet because they were waiting on the 5G or 6G network. This chip will keep your medical information on it. The Lord also revealed to me the chip will be able to send messages to your brain, and your brain will react to whatever message it receives. This means someone can control your thoughts once you take this chip. Just think of it like this: once you women take the chip, they can make you have sex with anybody they want you to have sex with! And there is nothing you can do to stop them because the chip will control your thoughts! Or they can send you a message and make you turn your child over to them so they can molest your child! That is horrifying! They can send a heterosexual message to enjoy having sex with the same sex, and instantly, that person will become a homosexual! Now, that is truly horrifying! They will be able to tell you to do anything they want you to do once you take the chip, and you will do it. If they send a message to your chip to kill, then you will kill once your chip receives the message!

Luke 10:18 reads, "He (Jesus) replied, I saw Satan fall as Baraq Ubamah (Barack Obama)."

When Jesus Christ, the Son of God, leaves a message in the Bible two thousand years ahead of time for you, I hope you have enough sense to take heave to the message! The message left for you in Luke 10:18 is one of those hidden messages I told you about in the Bible. In Chapter 72, titled "Hidden Messages In the Bible," I told you there are hidden codes and messages in the Bible. Well, Luke 10:18 is one of those hidden codes I was telling you about. To the naked eye, Luke 10:18 doesn't look like it is saying much, but once you translate a few words to Hebrew, it tells you who Satan will come as. There are many hidden codes in the Bible just like this. It's so many codes in the Bible, it is unbelievable! There are codes in the Bible that are right in front of your face! And you have no clue what it is truly telling you! The Lord has given me the wisdom and knowledge to crack the code of all codes that are in the Bible. I mean, I have the answers to mankind's questions! The code of all codes is in the Old Testament in the Holy Bible. What I must tell you is going to blow you away! What I have told you so far is nothing compared to what the code of all codes tells you! Just continue to read and I will crack the code of all codes for you! But for now, we must stay on point!

So, Jesus Christ names Barack Obama as Satan in the Holy Bible. And those scriptures date back almost two thousand years ago. But when Barack Obama was elected, I heard so many Christians say Barack Obama was sent by god! I heard so many Christians say this time and time again. Many Christians didn't understand that Satan sent Barack Obama to do Satan's will! That's why Barack Obama made sure a law was passed making it mandatory for you to take the Mark of the Beast (216 MHz chip)!

The Most High God Jehovah did not send Barack Obama, nor did the Lord Jesus Christ send him. Barack Obama was sent into this world by Satan so he could do Satan's will, but Barack Obama masquerades as an angel of light! So if your god is Satan, then the false god Satan did send Barack Obama into this world. But the Most High God Jehovah and the Lord Jesus Christ didn't send Barack Obama into this world! The Most High Jehovah and the Lord Jesus Christ sent me, the Prophet Elisha, here to warn his people and to save you from the Illuminati and Barack Obama! Just to let you know, Barack Obama wife Michelle Obama is truly a man, his name is Michael Robinson. Michael Robinson transgendered from a man to a woman name Michelle Obama. And that's 100% truth in the name of Jesus Christ. They pulled off one of the biggest scandals ever by a U.S. President! Those kids probably came from some kind of orphanage! Michelle Obama is a man that acts and speaks like a woman, his true name is Michael Robinson. Now do you understand why Barack Obama pushed and passed so many laws for homosexuals and transgenders! He passed the laws because he is a homosexual and Michael Robinson (Michelle Obama) is a transgender.

I ask this prayer for the people in this world, "Lord, I ask you to please answer any prayers from anybody who asks you any of these questions. Is Barack Obama the abomination that causes desolation? Is Barack Obama the evil one? Is Michelle Obama a man name Michael Robinson? I ask my Lord to please tell all those who consult you the absolute truth about who Barack Obama and Michelle Obama truly is. I ask this in the name of Jesus Christ!" Amen

Luke 10:18 He (Jesus) replied, "I saw Satan fall like lightning from heaven." (NIV, BibleGateway.com)

Luke 10:18 He (Jesus) replied, "I saw Satan fall as Baraq Ubamah (Barack Obama)."

Public Service Announcement

**** The Lord sent me the Prophet Elisha as an African American, so no one race can't be demonized as evil. Just because Barack Obama is the abomination that causes desolation, the son of Satan, there is no reason to demonize all African Americans or Africans as evil. Just to prove to you that African and African American people should not be perceived as evil, the Lord sent me the Prophet Elisha from the Old Testament as an African American man. So how could all black people be evil since I, the Prophet Elisha, is black? Stop all the hate! To white people, black people, and everyone else, your hate for Black People comes directly from SATAN! This is a public service announcement! ****

124. The Artist Part 2

The Most High God Jehovah told me Barack Obama is the abomination that causes desolation. Then Jesus Christ left us a message in the Holy Bible saying Satan would come as Barack Obama (Luke 10:18). Then, on top of all that, the Lord reminded me of the day when this boy in my High School drew this picture of a Barack Obama back in 1988. In Chapter 32, titled "The Artist Part 1," I told you about this boy who went to high school with me, that had this extraordinary gift to draw lifelike pictures. This guy was only in high school, but he could draw pictures that looked like they could jump off the paper and come to life.

The year was 1988. One day, I had a class with this guy and saw him drawing some pictures. First, he drew some cars that were the sharpest I had ever seen. So I stood over him as he drew the pictures. I was amazed at his ability to draw lifelike pictures. He drew futuristic cars. He drew a picture of these two-door muscle sports cars. The cars were authentic, and they looked so real. Then he drew the front of this truck, which was so bold and distinguished. It didn't look like any truck I had ever seen. The truck had this emblem of a Ram's head. But the Ram's head had a 3D effect. It was raised off the emblem. I asked him what that was, and he said, "This is an emblem of a ram's head, and it is raised up to give it a 3D effect." And the emblem of the 3D Rams head was on the front of the truck. And a larger emblem of the 3D Rams head was on the back of the tailgate.

As he drew those vehicles, I sat there and watched in amazement. I asked the boy, "How do you come up with these things you are drawing?" He said, "The images just come to my mind, and a story is always being told about the things I see." After he said this to me, he continued to draw. Then he started to draw a picture of this black man on the same page. He drew a very distinguished truck with the 3D Ram emblem. Once he was finished drawing the pictures of this black man. I asked him, "Who is that man?" He then looked at me with this stare in his eyes and said these exact words to me, "This man is going to come, and he is going to deceive everyone. Everyone is going to think he is good. But this man is not good; he is evil. He is going to come and try to take over the entire world. Somebody has to stop this man!" Then the Lord said to me, "It's your job to stop this man!"

The guy had this stare in his eyes while he was talking to me. The guy had the same stare in his eyes everyone has when the Lord speaks through them. The guy's mouth and eyes said, "Somebody has to stop this man!" Then the Lord said to me, "It's your job to stop this man!" When I heard the Lord say, "It's your job to stop this man!" I knew everything that was spoken to me was the absolute truth. I just stared at the picture. I kept looking at the face of the black man he drew. The drawing was so lifelike and oh-so-real. As the guy continued talking, I stood there staring at the picture. I got a good look at the black man in the picture. And I also looked at the truck with the Ram 3D emblem on it because it was drawn on the same page as the black man. Many years later I saw the same man drawn in the picture in real life. The man in the picture was Barack Obama!

Those events took place when I was at A. H. Parker High in 1988. Now let me explain to you what it means. The cars the boy drew were futuristic looking cars. But the cars he drew were the same cars that you and others are driving today! This boy drew the brand-new Camaro body style that came out in 2009 back in 1988. The same Camaro that everyone was driving in in 2009 and today. This guy drew the same Dodge Charger that you all are driving today back in 1988. Also, this boy drew the bold-looking Dodge Ram 1500 truck that came out in 2009 back in 1988.

This boy drew these vehicles more than twenty years before they were introduced to the public. By drawing these vehicles, the boy set a time frame for the things he said about the man to take place. The big 3D emblem of the Dodge Ram was placed on the front and rear of the Dodge Ram in 2008, the same year Barack Obama got elected! The new Camaro body style came out in 2009, the same year Barack Obama took office! The pictures the boy drew set a timetable for what the boy said about the man he drew in the picture. You must remember what the boy said about the man he drew in the picture. The boy said, "This man is going to come, and he is going to deceive everyone. Everyone is going to think he is good. But this man is not good; he is evil. He is going to come and try to take over the entire world. Somebody has to stop this man!"

The man that the boy drew in the picture was Barack Obama! The man the boy said would come and deceive the world is Barack Obama! The man the boy said would try to take over the entire world is Barack Obama! Barack Obama will attempt to take over the entire world once he is appointed as a One World Leader (Emperor)! Also, you must remember the boy said, "...He is going to come and try to take over the entire world. Somebody has to stop this man!" Then the Lord said, "It's your job to stop this man!" Meaning I Kennedy King Brown must stop him!

It was no coincidence this boy who went to high school with me drew pictures of cars in 1988 that you all are driving today. He drew these cars twenty years before they were introduced to the public. And it was also no coincidence that this boy drew a picture of Barack Obama twenty years before Barack Obama was elected President of the United States! These events that took place over my lifetime are not coincidences.

It's no coincidence that God told me Barack Obama is the abomination that causes desolation. It's no coincidence that Jesus Christ named Barack Obama as Satan in the Holy Bible, in Luke 10:18. And it is no coincidence all these supernatural things happen to me in my life! It's no coincidence that the Lord told me I am the Prophet Elisha. It also is no coincidence that I, the Prophet Elisha, and the son of Satan Barack Obama are in this world at the same time. These are not coincidences; these are spiritual truths! The reason Barack Obama is here is because, in the last days, Satan has sent his son into the world to make sure the people of this world take the mark of the beast (the chip) and worship the image of the beast. The Lord has sent me here to stop him! This is why the Lord said to me, "Save my people!"

125. Out of Israel Came Jesus Christ–Out of the Illuminati Came Barack Obama

Since I was a child, I have always seen a similarity between African Americans' journey and the Israelites' journey. One of the similarities I saw was how Israelites and African Americans had to endure a journey as hated people in this world. Another similarity was the Israelites were enslaved in the foreign land of Egypt, and African Americans were enslaved in the foreign land of the United States of America. Also, I saw a similarity in how the Israelites were enslaved for hundreds of years and how African Americans were enslaved for hundreds of years. The Israelites and African Americans were enslaved in a foreign land for hundreds of years. I saw these similarities between the Israelites and African American people when I was a child.

When I was in the fourth grade, the Lord revealed to me that I had been born in both races that were slaves. In Chapter 20, titled "I Have Been to This World Before," I told you how I was in the fourth grade and was thinking about the similarities between the Israelite people and African American people. As I was thinking about the similarities, the Lord spoke to me in my left ear and said, "You were born into both races that had been slaves." When I was in the fourth grade, I couldn't truly grasp nor understand how I could be born into both races that had been slaves. But now, as an adult, I understand what the Lord told me. And what the Lord was telling me was this. When I was born as Elisha in the Old Testament, I was born an Israelite. And the Israelites were once slaves in Egypt! And when I was born as Kennedy King Brown, I was born an African American. And African Americans were once slaves in the United States of America! When the Lord said to me, "You were born into both races that had been slaves." The Lord spoke the absolute truth. I was born into both races that had been slaves. And while I was in my forties the Lord came to me and said I am a direct descendant of the tribe of Judah. I am an Israelite from the tribe of Judah.

So once the Lord blessed me with more knowledge, wisdom, and understanding, the Lord revealed to me who Barack Obama truly was. I saw more than a similar pattern between the Israelites and African American people. I saw Satan's plan of symmetry and how he is going to attempt to persuade the world Barack Obama is the second coming of the Messiah. For Satan to pull off the second biggest lie ever told, Satan must show you a path of symmetry or a very close likeness to the path of Jesus Christ! The Israelites were God's chosen people, and from God's chosen people came Jesus Christ the Messiah! Now Satan, the Illuminati, and Barack Obama are trying to duplicate the path of Christ, and they are using the African-American race to do it. Let me show you this path of visual symmetry Satan and the Illuminati are trying to show you.

First, let's understand the Israelites and their journey of the past. I want to go through the entire journey but I will show you a sketch. I will pick up with the story of Joseph. Joseph was an Israelite who was sold into slavery by his brothers. Joseph's brothers sold him into slavery, and he was enslaved in Egypt, a foreign country. After Joseph was in Egypt for many years, Pharaoh made him second in command over all of Egypt. While Joseph was second in command of all of Egypt, he moved the Israelites into Egypt (his father, brothers, and their entire family into the province of Egypt into a land name Goshen).

Many years after Joesph died, a new Pharaoh was king over Egypt. This new Pharaoh enslaved the Israelites. They stayed in slavery for hundreds of years in Egypt, which was a foreign land. Egypt was a foreign land because God had promised Abraham that he would give his descendants a land flowing with milk and honey! And that land was not Egypt. While the Israelites were in slavery, the Egyptians were beating and mistreating the Israelites. After the Egyptians stayed in slavery for hundreds of years, the Lord sent Moses to "Free his people." The Lord's people are the true Israelites. Moses freed the Israelites, and they left Egypt. After the nation of Israel wandered the desert for forty years, they entered the promised land. The land God had promised Abraham. Then, many years later, the Son of the Living God, thy Lord and Savior Jesus Christ, was born an Israelite.

Since we have seen a sketch of Israel's journey, let's look at African Americans' journey. Just like Joseph's brothers sold him into slavery, Africans were first manipulated into slavery by white people. Slaves were supposed to be indentured servants for seven years when they came to America. But the white man didn't let the Africans go free after seven years. Africans were forced into slavery for life. Once the slave trade started, some Africans helped sell their fellow brothers into slavery. Africans captured other Africans for them to be sold into slavery! Then, Africans were brought to the foreign land of America, where they were sold as slaves. During this time of slavery, African Americans were brutally beaten and mistreated, just like the Israelites.

African Americans were then enslaved for hundreds of years, just like the Israelites. Then God sent his servant Abraham Lincoln to free his people! Abraham Lincoln was to African American people like Moses was to the Israelites. A war was started between the North and South to free African American people from slavery. After the end of the Civil War, President Abraham Lincoln signed the Emancipation Proclamation that ended all slavery on January 1, 1963. And just like Moses, Abraham Lincoln did not live to see the free slaves into the promised land. Abraham Lincoln was shot in the back of the head by a coward. On April 15, 1865, Abraham Lincoln died.

The Emancipation Proclamation did end slavery, but it didn't give inalienable rights to African American people. So many years later, Martin Luther King Jr. came and led African American people out of the darkness of unjust social and economic laws. Martin Luther King Jr., has been called the black Moses of today. Then, forty years later, after the death of Martin Luther King Jr., Barack Obama entered the Promise

Land, which was the White House and the Presidency of the United States of America.

Now, do you want to know where I am going with this? Let me show you. It has been well prophesied that when the antichrist (abomination that causes desolation) comes, he will declare himself "The Messiah". The only way Satan and the Illuminati can attempt to pull this off is by showing you a visual image of the Israelites' journey and the rise of Jesus Christ from people who were once slaves and comparing it to the journey of Barack Obama who will come from African America people who was once slaves. Satan must attempt to give you a visual image of symmetry or likeness of the rise of Jesus Christ from an enslaved race of people. The African American people's journey is very similar to the journey of the Israelites. It's a reason for that! Let's look at this visual image of symmetry.

First, the Israelites (Hebrew people, Jewish people) have always been a hated people of many nations. Then, the African people (African American people, black people) have always hated people of many nations. The Israelites were enslaved for hundreds of years, and African Americans were enslaved for hundreds of years. Then, God sent Moses to free his people. Then, God sent Abraham Lincoln to free his African American people from slavery.

The Israelites stayed in the desert for forty years until they entered the Promise Land, the Canaan land. Then African Americans wandered America forty years after the death of Martin Luther King Jr. until Barack Obama entered the promised land, which came in the form of the White House and the Presidency! With that, the stage was set! But Barack Obama entering the promised land was all staged and planned by the Illuminati so they could set it up for Barack Obama to declare himself to be the messiah one day!

So, out of the Nation of Israel came Jesus Christ, the Messiah. Then, out of the Nation of African American people by way of the Illuminati came the false Messiah Barack Obama. Do you now see how Satan and the Illuminati have been setting this all up? Satan and the Illuminati are showing you a visual image of symmetry of the rise of Barack Obama that looks like the original journey of the Israelites and the Lord Jesus Christ. The path has been cleared for Barack Obama to declare himself the Messiah or for others to declare him the Messiah. Barack always tries to quote Bible scriptures to give you the impression he is holy! But Barack Obama has never given glory to the Most High God Jehovah, nor does he give glory to the Lord Jesus Christ! So how could he be a holy man of God Jehovah if he never gives glory to the Most High God Jehovah and the Lord Jesus Christ! Barack Obama is not holy; he is the Son of Satan! Barack has always talked against the Lord Jesus Christ and his word!

Now, let's ask ourselves some very simple questions. Who do you think caused white people to enslave and mistreat African American people? Was it Jesus Christ, or was it Satan? The answer is Satan! You must ask yourself the question, why did Satan want African Americans to be enslaved? Satan wanted African Americans to be enslaved so he could show you a visual path of symmetry between the Israelite people being enslaved in a foreign land for hundreds of years and African American people being enslaved in a foreign land for hundreds of years. Since we see it was Satan who wanted white people to enslave black people, let's understand everything Satan is trying to do!

White people have been doing Satan's will for hundreds of years. It was Satan who wanted white people to enslave African Americans! It is Satan that is driving that hatred in you! That is not Christ telling you to hate African American people! It is not Jesus Christ giving you those thoughts not to hire that black person; it is Satan who gives you those thoughts! It is Satan that promotes racism. It is Satan who convinced white people to do all the inhumane things they have done to black people over the years. It is Satan! Let the truth be the truth! It has been Satan placing that hate and malice into white people's hearts toward BLACK people! To be honest, white people look up your history. You have slaughtered and massacred almost every race of people on this earth! And you are the newest and youngest race of people on this earth! Just continue to read, and you will know the absolute truth. I will tell you the same way the Lord told me. Just continue to read and learn!

Now, let me show you what Satan did to box white people into a corner! Satan had many white people mistreat black people for hundreds of years, whether it was during slavery or after slavery. Satan used white people to set the path for the coming of his Son, Barack Obama, through slavery. Then, once, some white people recognized Barack Obama as the Son of Satan. White people couldn't even go public and say Barack Obama is the Son of Satan because they would appear to be the biggest racist on the face of this earth. They would appear to be the biggest racist on the face of this earth because of all the things white people have done to black people in the past as well as the present. This means Satan has used white people to do his dirty work through slavery and racism. And after Satan has used white people to do his dirty work, Satan boxes white people into a corner because they can't even speak the truth about who Barack Obama is without them appearing to be racist! Wow!

If white people would speak publicly about Barack Obama being the Son of Satan, no other ethnicity would believe them because their credibility has been shot because of all the racist acts they have done against African American people throughout the years. Because if I didn't know all these things I know, I wouldn't believe you either if you said Barack Obama was the Son of Satan. I would think it was just another racist move white people are making because Barack Obama was an African American President!

Many Christians can't phantom the thought that Barack Obama is the Son of Satan because many Christians thought when the Son of Satan came, they wouldn't be here on earth because they would have been Raptured up into heaven. Many Christians have been misled by this false doctrine of people being called up into heaven **before** the Great Tribulation begins. This false doctrine of being Rapture up in heaven **before** the Great Tribulation started was placed into mainstream media and into churches by the Illuminati to deceive many Christians. The Rapture theory is misinformation used by the Illuminati to manipulate Christians into believing they will be called up into heaven **before** the Great Tribulation starts. I hate to be the barrier of bad news, but Christians will have to go through the Great Tribulation just like nonbelievers! Let me teach you the same way God taught me.

126. Rapture and The First Resurrection

I must be honest with you; the Illuminati has purposely misled this entire generation about the Rapture. The Illuminati misled you about when the Rapture would occur. The Illuminati misled you because if you are looking for people to start disappearing before the son of Satan (the abomination that causes desolation) takes power, then you wouldn't believe that Barack Obama was the abomination that causes desolation! Many of you don't think Barack Obama is the son of Satan (the abomination that causes desolation) because people haven't started disappearing like the movie "Left Behind" taught you. And that's exactly what the Illuminati and Satan wanted you to think! I have shown you how the Illuminati caused the United States and the world's stock market to crash. I have shown you how the Illuminati released COVID-19 on the world and manipulated most of the world's population to take their vaccine. So, if they conjured up a way to crash the U.S. Stock market and the world's stock market all at the same time and manipulated most of the world's population to take its COVID-19 vaccine, do you think it would be difficult for them to circulate a false prophecy in the media and churches?

Let's examine the Rapture theory, and I will prove to you with scriptures that the Rapture will not happen at the beginning of the Great Tribulation but at the end. And since the Rapture will happen at the end of the Great Tribulation, that means Christians will have to endure the Great Tribulation! What the Illuminati did was confuse Christians on when they would be called up into Heaven, which led Christians to believe they wouldn't have to endure the Great Tribulation. If Christians were called up into Heaven at the beginning of the Great Tribulation, they wouldn't have to endure all the horrors of the Great Tribulations. But if Christians are called up at the end of the Great Tribulation, then they would have to endure all the horrors of the Great Tribulations. Many Christians aren't concerned about national and world events that are going on now because they think they won't have to endure all the horrors of the Great Tribulation because they will be Raptured into Heaven before the Great Tribulation starts. And that's exactly what the Illuminati want you to think.

The current Pretribulation Rapture theory says that Christians will be called up to heaven before the antichrist takes power at the beginning of the Great Tribulation or right before the start of the Great Tribulations. That means Christians wouldn't have to endure the suffering of the Great Tribulations. Which is a lie. But many Christians like the sound of that lie, so many Christians willingly bought into the lie of no pain and no suffering! Because no pain and no suffering sounds better to them than lots of pain and lots of suffering!

We are going to examine the Pretribulation Rapture theory as you know it and examine the scriptures in the Bible. Then, I will prove to you without a doubt that Christians won't be called up into Heaven until the end of the Great Tribulation. This means Christians will have to endure all the pain and suffering of the Great Tribulation. When I am finished laying out all the evidence, you will see how the Illuminati used the media to program you to believe another one of their lies! The media is the Illuminati tool to program you and to tell you what to believe! You allowed yourself to buy into a lie of being called up into Heaven before the Great Tribulation starts when the Bible tells you the Saints (Christians) won't be called up into Heaven until Jesus returns. And the Bible clearly states that Jesus doesn't return until the end of the Great Tribulation. The Most High God Jehovah and the Lord Jesus Christ revealed this to me.

Between the years of 1998 and 2008, the Illuminati-controlled media talked about the Rapture a lot. The Illuminati-controlled media did this on purpose so they could program you years in advance. They needed you to be trained and taught that all Christians will be called up into Heaven before the antichrist comes. They needed you to believe this before 2008 because the Illuminati was sending Barack Obama to be President in 2008. The Illuminati had to program your mind years in advance before they sent the son of Satan, Barack Obama, to be elected as President of the United States. So, between the years of 1998 and 2008, the media trained you to believe Christians would be called up into Heaven before the antichrist came.

While the Illuminati-controlled media was teaching you this false doctrine about the Pretribulation Rapture through the media, many Pastors were also teaching you this false doctrine. And the false doctrine was planted into the Church by the Illuminati! Then, at the same time, many Pastors were teaching you the antichrist would be a white man out of Europe! So, the false doctrine of Christians being Rapture up before the antichrist takes power and the false doctrine of the antichrist will be a white man out of Europe were working together at the same time! And both of those false doctrines were placed into the Church by the Illuminati! There are some Bishops, Archbishops, Pastors, and Ministers who are members of the Illuminati. Many Illuminati members have infiltrated the Church.

Do you know the word "Rapture" does not appear in the Bible? If you don't believe me, look it up for yourself. Then let me know when you find the word Rapture in the Bible! If the word Rapture appears in your Bible, you better throw that Bible away and go and get yourself a new Bible. The word Rapture came from a preacher who preached in the 1800s about people being called up to Heaven before the days of the Great Tribulation. The preacher's name was John Nelson Darby. He is said to be the first to preach about Christians being called up into Heaven before the days of the Great Tribulation and how Christians wouldn't have to endure the Great Tribulation. This is the same theory circulating in many churches and ministries today. Just to put it plainly to you, the theory is wrong!

If Christians were going to be raptured up before the Great Tribulation started, that means the Lord didn't have to send me here to warn you! And if you were going to be called up before the Great Tribulation started the Lord would have never said to me, "Save my people!" Why would the Lord tell me to save his people if you were Raptured up into Heaven before the Great Tribulation started? There would be no need for the Lord to tell me to "Save my people" if you were going to be called up into Heaven before the Great Tribulation started! Christians, Jews, and Muslims who believe Jesus Christ is the son of God will be saved! Christians, Jews, and Muslims are the ones God references as saints in the Holy Bible. My Jewish and Muslim brothers believe Jesus was a Prophet of God. But they will soon know that Jesus is the Son of God! And all Muslims and Jews who accept Jesus Christ as the Son of God will be saved. All that I say about Muslims and Jews was given to me by the Most High God Jehovah.

Let's get to the absolute truth! The Rapture Theory comes from these primary scriptures from the Bible: Matthew 24:30-31, Matthew 24:36-41, and 1 Thessalonians 4:15-17. We will go through these scriptures one by one, and I will prove to you that Christ won't call people up into Heaven until after the end of the Great Tribulation. Let's go through the scriptures to see what the scriptures say. In Matthew 24:30-31, Jesus talked to his disciples about signs of the end, referring to the Great Tribulation.

Jesus said in Matthew 24:30-31, [30] "Then will appear the sign of the Son of Man in Heaven. And then all the peoples of the earth will mourn when they see the Son of Man coming on the clouds of Heaven, with power and great glory. [31] And he will send his angels with a loud trumpet call, and they will gather his elect from the four winds, from one end of the heavens to the other." (NIV, BibleGateway.com)

First, the term Son of Man is referring to Jesus Christ. Heaven in Matthew 24:30 means high place, heights, or elevation! The word Heaven is referring to the high place in the sky! So verse 30 tells you Jesus will appear in the sky riding on a cloud! And once all the people see Jesus riding on a cloud, they will all mourn. Then, in verse 31, Jesus will send his angels with a loud trumpet call, and they will gather his elect. Did you see that verse 31 said Jesus sent his angels with a loud trumpet call to announce his return? Jesus' return is called the second coming of Christ! After the angels announced Jesus' return with a loud trumpet call, then the angels gathered **Jesus' elect**. The scriptures tell us that Jesus Christ must first return, then Jesus will send his angels to gather his elect. Jesus's second coming must happen before you are called into Heaven (gather his elect).

We must understand some terminology in the scriptures above before moving on. The scriptures used the term "gather his elect". We all know the word gather means to collect. But who are the elect? The elect are the saints (Christians, Jews, Muslims who believe Jesus Christ is the son of God) who are still alive, as well as those saints (Christians, Jews, Muslims) who were beheaded because of their testimony of Jesus Christ during the Great Tribulation. Many saints (Christians, Jews, Muslims) will be beheaded (killed) because they testify Jesus Christ is the Son of the Most High God Jehovah. I know what you are thinking. Many Jews and Muslims don't believe Jesus Christ is the Son of God. Don't worry. The time is coming when they will confess with their tongues and hearts that Jesus is the Son of God!

When the scripture says, "gather the elect," that means Jesus is going to call up those who were killed because they held to the testimony that Jesus Christ is the son of God, and then Jesus is going to call up some of the Christians, Jews and Muslims who are still alive. The phrase "gather the elect" is the same thing you all refer to as being Rapture up into Heaven! Let's read the scripture again so you can see what will happen and how it will happen.

Jesus said in Matthew 24:30-31, [30] "Then will appear the sign of the Son of Man in Heaven. And then all the peoples of the earth will mourn when they see the Son of Man coming on the clouds of Heaven, with power and great glory. [31] And he will send his angels with a loud trumpet call, and they will gather his elect from the four winds, from one end of the heavens to the other." (NIV, BibleGateway.com)

The scriptures tell us Jesus will return riding on clouds; then he will send his angels with a loud trumpet call to announce his return and gather his elect. The scripture tells us that the whole world will mourn when they see Jesus (the Son of Man) coming on clouds of Heaven with power and glory. The scriptures said the whole world will mourn when they see Jesus. But the movie Left Behind didn't say anything about the entire world mourning when they saw Jesus in the sky riding in on a cloud! The movie Left Behind just says people will disappear before the start of the Great Tribulation. So that's a huge discrepancy between scripture and the movie Left Behind! The movie Left Behind purposely left out the information of Jesus' returns must happen first before Christians are called up into Heaven. Also, the Movie Left Behind didn't say anything about angels riding horseback with a loud trumpet sound. Matthew 24:30-31 disproves the movie Left Behind.

Let's continue to look at the scriptures so I can give you proof that their first must be the first resurrection of those who died because they held to their Testimony that Jesus Christ is the Son of God. John tells us about the first resurrection in the Book of Revelation's 20th Chapter. The first resurrection is when all those who were beheaded because they held to their testimony of Jesus Christ will be called up into Heaven with Christ right before the Christians who are still alive are called up into Heaven.

Revelation 20:4-5 reads, [4] "And I saw thrones, and they sat on them, and judgment was committed to them. Then *I saw* the souls of those who had been **beheaded for their witness to Jesus and** for the word of God, who had not worshiped the beast or his image and had not received *his* mark on their foreheads or their hands. And they lived and reigned with Christ for a thousand years. [5] But the rest of the dead did not live again until the thousand years were finished." (NKJ. Biblegateway.com)

If you noticed those people who stayed firm to the word of God, those people who died for Christ, and held to their testimony that Jesus Christ is the true Son of God were taken into Heaven! Also, if you noticed, the scripture said that those people who did not worship the beast (Satan) or the image of the beast and those who did not receive the mark of the beast (the chip) were the souls that reigned with Christ for a thousand years. If you noticed, the scripture references the mark of the beast, which will take place during the Great Tribulation, and worshiping the image of the beast, which will also occur during the Great Tribulation.

Since all of this is taking place during the Great Tribulation, that means the souls that were beheaded because they gave their testimony that Jesus Christ is the Son of God happened during the Great Tribulation. And that means those souls (Christians, Jews, Muslims) are here on earth during the times of the Great Tribulation. Because how could those souls be beheaded during the time of the Mark of the Beast if they were already Raptured up according to the Rapture theory? The Christians that were beheaded during the times of the Great Tribulation will be called up first. And if they were beheaded during the Great

Tribulation, that means Christians were here during the Great Tribulation. The Rapture theory does not stand up to scripture.

Revelation 20:4-6 tells you of the account of the first resurrection (the saints who were killed during the Great Tribulation because they held to their testimony that Jesus Christ is the Son of God). Revelation 20:4-6 tells you who will come to life and reign with Jesus for a thousand years. In 1 Thessalonians 4:15-17, the Apostle Paul tells you how those who had been beheaded (killed) because of their testimony of Christ will be called up into the sky first. Then, those still alive at the end of the Great Tribulation will be called up into Heaven next.

1 Thessalonians 4:15-17 reads, [15] "According to the Lord's word, we tell you that we who are still alive, who are left until the coming of the Lord, **will certainly not precede those who have fallen asleep**. [16] For the Lord himself will come down from Heaven, with a loud command, with the voice of the archangel and **with the trumpet call of God, and the dead in Christ will rise first.** [17] **After that, we who are still alive and left will be caught up with them in the clouds to meet the Lord in the air**. And so we will be with the Lord forever." (NIV, BibleGateway.com)

If you noticed, 1 Thessalonians 4:15-17 told you, everything Matthew 24:30-31 told you about Jesus' returns. It tells you how Jesus will be introduced with a loud trumpet call in verse 16. The same trumpet call is described in Matthew 24:31. Then verse 15 says, "According to the Lord's word, **we tell you that we who are still alive…**" Did you see that? The Apostle Paul said in verse 15, "…we tell you that **we who are still alive…**" Why did Apostle Paul say, "…we tell you that **we who are still alive…**"? Paul made that statement because, by the end of the Great Tribulation, many people will be dead. Many people will be killed by the abomination that causes desolation (Barack Obama), the image of the beast will kill many people, and many people will be killed by the cataclysmic events that will happen during the Great Tribulation.

Many people will be killed and beheaded because of their testimony of Christ! Not all of us will see the coming of the Lord Jesus Christ. If the Rapture was going to happen before the abomination that causes desolation takes power, then the Apostle Paul wouldn't have made the statement, **"we tell you that we who are still alive…"** Because if the saints were going to be Rapture up into Heaven before the abomination that causes desolation took power, not many people would be dead. Which means the Apostle Paul wouldn't have had to say, "…**we** tell you that we who are still alive, who are left until the coming of the Lord..." Paul phrased his words that way because he realized many saints would be dead by the end of the Great Tribulation when Jesus returned! Since we understand why Paul made that statement, let's go over verse 15 again.

1 Thessalonians 4:15 "According to the Lord's word, we tell you that we who are still alive, **who are left until the coming of the Lord, will certainly not precede those who have fallen asleep.**" (NIV, BibleGateway.com)

In verse 15, the Apostle Paul tells us that all of us who are still alive until the coming of the Lord will certainly not precede those who have fallen asleep (which means dead)! That means Christians who are still alive when Jesus returns won't be called up into the air first. The ones who are asleep, meaning dead, will be called up or raptured up first. So those who had been killed (fallen asleep) because they held to their testimony that Jesus Christ is the Son of God, will be called up first (raptured up first). Then, those who are still alive will be called up. In verse 16 it tells you the dead in Christ will rise first. That's why it's called the first resurrection.

1 Thessalonians 4:16 reads, For the Lord himself will come down from Heaven, with a loud command, with the voice of the archangel and **with the trumpet call of God, and the dead in Christ will rise first.** (NIV, BibleGateway.com)

Those who had been killed in the Great Tribulation because they held to their testimony that the Lord Jesus Christ is the Son of God will be called up first into the sky, and then those Christians who are still alive will be called up next. So, according to Paul, the first people to be called up to Heaven once Jesus returns are those people who were killed and beheaded because they held to the testimony that Jesus was the Christ. Then, those Christians who are still alive will be called up into the sky.

So once the first resurrection happens, the Saints who are still alive will be called up into the sky. This means no one can be called up into Heaven until the first resurrection happens, and the first resurrection cannot happen until saints (Christians, Jews, Muslims who believe Jesus Christ is the Son of God) are beheaded and killed during the Great Tribulation. This means you can't have the Rapture without having a first resurrection, and you can't have a first resurrection without the saints being beheaded during the Great Tribulation! The saints will have to go through the Great Tribulation. They brainwashed you in the movie Left Behind! Stop believing Christians will be called up into Heaven before the Great Tribulation starts! Stop believing the lie that Christians won't have to go through the Great Tribulation. That was a lie put into the mainstream media and churches by the Illuminati!

Some of the Christians who are still alive will be taken up into the heavens, and some will be left behind to experience the thousand years of peace here on earth. Those who are left behind are the meek that will inherit the earth!

Matthew 24:40 reads, [40] "Two men will be in the field, one will be taken and the other left." (NIV, BibleGateway.com)

Jesus said in Mathew 5:5, [5] "Blessed are the meek, for they will inherit the earth." (NIV, BibleGateway.com)

Psalms 37:11 reads, [11] But the meek will inherit the land and enjoy peace and prosperity. (NIV, BibleGateway.com)

Mathew 24:40, Matthew 5:5, and Psalms 37:11 refer to the thousand years of peace when the meek shall inherit the earth. The thousand years of peace do not happen until the end of the Great Tribulation! But did you notice in Mathew 24:40 it said, "...one will be taken and the other on left." Watch this: if the meek will inherit the earth, that means the wicked must have been destroyed. And we all know the wicked will be destroyed during the times of the Great Tribulation. So that tells us that the calling up of those saints into the sky has to happen at the end of the Great Tribulation. Because God is only leaving the meek on the earth at the end of the Great Tribulation, the wicked would have been destroyed by the end of the Great Tribulation. I can prove it with scripture. Psalms 37:10 tells you that the wicked want be found during the thousand years of peace.

Psalms 37:10 reads, [10] A little while, and the wicked will be no more; though you look for them, they will not be found. (NIV, BibleGateway.com)

The meek are those saints (Christians, Muslims, Jews who believe and accept Jesus Christ is the Son of God.) who will be left behind after the Great Tribulation is over and the thousand years of peace begin. And the earth will be made new, and the earth will be an inheritance, which is a reward for those who stayed truthful to the Most High God Jehovah and the Lord Jesus Christ during the Great Tribulation. There will be no more sickness and pain! All the curses of this world will be done away with by the Most High God Jehovah. I know the world has told you the world will end after the Great Tribulation. But God didn't say that man did! In the chapters to come, I will tell you exactly what will happen after the Great Tribulation is over because God has already shown it to me, and I will prove it with scriptures. But for now, we must stay on point! Now, let's continue with the rest of 1 Thessalonians 4:16-17.

1 Thessalonians 4:16-17 reads, ⁱ⁶ For the Lord himself will come down from Heaven, with a loud command, with the voice of the archangel and with the trumpet call of God, **and the dead in Christ will rise first.** ⁱ⁷ **After that, we who are still alive and are left will be caught up together with them in the clouds to meet the Lord in the air**. And so we will be with the Lord forever.

Also, if you noticed, everything that was said in the scriptures concerning a loud trumpet sound, Jesus riding in on a cloud, and the dead being raised was already revealed to me in a vision when I was a student at Jacksonville State University. Do you remember the vision I told you about in Chapter 45, titled "I Witness the Second Coming of the Lord?"

In that Chapter, I told how I went to sleep one night, and the Lord took me into the spirit and showed me at a class reunion picnic. Then I was talking to two guys named Lando and Fred and I heard a loud trumpet sound. Then I turned to see where this loud trumpet sound was coming from, and I looked to the sky and saw Jesus standing on a cloud, riding the cloud. Remember I told you I saw everything about Jesus except for his face. The Lord wouldn't allow me to see his face. The sun's brightness blocked his face because the sun was directly behind him Then, I saw the angels following Jesus on horses. Then I turned around to the two guys, Lando and Fred, and they instantly caught on fire and began to burn right before my eyes. After they began to burn, I turned and saw a cemetery, and I saw spirits coming out of the graves. The spirits coming out of the graves were the saints (Christians who were beheaded because of their testimony of Christ being the son of God). The spirits coming out of the graves were Christians who took part in the first resurrection when Jesus returned. The Lord had already shown me in a vision everything I needed to know about the second coming of the Lord Jesus Christ and the first resurrection. I saw in my vision concerning Jesus Christ's return and spirits coming out of the grave was the same thing described in 1 Thessalonians 4:16.

1 Thessalonians 4:16 reads, ⁱ⁶ "For the Lord himself will come down from Heaven, with a loud command, with the voice of the archangel and with the trumpet call of God, **and the dead in Christ will rise first.**

In my vision of the return of Jesus Christ, once I heard the loud trumpet sound, I turned and looked to the sky. Then I saw Jesus standing on a cloud and angels following Jesus on horseback. After I saw Jesus and the angels, I turned and looked at the two guys, Fred and Lando, and at that very moment, those two guys instantly caught on fire right before my eyes! Then I turned and saw a cemetery and spirits coming out of the graves. If you just noticed, I said the two guys caught on fire before the spirits came out of the graves. But 1 Thessalonians 4:16 does not say anything about people catching on fire. But if you look at Matthew 13:30 and Matthew 13:38-40, those scriptures explain what will happen once Jesus returns and how people will be burned up. Many people don't understand Matthew 13:30 and Matthew 13:38-40 because Jesus talked to his disciples in parables. The Parables Jesus used in Matthew 13:30 and Matthew 13:38-40 referred to Jesus' return.

Jesus said in Matthew 13:30, ^{30} "...Let both grow together until the **harvest**. At that time, I will tell the **harvest**ers: **First collect the weeds and tie them in bundles to be burned**; then gather the wheat and bring it into my barn.'" (NIV, BibleGateway.com)

The weeds described in the scripture are those who choose not to believe in the Lord Jesus Christ and those who choose not to be faithful to Jesus Christ. All those people who worshiped the beast and worshiped the image of the beast and took the mark of the beast (the chip) and those who rejected Jesus Christ as the son of God are the weeds being described in Matthew 13:30. And the weeds are burned up which means they caught on fire like the two guys Lando and Fred.

The wheat described in the scripture are faithful saints. So those saints called up into Heaven are the same as the wheat brought into the barn, described in Matthew 13:30, "...then gather the wheat and bring it into my barn." The wheat is those who were being beheaded or killed because they held to the testimony that Jesus Christ is the son of God and those saints who are still alive (the meek). So the wheat is those who were called up into the sky to be with Jesus. Then Jesus explains the parable in Matthew 13:30.

Matthew 13:38-40, ^{38} "The field is the world, and the good seed stands for the people of the kingdom. **The weeds are the people of the evil one**, ^{39} and the enemy who sows them is the devil. **The harvest is the end of the age, and the harvesters are angels.** ^{40} "**As the weeds are pulled up and burned in the fire, so it will be at the end of the age.**" (NIV, BibleGateway.com)

Jesus just explained to you who the weeds were in verse 38. Jesus told you the weeds are people of the evil one, which means the people of Satan! Then, in verse 39, Jesus tells you the angels are the harvesters. Jesus tells you that when he returns, there will be a great harvest when he sends his angels to burn the weeds. The weeds are the people of Satan: those who took the mark of the beast (the chip), those who worshiped the image of the beast, those who worship Satan as God, and those who reject Jesus Christ as the son of God! While the children of Satan are being burned with fire. The wheat are the children of the Lord Almighty who will be called up into Heaven. Also, you should have noticed that Jesus said this will happen at the end of the age. The end of the age is at the end of the Great Tribulation!

In my vision, the Lord showed Fred and Lando burning in a blaze of fire once Jesus returned. They were the weeds described in Matthew 13:30; their names are not written in the Book of Life. These scriptures I just gave you give you further proof that people won't be called up into Heaven until towards the end of the Great Tribulation when Jesus returns. Jesus told you in Matthew 13:39-40 that all these things will happen at the end of the age. The end of the age happens at the end of the Great Tribulation! Since Jesus Christ himself told you the angels will gather the weeds (children of Satan) to burn at the end of the age, and angels are going to gather the wheat (Christians) at the end of the age, we should understand the end of the age doesn't occur until towards the end of the Great Tribulation.

Matthew 13:39-40 reads, [39] **"The harvest is the end of the age, and the harvesters are angels.** [40] "As the weeds are pulled up and burned in the fire, so it will be at the end of the age." (NIV, BibleGateway.com)

Revelation 7:14 reads, [14] "...And he said, "These are they who have come out of the great tribulation; they have washed their robes and made them white in the blood of the Lamb." (NIV, Biblegateway.com)

In Revelation 7:14, the phrase, "These are they who have come out of the great tribulation..." has been misinterpreted to mean those people came out of the great tribulation before the great tribulation started. But that is not what Revelation 7:14 means. The phrase "These are they who have come out of the great tribulation..." means they came out of the Great Tribulation after **they went through the Great Tribulation**. In order to come out of something, you must first **go through something**. You cannot come out unless you go through! I couldn't come out of the trials and tribulations of my life until I went through the trials and tribulations of my life. If you continue to read Revelation 7:14-17, you will truly understand the meaning of verse 14.

Revelation 7:14-17 reads, [14] "I answered, "Sir, you know." And he said, "These are they who have come out of the great tribulation; they have washed their robes and made them white in the blood of the Lamb. [15] Therefore, "they are before the throne of God and serve him day and night in his temple; and he who sits on the throne will shelter them with his presence. [16] 'Never again will they hunger; never again will they thirst. The sun will not beat down on them, nor any scorching heat. [17] For the Lamb at the center of the throne will be their shepherd; 'he will lead them to springs of living water. And God will wipe away every tear from their eyes." (NIV, BibleGateway.com)

If you noticed, verse 16 explains the ordeal they just came out of. Verse 16 reads, 16 "Never again will they hunger; never again will they thirst. The sun will not beat down on them, nor any scorching heat." These things described in verse 16 are what they endured during the time of the Great Tribulation. Many will hunger and thirst during the Great Tribulation, and the sun will scorch many. Then, the ending part of verse 17 says, "And God will wipe away every tear from their eyes." The reason why God will have to wipe the tears away from everybody's eyes is because they had just endured the most horrendous, treacherous, and destructive times mankind has ever seen. The pain and suffering that will be experienced during the times of the Great Tribulation will be unmatched by anything ever seen before! Verse 17 tells you how God had to wipe away every tear from their eyes! The Great Tribulation was so hard and bad on Christians that God himself had to wipe away every tear!

Now let me show you the scriptures that tell how the beast made War against the saints (Christians, Muslims, Jews who believe and accept Jesus Christ is the Son of God). The name the Beast is just another name the Holy Bible uses to reference Satan or Barack Obama. The scripture below refers to Barack Obama as the beast. So let me ask you this question before you read Revelation 13:5-10. How could the beast (Barack Obama) make War against the saints if the saints had been Raptured up into Heaven before the beast took power? Think about it!

Revelation 13:5-10, [5] "**The beast** was given a mouth to utter proud words and blasphemies and to exercise its authority for forty-two months. [6] It opened its mouth to blaspheme God and to slander his name and his dwelling place and those who live in Heaven. [7] **It was given**

power to wage war against God's holy people and to conquer them. It was given authority over every tribe, people, language, and nation. [8] All inhabitants of the earth will worship the beast—all whose names have not been written in the Lamb's book of life, the Lamb who was slain from the creation of the world. [9] Whoever has ears, let them hear. [10] "If anyone is to go into captivity, into captivity they will go. If anyone is to be killed with the sword, with the sword they will be killed." **This calls for patient endurance and faithfulness on the part of God's people."** (NIV, BibleGateway.com)

So, according to the Rapture theory, Christians are going to be called up into Heaven before the antichrist takes power, which means Christians won't have to go through the Great Tribulation. If that is so, why did verse 7 say the beast was given power to wage War against God's holy people and to conquer them? Revelation 13:7 reads, [7] **"It was given power to wage war against God's holy people and to conquer them..."** If Christians were called up into Heaven at the beginning of the Great Tribulation like the Rapture theory has taught, you. Why does the scripture tell you the beast was given the power to wage War against God's holy people and to conquer them? God's holy people are Christians, Jews, and Muslims, those people who truly believe and accept Jesus Christ is the Son of God. Revelation 13:7 tells you the saints will still be here on earth during the Great Tribulation because the beast was given the power to wage War against them. The power given to the beast was a position of power and that position of power was a One World Leader for a One World Government! New World Order! And the beast (Barack Obama) used his position of power as a One World Leader (Emperor) to make War against all the Christians in the world!

That's why Revelation 13:7 said, [7] **It was given power to wage War against God's holy people and to conquer them. And it was given authority over every tribe, people, language and nation.** (NIV, Biblegateway.com)

So, for the beast to be given the power to wage War and conquer God's holy people, that means God's holy people (Christians, Muslims, Jews who believe and accept Jesus Christ is the Son of God) are still here on earth during the times of the Great Tribulation! Revelation 13:7 disproves the Rapture theory that says Christians will be called up into Heaven before the Great Tribulation starts!

Then Revelation 13:10 also provides a key piece of information that lets you know Christians will be on earth during the Great Tribulation.

Revelation 13:10 reads, [10] "This calls for patient endurance and faithfulness on the part of God's people." (NIV, Biblegateway.com)

Now you must ask yourself, why would God's people (Christians, Muslims, Jews who believe and accept Jesus Christ is the Son of God) must have patience, endurance, and faithfulness during the Great Tribulation if they have been called up into Heaven like the Rapture theory taught you? The question I just ask you is so good I must ask you again. Why would God's people (Christians, Muslims, Jews who believe and accept Jesus Christ is the Son of God) must have patience, endurance, and faithfulness during the Great Tribulation if they have been called up into Heaven as the Rapture theory taught you? Revelation 13:10 says, **"This calls for patient endurance and faithfulness on the part of God's people."** Christians must have patience, endurance, and faithfulness because they will be here on earth going through all the hell of the Great Tribulation just like everybody else. Christians will be here on earth going through hell because they won't be called up into Heaven until Jesus returns, which is at the end of the Great Tribulation! **You must walk by faith during the Great Tribulation and not by sight.** Your Pastors have taught you many lessons on faith, so you must put your faith lessons to work during the Great Tribulation!

Throughout this Chapter I have told you Jesus Christ is not returning until the end of the Great Tribulation. I have given you very specific scriptures that point to the same thing. And all the scriptures I have given you have supported each other. None of the scriptures contradicted each other. To understand when Jesus will return, you must completely understand when the War of Armageddon occurs. Armageddon is a war between Jesus Christ's army and the abomination that causes desolation army (Barack Obama's army). The War of Armageddon does not occur until the end of the Great Tribulation once Jesus returns.

Once you understand that the War of Armageddon doesn't take place until the end of the Great Tribulation, you can understand that Jesus Christ returns at the end of the Great Tribulation to fight the War of Armageddon. The scriptures in Revelation 16:12-16 prove that Jesus Christ doesn't return until the War Armageddon is about to occur.

Revelation 16:12-16 reads, [12] "The sixth angel poured out his bowl on the great river Euphrates, and its water was dried up to prepare the way for the kings from the East. [13] Then I saw three impure spirits that looked like frogs; they came out of the mouth of the dragon, out of the mouth of the beast and out of the mouth of the false prophet. [14] They are demonic spirits that perform signs, and they go out to the kings of the whole world to gather them for the battle on the great day of God Almighty. Then Jesus said in verse [15] "Look, I come like a thief! Blessed is the one who stays awake and remains clothed so as not to go naked and be shamefully exposed." [16] Then they gathered the kings together to the place that in Hebrew is called Armageddon." (NIV, BibleGateway.com)

If you noticed the scriptures said all the kings of the earth gathered at the place that is called Armageddon. Then Jesus said in verse 15, he is coming like a thief, and blessed is the one who stays awake and remains clothed, so they want to be shamefully exposed. If you notice, verses 12 through 14 discuss the gathering of the great battle at Armageddon. Then, in verse 15, Jesus speaks of his return. Jesus tells people he is coming like a thief in the night. This means Jesus is coming when you least expect it. Just like a thief comes when you least expect it! Then Jesus tells you in verse 15 that blessed are the ones who stay awake and remain clothed so they won't be naked and shamefully exposed when they are taken. Verse 15 refers to people being called up and taken into the sky. So Jesus will return when they prepare to make War against him at Armageddon.

If you noticed, verse 15 is bracketed between verses 12, 13, 14, and 16. Verses 12, 13, 14, and 16 tell you about the War of Armageddon. Then, Verse 15 has Jesus speaking to you about his return. This is done to give you a timetable of when Jesus Christ will return and when people will be called into Heaven. If you look at the information given to you in Revelation 16:12-14,16 it tells you Jesus doesn't return until the War of Armageddon is about to take place. Then, in verse 15, Jesus warns you to be clothed when he comes so you won't be naked when you are taken so you won't be shamefully exposed! The battle of Armageddon cannot take place unless Jesus returns. And that means, saints cannot be called up into Heaven until Jesus returns. Jesus isn't returning until the end of the Great Tribulation when the battle of Armageddon is about to take place. Also, if you read Revelation 19:11-21 it gives you more details of Jesus return and the battle of Armageddon.

Revelation 19:11-21 reads, [11] I saw Heaven standing open and there before me was a white horse, whose rider is called Faithful and True. With justice, he judges and wages war. [12] His eyes are like blazing fire, and on his head are many crowns. He has a name written on him that no one knows but he himself. ¹³ He is dressed in a robe dipped in blood, and his name is the Word of God. ¹⁴ **The armies of Heaven were following him,** riding on white horses and dressed in fine linen, white and clean. ¹⁵ Coming out of his mouth is a sharp sword with which to strike down the nations. "He will rule them with an iron scepter." He treads the winepress of the fury of the wrath of God Almighty. ¹⁶ On his robe and on his thigh, he has this name written: king of kings and Lord of lords. ¹⁷ **And I saw an angel standing in the sun, who cried in a loud voice to all the birds flying in midair, "Come, gather together for the great supper of God, ¹⁸ so that you may eat the flesh of kings, generals, and the mighty, of horses and their riders, and the flesh of all people, free and slave, great and small."** ¹⁹ Then I saw the beast and the kings of the earth and their armies gathered together to wage War against the rider on the horse and his army. ²⁰ **But the beast was captured, and with it, the false prophet who had performed the signs on its behalf. With these signs he had deluded those who had received the mark of the beast and worshiped its image. The two of them were thrown alive into the fiery lake of burning sulfur.** ²¹ The rest were killed with the sword coming out of the mouth of the rider on the horse, and all the birds gorged themselves on their flesh. (NIV, BibleGateway.com)

Revelation 19:11-21 tells of Jesus' returns, and it tells of the battle of Armageddon. This also proves that Jesus doesn't return until the battle of Armageddon, which is at the end of the Great Tribulation. This means Christians want to be called up into Heaven until Jesus returns at the end of the Great Tribulation. And if that is not enough proof for you, I have one more scripture I want to give you.

In Matthew 24:15-22 Jesus Christ tells how awful it will be during the Great Tribulation. It is so awful that the Lord had to cut the Great Tribulation short because of the elect (Christians, Muslims, Jews who believe and accept Jesus Christ is the Son of God). Jesus said no one would have survived if the Lord hadn't cut those days short. If the Great Tribulation was so awful, the Holy Father had to shorten the length of it for the sake of the elect (Christians, Muslims, Jews who believe and accept Jesus Christ is the Son of God). Why would the Lord have to cut those days short for elect if Christians had already been raptured up in Heaven as the Rapture theory taught you? The Rapture theory you were taught by the movie Left Behind and some pastors goes against scripture!

Jesus said in Matthew 24:15-22, [15] "So when you see standing in the holy place 'the abomination that causes desolation spoken of through the prophet Daniel—let the reader understand— **[16] then let those who are in Judea flee to the mountains.** [17] Let no one on the housetop go down to take anything out of the house. [18] Let no one in the field go back to get their cloak. [19] How dreadful it will be in those days for pregnant women and nursing mothers! [20] Pray that your flight will not take place in winter or on the Sabbath. [21] For then there will be great distress, unequaled from the beginning of the world until now—and never to be equaled again. [22] **"If those days had not been cut short, no one would survive, but for the sake of the elect those days will be shortened. (NIV, BibleGateway.com)**

You must remember the elect are Christians, Muslims, Jews who believe and accept Jesus Christ is the Son of God. The scripture say, when you see the abomination that causes desolation (Barack Obama) standing in the holy place, which is in Jerusalem or the temple in Jerusalem. The scripture tells the reader to flee to the mountains in Judea! This means when Barack Obama goes to Jerusalem, the beginning of the Great Tribulation is about to start, and it's about to go down! Also, the word flight in verse 20 talks about fleeing from their homes. And verse 22 tells you that God cut the days short of the Great Tribulation for the sake of the elect (Christians, Muslims, Jews who believe and accept Jesus Christ is the Son of God). This means the Lord showed mercy and cut those days short for the elect so some would survive the Great Tribulation. This means Christians are here on earth during the times of the Great Tribulation! This also means that the pretribulation Rapture theory and the movie Left Behind is a lie and false doctrine!

So now you should have a complete understanding that Christians will not be called up into Heaven until the end of the Great Tribulation when Jesus Christ returns! The Illuminati purposely misled you about the Rapture with the movie "Left Behind"! The Illuminati planted the false doctrine of the pretribulation Rapture theory into CHURCHES so Christians would believe they don't have to endure the Great Tribulation. The Illuminati also wanted you to be looking for the Rapture as a sign of the coming of the antichrist. While Christians were looking for a Rapture as a sign for the coming of the antichrist. The Illuminati slip the abomination that causes desolation into power as the President of the United States of America (Barack Obama) in order to introduce him to the world! The time will come when they will start World War III. After the war has gone on for a while they will have Barack Obama settle a peace agreement between nations. Then they will crown Barack Obama as a One World Leader. He will be like an Emperor! This is what the Lord told me. The Lord gave me all this knowledge, wisdom, and understanding to give you!

Now that you are starting to understand who Barack Obama truly is. Let me explain what they are truly doing. First, you must remember the rule God taught me. Satan always sends a decoy before God sends the real thing. God taught me that rule in Chapter 39 titled, "Sandra". For you to believe Barack Obama is some type of Savior or a messiah. The Illuminati must create certain events here on earth to make you believe the Great Tribulation has already started. The Illuminati has already planned key events to take place. The Illuminati will cause food and water shortages. Remember, in Chapter 66, titled "The Illuminati Corporation Structure," I told you how the Illuminati has seized control over the United States food and water supply through acquisitions and mergers of Corporations. Then, they buy up the farmland so no food can be grown. They use the software guy name "Ga" to do this. They are forcing farmers to kill off chickens and cows and forcing them to stop growing food. Then the Illuminati will cause a mass amount of people dying and calling it the Rapture; they will cause these deaths by the viruses they injected into when you took the COVID-19 vaccine. It will be a worldwide outbreak of the Marburg virus, and they will call it a plague from God. Then they will use their weather modification devices to manipulate the weather all across the globe (they can make it snow in the desert and cause hurricanes, floods, and droughts).

When all these things started happening simultaneously, you would believe all those things were plagues sent by God. Just like you all believed COVID-19 was a plague by God. COVID-19 was not a plague sent by God Jehovah. It was a biological weapon released by the Illuminati! And once they released the biological weapon named COVID-19, the Illuminati gave you their solution for COVID-19. The Illuminati's solution for COVID-19 was to give you another biological weapon, which was the COVID-19 vaccine. Inside that COVID-19 vaccine, they implanted nanotechnology, the Marburg virus, and other bacteria and diseases.

So after so many people have died from the plagues, diseases, and World War III, and after so many people have starved from the food and water shortage that the Illuminati caused. The Illuminati will have Barack Obama present a prearranged peace agreement to stop World War III. Then the Illuminati and Barack Obama will give you food to eat and water to drink, and you will be so happy. Then Barack Obama will be accredited for stopping the food shortages, the Marburg virus (Disease X) outbreak, and World War III. The people would look at Barack Obama as some great savior. Then, the Illuminati will crown him as a One World Leader and call him the prince of peace. But there is only one Prince of Peace, and his name is Jesus Christ the Messiah.

Satan always sends a decoy before God sends the real thing. Barack Obama is the decoy that Satan sent. Satan had to send his false messiah first because you would never believe Barack Obama was a messiah once Jesus Christ returned. The scriptures tell of all the supernatural things that will happen upon Jesus Christ's return. Satan sent his false messiah, Barack Obama! Because the decoy almost always looks and sounds like the real thing. Satan sends the decoy to keep you away from the real thing, which is Jesus Christ. The decoy always comes to steal, kill, and destroy while it appears to be an angel of light. The Lord told me Barack Obama is the abomination that causes desolation. Then Jesus Christ said he saw Satan come as Barack Obama (Luke 10:18)

The Illuminati has set the stage for you to believe Barack Obama is the messiah. The Illuminati are about to cause a lot of problems in this nation and globally, so they can give you the answer. For example, they created Mortgage Derivatives to crash the stock market and the housing market, so they could force you to want change and elect Barack Obama as President. Then they weaponized and released the coronavirus (COVID-19) so millions would get sick and die. Then, after so many people got sick and died, they gave you the answer, which was the COVID-19 vaccine, which is a biological weapon that will kill off the world's population. They will purposely crash the economy, cause World War III, create food and water shortages, and release plagues and diseases, so you will accept Barack Obama as their Messiah! The rule the Most High God Jehovah taught me was this. The Illuminati always use CHAOS to gain power, and Satan always sends a decoy before God sends the real thing. To the Illuminati, how did I do in explaining your plan?